# Silent Revolution

## THE RISE AND CRISIS OF MARKET
## ECONOMICS IN LATIN AMERICA

*Second Edition*

DUNCAN GREEN

 MONTHLY REVIEW PRESS  *New York*

 LATIN AMERICA BUREAU  *London*

*Copyright* © 2003 by MONTHLY REVIEW PRESS
*All Rights Reserved*

Library of Congress Cataloging-in-Publication Data

Green, Duncan.
   Silent revolution: the rise and crisis of market economics in Latin America /
Duncan Green.– 2nd ed.
      p. cm.
   Includes bibliographical references and index.
   ISBN 1-58367-091-2 (pbk.)
      1. Latin America–Economic conditions–20th century. 2. Latin America–
Economic policy. 3. Capitalism–Latin America. I. Title.
      HC125.G66 2003
      2003018732


ISBN 1-58367-091-2

MONTHLY REVIEW PRESS
122 West 27th Street
New York, NY 10001
www.monthlyreview.org

ISBN 1-899365-60-5

LATIN AMERICA BUREAU
1 Amwell Street
London, EC1R 1UL
United Kingdom


*Printed in Canada*      10 9 8 7 6 5 4 3 2

19/SLC

# SILENT REVOLUTION

# CONTENTS

FOR CATHERINE, CALUM AND FINLAY

# PREFACE

As I finish this new edition, in a hotel room in Buenos Aires, it is twenty years since Mexico's default on its foreign debts precipitated the continent's debt crisis and the deeper market restructuring that this book terms a "Silent Revolution." Most of today's Latin Americans were not even born then—they have grown up to a world of "permanent adjustment."

After twenty years of so-called stabilization and adjustment, Latin America is once again facing a chaotic and uncertain future. Argentina is currently enduring the worst peacetime economic crash in Latin America's history. Across the border in Brazil, Lula's fledgling progressive government is beginning its high-wire act of trying to reassure international investors, while at the same time confronting the crushing inequities and injustices of the world's most unequal society. In the past year, riots against government austerity and privatization plans have erupted in Uruguay, Peru, Bolivia, and Paraguay. Across the region, grassroots opposition to the proposed Free Trade Area of the Americas is burgeoning.

When I wrote this book, in the early 1990s, critics of neoliberalism were derided as fools or nostalgics, hankerers after the bad old days of statism and inflation. A decade later, some of that arrogance is gone. As well as "adjustment fatigue" among the continent's politicians, there is doubt at the intellectual core of the neoliberal crusade, the Washington–based international financial institutions and the U.S. administration. A few voices still claim the problem is that the region has not adjusted *enough*, but as the years and the adjustment programs pass by, and the promised land of stable growth and prosperity comes no closer, their conviction and credibility are fading.

In a rational, humane world, Latin America's decision makers would be encouraged and supported in exploring new approaches. Instead, with only minor alterations, the policy prescriptions remain

7

unchanged, and the world's governments continue to negotiate new obstacles to a change in direction, locking in the discredited nostra of market fundamentalism at the WTO, the Free Trade Area of the Americas, and innumerable smaller treaties and agreements. This is not yet set in stone—the negotiations are still under way. Decisions made by politicians can be changed by politicians, if the will is there. The very least the powerful nations of the North can do is recognize the failures of the past, and not prevent Latin Americans from finding their own, more successful, path to development.

A number of people gave invaluable advice and commentary on this new edition. In particular, I would like to thank Victor Bulmer-Thomas, Ha-Joon Chang, Clare Dixon, James Dunkerley, George Gelber, Robert Gwynne, Cristóbal Kay, Richard Lapper, Fernando Leiva, Peter Lloyd-Sherlock, Matthew Lockwood, Claire Melamed, Andrew Nash, James Painter, Manuel Pérez Rocha, Nicola Phillips, Sarah Smith-Pearse, Alistair Smith, Jane Turner, and Alex Wilks. All opinions and errors are, of course, my own.

*Buenos Aires*, February 2003

# INTRODUCTION

Not many nascent political parties use a toilet bowl as their logo, but the Giant Toilet Committee in Argentina's second city of Córdoba is both a witty protest movement and an apt metaphor for the dire state of the country.

The Committee's barrio was nicknamed "the giant toilet" after the water table rose and sewage started flooding the houses and roads. For years, residents fruitlessly lobbied the local council for a sewage system. An outbreak of hepatitis in 2001 was the last straw. A protest committee formed, opting for irony rather than road blockades. They started off by parading outside the town hall with a thirty-foot-high toilet. On its lid was written "Promises" with an arrow pointing downward into the bowl. They made the front page of the national press.

Now they want to form a new movement called *Despertar* (Awakening), but plan to keep the logo. As one of its leaders, mechanic Oscar Perassi, puts it, "All the other political parties end up down the toilet, but we're emerging from one!"

The Giant Toilet Committee is just one of thousands of self-help and protest groups confronting the worst crisis in Argentina's history. The end of 2001 saw mass demonstrations oust five governments in the space of two weeks and a chaotic devaluation. In 2002, the GDP fell by anywhere from 11 to 15 percent, unemployment and underemployment rose to about half the working population, and 20,000 people a day slid below the poverty line. A quarter of Argentines no longer earn enough to feed themselves or their families. The cities are littered with boarded-up shops and factories, while the poorer barrios look more like Bolivia than the old self-confident Argentina that was one of the world's most prosperous economies.[1]

The collapse was all the more shocking because during the 1990s, Argentina was lauded by the U.S. government and International Mone-

9

tary Fund as a model for the rest of the developing world. In October 1998, in the middle of the Asia crisis, the Fund's then-managing director, Michel Camdessus, invited President Menem to join Bill Clinton in opening the IMF annual meeting in Washington—the ultimate pat on the back. IMF sources said Argentina was being held up as an example to other countries of how to manage their economies in turbulent times.

Argentina's boosters portrayed it as the fearless avant-garde of a "silent revolution" that began in the region in the early 1980s. It is a revolution that has gone largely unreported outside Latin America, except in the pages of the *Financial Times* and other media catering to foreign investors. As in any revolution, the old order was turned upside down, but this economic transformation does not aspire to create a socialist utopia. Instead, it has enshrined market forces at the heart of the region's economy through a combination of deregulation and liberalization.

## WHAT IS NEOLIBERALISM?

In Latin America, the pro-market school of thought is known as neoliberalism, but even the name is confusing. Outside the region, the word *liberal* often describes people who support civil rights and a stronger sense of community values, but in this case, the liberalism is economic, not political. The overriding freedom in the neoliberal canon is that of the "free" market, and where freeing the market is incompatible with freeing the people, the market usually takes precedence. The notorious Chilean dictator General Pinochet was a crusading neoliberal.

The *neo* prefix is needed because after the 1930s liberalism went out of fashion in Latin America, dropped in favor of an economic model known by the unlovely name of "import substituting industrialization," or import substitution for short. Import substitution changed the economic face of the continent through a strategy of state-led development of domestic industry, but for the neoliberals it was a big mistake. Their diagnosis of Latin America's economic ills was simple: too much state, too much regulation, too much government spending, and not enough emphasis on the private sector and foreign trade.

The neoliberals drew their inspiration from the great classical traditions of economic thought. The bible of classical economics is Adam Smith's *An Inquiry into the Nature and Causes of the Wealth of Nations*, published in 1776. Smith's work reflects the rise of a new entrepreneurial class in the early years of Britain's industrial revolution, and many of its themes have remained central to economic debate ever since.

Refined in succeeding generations by other great economic thinkers such as David Ricardo, Thomas Malthus, and John Stuart Mill, Smith's book endeavored, in contemporary language, to explain the origins of economic growth. He found them in the unhindered operation of the market, which he memorably described as an "invisible hand," working to maximize economic growth and human happiness. Smith and his followers fiercely criticized any attempt by government to interfere with the benign workings of the market as likely to damage the prospects for growth.[2] Subsequently, Ricardo extended such ideas to trade between nations and wages, arguing that "like all other contracts, wages should be left to the fair and free competition of the market, and should never be controlled by the interference of the legislature."[3]

The second strand of neoliberalism is monetarism, essentially the theory that a change in the money supply leads to a corresponding change in the overall level of prices, but does not affect output or employment. This theory is said by one author to be "at least 500 years old and ... sometimes claimed to date from Confucius."[4] The theory was formalized by Irving Fisher as the quantity theory of money, which was revived by Milton Friedman in the 1960s, following the successful challenge launched by Keynes's *General Theory* in 1936.[5] Monetarism underlies the monetary approach to the balance of payments which forms the theoretical basis for IMF programs.

Classical economics provided the intellectual foundations for the laissez-faire capitalism of the Victorian age. The trauma of the great depression in the 1930s convinced many people that the untrammeled workings of the market were anything but benign, and the classical school suffered a temporary eclipse in favor of the ideas of its two greatest adversaries, Karl Marx, who challenged the supremacy of the market, and John Maynard Keynes, who challenged monetarism. Both men argued for a far more central role for the state in economic management. As the state-led models of these two thinkers ran into trouble in the 1960s, a new generation of economists and politicians were once again drawn to the attractive simplicity of Smith's view of the world.

The neoliberal recipe has evolved as the silent revolution has unfolded, and not all countries have followed every recommendation, but the core message never varies. The solution to the region's underdevelopment lies in a three-stage economic transformation: stabilization, structural adjustment, and export-led growth.

STABILIZATION: Stabilization means curbing inflation, seen as the single greatest obstacle to economic recovery. In neoliberal eyes, the way to fight inflation is the monetarist path of reducing the growth in the money supply by cutting public spending and raising interest rates. Wage controls are also used to reduce demand in the economy. In practice, usually under IMF tutelage, stabilization pursues a second, often contradictory objective—making sure the country does not default on its debt repayments to the northern commercial banks, the IMF, and the World Bank. This usually entails a large devaluation to generate a trade surplus with which to keep up its debt repayments.

STRUCTURAL ADJUSTMENT: In the longer term, stabilization should coincide with or be swiftly followed by "structural adjustment." The aim here is to implant a functioning market economy in the country by "getting the prices right," removing artificial distortions such as price controls or trade tariffs, allowing the unregulated market to determine the most efficient allocation of resources. Because of its role in distorting prices and generally interfering with the free operation of the market, the state is seen as part of the problem, not part of the solution, and the economy has to be restructured to reduce the state's role and unleash the private sector. This means privatizing state firms and the broader deregulation of trade and investment. Deregulation should also remove "structural rigidities" in the workforce. In practice this often means cutting labor costs by making it easier to hire and fire employees, restricting trade union activities, and encouraging greater "flexibility" through short-term contracts and subcontracting. Like stabilization, structural adjustment supports eliminating government spending deficits, which are seen as inflationary, but adjustment differs in that it more frequently involves closing the deficit by enhancing revenue as well as cutting spending. This is usually achieved by a mixture of privatization proceeds and raising sales taxes such as the VAT. In the 1990s, as structural adjustment failed to deliver growth, new candidates for a "second generation" of reforms emerged, in areas such as property rights, the criminal justice system, or anti-corruption measures.

EXPORT-LED GROWTH: Structural adjustment paves the way for an export-led economic recovery. The government should give priority to exports, encouraging the private sector to diversify and find new markets for its products. This sometimes involves suppressing domestic demand (which diverts goods away from exports to local consumption). Removing all trade barriers (on both imports and exports) will, argue the neoliberals, ensure that resources are allocated efficiently, and that exports are made more competitive because their producers will be able to cut costs by importing the cheapest inputs available, whether fertilizers and pesticides for agroexports or manufactured inputs for industry. Export-led growth generally means encouraging foreign investors to bring in new technology and capital.

## ARGENTINA: WHAT WENT WRONG?

Walking past the heavily shuttered, graffiti-spattered banks in the imposing center of Argentine's capital city Buenos Aires in early 2003, it was hard to believe that for much of the 1990s this rapidly disintegrating nation was the darling of the Washington Consensus, held up as a shining example of successful structural adjustment. What went wrong?

The depth of *La Crisis* was hard to exaggerate. According to government figures, by late 2002, poverty affected 58 percent (21 million) of the population, while 28 percent (10 million people) were classified as "indigent," earning too little even to cover their families' food requirements. Over the previous year, Argentinians had slid below the poverty line at the rate of 20,000 per day.

Poverty hit both the middle and poorer classes. The middle classes saw their jobs disappear and had their savings in dollar accounts frozen by the government in a measure known as the *corralito*. Two million of the poorest families were dependent on state handouts under the "Head of Household Scheme," a work program that paid out $150 per month (U.S. $50), less than half the amount required to feed a family. Hundreds of soup kitchens sprang up in the cities, playing a crucial role in staving off mass hunger. Families still sent their children to primary school, not least because they provided at least one solid meal a day, but many more were dropping out of secondary school, where free food was not an offer.

The crisis stemmed from a disastrous combination of bad economic policies (often at the behest of the international financial institutions), political paralysis, and external pressures beyond the government's control.

In 1991, the government ended inflation by pegging the peso to the dollar in the "Convertibility Plan." This step, which effectively made devaluation illegal, also said that the government could issue pesos only if they were backed by dollar reserves. In the event of a fiscal deficit, the government's only option was therefore to borrow dollars to cover the gap.

The government proved unable or unwilling to curb its fiscal deficit. This was partly because of the hubris of the 1990s—with inflation curbed, and the economy growing strongly from 1991 to 1997, the government felt sure it could grow its way out of debt and did not want to cause political turmoil by curbing spending even further.

The biggest single cause of the fiscal deficit was, however, one of the policies commonly included in the Washington Consensus package of neoliberal reforms, namely pension privatization. This involved moving from a "pay as you go" scheme in which the government used income from those working to fund its pension commitments, to a funded scheme, where individuals saved for their own retirement. However, during the transition period, the government faced a dilemma—it no longer received pension contributions, but still had to pay out to current pensioners. In the Argentine case, decades of state patronage had led to a massive pension bill, and the switch to funded schemes accounted for 70 to 80 percent of the deficit during the 1990s.

A number of other adjustment measures increased Argentina's vulnerability: bungled privatization led to a high-cost economy, with tariffs for phones and electricity running at up to ten times the international rates. This, plus an overvalued currency and trade liberalization led to a surge of imports that destroyed swathes of Argentine industry and an increasing trade deficit.

Financial deregulation, the privatization of the banking system, and the liberalization of capital flows meant that the government effectively lost control over the economy. As its need for dollars to fill the fiscal deficit rose, it was forced to push interest rates ever higher. Owners of capital stopped investing in production, as playing the capital markets was far more profitable, and high interest rates effectively squeezed industries out of the credit market.

The vulnerability of the newly adjusted Argentine economy was exposed by the slump in capital flows following the Mexican "Tequila crisis" of 1994, and again in the Asia crisis of 1997–1998. The Tequila crisis prompted massive capital flight, which was all the easier in Argentina due to the prior deregulation of capital markets. Another victim of the Asia crisis was Brazil's own currency, which was forced to devalue in January 1999. This added to the pressure on the peso by suddenly making Argentina's exports uncompetitive in the Brazilian market.

During much of the 1990s, the IMF held up Argentina as a model for the rest of the developing world, turning a blind eye to the looming crisis. When the crisis hit, the Fund made matters worse by pressuring Argentina to apply its standard pro-cyclical recipe of trying to balance budgets during a recession by cutting public spending. In January 2003, the Fund's agreement with the Duhalde government included the requirement to generate a $13 billion surplus in 2003. To achieve this, public sector wages and pensions were frozen in nominal terms, despite the government's own prediction of 35 percent inflation over the year. Sales tax and utility charges were also set to rise.

Although much of Argentina's crisis is homegrown, aspects of its travails can be recognized across the region. For a few years in the early 1990s, the new model appeared to offer a return to economic growth, but it proved short-lived. By the early years of the new century, the UN was talking of a new "lost half-decade" (1997–2002), a return to the slump of the 1980s. Capital inflows had dried up after the Asia crisis of 1997–1998; popular disenchantment with economic reform was growing. Latin America's twenty-year affair with the market seemed to be heading for the rocks.

## ABOUT THIS BOOK

*Silent Revolution* shows the all-encompassing nature of the economic transformation of Latin America in recent decades and the growing social and economic crisis that has in part been caused by the new model. Outside the region, public discussion has concentrated almost exclusively on the region's debt crisis and the role of the international financial institutions, in particular the IMF, cast by its critics as the neocolonial villain of the piece. Much less attention has been paid to the role of the debt crisis as midwife to a profound restructuring of the region's economy, a process that is still under way throughout the continent.

Central to the restructuring was the belief that the state's role in the economy should be reduced. This book looks at the successes and failures of state and market in Latin America's recent past and contrasts the past failings of state involvement in the region with the record of Southeast Asian economies such as Taiwan and South Korea. Apart from a slump in 1997–1998, from which they rapidly recovered, both have boomed, while relying on a hands-on role for the state that is anathema to neoliberal orthodoxy.

From the earliest days of the debt crisis the IMF and, increasingly, the World Bank, were key players in persuading or forcing Latin American policy makers to adopt the neoliberal agenda. *Silent Revolution* explores the structure, thinking, power, and policies of the Fund and the Bank. It analyzes the real extent of their policy changes since the mid-1990s, made in response to a rising chorus of criticism over the human costs of their policies, and explores the likelihood of new economic models emerging from the current crisis.

Most information on this phenomenon, arguably the most important political and economic issue facing the region today, is written in impenetrable language designed by and for professional or apprentice economists. This book aims to tell the story in plain English. Although this will doubtless run the risk of oversimplifying complex processes, losing some "shades of gray" along the way, the exercise will be worthwhile if it helps a wider audience grasp the human and economic impact of the silent revolution.

The period of reform breaks down roughly into two equal periods. That of 1982 to 1991 has been termed the "lost decade" of debt crisis, recession, and austerity. From 1991 on, foreign capital started once again to flow into the region, and growth took off, only to slump again after the Asia crisis of 1997–1998 led to an abrupt end to net capital flows to all "emerging markets," including Latin America. Throughout the period, structural adjustment gathered pace. *Silent Revolution* looks at both phases, but places most attention on the wider changes of the 1990s.

One of the central assumptions of the silent revolution is that the unregulated flow of goods and capital will enhance prosperity for all those who participate in it. This book analyzes Latin America's position

in a changing global economy and shows how countries have special-
ized in two main areas of exports: the South American economies have
concentrated on primary commodities like oil, minerals, and agricultural products, while Mexico, Central America, and the Caribbean have
become a low-cost manufacturing platform for the U.S. economy. *Silent
Revolution* explores the impact of trade liberalization on the region's
workforce, surveys the flurry of regional trade agreements, which have
become an essential part of the region's economic hopes, and looks at
the prospects for the Free Trade Area of the Americas negotiations.

The abstraction of most economic debate on the issue also tends to
downplay the impact of economic change on those it is supposed to
benefit—ordinary Latin Americans. While examining neoliberalism's
macroeconomic record at regional and national level, *Silent Revolution*
also reveals the human costs of the region's experiment in market economics, even before the crisis of neoliberalism. It describes some of the
ordinary men and women whose jobs and lives have been changed for-
ever by structural adjustment. In doing so, this book tries to answer
two central questions: Is the region's economy better off after twenty
years of adjustment, and are Latin Americans themselves leading better
lives as a result?

Most criticisms of structural adjustment are written by dissident
economists from the North, who then offer their own alternatives with
scant recognition for the opinions of those suffering adjustment's
impact in the South. *Silent Revolution* shows how Latin Americans are
themselves actively involved in the search either for more effective and
socially inclusive versions of market-led growth, or for a completely different model of "people-centered development" and analyzes the political constraints on the changes they propose.

## THE POWER OF LANGUAGE

In any debate over the costs and benefits of neoliberalism, its supporters start out with a distinct advantage, for the silent revolution has
managed to get language on its side. Calling unregulated commerce
"free trade" and unfettered capitalism "the free market" automatically
confers legitimacy on the ideas. Likewise, "removing trade barriers,"
"enhancing efficiency/competitiveness," "getting the prices right," and
"improving growth" sound essentially positive, even if the listener is

vague on the details, and even vaguer on the consequences. Critics are forced to choose between adopting neoliberal terminology which automatically works against them (usually reducing them to strewing dozens of inverted commas around terms like "free trade" and "efficiency") or trying to frame an entirely different language for the debate, which inevitably means that they are written off as more concerned with political correctness than the real world.

Neoliberalism's advocates are also adept at the use of euphemism and obfuscation. "Protection" might sound like something positive (after all, a mother protects her children), but call it *protectionism* and there is nothing to stop free-market *machismo* from stigmatizing it as a sign of political cowardice. A linguistic sleight-of-hand has seen U.S. politicians and policy makers emphasizing Washington's support for "market democracies." Democracy is clearly something no one can oppose, and Washington's push to spread market forces into every corner of the world economy wins public support on its coat-tails.

In massacring language and baffling almost any non-economist, the IMF is unsurpassed: loans become "arrangements" or "facilities," part payments are "tranche disbursements." The IMF's "stabilization programs" frequently achieve exactly the opposite. The queen of all euphemisms is undoubtedly "structural adjustment," a stunningly bland name for the brutal surgery that lies at the heart of the silent revolution.

Rather than trying to invent a whole new vocabulary, this author chooses to debate on the linguistic terrain of the free-marketeers in an effort both to demystify the language and to show that, even on its own terms and in its own words, after twenty years of near total ideological dominance, neoliberalism can claim remarkably few successes in return for far too many failures in both human and economic terms.

# 1—State vs. Market

## The Rise and Fall of Import Substitution

Anybody who had reason to use a Brazilian disposable diaper in the early 1990s had firsthand experience of how import substitution failed the consumer. The diapers didn't work. Until recently, Brazil's diapers were treacherous things, liable to leak or spring open with disastrous consequences for your carpet. The tale of the Brazilian disposable is a microcosm of what went wrong with much of Brazil's industry, and it stems from the flawed model for economic development adopted in Latin America after the 1930s.

The offending items were made by Brazilian workers in a Brazilian factory. They were protected by import taxes against competition from better quality foreign varieties. The taxes were originally designed to encourage the development of a Brazilian diaper industry, thereby reducing the economy's reliance on manufactured imports. However, protection also absolved the manufacturer from having to worry about quality or keeping prices down.

This was particularly true because the market was so small in Brazil. Only one Brazilian baby in forty wore disposables—the poor majority couldn't afford them, and many of the rich preferred to pay the poor to wash their babies' cloth nappies rather than buy disposables.[1] Consequently, there was little room in the market for more than a few producers, who could fix prices between themselves to prevent competition. The consumer was the loser.

Like many of the beneficiaries of Brazilian protectionism, the producer was a transnational company, Johnson & Johnson. It had built a factory in Brazil in 1975, "tariff hopping" to take advantage of the protected market, where it had an effective monopoly. It could undoubtedly have invested to upgrade the quality, but in the absence of competition, why bother? When the Brazilian government tried to open up the economy to imports, Johnson & Johnson did their utmost to prevent it:

> The Argentine nappies on sale in Mappins, one of the country's largest store chains, at half the price of Brazilian ones, required a long battle. When Mappins began the imports, trucks were held up on the border while Johnson & Johnson, which monopolizes the Brazilian nappy market, found a helpful bureaucrat with an ancient regulation classifying nappies as pharmaceutical products which could be imported only if accompanied by a qualified pharmacist, transported and kept in cold storage.[2]

Faced with a small local market, Johnson & Johnson might have tried to cut costs by exporting to other countries. This would allow them to increase output, bringing economies of scale that would lower the unit cost. But who would buy an overpriced, substandard Brazilian diaper? The problem recurred throughout Brazilian industry. A 1990 study of the performance of 220 Sao Paulo companies showed them to be "generally dozens or hundreds of times worse than that necessary to compete on world markets."[3]

Yet even in Brazil, at the time routinely branded by the financial press as the laggard of the silent revolution, times were changing. The imports from Argentina eventually got past the bureaucratic hurdles and broke Johnson & Johnson's monopoly. In the years that followed, a number of competitors got in on the act, both importing and producing locally. Prices promptly fell to about a third of their former levels and Johnson & Johnson were driven into third place in the diaper market, behind brands such as Procter & Gamble's Pampers.[4] The quality of life (and carpet) of a small number of disposable-dependent foreigners and wealthy Brazilians undoubtedly improved, lending further support to the arguments in favor of the switch from import substitution to the free market.

Brazil was something of a late convert to the merits of the market. In the rest of Latin America the state-versus-market pendulum, which had swung so completely to the side of the state in the 1950s, reached the opposite extreme in the 1980s, in the darkest days of the debt crisis. Free-marketeers in the United States and Latin America hailed the demise of import substitution as proof that the state should stay out of running the economy. Governments were inherently bureaucratic, inefficient, and corrupt and always put short-term political advantage before long-term economic prosperity, they argued. The only way forward was the standard IMF recipe of deregulation, privatization, and free trade, which would free the region from the dead hand of statism and let Adam Smith's "invisible hand" of the market lead it to a golden dawn of prosperity and growth.

One of the strongest cards in neoliberalism's hand is its self-belief. Its diagnosis and cure were presented as common sense: the market was obviously more efficient than the state; free trade had to be better for growth than protectionism; the state should not spend more than it earned. As one U.S. critic complained, "So completely do the free market ideas of neoliberalism dominate the current Latin American debate that opposing ideas are increasingly treated with the bemused condescension usually reserved for astrological charts and flat-earth manifestos."[5] At an early 1990s seminar in London's Institute of Latin American Studies, Paul Luke of Morgan Grenfell Debt Arbitrage and Trading, (a man introduced as "the leading City analyst on Latin America") caused barely a stir when he informed his audience in urbane tones of absolute certainty that "protectionism is obviously bad for growth" (Japan? Taiwan?) and that in Latin America only those of "low IQ" (among whom he included the recently elected Venezuelan president) dissented from the basic neoliberal recipe. The arguments convinced because they were seductively simple and endlessly repeated. But were they right?

Since independence in the early nineteenth century, debt crises have scourged Latin America at roughly fifty-year intervals—the 1820s, 1870s, 1930s, and 1980s.[6] Each crisis has swept away the previous economic model and laid the basis for the next fifty-year experiment. Each birth has been painful and each model has left both losers and winners in Latin America's historic search for the road to long-term development. Echoing Garcia Marquez's great novel *One Hundred Years of Solitude*, an unusually lyrical World Bank study described Latin American economic history as "irregular and magical cycles of sorrow and frustration."[7]

After the crisis of the 1820s, Latin America chose an export-led model based on selling raw materials (commodities) to North America and Europe. After the second crisis in the 1870s, the larger republics began some modern manufacturing. The disastrous world depression of the 1930s set Latin America on the path of vigorous import substitution, which duly came unstuck in the "lost decade" of the 1980s. At the begin-

ning of each change of direction, successive generations of economists
and politicians were convinced that their way was the only way; it was
just "common sense."


## IMPORT SUBSTITUTION

Up until the 1930s Latin America's economy depended on exporting
raw materials to the industrialized world in order to earn hard currency with which to buy manufactured products. Following the Wall
Street crash of 1929 and the ensuing depression in Europe and North
America, this classic free-trade model fell apart. World coffee prices fell
by two-thirds, cutting Brazil's exports from $446 million in 1929 to just
$181 million by 1932.[8] In El Salvador the coffee slump drove impover-
ished workers to rebel in 1932, ending in an army massacre of 30,000
peasants that virtually wiped out the country's Indian population.
Most of Latin America in the 1930s experienced growing poverty, social
unrest, repression, economic recession, and defaults on the foreign
debt. Latin America's export markets disappeared, and economies
starved of hard currency had to drastically curtail imports.

What began as emergency measures to produce goods that could no
longer be bought abroad eventually grew into the fully fledged model of
import substitution, which became the unchallenged economic gospel
in Latin America after the Second World War. Import substitution's theoretical foundations were mainly laid by the UN's Economic Commission for Latin America and the Caribbean (known by its Spanish
acronym, CEPAL). Free trade had failed the region, and "common sense"
dictated that the state should intervene to encourage national industry
and protect its citizens from the cold winds of the world market.

Import substitution built on the ideas of John Maynard Keynes,
whose arguments for state management of the economy had inspired
New Deal economics in the United States and the creation of the welfare state in Britain. At its height, import substitution's brand of state-
led development was the unquestioned orthodoxy of the age.
According to Humberto Vega, a donnish former chief of the Chilean
Treasury, "In the 1960s the economics department taught you Keynes
and *Cepalismo*. Classical economics was only taught in economic history! The role of the state was obvious, no one argued with it, not even
the right, which was very protectionist."[9] Soviet industrialization and

the heavily state-led revival of the European economy after the Second World War had further established the centrality of the state in successful economic planning.

The state stepped in with a "big push" to redirect the economy away from its dependence on primary exports and kick-start it into producing manufactured goods for the domestic market. To achieve this, it

- invested heavily in the kind of infrastructure required by industry, such as new roads, water, and electricity supplies;

- kept labor costs down in urban areas by subsidizing basic foods and imposing price controls;

- protected local industries against foreign competition by imposing import taxes and "non-tariff barriers" such as import quotas;

- nationalized key industries such as oil, utilities, and iron and steel, and established new ones. This produced a large state sector, intended to play a leading role in developing the economy;

- supported an overvalued exchange rate, making Latin America's exports expensive and imports cheap. This hurt exports, but helped industry by reducing the price of imported machinery and inputs, while tariff and non-tariff barriers ensured that the relative cheapness of imports did not undercut their products. An overvalued exchange rate also kept inflation down by ensuring cheaper imports.

The new economic model went hand in hand with the political phenomenon known as populism. Charismatic leaders such as Juan Domingo Perón (Argentina), Lázaro Cárdenas (Mexico), or Getulio Vargas (Brazil) preached a message of nationalist development and became the darlings of the new urban masses. Such men made brilliant leaders, but poor economists. They avoided politically divisive decisions over how to distribute wealth, preferring to print enough money to keep everyone happy in the short term. They bequeathed an inflationary legacy with which the region has been grappling for much of the last twenty years.

Although now widely derided by today's generation of liberal economists, import substitution transformed the region's economy. By the early 1960s, domestic industry supplied 95 percent of Mexico's and 98 percent of Brazil's consumer goods.[10] From 1950 to 1980 Latin America's industrial output went up six times, keeping well ahead of population growth. Infant mortality fell from 107 per thousand live births in 1960 to 69 per thousand in 1980;[11] life expectancy rose from 52 to 64 years. In the mid-1950s, Latin America's economies were growing faster than those of the industrialized West.

Industrialization transformed the continent's economy. In what had previously been a predominantly rural, peasant society, great cities sprang up in an unplanned sprawl of cheap concrete tower blocks, dirty factories, flyovers, and congestion. Rich, smart central districts with luxury shopping malls and mirror-glass skyscrapers were dwarfed by the vast shanty towns of the poor which ring all the major cities, epitomizing the sharp inequalities of wealth in the region. Convinced by their own boom-time, we-can-do-anything rhetoric, the Brazilian military embarked on huge road- and dam-building sprees. In 1968 and 1970 Mexico City hosted the Olympics and World Cup to announce its arrival as an international capital. The state played the pivotal role in achieving this transformation.

Import substitution also changed the political face of the continent, as leaders like Perón and Vargas built their support on the burgeoning urban working class. Especially in its earlier phase (before the Brazilian military coup of 1964), this broadened political participation to new areas of society, building up a strong trade union movement (albeit often with an unhealthily close relationship with the state) and greatly strengthening democratic politics.

Brazil and Mexico were the success stories of import substitution. Between 1960 and 1979 they increased their share of Latin America's industrial output from 50 to over 60 percent and attracted over 70 percent of foreign direct investment over the same period.[12] Brazil, whose industrial output per person went up more than fourfold between 1950 and 1970,[13] became Latin America's economic giant, producing a third of the regional GDP by 1981,[14] making it the seventh-largest industrial producer in the world.[15]

While other developing countries, such as South Korea and Taiwan, found ways to move from import substitution to a new phase of export-led growth (see chapter 8), in Latin America these efforts foundered. The cracks were already beginning to show by the late 1950s. Industrialization was capital intensive and failed to generate the expected number of new jobs for the region's unemployed masses. Transnational companies proved particularly ineffective in creating new jobs. The result was a two-tier labor force, a small "aristocracy of labor" employed in the modern industrial sector of the economy, and a mass of unemployed or underemployed workers elsewhere.

Sheltered by tariff barriers, industries became inefficient, producing shoddy and expensive goods for consumers who had no choice. In 1969 the Chilean domestic prices of electric sewing machines, bicycles, and home refrigerators were respectively three, five and six times higher than international prices.[16] The small domestic markets for such goods were usually dominated by a few companies, who established "oligopolies," fixing prices between themselves and thereby avoiding the pressures of competition that might have forced them to invest more and produce better-quality goods. "Before, it was easy to be a businessman in Argentina, with subsidies, speculation, and protection," recalled ex-president and leading neoliberal crusader Carlos Menem. "This was a country of rich businessmen and poor companies."[17] Local middle classes soon came to equate local manufacture with low standards. When Argentina liberalized imports in the late 1970s, the shops of Buenos Aires would plaster their windows with signs saying *Todo Importado*, "Everything Imported," to attract customers.

Although import substitution successfully ended the need to import some goods, especially consumer durables like cars and TVs, it merely replaced that dependence with a new kind, stemming from industry's reliance on imported capital goods such as heavy machinery, turbines and cranes. This meant that Latin America did not solve its trade deficit. The overvalued exchange rates and priority given by government to producing for the domestic market made matters worse, as neglected and uncompetitive exports failed to keep up with booming imports.

Countries undergoing import substitution were dogged by the economic consequences of inequality, which the model further exacerbated. Only a small proportion of the people in most Latin American republics actually functioned as consumers for the new industries—the great majority were too poor to buy anything. In all but the largest countries, such as Brazil and Mexico, the domestic market was therefore too small for fledgling industries to achieve the necessary economies of scale. Foreign companies were particularly reluctant to invest outside the big economies for this reason. Few governments were willing to undertake the kind of fundamental redistribution of wealth required to create a sizable domestic market. Instead, they opted for regional free trade agreements, hoping that by grouping the middle classes of, for example, all the Central American countries, they could reach the market size required for industrial takeoff. In practice, these agreements soon foundered, as they worked to the benefit of the stronger economies, and the weaker ones quickly pulled out.

Knowing that the government would always bail them out in the end, many (though not all) state industries proved inefficient producers, saddling the treasury with large operating losses. The widespread subsidies and increased state spending on social services as well as state investment further contributed to chronic government spending deficits. When governments covered these by printing money, inflation started to gather pace.

Import substitution was particularly disastrous for the countryside, which was starved of public investment and social services as the government gave priority to urban areas. Peasants selling their harvests suffered when price controls were imposed on their crops, while import substitution's overvalued exchange rates also encouraged a flood of cheap food imports that undercut local farmers. The deepening misery in the countryside, coupled with the industrial boom in the cities, provoked a massive spate of migration. Between 1950 and 1980, 27 million people left their farms and villages and joined the great exodus to the cities.[18]

Other aspects of government policy benefited rural areas, however. In the wake of the Cuban revolution, the United States promoted land reform throughout the region via President Kennedy's Alliance for Progress. Limited amounts of land were distributed, and credit was provided for small farmers through the state banking system in countries such as Chile, Colombia, and Venezuela.

The neglect of the countryside, where most of Latin America's poorest people live, along with the failure to generate jobs, meant that import substitution had a negative effect on income distribution. The region became increasingly polarized between rich and poor, the worst offender being Brazil, where from 1960 to 1970 every social class increased its income, but the bulk of the increase went to the rich. The richest 10 percent of Brazilians increased their share of total income from 28 to 48 percent.[19] Modern Brazil remains a country of extraordinary contrasts, from the blighted rural northeast, where conditions are as bad as many of the poorest parts of Africa, to the high-rise opulence of downtown Rio or São Paulo.

Import substitution also deepened Latin America's love-hate relationship with transnational companies. Although nationalists objected to the transnationals' repatriation of profits and the limited benefits they brought to the rest of the economy, Latin America's leaders saw them as a vital source of technology and capital, both in short supply in the region. Especially from the 1960s, transnationals extended their grip on the most dynamic sectors of the economy, leaving the more sluggish industries to local capital. The stranglehold exerted by the transnationals allowed the state to neglect spending on research and development (R&D), leading to a growing technology gap between Latin America and the North. This gap made it even more difficult for Latin American–owned companies to break into the fastest-growing areas of world trade, such as electronics and pharmaceuticals, which were also the areas of most rapidly developing technology.

As the flaws in the model became apparent, governments modified their policies. From the late 1960s onward, countries such as Brazil and Mexico gave increased priority to manufactured exports to try to fill their growing trade gaps. Although Mexico's sudden oil bonanza in the late 1970s meant it temporarily lost interest in industrial exports, Brazil achieved some extraordinary results. Following the military coup of 1964, a combination of devaluation (to increase exports' competitiveness) and the army's ruthless suppression of labor to bring down wages, led to the "economic miracle" of 1967–1973; manufacturing exports tripled in the three years to 1973. Having already built factories in Latin America to produce for the protected local markets, transnational companies were best placed to turn their attention to exports and dominated the export boom in Mexico and Brazil. In the region as a whole, manufactured exports increased forty-fold from 1967 to 1980,[20] but even then they represented only a fifth of industrial output, which remained predominantly directed at the local market, and the continued reliance on imported capital goods meant that the trade gap in manufactures continued to grow.[21]

## THE DEBT CRISIS

The final decline of import substitution began with the sudden rise in world oil prices in 1973. The billions of "petrodollars" that OPEC countries recycled into the world's financial markets had to go somewhere,

and Western banks fell over themselves to lend to third world governments. The banks fell into the trap of believing, in the words of Citicorp
chairman Walter Wriston, that "a country does not go bankrupt" as a
private company could.[22] Understandably, the Latin American governments flocked to borrow at the low or even negative real interest rates
being offered by the banks. They believed such rates would be permanent, enabling them both to grow their way out of poverty and pay off
their debts. Almost everyone had a good reason to borrow. Brazil was
faced with an acute foreign exchange crisis, and as its oil import bill
soared it chose to borrow abroad to keep importing the oil, machinery,
and inputs it needed for its industrial growth. The economy kept on
growing, but so did Brazil's foreign debt. By 1978 its debt service took
up 64 percent of its export income.

> [From 1978 to 1982] Brazil borrowed $63.4bn, well over half of its total gross for-
> eign debt, in a frenzied, and eventually useless attempt to avoid default. Almost
> all of this money did not even enter Brazil, but stayed with the foreign banks
> ($60.9bn).... [Brazil was forced to] contract a huge paper debt that it would later be
> forced to honor through the export of real goods. It was a financial con trick on
> an unprecedented scale.[23]

In other oil importing countries such as Chile and Argentina the
neoliberals made their first appearance on the scene following bloody
military coups in 1973 and 1976 respectively. The military governments
chose to abandon import substitution in favor of the sudden removal
of import barriers. The results were catastrophic, as both countries
went through a swift deindustrialization involving a spate of bankrupt-
cies and job losses. The Argentine military opted for a particularly spectacular form of industrial suicide by removing import controls and
tariffs at the same time they left the peso massively overvalued; the
result was a flood of artificially cheap imports. Argentina's consumer
goods imports increased over five times between 1975 and 1981 while
local industrial output fell by 3 percent a year over the same period.[24]
Since the import boom had to be paid for with foreign borrowing, the
Argentine and Chilean debts rose just like the Brazilian one, but without the benefit of industrialization.

In Mexico, the advent of the OPEC price rise just as massive new oil
finds came onstream ought to have been good news. But the govern-

ment borrowed massively to build up the oil industry. Pemex, the state oil giant, ran up a company debt of $15 billion by the early 1980s.[25]

Although some of the proceeds from aid and oil exports went into building up heavy and export industries, far more was spirited out of the country into U.S. banks as capital flight. As loans poured in, dollars also poured out, as government officials or business leaders siphoned as much as possible into U.S. bank accounts. In many cases this involved corruption, such as taking kickbacks on government con- tracts, but in Venezuela and Mexico, for example, it was quite legal to export dollars into a U.S. account. Estimates of the extent of capital flight vary wildly, but according to one World Bank report, "between 1979–82, $19.2bn left Argentina, $26.5bn left Mexico and $22bn left Venezuela: 64 percent, 48 percent and a staggering 137 percent respec- tively of the gross capital inflows to those countries." The Bank con- cluded "much of the money being borrowed from abroad was funneled straight out again."[26] Even in 1986, at the height of austerity, one banker confessed that his bank regularly "sends a guy with two empty suitcases" to Mexico City to pick up dollar deposits.[27]

The "dance of the millions," as the influx of petrodollars became known, also coincided with a period of military rule in Latin America; from 1972 to 1982 arms imports grew at an annual rate of 13 percent. In 1986, the Peruvian foreign minister estimated that Latin America's total defense spending over the previous ten years came to over $114 billion, roughly half the region's entire foreign debt.[28]

It seemed that whatever a Latin American government's policies, the temptation of cheap foreign capital seduced it into running up huge debts in the 1970s. One of the few exceptions was Colombia, which refused to be sucked into the borrowing frenzy and consequently, in eco- nomic terms at least, was an island of growth and falling poverty and inequality throughout the 1980s. Even Chile's first attempt at neoliberal reform under Pinochet foundered under the weight of debt—Chile's economy was actually worse hit than any other by the initial shock of the debt crisis. Brazil, Mexico, and Argentina became the third world's top three debtors. The flood of foreign borrowing allowed Latin America to stave off the collapse of import substitution for a few more years, but the delay proved expensive in both financial and human terms.

It is worth noting that import substitution alone did not lead to this collapse—countries such as South Korea managed to combine import substitution with manageable levels of foreign debt. According to a study by the UN Development Program, the main cause of the Latin American crisis was not its industrial policy per se, but its inability to cope with the economic shocks of the oil crisis by cutting spending to avoid a fiscal deficit. This in turn led to high inflation, shortages of foreign exchange, and eventually a debt crisis.[29]

Outside the region, the world economy and political thinking had changed radically since the days of Keynesian consensus in the 1950s. In the late 1960s, the unprecedented global economic boom of the postwar years began to run into trouble, and both Keynesianism and import substitution came under academic siege from a new generation of economic liberals. The resurgent free-marketeers argued for a sharp cut in the state's role in the economy, and took over the commanding heights of the world economy with the elections of Margaret Thatcher (1979) and Ronald Reagan (1980). The monetarist obsession with reducing inflation supplanted Keynesian concerns with full employment and the welfare state. In just twenty years, the roles had been reversed: neoliberalism had become the common sense of the day, and statism was consigned to the junkyard of history.

For Latin America the problems began with the second big oil price rise of 1979. A new generation of first world conservative leaders reacted to rising global inflation by raising interest rates. The move prompted a deep recession in their own economies, which formed the main markets for Latin American exports. Latin America had to pay higher interest rates on its debt just as its exports began to fall; the sums no longer added up. In August 1982, the crash finally came when Mexico announced it was unable to meet its debt repayment obligations. Latin America's "lost decade" had begun.

The debt crisis that broke over the continent in August 1982 brought in its wake recession and hardship for millions of Latin Americans. But for Sir William Ryrie, a top World Bank official, it was "a blessing in disguise."[30] The debt crisis forced Latin America into a constant round of debt negotiations, providing the Reagan government, along with the IMF and the other international financial institutions with all the leverage they needed to overhaul the region's economy, in alliance with northern commercial creditor banks and the region's homegrown free-marketeers. Latin America was ripe for a free market revolution.

## WINNING THE ARGUMENT

Ideas are powerful, as Keynes observed:

> The ideas of economists and political philosophers, both when they are right and when they are wrong, are more powerful than is commonly understood. Indeed the world is ruled by little else. Practical men, who believe themselves to be quite exempt from any intellectual influences, are usually the slaves of some defunct economist. Madmen in authority, who hear voices in the air, are distilling their frenzy from some academic scribbler of a few years back. I am sure that the power of vested interests is vastly exaggerated compared with the gradual encroachment of ideas.[31]

Critics of neoliberalism often talk as if Washington, the IMF, and the World Bank have single-handedly imposed neoliberalism on a uniformly reluctant continent. While the Fund has undoubtedly played an important role, it would never have been possible without the support of local economists and politicians, the preexisting crisis in import substitution, and the perceived lack of alternatives. Except in the worst meltdowns, such as Argentina's in 2002, a sizable elite in Latin America, perhaps 20 to 30 percent of the population, have gained from access to first world consumer goods, jobs with international companies, and the opportunities brought by deregulation and increased trade. As one veteran Central American intellectual observed, "neoliberalism has united the elites of the South with those of the North and created the biggest convergence of financial, technological, and military power in history."[32] By the time the debt crisis swept away the remnants of import substitution in the early 1980s, neoliberalism enjoyed an unstoppable coalition of influential supporters and potential beneficiaries both inside and outside the region, and had the intellectual high ground to itself. According to the eminent historian Eric Hobsbawm, "The most dangerous legacy of the 1970s and 1980s has been the conversion of most economists to the theology of absolute neoliberalism."[33]

Ideological shifts are partly generational. The young men and (occasionally) women who end up as policy makers grow up, go to school and usually university, read the newspapers, argue and debate the new ideas of the time, and often go on to post-graduate studies. By the time they leave university for their first job, their mental frameworks are well established and do not easily change in later years, barring the occasional road-to-Damascus style of conversion. For the academic generals grooming new generations of ideological warriors for the fray, the message is, get them young.

Fresh from university, the eager, young would-be policy makers join up for the war of ideas, where the battalions from the university economics departments, private think tanks, government ministries, banks, and international institutions meet and argue their case in a global merry-go-round of conferences and seminars. To the winners, the spoils: jobs in universities, government departments, international agencies, and eventually, perhaps, Minister of Finance or one of the other key posts in the economic cabinet. With them, the chance to change the nature of the economy and influence the fate of millions of citizens, followed by a well-paid directorship or two after leaving office. For the losers, unless they switch sides, years in the intellectual wilderness, trying to build up a critique and an alternative model that will eventually drive the pendulum back in their direction. In this world, the big institutions like the World Bank and IMF command enormous influence; when it comes to the broad issue of "development," their huge research budgets decide what is researched and by whom, both by their own staff and an army of thousands of consultants. The arrangement has been described by one critic as an "intellectual-financial complex,"[34] enabling the Bretton Woods institutions to set the parameters, and to some extent conclusions of the debate on world development. As the executive secretary of the UN Economic Commission for Latin America (CEPAL), José Antonio Ocampo, sees it, "whereas the center is made of 'policy *making*' economies, the periphery is largely 'policy *taking*.'"[35]

Chile provides a good example of the connections among academic research, institutional power, and the harsh realities of politics. There, the first steps in the neoliberal counterattack against the state took place almost twenty years before General Pinochet seized power. In the mid-1950s the economics faculty in the far-off University of Chicago was nurturing the flame of liberalism at a time when Keynes's thinking was the orthodoxy of the age. In their academic redoubt, the high priests of Chicago, Friedrich von Hayek, Milton Friedman, and Arnold Harberger, laid the intellectual foundations for the liberal crusade that swept the world in the 1970s.

Friedman and Harberger were the economists, specializing in fierce critiques of state intervention and laying the theoretical basis of monetarism. Von Hayek was the philosopher, expanding liberal ideas to include the social and political arguments for "taking the politics out of politics": using an authoritarian state to prevent pressure groups such as trade unions and political parties from interfering with a government's ability to make decisions free from immediate political pressures. Such interference, they argued, could only inhibit the efficiency-maximizing role of the market and hinder growth. The combination of reducing the state's role in the economy, while greatly strengthening its powers to undermine trade unions and other potential opponents became the hallmark of neoliberal rulers such as General Pinochet or Mrs. Thatcher.

Taking note of CEPAL's growing influence, Chicago decided to launch a counterattack on its doorstep. In 1955 Professor Theodore W. Shultz, president of the Department of Economics, visited the Catholic University of Chile to set up a scholarship system for a select group of Chilean post-graduate students.[36] Between 1956 and 1961 at least 150 promising Chilean students received U.S. government-sponsored fellowships to study economics at Chicago.[37] It was money well spent. Many of the students went back to academic posts in the Catholic University, which became the intellectual powerhouse for neoliberal ideas as Chile's statist experiment ended in spectacular economic collapse (helped by Washington's destabilization program and other forms of sabotage) during the years of Salvador Allende.

In 1973 General Augusto Pinochet overthrew Allende in a military coup. Within three months, the army had killed at least 1,500 people in a savage assault on trade unionists and political activists.[38] Whatever their feelings about the massacre, the coup was a golden opportunity for the neoliberals. The inexperienced technocrats faced initial skepticism from both the military and Chile's business community until March 1975, when they flew in Milton Friedman and Arnold Harberger for a high-profile lobbying effort. A month later Pinochet ditched his initially cautious economic team and put the "Chicago Boys" in charge.[39] Chile has not been the same since. From 1975 to 1982, the country pioneered a particularly savage form of neoliberalism, ending in a spectacular financial crash in 1982. After that, a more cautious and successful model emerged from the rubble, turning the country into the region's economic success story over the next two decades, albeit with severe social costs (see chapter 5).

initial extreme neolibralism failed; more cautious
succeeded - but with social cost

Ever since the Chicago Boys arrived, the running of the Chilean economy has remained firmly in the hands of the technocrats. After 1973, a mirror image of the rise of the Chicago Boys got under way as a new generation of anti-Pinochet technocrats began to assemble in the wings. Many were driven into exile and had little option but to enroll in post-graduate studies in order to earn a living. In Chile, intellectual opponents of Pinochet set up private think tanks, often with funding from international aid agencies. By 1985 there were thirty private research institutes in Chile working in the social sciences, employing 543 researchers. Of these, 30 percent held M.A. or Ph.D degrees from foreign universities.[40] Academic rigor in their work was essential to fend off accusations that the new think tanks were mere front organizations for proscribed left-wing political parties, and as a result their analyses and opinions won widespread respect.

In the libraries and cafes of exile, and later back in Chile after the early 1980s, Chile's intellectuals endlessly argued over the reasons for the collapse of the Allende government, the world's first elected Marxist government. The failure of Allende's economic program could not wholly be blamed on the saboteurs, and a radical rethink gathered pace, further fueled after 1985 by the swift growth of the Chilean economy under Pinochet and the startling collapse of statist systems in Eastern Europe.

By the time General Pinochet left power in 1990, the opposition had accepted many of the Chicago Boys' ideas: the state should be kept out of economic management where possible; foreign investment and economic stability, including low inflation, are essential for growth; the government should not spend its way into a deficit. However, the "CIEPLAN monks" as they became known (named after one of the leading think tanks) took a more pragmatic approach to economic planning, and believed the benefits of growth had to be more fairly distributed than during the Pinochet years, which had seen a sharp increase in inequality within Chile. This also involved a real commitment to democratic government.

As the soldiers retired to their barracks, a new generation of technocrats moved smoothly from think tanks to ministries and Chile's economy continued to grow with scarcely a blip. They were still almost all post-graduates from U.S. and European universities, but fewer of them came from Chicago. Within weeks of their defeat, General

Pinochet's leading economists were busily setting up a new series of think tanks in which to lick their wounds before mounting an eventual counteroffensive.

## ON ECONOMICS AND ECONOMISTS

The rise of Latin America's technocrats is part of a worldwide phenomenon in recent decades, the exaltation of economists as the natural leaders of the world order. While some leading academic economists, such as Joseph Stiglitz or Dani Rodrik, are well aware of the limitations of their craft, many government policy makers, with only a few years of study under their belts, demonstrate all too clearly that a little learning is a dangerous thing. Their self-belief and their promise to turn the dross of underdevelopment into the pure gold of high-speed growth, turns them from economist into alchemists (alconomists?), with an apparently hypnotic power over the minds of political leaders.

A profound identity crisis lies at the heart of economics—is it an art or a science? In the past, great economists such as Friedrich List (1789–1846) and Karl Marx (1818–1883) followed a historical approach. One modern-day disciple, Ha-Joon Chang, an economist at Cambridge University, describes their method as

> searching for historical patterns, finding explanations behind them, distilling theories from them, and finally applying the theories just constructed to contemporary problems.... The approach is concrete and inductive, and contrasts with the currently dominant Neoclassical approach based on abstract and deductive methods.[41]

Unfortunately, as Chang suggests, today's economists want to be more like Isaac Newton than Friedrich List. Since the days of Newton, physics has been a role model for other disciplines because of its elegance, simplicity, and above all its ability to predict events in the real world. Physics moves from hypothesis to prediction using mathematics, then checks the prediction against reality. Andrew Lo, an economist at MIT, believes his peers are suffering from "a peculiar psychological disorder known as 'physics envy.'. . . We would love to have three laws that explain 99 percent of economic behavior; instead we have about 99 laws that explain maybe 3 percent of economic behavior. Nevertheless, we like to talk as if we are dealing with physical phenomena."[42]

Academic prestige (including the lion's share of Nobel laureates) within the economics establishment increasingly stems from mathematical wizardry, not from engaging with real world events or people. As one economist admitted, "I must confess to an instinctive conviction that what cannot be measured may not exist."[43] So much for human happiness, job satisfaction, anxiety and stress at the workplace.

To enable mathematics to be applied, a series of assumptions must be made to simplify the real world into a model fit for the computer. Wassily Leontieff, a Nobel Prize-winning mathematical economist, poured scorn on the whole idea:

> Page after page of professional economic journals are filled with mathematical formulas leading the reader from sets of more or less plausible, but entirely arbitrary assumptions to precisely stated but irrelevant theoretical conclusions.[44]

At the cutting edge, neoliberal practitioners like Harvard's Larry Summers prefer to be seen as engineers rather than physicists. In a speech to delegates at the joint IMF–World Bank meeting in Bangkok in 1991, Summers revealed the origins of his self-belief:

> The laws of economics, it's often forgotten, are like the laws of engineering. There's only one set of laws and they work everywhere.[45]

At that time Summers was the Bank's chief economist and vice president for development economics. In 1993 he became President Clinton's under secretary to the Treasury, before becoming president of Harvard University in 2001. Other Harvard economists are much more skeptical over their discipline's claims to scientific status, above all its poor record as a predictive tool. Dani Rodrik, of the university's John F. Kennedy School of Government caustically observes, "Economists rank second only to astrologers in their predictive abilities."[46] In practice, economic policy making is like "driving a car only looking in the rearview mirror," according to one senior IMF analyst.[47]

The most basic subject of orthodox economics is *homo economicus*, an abstraction of the human being.[48] *Homo economicus* has no friends, family, community, nor any other non-economic links. S/he has an insatiable urge to acquire goods and his/her happiness is directly

proportional to consumption. A person with ten cars is ten times hap-
pier than a person with one. S/he acts purely on the basis of short-term
self-interest. With assumptions like these, it is small wonder that the
end result—neoclassical economics—leads to a society that is strong on
materialism and fails miserably on issues like justice, inequality or
quality of life. Small wonder that Thomas Carlyle famously labeled the
discipline "that Dismal Science."

The variables used by economists to describe the world around
them are themselves open to question. Most governments and commentators measure a country's economic performance in terms of
Gross Domestic Product (GDP), the sum of all the goods and services
produced by a country. Yet as an indicator of well-being or misery, GDP
leaves out almost as much as it describes:[49]

- It excludes important areas of activity that lie outside the money economy, such
  as unpaid domestic labor, thereby ignoring a large part of women's contribution
  to the economy. If women are forced out to work and end up paying for their
  child care, GDP goes up for both the job, and the paid child care, distorting the
  picture as well as ignoring the impact of a "double day" on women's lives.

- It excludes issues of wealth or income distribution within a country (although
  other standard, if rarely used, indicators can fill in the gap).

- GDP assumes nature is infinitely bountiful, and excludes the exhaustion of natural resources. "Costa Rica between 1970 and 1990 lost natural capital (such as soils
  and forests) amounting to more than 6 percent of its total GDP in that period. Yet
  the national accounts were silent on this continuing hemorrhage."[50] GDP also
  fails to allow for depletion of natural capital caused by using nature as a "sink"
  for dumping waste. In fact, waste disposal is classed as a productive activity and
  therefore contributes positively to growth.

- GDP compares different countries by converting at the official exchange rate,
  even though this can be massively over or undervalued. This weakness is now
  widely recognized, and the UN Development Program produces annual estimates
  of per capita GDP at "purchasing power parity" that attempt to compensate for
  exchange rate distortions. To date, however, the World Bank has largely insisted
  on using conventional measures of GDP.

Unfortunately, no one has yet come up with a better alternative. For the
time being, whatever its flaws, GDP growth will continue to be used as

the yardstick of economic success and this book will be forced to talk in terms of free markets, free trade, and GDP, despite serious reservations as to their value as objective and useful concepts.

A further myth arising from the mathematical pretensions of the discipline is that of objectivity. In fact, a political choice is implicit in any technical debate over the rival merits of state and market. States are, to some degree, accountable and representative. Markets are not. Whatever the flaws of the Latin American state, many grassroots organizations and other pressure groups have spent decades learning how to pressure it into listening to their needs and demands. Replacing the state with the market disenfranchises them, unless they are to acquire genuine influence over the decisions of transnational corporations, large local companies, and others, an implausible scenario that the technocrats seek to avoid at all costs in the name of economic efficiency. Some critics believe that the central purpose of neoliberalism is political rather than economic:

> The aim of the last generation of free market thinkers, notably Hayek and his followers, was less to build a robust view of what actually happens in a market economy than a model that could compete with Marxism. The aim was ideological and required all kinds of contortions to produce the desired result. As a source of inspiration in a battle of ideas which the West needed to win, it worked; as a source of policy recommendations, millions have reason to curse the theory for the avoidable suffering exacted in its name.[51]

Such matters would be of little concern if the rise of the technocracy had not given economists such enormous (and growing) influence over the way governments decide policy. In extreme cases, as in Pinochet's Chile, the economic cabinet can end up resembling Aztec high priests, sacrificing thousands of lives on the altars of the unfathomable gods of monetarism or structural adjustment.

# 2 — Poverty Brokers

## The International Monetary Fund and the World Bank

The acronyms of faceless international organizations do not usually start riots, but the three letters IMF (International Monetary Fund) provoke explosive reactions throughout Latin America. Since 1982 and the start of the debt crisis, "IMF riots" have periodically ravaged the region's cities from Buenos Aires to Caracas, leaving hundreds of dead and wounded and losses of millions of dollars in damaged and looted property.

The riots have been a response to the IMF's role in orchestrating (some say imposing) neoliberal reforms in response to the region's debt crisis. These have involved austerity measures to "stabilize" the crisis, followed by the wider restructuring of "structural adjustment." Since the mid-1980s, other institutions, notably the World Bank and Inter-American Development Bank, have joined the IMF in its crusade. Critics charge that such policies have failed to produce a return to sustained growth, while exacerbating poverty and inequality. Such claims have led to a growing international clamor for the reform of the two institutions and their policies, but so far behavior on the ground suggests that little has changed in the institutions' underlying policy prescriptions.

One of the bloodiest IMF riots took place in 1984 in the Dominican Republic, which shares a troubled island with Haiti in the Caribbean. After a year of wrangling over the Dominican government's failure to fulfill its promises to the Fund, the IMF retaliated with a virtual financial blockade of the country. On April 19, 1984, the Dominican government caved in and announced that food and medicine prices would be "liberalized." Overnight, medicine went up by 200 percent, while milk, rice, and cooking oil all doubled in price. Four days later riots started in the capital, Santo Domingo, then spread to thirty other towns. By the night of April 25, 112 civilians were dead and 500 wounded.[1]

The hunger and carnage in Santo Domingo and Caracas (300 to 1,500 dead in IMF riots in 1989, depending on whom you believe) are a far cry from the gleaming opulence of the joint annual meetings of the Fund and its sister organization, the World Bank.

These meetings are extraordinary events, half cult gathering, half beauty contest. One such beauty contest took place in September 1999 in the darkened seminar rooms of the palatial Marriott Hotel in Washington as one third world official after another stepped up to the podium and pitched to the bankers and fund managers who made up the audience. Reforms were on track. Political will was there. Inflation was coming down. Banks were being overhauled. This was the quest for that elusive beast, "market confidence." By publicly swearing fealty to the market, the officials hoped to reassure investors and prevent the kind of disastrous capital flight that had brought down economies in Asia, Latin America, and Eastern Europe over the previous two years.

The cult is built on the endless repetition of free market mantras (liberalize, privatize, encourage foreign trade and transnational corporations) combined with attacks on the cult's enemies—protectionism, government interference, capital controls. One investment banker in a seminar on Korea added to the quasi-religious feel by demanding that the government "respects the sanctity of contracts." The uniform dark suits and neat haircuts ensured that the delegates even *looked* like cult members. After a week of mutual brainwashing, thousands of them emerged blinking into the sticky Washington air, fortified and resolute, and scattered across the globe to continue leading their peoples on the long march toward the market.[2]

According to its founding articles, the IMF's purposes include:[3]

- to "promote international monetary cooperation"
- to "facilitate the expansion and balanced growth of international trade and to contribute thereby to the promotion and maintenance of high levels of employment and real income"
- to "promote exchange stability" and "avoid competitive exchange depreciation"
- to help eliminate foreign exchange restrictions "which hamper the growth of world trade"
- to provide members with loans "under adequate safeguards" when they get into balance of payments difficulties
- to lessen and shorten imbalances in the international balance of payments of member countries.

At first sight, such apparently laudable aims make the IMF sound like a philanthropic institution, smoothing the path of world trade and lending a helping hand to members who get into difficulties. It hardly seems the stuff to provoke mayhem and bloodshed on the streets of the third world. But the IMF's enormously increased power after the onset of the debt crisis in 1982, coupled to its hard-line interpretation of its role in "adjusting" troubled economies, has turned it into an "Institute of Misery and Famine" in the eyes of much of the developing world.

Like the United Nations, the IMF and its sister organization, the World Bank, were born at the end of the Second World War as part of an attempt by the victorious Western powers to prevent a repeat of the trade disputes of the Great Depression, which had sown the seeds of war. Although constitutionally they are part of the UN system, in practice the structure and role of the giant multilateral organizations demonstrate two radically opposed approaches. While the UN and its organizations largely subscribe to a "one country, one vote" principle (at least in the General Assembly), decisions at the IMF and World Bank are taken on the basis of "one dollar, one vote," guaranteeing the dominance of both by the U.S. government.

With Europe largely reduced to rubble, the United States emerged from the war as the world's economic superpower, able to dictate the rules of the game. At the IMF and World Bank's founding conference in Bretton Woods, New Hampshire, in July 1944, the U.S. delegation swiftly quashed the suggestions of John Maynard Keynes, the illustrious economist who headed the British delegation, and imposed Washington's blueprint for the postwar world economy and the institutions that would guide it. Half a century later, the third world (which at the time was still emerging from colonial rule) is still paying the price for that fateful clash between a triumphant United States and a bankrupt Britain.

Bretton Woods established the U.S. dollar as the international currency, although Keynes had argued for a new, neutral world currency. The arrangement simplified U.S. investment overseas, allowing the U.S. government to fund both investment and military spending by printing dollars as required. At the same time, in the third Bretton Woods institution, the General Agreement on Tariffs and Trade (GATT), founded in 1947, a body was created to press for fewer restrictions on world trade. In 1995, following the Uruguay Round of trade negotiations, the GATT agreement finally evolved into a new institution, the World Trade

Organization (WTO), which quickly acquired a public notoriety on a par with that of its older siblings.

The IMF and World Bank, officially named the International Bank for Reconstruction and Development, at first confined their attentions to rebuilding Europe with loans to Denmark, France, and Holland. As Europe began to recover, the Bretton Woods institutions began to look further afield. The Bank's first loan to a developing country went in 1948 to Chile.[4]

Bretton Woods enshrined "might is right" at the heart of global economic management. Voting power at the international financial institutions, as the IMF and World Bank are known, is determined by contribution to working capital. As of 2002 the United States had 17.16 percent of the vote,[5] sufficient to guarantee it the right to a veto over major IMF policy decisions, which require at least 85 percent support.[6] In contrast, no other country has more than 6.5 percent of the voting rights. In the real world, U.S. economic supremacy has dwindled, but the IMF has frozen the 1944 balance of power and Washington's veto into its voting system. As a sop to European sensibilities, the managing director of the IMF has traditionally been a European (currently Horst Köhler from Germany), while the World Bank president has always been an American (since 1995, James Wolfensohn, a former investment banker and patron of the arts).

The U.S. government even won the symbolic squabble over where to locate the offices of the international financial institutions, which ended up in Washington, under the wing of the U.S. government and well away from the UN headquarters in New York. Locating the global financial institutions in the U.S. political capital, rather than its financial center, further underlined the political importance Washington attached to the international financial institutions' role in building a new global economic order along U.S. guidelines.


## THE IMF

In theory, the IMF concerns itself with short-term stabilization, while the World Bank deals with longer-term issues like project funding and structural adjustment. In practice, the distinction has become increasingly blurred in recent years. Starting operations with 44 member governments,[7] by 2002 the IMF's membership had expanded to 183,[8] swollen by the rapidly escalating number of Eastern European republics desperate to rejoin the capitalist fold.

In normal times, the IMF oversees members' economic performance with regular visits to discuss policies and put pressure on member governments to observe Fund rules on issues like free trade and capital transfers. In such periods of tranquility, the IMF does not need to impose sanctions, but does have considerable influence over the weaker economies, not least through its gamut of "technical aid" services, including conferences, training, and the secondment of economic advisers to member governments.

However, the Fund only really comes into its own as a "lender of last resort," when a member gets into balance of payments difficulties—which usually means it cannot borrow sufficient money abroad to cover its trade deficit *and* keep up with debt service payments. In these circumstances, a member government can approach the IMF for a loan to bridge the financial gap, a procedure known as a "standby arrangement." In return for the loan, the Fund imposes conditions on the borrower, intended to make it pursue policies that will eliminate the balance of payments problem. The borrower's promises are enshrined in a "letter of intent" to the IMF. The letter is almost invariably drafted by IMF officials, leaving the government to try to negotiate modifications to the document.[9] Once the letter is "received" by the Fund, it releases ("disburses") the loan in staggered installments ("tranches"). If at any point the country fails to comply with the promises and targets ("performance criteria") laid out in the letter of intent, the Fund can suspend payments. Stand-by arrangements usually run from twelve to eighteen months, and can then be renewed if the balance of payments problem has not been solved. It frequently isn't—confirmed addicts like Honduras and Bolivia are now approaching the end of their second decade of almost continuous IMF loans.

From 1982, in the first years of the debt crisis, the IMF worked closely with creditor banks, which embarked on a seemingly endless round of negotiations to reschedule the debts of most Latin American nations. Rescheduling postponed a debtor's repayments (often at the cost of increasing a country's overall debt) and saved the commercial banks from having to write off their Latin American loans, which would have spelled disaster for their images on their home stock markets. For each debtor country, the banks formed advisory committees of creditors who undertook negotiations with individual debtors on a "case-by-case" basis. In the language of the school playground, the banks ganged up on the debtors, using divide-and-rule tactics to prevent any chance of a debtors' cartel forming. The advisory committees worked with IMF officials also engaged in negotiations with the government, creating what one critic has called "the Consortium" of commercial banks, Northern governments and international financial institutions that spoke with one all-powerful voice to the financially crippled nations of the South.[10]

It is its role as a leading agency in the Consortium that gives the Fund its real power, for the amounts of money it loans are often small compared to capital flows in and out of the third world. Instead, its clout stems from its role as international financial policeman. Most other potential lenders, such as the World Bank and the governments and banks of the rich industrialized world, usually make their loans conditional on an agreement with the IMF. International investors also see an IMF deal as a clean bill of financial health. The equation is simple: no standby arrangement, no cash. For any debtor country, the Fund is thus able to turn the taps of world finance off and on at will, turning it into "the most powerful international organization of the twentieth century, decisively influencing the well-being of the majority of the world's population."[11]

This was particularly the case in the first years of the 1980s, when most other sources of capital had dried up. When private capital flows surged back into the larger economies of Latin America in the early 1990s, the IMF's supremacy declined temporarily, but since foreign investors and the Fund frequently share the same view of what constitute "sound policies" in Latin America, the impact of this change was limited. Many of the smaller economies, however, remain starved of capital and as dependent on the IMF as ever. From 1995 on, a series of spectacular financial crashes in the larger economies (Mexico, 1995; Brazil, 1998; Argentina 2002) all involved massive IMF bailouts and a reassertion of the Fund's influence with even the largest players.

The IMF's elaborate strategy of carrots and sticks was not devised at Bretton Woods. Conditions were not attached to the European borrowers in the international financial institutions' initial phase of postwar reconstruction. Conditionality, as it is known, began in the 1950s and has grown steadily more stringent and all-pervasive ever since. In the aftermath of the debt crisis of the 1980s, the IMF and later the World Bank's use of conditionality allowed the powerful industrialized nations to revamp one third world economy after another along free market lines. Critics believe that in the process, the IMF and World Bank have systematically put the powerful nations' self-interest before the welfare of the third world poor, allowing Washington, London, and Frankfurt to exert huge leverage over other countries at arm's length through the mechanism of a "deniable" and nominally impartial international organization. In the words of one U.S. deputy trade secretary on the virtues of the Bank's role in the Philippines:

> We have not been particularly successful ourselves in winning policy reforms from the Philippines. Because it is something of a disinterested party, however, the World Bank has been enormously successful in negotiating important policy changes which we strongly support.[12]

The fewer the options open to the bankrupt government, the greater the Fund's ability to dictate terms. The Argentine crisis of 2002 demonstrated how the Fund's power waxes and wanes even within individual countries. When the economy was booming and private capital was flowing into the country in the early 1990s, the Fund's calls for spending restraint made more sense, but were ignored by a government flushed with success that proceeded to run up massive debts. When capital dried up, the government was finally forced to listen to the Fund and cut spending, but at just the wrong time for an economy desperate for some kind of stimulus.[13]

With few exceptions (such as when the British Labor government was forced to go to the IMF in 1976), the IMF is unable to influence the policies of the powerful nations, despite their often outrageous double standards, and has not lent to a developed country since Australia and Iceland in 1982. The powerful patrons of the international financial institutions rarely practice what they preach. Throughout the debt crisis of the 1980s, the United States was running up the world's largest trade and fiscal deficits and a national debt far greater than that of the whole third world put together, yet the IMF was powerless to make its most powerful and out-of-control member take a dose of its own neoliberal medicine. Looking back on his achievements, Eddie Bernstein, the key U.S. negotiator at Bretton Woods, reflected that U.S. double standards had damaged the credibility of the IMF: "It suffers from having never been able to discipline its principal member, the United States."[14]

Many believe the United States was right to avoid following the IMF recipe. As Arthur Schlesinger, the U.S. historian who worked for President Kennedy, pointed out:

> If the criteria of the International Monetary Fund had governed the United States in the 19th century, our own economic development would have taken a good deal longer. In preaching fiscal orthodoxy to developing nations, we were somewhat in the position of the prostitute who, having retired on her earnings, believes that public virtue requires the closing down of the red-light district.[15]

Since its first loan to Chile in 1948, the IMF had periodically been involved in Latin America. When the debt crisis broke in August 1982 this occasional involvement rapidly escalated. During 1982 and 1983, seventeen Latin American governments signed IMF agreements, the only significant exceptions being Venezuela, Colombia, Paraguay, and Nicaragua,[16] which throughout the period of Sandinista rule was effectively boycotted by the international financial institutions under political pressure from Washington. By the mid-1980s, the Fund was involved in almost every country in the region (see table 2.1).

## HOW THE FUND THINKS

The IMF was created to help countries sort out occasional balance of payments problems, which occur when a country's foreign exchange receipts (through both export income and capital inflows) are no longer sufficient to cover its foreign exchange requirements (for imports and capital outflows such as debt repayments). The Fund sees balance of payments problems as stemming from what it calls "excessive demand"—a diagnosis that, whatever its technical merits, must sound perverse to the poverty-stricken masses of the South. In IMF eyes, too much demand is chasing too few goods. This sucks in imports, creating an unsustainable trade deficit that then feeds the balance of payments crisis.

Excess demand also forces up prices, and the IMF believes that inflation also adds to the balance of payments problem. Since the causal connection between inflation and a balance of payments deficit is at first sight not at all obvious, it is worth spending some time to understand the IMF's reasoning.

Inflation at home erodes the real value of the national currency. If the government is to ensure that goods produced inside the country are to remain competitive with imports and competing exports from elsewhere, the exchange rate must fall by the same amount, but this rarely happens since exchange rates are seldom completely free to float. Over the whole economy, the process will thus encourage imports and deter exports, exacerbating the balance of payments deficit. Price distortions generally contribute to inefficiency in the economy, by skewing the way producers and consumers make decisions.

TABLE 2.1. IMF Adjustment Loans to Latin American and Caribbean Countries, 1981–2001

The various kinds of IMF loans are:

- STAND-BY ARRANGEMENT (SBA): The traditional short-term loan described in the text. Covers from one to two years.
- EXTENDED FUND FACILITY (EFF): A medium-term loan, usually for three years, with annual reviews to assess compliance with performance criteria and to 'spell out' policies for the next year.
- STRUCTURAL ADJUSTMENT FACILITY (SAF): A concessional medium-term loan for low-income countries, usually for a three year period.
- ENHANCED STRUCTURAL ADJUSTMENT FACILITY (ESAF): Similar to the SAF in terms of objectives and conditions for eligibility, but differs 'in the scope and strength of structural policies'.
- POVERTY REDUCTION AND GROWTH FACILITY (PRGF): Replaced ESAF in 1999 as the name for the IMF's concessional lending arm. Provides the finance to back Poverty Reduction Strategy Paper (PRSP)-based lending.

| APPROVAL DATE | AMOUNT APPROVED | Type of Loan (mn SDRs²) | | APPROVAL DATE | AMOUNT APPROVED | Type of Loan (mn SDRs²) |
|---|---|---|---|---|---|---|
| **ARGENTINA** | | | | **BARBADOS** | | |
| 1983 | 1,500 | SBA | | 1982 | 32 | SBA |
| 1984 | 1,419 | SBA | | | | |
| 1987 | 948 | SBA | | **BELIZE** | | |
| 1989 | 736 | SBA | | 1984 | 7 | SBA |
| 1992 | 2,483 | EFF (3 year) | | | | |
| 1996 | 720 | SBA | | **BOLIVIA** | | |
| 1998 | 2,080 | EFF | | 1986 | 50 | SBA |
| 2000 | 10,850 | SBA | | 1986 | 58 | SAF (3 year) |
| | | | | 1988 | 36 | ESAF (3 year) |
| | | | | 1991 | 27 | 2 year extension to ESAF |
| | | | | 1994 | 101 | ESAF |
| | | | | 1998 | 101 | ESAF/PRGF |

| APPROVAL DATE | AMOUNT APPROVED | Type of Loan (mn SDRs²) |
|---|---|---|
| **BRAZIL** | | |
| 1983 | 4,239 | EFF (3 year) |
| 1988 | 1,096 | SBA |
| 1992 | 1,500 | SBA |
| 1998 | 13,024 | SBA |
| 2001 | 12,144 | SBA |
| **CHILE** | | |
| 1983 | 500 | SBA |
| 1985 | 750 | EFF (3 year) |
| 1988 | 75 | 1 yr extension of EFF |
| 1989 | 64 | SBA |
| **COLOMBIA** | | |
| 1999 | 1,957 | EFF |
| **COSTA RICA** | | |
| 1981 | 276 | EFF (3 year)3 |
| 1982 | 92 | SBA |
| 1985 | 54 | SBA |
| 1987 | 40 | SBA |
| 1989 | 42 | SBA |
| 1991 | 34 | SBA |
| 1993 | 21 | SBA |
| 1995 | 52 | SBA |
| **DOMINICA** | | |
| 1981 | 9 | EFF (3 year) |
| 1984 | 1 | SBA |
| 1986 | 3 | SAF (3 year) |
| **DOMINICAN REPUBLIC** | | |
| 1983 | 371 | EFF (3 year) |
| 1985 | 79 | SBA |
| 1991 | 39 | SBA |
| 1993 | 32 | SBA |
| **ECUADOR** | | |
| 1983 | 158 | SBA |
| 1985 | 106 | SBA |
| 1986 | 75 | SBA |
| 1988 | 75 | SBA |
| 1989 | 110 | SBA |
| 1991 | 75 | SBA |
| 1994 | 174 | SBA |
| 2000 | 227 | SBA |
| **EL SALVADOR** | | |
| 1982 | 43 | SBA |
| 1990 | 36 | SBA |
| 1992 | 42 | SBA |
| 1993 | 47 | SBA |
| 1995 | 38 | SBA |
| 1997 | 38 | SBA |
| 1998 | 38 | SBA |
| **GRENADA** | | |
| 1981 | 3 | SBA |
| 1983 | 14 | EFF (3 year) |
| **GUATEMALA** | | |
| 1981 | 19 | SBA |
| 1983 | 115 | SBA |
| 1988 | 54 | SBA |
| 1992 | 54 | SBA |
| **GUYANA** | | |
| 1990 | 50 | SBA |
| 1990 | 82 | ESAF (3 year) |
| 1994 | 54 | ESAF |
| 1998 | 54 | ESAF/PRGF |
| **HAITI** | | |
| 1982 | 35 | SBA |
| 1983 | 60 | SBA |
| 1986 | 28 | SAF (3 year) |
| 1989 | 21 | SBA |
| 1995 | 20 | SBA |
| 1996 | 91 | ESAF |
| **HONDURAS** | | |
| 1982 | 77 | SBA |
| 1990 | 31 | SBA |
| 1992 | 47 | ESAF |
| 1999 | 157 | ESAF/PRGF |

| APPROVAL DATE | AMOUNT APPROVED | Type of Loan (mn SDRs²) |
|---|---|---|
| **JAMAICA** | | |
| 1981 | 478 | EFF (3 year) |
| 1984 | 64 | SBA |
| 1985 | 115 | SBA |
| 1987 | 85 | SBA |
| 1988 | 82 | SBA |
| 1990 | 82 | SBA |
| 1991 | 47 | SBA |
| 1992 | 109 | EFF (3 year) |
| **MEXICO** | | |
| 1983 | 3,411 | EFF (3 year) |
| 1986 | 1,400 | SBA |
| 1989 | 3,263 | EFF (3 year) |
| 1992 | 466 | 1 yr extension to EFF |
| 1995 | 12,070 | SBA |
| 1999 | 3,103 | SBA |
| **NICARAGUA** | | |
| 1991 | 41 | SBA |
| 1994 | 120 | ESAF |
| 1998 | 149 | ESAF/PRGF |
| **PANAMA** | | |
| 1982 | 30 | SBA |
| 1983 | 150 | SBA |
| 1985 | 90 | SBA |
| 1992 | 94 | SBA |
| 1995 | 84 | SBA |
| 1997 | 120 | EFF |
| 2000 | 64 | SBA |
| **PERU** | | |
| 1982 | 650 | EFF (3 year) |
| 1984 | 250 | SBA |
| 1993 | 1,018 | EFF (3 year) |
| 1996 | 300 | EFF |
| 1999 | 383 | EFF |
| 2001 | 128 | SBA |

| APPROVAL DATE | AMOUNT APPROVED | Type of Loan (mn SDRs²) |
|---|---|---|
| **TRINIDAD & TOBAGO** | | |
| 1989 | 99 | SBA |
| 1990 | 85 | SBA |
| **URUGUAY** | | |
| 1981 | 32 | SBA |
| 1983 | 378 | SBA |
| 1985 | 123 | SBA |
| 1990 | 95 | SBA |
| 1992 | 50 | SBA |
| 1996 | 100 | SBA |
| 1997 | 125 | SBA |
| 1999 | 70 | SBA |
| 2000 | 150 | SBA |
| **VENEZUELA** | | |
| 1989 | 3,857 | EFF (3 year) |
| 1992 | - | 9 month extension of EFF |
| 1996 | 976 | SBA |

SOURCES: IMF Annual Reports, www.imf.org

1   Although the World Bank and IADB also make many adjustment-related loans, the sheer number of such loans, and lack of clarity over what is/is not adjustment-related makes it impossible to include them in this table.

2   IMF loans are measured in Special Drawing Rights (SDRs), the Fund's international unit of account. As of 29 May 2002, 1 SDR was worth $1.286

3   cancelled following year and replaced by SBA

Overvaluation also contributes to the balance of payments problem by encouraging capital flight, as peso holders try to convert them into dollars and get them out of the country before the impending devaluation reduces their value. The general mood of uncertainty and instability created by inflation and devaluation also discourages foreign investors, who will be reluctant to convert their dollars into depreciating pesos.

The Fund also rightly claims that high inflation is a tax on the poor, since they are worst hit by price rises and have no means of defending their income levels, whereas better-off wage earners can usually index their incomes to inflation, or convert them into dollars. High inflation often provides rich pickings for investors able to play the financial system; for example, by jumping between different interest-bearing accounts and currencies to take advantage of the short-term distortions that inflation produces.

However, the Nobel Prize–winning economist Joseph Stiglitz, himself a former chief economist at the Bank, believes the IMF has become too fixated with inflation. He draws a distinction between high inflation (over 40 percent a year), where firm evidence exists for the harmful effects on growth, and lower levels where no conclusive evidence exists. The IMF, it seems, has been tilting at windmills for much of the last decade (Latin America's level of regional inflation fell below 40 percent in 1995).[17] When it should have been arguing for increased spending and reflation, the Fund continued to demand austerity, at enormous social cost.[18]

In the debt crisis of the 1980s, an obvious way for Latin American countries to ease their balance of payments problems would have been to declare a moratorium on their escalating debt service payments, but the IMF used all its influence to prevent this from occurring, arguing that countries that defaulted would become international financial pariahs who would be unable to borrow in the future. Instead, the Fund argued for a further reduction in demand and devaluation, this time to cut imports and diversify the economy's efforts to exports, in order to generate a trade surplus with which to pay the debt service. The result was a "double whammy," driving Latin America into an acute recession.

Beyond the immediate objective of correcting a balance of payments deficit, the IMF clearly has a much broader agenda, namely imposing "sound" (i.e., neoliberal) economic policies on the country concerned. IMF conditions demand a smaller role for government, a switch in power and resources to the private sector, the privatization and deregulation of industry, and the opening up of the economy to foreign trade, investment, and capital flows. In return, a successful IMF program promises to enable a country to move smoothly from "stabilization," through "structural adjustment" to reach the promised land of "export-led growth."

## WHAT THE FUND DOES

In the short term, rather than increasing supply to bring supply and demand into balance, the Fund responds to a balance of payments crisis by proposing a swift but painful cure of recession and reduced demand, provoking two otherwise sober economists to write, "To many people who have witnessed the consequences of IMF programs on the poor, this cure seems about as sensible as the idea of bleeding a feverish patient."[19]

The Fund's measures can broadly be divided into two groups, those aimed at achieving short-term stabilization and those concerned with longer-term changes in the economic structure. Stabilization aims to control inflation and rapidly create a large trade surplus with which to continue debt service payments. Measures include:

- Cutting consumer spending power by raising interest rates to limit domestic credit. High interest rates also discourage capital flight and encourage inward investment. In practice, the Fund is also willing to tolerate wage controls as a means of controlling inflation, though it claims to disapprove.

- Curtailing the fiscal deficit by cutting government spending. This involves removing state subsidies on food, fuel, and public transport and reducing social spending on health, housing, and education, measures that also help cut demand in the economy as a whole. Measures can also include raising government revenue by increasing charges on state-run utilities such as electricity and water and charging "user fees" for hitherto free education and health services.

- Devaluing the currency to encourage exports and discourage imports (which, since they are priced in dollars, become more expensive in terms of the local currency).

Structural adjustment is a more profound and longer-term process, through which the international financial institutions try to implant a functioning free market economy in the country concerned. Controls on prices, wages, interest rates, investment, trade and exchange rates are removed since the IMF believes in letting the unregulated market decide prices to maximize the efficient allocation of resources. Governments are forced to cut back on state investment in the economy, as part of the effort to reduce state spending, but also in the belief that the state is both less efficient and "crowds out" private-sector investment by soaking up the available credit. The full repertoire of structural adjustment measures did not come into force until the late 1980s, once the World Bank had become fully immersed in the adjustment process. As the 1990s wore on, new kinds of conditions were added, specifying a broader range of institutional and legal changes, which the Bank and Fund deemed necessary to build a modern, functioning economy.

## THE WORLD BANK

From the Mexican default in August 1982 until mid-1985, the IMF and its short-term stabilization approach dominated the response to the debt crisis. The continent was forced to cut back on imports and use the dollars it saved to pay debt service, and to go through a fierce recession to curb inflation. The scheme saved the banks and Northern financial markets from collapse, but at huge social cost in the South.

By 1985, it had become obvious that the commercial banks had no intention of renewing lending to Latin America, and resistance was growing among debtor countries that saw no point in squeezing their people to pay endless tribute to the rich nations while receiving nothing in return. In the second half of 1985, Peru's President Alan García defied the IMF by announcing that "Peru's main debtors are its people" and unilaterally limited debt repayments to 10 percent of the value of Peru's exports, calling on other Latin American debtors to join him.[20] Peru was duly punished for its presumption, but the West realized that a change of tack was needed to prevent its whole debt strategy from crashing.

U,S. Treasury Secretary James Baker retook the initiative within months of García's move. In October 1985, at the annual IMF–World Bank meeting in Seoul, South Korea, he unveiled his "Baker Plan" for shifting from recessive to growth-oriented adjustment. The plan, which applied only to the fifteen largest debtors, entailed asking the private banks to renew lending to the South (a request they largely ignored). It also gave the World Bank and regional development banks like the InterAmerican Development Bank (IDB) a greatly increased role in lending and overseeing longer-term structural adjustment.

The World Bank, the second of the Bretton Woods "heavenly twins" has traditionally played the role of Mr. Nice Guy in contrast to the IMF's Mr. Scrooge. It has also proved far more of a chameleon, regularly changing its stated aims and policies during its fifty years of operation in accordance with the prevailing political wind, although the impact of the new rhetoric on its policies on the ground remains debatable.

> In recent years the Bank has adopted—if only superficially—virtually every sugges-
> tion its supporters and critics have offered, with one exception: that the Bank
> practice self-restraint. It is now committed, at least on paper, to helping the pri-
> vate sector, women, and the poor; to working with non-governmental organiza-
> tions and the people directly affected by their projects; to increasing its lending
> for education, health, nutrition, and micro-enterprises; to protecting or improv-
> ing the environment; to reducing military expenditures and corruption; to pro-
> moting openness in government, the rule of law and equitable income
> distribution—and to doing it all "sustainably."[21]

Despite, or more likely because of this constant "mandate creep," the Bank is an organization racked by low morale and self-doubt. Periodical-ly, it responds to criticisms of its lack of focus with another organization-al restructuring that only adds to the "initiative fatigue" and low morale of its 10,000-member staff. In January 2001 one leaked memo from staff in the Middle East and North Africa Department, complained:

> The Bank today has no focus and is driven by an ever growing list of mandates
> imposed on it through a variety of means. . . . [The World Bank] President's
> favorite subjects as mentioned above, Board sentiments as discerned from time to
> time, public pressures, ideas generated by internal constituencies, and even fads.
> These are all cumulative with nothing ever taken off.[22]

The Bank's organizational traumas stand in marked contrast to the complacent insularity of the Fund, whose staff, despite all evidence to the contrary, continue to believe that they know best.

The Bank played a minor role in European reconstruction, lending for large infrastructure projects, then adopted the same "big is best" philosophy in the South. Until shortly before the debt crisis, the Bank remained a project lender, concentrating on giant projects such as road- and dam-building. By backing such "mega-projects" it has become notorious among environmentalists for its role in deforestation, flooding out indigenous communities and supplanting peasant agriculture with large agribusiness schemes. Such projects still constitute a significant proportion of the Bank's loans, a vast global enterprise that churned out over \$2.9 million an hour in 2000.[23] Latin America claimed a larger portion of Bank lending than any other region, accounting for \$5.3 billion in 2001.[24]

The Bank's own articles of agreement specify that "loans made or guaranteed by the Bank shall, except in special circumstances, be for the purpose of specific projects of reconstruction or development."[25] Nevertheless, the onset of the debt crisis saw a shift from project-based lending to structural adjustment, a process that accelerated sharply with the Baker Plan. In 1980 the World Bank created a new credit line of Structural Adjustment Loans (SALs) to support economic reform programs. SALs remained a minor part of the World Bank's loans portfolio until the Baker Plan was announced, but by 1987 these and other forms of policy-based lending had risen to 20 percent of the Bank's loans to Latin America.[26]

SALs came with a new checklist of conditions and performance targets attached. The Bank usually made SALs conditional on countries having already put in place an "appropriate macroeconomic framework." In practice, this usually meant having agreed a stabilization program with the IMF.[27] The phenomenon of "cross-conditionality" was born, whereby a country had to satisfy simultaneously two different but interconnected sets of conditions from the IMF and World Bank. Were it to break either set, the result could be a suspension of the program and an economic boycott by world capital markets. While the Fund's conditions tended to be quantified and precise, the Bank's were more qualitative and negotiable. The result was an administrative nightmare, as recipient government officials spent more time trying to satisfy the international financial institutions' endless requirements than on running their own economies.

The debt crisis of the 1980s accelerated the convergence of the two institutions. In the years following Bretton Woods, there was a clear division of roles: the IMF was placed in charge of finding short-term, economy-wide solutions to balance of payments crises; the World Bank promoted long-term development via project funding. Since the early 1970s, this division of labor has become increasingly blurred. In 1974 the IMF moved into medium-term lending with its EFF (Extended Fund Facility). Later it added SAFs (Structural Adjustment Facility) and ESAFs (Enhanced Structural Adjustment Facilities), new kinds of concessional loans geared even more directly to structural adjustment policies. In 1999, their paths converged still further when ESAFs were replaced with the Poverty Reduction and Growth Facility (PRGF), while the Bank subsequently introduced the Poverty Reduction Support Credit (PRSC). The Bank and Fund agreed that from 2002, both institutions' funding to low-income countries such as Bolivia and Nicaragua would be based on the Poverty Reduction Strategy Paper process (see below).

At the same time, the shift to SALs brought the World Bank into competition with the Fund on short-term, economy-wide reform. With the creation of Sectoral Adjustment Loans (SECALs) in 1983, the Bank further increased its ability to intervene in third world economies by lending in return for reforms in specific sectors, such as privatization, "rationalization," or stimulating exports.[28] The Bank can now throw its weight around in the economies of the South to manage the fine detail of policy in a far more all-pervasive way than the IMF's efforts, which are restricted to macroeconomic targets like the fiscal deficit or exchange rate. It has become a more effective neoliberal battering ram, while its more sensitive handling of publicity and its own image have so far allowed it to escape the IMF's global notoriety.

The Bank's adjustment-related lending promoted very specific reforms, such as:

- DEREGULATING FOREIGN TRADE. The international financial institutions believe that protectionism spawns inefficiency, so import taxes and quotas are removed as part of the wider effort to "get the prices right." The market can then allocate resources more efficiently and comparative advantage becomes the basis for a country's trade.

- LIBERALIZING THE FINANCIAL MARKET. The Fund and Bank believe that the freest possible flow of capital would lead to the most efficient allocation of investment, so they pressured countries to open up to foreign capital flows and deregulate their domestic financial institutions.

- PRIVATIZING STATE-OWNED COMPANIES. This has proved an extremely attractive option to both governments and the international financial institutions from the mid-1980s onward, since it sheds loss-making companies that contribute to the fiscal deficit, while the proceeds from sales create a one-off boost to government revenue (not to mention plentiful opportunities for corruption). The international financial institutions also believed that privatization would lead to a more efficient economy, since it would encourage the private sector (especially transnational companies) to inject new capital and technology, and "muscular management," free from political considerations, could sack staff deemed surplus to requirements.

- DEREGULATING THE LABOR MARKET. This involved making it easier for employers to hire and fire at whim, an assault on the power of trade unions that enabled employers to cut salaries, reducing "red tape" such as health and safety legislation which pushes up employers' costs, and encouraging a range of "flexible practices" such as subcontracting, self-employment, and part-time work, all of which increase business competitiveness, while reducing workers' wages and job security.

- Tax reform and higher charges for state-produced goods like electricity and water were both introduced as a means of balancing government budgets. Most tax reforms involved increasing sales taxes, such as VAT, which proportionally hit the poor hardest.

Just as with the initial stage of IMF-run stabilization, the Baker Plan may have failed to fulfill its stated aims, but the World Bank's plunge into structurally adjusting the South proved remarkably successful in opening up the Latin American economy to the traders and investors of the rich nations, and reforming it along neoliberal lines, while further eroding Latin America's economic sovereignty.

## THE IDB

A lesser-known international financial institution, the Inter-American Development Bank (IDB), also plays a leading role in the region's adjustment process. Founded in 1959, the IDB has stuck closer than the World Bank has to its original role in providing finance for specific projects. During its first twenty years it concentrated on agriculture and social sector projects, leaving the World Bank to its romance with infrastructural "megaprojects" such as giant dams and roads. With the onset of the debt crisis, the IDB lost favor in Washington, as structural adjustment took over from project lending as the policy makers' favorite, but since the late 1980s it has made a comeback and gained new funding for its lending. To get the new funds from the United States, it was forced to clamber aboard the structural adjustment bandwagon, but opposition from Latin America limited the extent of its adjustment-oriented sectoral loans.[29] In 2000, of total lending of $5.3 billion, the IDB classified $1.9 billion as "reform and modernization of the state."[30] By comparison, gross disbursements to the region by the World Bank came to $4.1 billion in that year.[31]

As with the IMF and World Bank, the U.S. government exerts a high level of control over the IDB, which is conveniently headquartered in Washington. The United States has just enough votes (30.008 percent in 2002)[32] to veto loans financed through the Fund for Special Operations, IDB's "soft window" for concessional loans.

## CRITICISMS OF STRUCTURAL ADJUSTMENT

The human and economic impact of structural adjustment is examined in detail in subsequent chapters. The Bretton Woods institutions argue their case on the basis of "no pain, no gain." While the model invariably produces the pain through increased poverty, inequality, and unemployment, the gains have so far proven more elusive. The Fund and Bank still avow that they will be proved right in the long run, but as Keynes acerbically remarked, "In the long run, we are all dead."[33] The model can be criticized both in terms of its recipe for stabilization and the model of trade underpinning its advocacy of growth based on exports.

In the short term, while nominally attacking inflation, the devaluation which almost invariably accompanied an IMF agreement led to a surge in prices as imports suddenly rose in price. These policies plunged much of Latin America into a "stagflation" cycle of recession and high inflation during the 1980s. As pointed out earlier, the Fund's obsession with even moderate levels of inflation prevented it from trying to reflate recession-hit economies.

In the 1990s, structural adjustment took over from stabilization as the focus for most Bank and Fund loans, liberalizing trade and capital flows, and deregulating and privatizing the domestic economy. The results demonstrated that financial liberalization brings with it even greater risks and instability than liberalization of areas such as direct investment or trade. Financial deregulation combined with liberalization of countries' capital accounts produced an explosive mix of high-volume flows of short-term capital. When, for whatever reason, investors of this "hot money" took fright and fled, they triggered national crises and banking collapses, which almost inevitably ended in huge public bailouts and a legacy of increased debt payments.

The Bretton Woods institutions' advice on trade, based on orthodox notions of comparative advantage, ignores what is known as the "fallacy of composition." In dealing with each country separately, they assume the rest of the world economy remains unchanged so that devaluing and boosting both traditional and nontraditional exports will improve a country's trading performance. But if the whole third world follows the same policies, it risks flooding the market with new agricultural products, with the inevitable impact on prices; if Kenya and Vietnam and Guatemala all decide to compete in exporting coffee or nontraditional products such as mange tout (snow peas), it may be good news for shoppers in the North's supermarkets, but leaves developing countries with falling incomes despite increased export volumes. Under Washington's tutelage, third world economies were forced to run just to stand still, as their terms of trade continued to deteriorate.

Reviews of SAPs, including some commissioned by the Fund, repeatedly found serious flaws in their design. In 1997–1998 internal and external reviews of the Fund's ESAF lending found that programs with large number of conditions tended to perform poorly, often due to policy disagreements between IMF staff and borrower governments.[34]

The Fund and the Bank's standard policy packages take little account of local political or economic conditions. As one local expert complains, "Even before they arrive in a given Latin American country, the experts of the IMF know better than Latin American economists how to tackle the problem."[35] Typically, IMF "missions" from Washington fly in for three weeks with a blueprint for the country's future economic policy already in their briefcases. Once in the country, they negotiate with local technocrats from the Finance Ministry, often themselves former IMF or World Bank employees, but they do not consult other bodies like the Agriculture Ministry or the UN Food and Agriculture Organization, which have a far better understanding of how the Fund's economic prescriptions will affect people on the ground.[36] Still less do they talk to the peasants' organizations, community associations, trade unions, or NGOs who are most in touch with the poor communities the Fund is supposed to be helping. The Fund's dismissive attitude toward "the field" was summed up by one of its executive directors, who recalled, "In the old days, if someone was no good, we would say, 'send them to Honduras!'"[37]

In a hundred-page open letter of resignation from his job as senior economist with the IMF, Grenadian economist Davison L. Budhoo lambasted the IMF mentality in the 1980s:

> Let us remove all elements of recipient discretion from our programs. Let us state explicitly and unequivocally what the third world blighters must be made to do, and when and how they must be made to do it Let us give the countries of the South specific things to do in specific months, and even during specific weeks of specific months. Let us finally put a particular cut-off point for completing our task of effecting Reaganomics and Thatcheromics in the South.[38]

One of the most ambitious reviews of the impact of SAPs on the ground was carried out by a network of NGOs, trade unions, and academics in a dozen countries that had gone through Bank-funded adjustment programs, including Mexico, El Salvador, and Ecuador in Latin America. The Structural Adjustment Participatory Review Initiative (SAPRI) began with a challenge to James Wolfensohn shortly after he became World Bank president. By the time the initiative was completed, it had come to include thousands of local organizations participating in national field exercises on four continents, the majority of which were carried out jointly with the Bank and the national government. The parties investigated, in a highly participatory fashion, the impact of a broad range of economic adjustment policies, such as trade liberalization, financial sector reform, agricultural-reform measures, and the privatization of public utilities.

The conclusions, published in April 2002, were damning, and can be found on the SAPRI website.[39] Unfortunately, according to the document summarizing the project's findings, even though it funded the exercise, the Bank

> went to extraordinary lengths to bury SAPRI and its findings within the institution, as well as to lower its profile to the outside world. After insisting on joint actions throughout the exercise, management decided to write its own final report, which focused as much on its own in-house research as on SAPRI fieldwork. . . . At the conclusion of the forum, it immediately closed down the SAPRI process without any commitment to follow up or any trace of the multi-year SAPRI analysis in any of its internal documents.[40]

Among the key findings of the study:

TRADE LIBERALIZATION has led to growing trade deficits, export growth typically based on natural resources and low-skilled labor, and the failure of many local manufacturing firms, particularly innovative, small and medium-sized firms that generate a great deal of employment. Transnational corporations have often been the principal beneficiaries.

FINANCIAL SECTOR LIBERALIZATION has increased inequality. Instead of helping producers that need capital to maintain or expand their operations, financial intermediaries have directed financing toward large (usually urban) firms and extended the largest share of loans to a few, powerful economic agents. Small and medium-size firms, rural and indigenous producers, and women have very limited access to the formal financial system, thereby exacerbating existing inequalities.

LABOR MARKET REFORMS have had adverse employment effects. "Flexibilization" policies have undermined the standing of workers generally. Reforms have led to fewer regulations concerning labor stability and firing practices, thus facilitating widespread use of temporary contracts and leaving workers with little recourse when employers choose to reduce their workforce. Labor rights have been affected by restrictions placed on the right to strike and to bargain collectively.

PRIVATIZATION earns mixed reviews. Civil society groups drew a distinction between the privatization of enterprises involved in production (which sometimes made economic sense) and those delivering basic services, such as water and electricity. As far as the latter category was concerned, access to affordable quality services did not improve for the societies as a whole and, in some cases, worsened. Privatization measures exacerbated inequality and failed to contribute to macroeconomic efficiency. In El Salvador, poor consumers saw their bills rise at nearly twice the pace of increases for high-end consumers.

AGRICULTURAL REFORMS have generally included the removal of subsidies on agricultural inputs and credit; liberalization of producer prices; privatization of state entities involved in marketing and the distribution of inputs and produce; liberalization of trade in agricultural inputs and commodities; and currency devaluation. The result has been increasing rural inequality, since only those producers with previous access to resources and economies of scale were able to benefit.

## REDISCOVERING POVERTY

As the human toll of the first wave of stabilization and structural adjustment policies in the 1980s became apparent, criticism grew. UNICEF conducted an impressive lobbying effort while always treating the IMF with "an appropriate degree of professional deference."[41] Its 1987 publication of *Adjustment with a Human Face* was a landmark critique of the international financial institutions' policies in the South.[42] One of its principal findings was that although structural adjustment had greatly increased poverty in the region, the international financial institutions' lending policies and conditions had paid "almost no attention to the special problems of the poor."[43] One high-ranking World Bank economist confessed, "We did not think that the human costs of these programs could be so great, and the economic gains so slow in coming."[44]

True to form, the Bank responded by agreeing with its critics. In 1990, World Bank President Lewis Preston described sustainable poverty reduction as "the overarching objective of the World Bank. It is the benchmark by which our performance as a development institution will be measured."[45] The new strategy aimed "to reduce poverty through broadly based labor-intensive growth to generate jobs and income for the poor; social investment to improve poor people's access to education, nutrition, health care, and other social services and social safety nets to protect the poorest and most vulnerable sections of society."[46] The Bank's annual flagship World Development Report reflected the extent of the intellectual overhaul. Its 1997 edition was devoted to arguing that an effective state was vital for development, marking an important change from the "market good, state bad" rhetoric of the early days of the Washington Consensus.

In the larger economies, criticism subsided somewhat in the early 1990s, as renewed capital flows led to a brief return to reasonably high levels of growth. However, the 1995 Mexican crash, rapidly followed by crises and bailouts in Brazil and Argentina, marked a new phase of apparently permanent instability. Along with crises in Asia and Russia, this prompted a much broader range of critics to take issue with structural adjustment policies.

In both Brazil and Argentina, multibillion-dollar bailouts proved unable to prevent a crash, raising suspicions that they were in fact designed merely to buy enough time for foreign investors to exit the country before the devaluation occurred. Nobel Prize-winning economist Joseph Stiglitz, who in recent years has become the Fund's most trenchant critic, is in no doubt:

> When the IMF and the Brazilian government spent some $50 billion maintaining the exchange rate at an overvalued level in late 1998, where did the money go? The money doesn't disappear into thin air. It goes into somebody's pocket—much of it into the pockets of the speculators. In a sense, it is the IMF that keeps the speculators in business.[47]

Stiglitz also points out that the IMF's standard policy of prescribing high interest rates and spending cuts to governments already in or approaching recession merely makes matters worse.[48] It is worth recalling that the Bush administration responded to the slowdown in the United States in 2001 in precisely the opposite way—cutting interest rates and boosting the economy with tax cuts.

In low-income countries such as Nicaragua and Bolivia, concerns also mounted about the levels of foreign debt. Unattractive to private investors, these countries, along with the poor countries of Africa and Asia, piled up debts to the Bank and Fund. In Bolivia, the proportion of public debt owed to the multilateral lenders like the Bank, Fund, and IDB rose from 32 percent in 1981 to 70 percent in 2001.[49] Critics pointed out that the crushing debt burden was preventing poor countries from achieving precisely the kind of sustained growth and development that the Bretton Woods Institutions were supposed to be promoting, and called for sweeping debt relief. Jubilee 2000, an international Church-based movement calling for cancellation of unpayable debts to mark the dawn of the new millennium, started to exert significant political pressure on Northern governments. When 70,000 people (many of them middle-aged churchgoers on their first demonstration) formed a human chain around the G7 summit in Birmingham in 1998, they succeeded in forcing debt onto the agenda and won significant concessions at the G7 summit in Cologne the following year.

The Asian crisis also prompted attacks from the Republican Right in the United States, which used the occasion to argue for a drastic reduction in the funding and scope of both Bank and Fund, for example pulling the IMF out of structural adjustment funding altogether.[50] Such pressures subsequently increased with the election of George W. Bush. On the eve of the Fund's 2002 Annual Meeting, *The Economist* reported, "A growing chorus of insiders, from staff members to Wall Street bankers, is asking whether the Fund and the rich countries that largely determine its policies know what they are doing. The reason for the disquiet is Latin America."[51] The magazine reported that the Fund was under attack on three fronts: for not pushing its policies hard enough, for flaws in the policies themselves, and for not being consistent in its message to developing countries. Such attacks posed an interesting challenge for left-wing critics of the Fund and Bank, who suddenly found themselves arguing for the same things as their erstwhile foes, albeit for different reasons!

The "growth versus equity" debate came to a bloody head around the 2000–2001 World Development Report, entitled "Attacking Poverty." Unfortunately, Bank staff drafting the report also spent a fair amount of time attacking one another. For the WDR exercise in 2000, the Bank took the unusual step of publishing the first draft and organizing a far greater degree of public consultation than is customary. As a result, onlookers were able to observe a full-scale war for the Bank's economic soul being fought between the old guard neoliberals headed by the appropriately named David Dollar and the new thinking on so-called second-generation reforms being proposed by Joseph Stiglitz and others.

The first draft was an exciting departure, concentrating much more on previously missing issues such as how to combine growth with equity as the best means of reducing poverty. The counterattack was fierce: the Bank's leading neoliberals publicly accused their rivals of getting their sums wrong and the WDR editor, Ravi Kanbur resigned.[52] The final version of the report dropped many of the sections criticizing standard Bank views on liberalization and added a whole new chapter rehashing orthodox Washington Consensus views. The result was a schizophrenic document that accurately reflected the confusion within the institution. Oxfam described the result as a "painful disjuncture between policy messages on equity and the macroeconomic message on growth."[53]

## PRSP—POVERTY REDUCTION OR PUBLIC RELATIONS?

Progress has been swiftest over the low-income countries still mired in debt to the Bretton Woods institutions. In September 1999, the World Bank and the IMF responded to the political pressure generated by Jubilee 2000 by agreeing that "nationally owned participatory poverty reduction strategies should provide the basis of all their concessional lending and for debt relief under the enhanced Heavily Indebted Poor Countries (HIPC) Initiative." In time, lending by both Bank and Fund would be based on Poverty Reduction Strategy Papers (PRSPs), drawn up by country authorities for submission to the Bank and Fund boards. By 2002, Honduras, Guyana, Nicaragua, and Bolivia all started to benefit from the new debt relief. The crucial point was that PRSPs were to be drawn up with full participation of the public, not agreed behind closed doors between finance ministry and IMF or Bank officials. The IMF duly rechristened its Enhanced Structural Adjustment Facility as the new, more cuddly-sounding Poverty Reduction and Growth Fund.

The Fund and Bank promised that poverty reduction would be placed at the heart of policy design, but the practice to date has been very different. Civil society organizations found themselves consulted when it came to "soft items" about public spending, but were not invited when the subject turned to broader economic policy issues. A study by Christian Aid of Bolivia's PRSP process, carried out in 2000, found that part of the reason for excluding even specialist economic policy NGOs was political—even some government employees admitted that if Bolivia had presented an alternative strategy to the Fund and Bank, it would have risked losing its debt relief. Although more than 100 Bolivian civic organizations subsequently appealed to the IMF not to approve the final document, it was endorsed in May 2001.[54]

CIDSE, an international alliance of Catholic development agencies, concluded:

> In countries producing PRSPs, poverty reduction is not being integrated into the heart of structural and macroeconomic policies. The same structural adjustment policies of the past dominate PRSPs, focusing on budget austerity, economic growth, and free market approaches, with little consideration of who benefits and who loses from these policies. Instead, poverty reduction is still treated as a new layer on top of the old policies, often reduced to increased investments in health and education and expansion of "safety nets."[55]

## IS THERE A POST–WASHINGTON CONSENSUS?

Much of the academic and policy debate in and around the Bretton Woods institutions has focused on what, if anything, should replace the ten commandments of the Washington Consensus reform program of the early 1990s. Insider critics such as Stiglitz argued that what was needed was a "post–Washington Consensus," where the focus was on building institutions, both state and private, to address the failings of the market:

> The policies advanced by the Washington Consensus are not complete, and they are sometimes misguided. Making markets work requires more than just low inflation; it requires sound regulation, competition policy, and policies to facilitate the transfer of technology and to encourage transparency.[56]

As usual, the change in tack was reflected in the theme of the Bank's flagship World Development Report, which in 2002 was titled "Building Institutions for Markets."

Table 2.2 shows one version of the policy areas covered by both the Washington Consensus and its successor, but the scramble to redefine the Washington Consensus included a large number of often mutually contradictory proposals. While the original consensus had been found wanting, there was clearly very little consensus on what should take its place beyond admitting that "life is more complicated than we thought."

TABLE 2.2. Washington Consensus and After[57]

| THE ORIGINAL WASHINGTON CONSENSUS: | THE AUGMENTED WASHINGTON CONSENSUS *The original list plus:* |
|---|---|
| • Fiscal discipline | • Legal/political reform |
| • Reorientation of public expenditures | • Regulatory institutions |
| • Tax reform | • Corruption |
| • Financial liberalization | • Labor market flexibility |
| • Unified and competitive exchange rates | • WTO agreements |
| | • Financial codes and standards |
| • Trade liberalization | • "Prudent" capital-account opening |
| • Openness to foreign direct investment | • Non-intermediate exchange rate regimes (i.e., fixed or floating) |
| • Privatization | • Social safety nets |
| • Deregulation | • Poverty reduction |
| • Secure property rights | |

Dani Rodrik, the economist who compiled table 2.2, is skeptical of what he calls, in order to stress the degree of ideological continuity with its predecessor, the "Augmented Washington Consensus":

> Operationally, these institutional reforms have two noteworthy features. First, they are heavily influenced by an Anglo-American conception of what constitutes desirable institutions (as in the preference for arm's-length finance over "development banking" and flexible labor markets over institutionalized labor markets). Second, they are driven largely by the requirements of integration into the world economy.[58]

One such second-generation issue is corruption, politely rechristened "governance" in World Bank parlance. The Bank's website proudly proclaims that though few Bank country programs discussed the issue prior to 1998, between January 1998 and June 1999, 78 percent of "country assistance strategies" mentioned governance.[59] On both political and practical grounds, Rodrik argues against trying to correct the failings of the 1980s by trying to build up a whole set of institutions from scratch:

> The practical difficulties of implementing many of the institutional reforms under discussion are severely underestimated. Today's developed countries did

not get their regulatory and legal institutions overnight. It would be nice if third world countries could somehow acquire first world institutions, but the safe bet is that this will happen only when they are no longer third world countries.[60]

Another observer, Moises Naim, questions whether any post-Washington Consensus exists, pointing to the "wildly gyrating ideas about controls on foreign capital or about exchange rate regimes" and stressing the constantly shifting demands on Southern governments:

> Reforming governments everywhere saw how the policy goals that just a few years, or even months, earlier had been specified as the final frontier of the reform process became just a mere precondition for success. New, more complex, and more difficult goals were constantly added to the list of requirements for an acceptable performance.[61]

Whatever the intellectual gymnastics in Washington, criticism has continued to mount over the gap between the new rhetoric and the reality on the ground. In January 2001, the Annual Review of Development Effectiveness, by the Bank's Operations Evaluation Department found that

> for most adjustment operations, the focus on public expenditures outweighs that of addressing economic distortions or safety nets, and the impact of reforms on the poorest is rarely considered.[62]

The third world governments that borrow money from the Bank confirmed that not much has changed. When an internal assessment by the Bank asked them what the Bank was good at, helping strengthen civic participation in national development efforts came bottom of the list, with 14 percent. At the top of the list came "Helping strengthen and maintain sound macroeconomic and trade policies" and "helping attract investment."[63]

## THE POLITICS OF ADJUSTMENT

The motive for Davison Budhoo's resignation was one of the most serious claims of fraud and bad faith leveled at the Fund in recent years. Budhoo worked for the IMF between 1985 and 1987, evaluating the economy of Trinidad and Tobago. He later resigned, charging that he had uncovered evidence that the Fund deliberately distorted the state of the country's economy in order to force it to adopt stronger adjustment measures. This included more than doubling the figures for Trinidad's fiscal deficit, vastly inflating the figures for the rises in the country's labor costs, and giving a distorted picture of the real exchange rate to strengthen its argument for devaluation of the local currency. Budhoo claimed that when he pointed out the mistakes, he was ignored, forcing him to conclude that the distortions were "premeditated and systematic" frauds.[64]

The Bretton Woods institutions invariably present their policy packages as an "objective" solution to a country's internal problems, yet self-interest is clearly involved, since powerful interests in the North reap rich rewards from structural adjustment, which opens up the economies of the South to first world traders and investors. In the massive privatizations of the 1990s, U.S. and European transnational corporations were able to snap up the pick of Latin America's airlines, banks, and telecommunications companies and also moved in on its oil sector. Structural adjustment's emphasis on export-led growth, along with its tendency to deindustrialize third world economies, leads to more abundant, and therefore cheaper, supplies of raw materials for the industrialized economies, locking much of the South into a neocolonial economic relationship with the North. Given the control by those same rich countries of the Fund and the Bank, it is hard to believe that this is pure coincidence.

Such suspicions are borne out by the spin the Bank puts on its presentations to U.S. audiences. One such briefing read: "The Bank's loans have helped develop these new markets [for U.S. exports]. . . . In Argentina, export diversification loans pushed the country to open closed markets, allowing average U.S. exports to increase from $862m to $3.7bn." [65] The briefing went on to quote the Congressional testimony of a vice president of the Caterpillar company:

> By encouraging—and at times pressuring—countries to lower trade barriers, privatize enterprises, and support democratic reforms, [the World Bank] is helping to develop markets for American products.

Often, it is impossible to disentangle political from economic criteria. The IMF and World Bank believe in the market and will not fund a government that rejects their ideas in favor of a more progressive a genda such as redistributing wealth or building up national industry through some measure of protection. Staff at the Bretton Woods institutions believe that their decisions are based purely on economic grounds, but in practice, they promote the U.S. agenda for the third world. Washington certainly sees it that way according to one U.S. official, who advised, "We must counter, both in the UN and within the framework of the North-South dialogue, any discussion of global problems which questions the validity of the free market and of free enterprise in the countries of the third world."[66]

The United States has regularly used the Fund and the Bank to reward its allies, however undeserving, and punish its enemies, however strong their case for a loan. In 1993, Mexico, emerging from a decade of neoliberal shock treatment, duly reaped its reward when it took over from India as the World Bank's all-time largest borrower.[67] A few years earlier, a leaked memo from the British Foreign Office provided a revealing account of political interference in the World Bank, at a time when Britain was faithfully toeing Washington's hard line against Nicaragua at the height of the Contra war. Stamped "Confidential," the memo stated, "There is no need to amend our voting policy toward Nicaragua for the time being. The problem of explaining it in public will, however, persist and we shall need to stick to our present line of claiming that our opposition is based on technical grounds." Underneath this paragraph, an exasperated civil servant had scribbled, "If we can find them!"[68]

Joseph Stiglitz traces the political problems back to the nature of the IMF's relationships with governments:

> The IMF's governance structure makes it accountable to finance ministeries and central banks, with close connections to the financial community . . . the IMF has pursued the *collective interests* of a subset of the international community, rather than serving the broader collective interests for which it was originally created.
>
> The IMF interacts with a country's finance ministry, which all too often largely reflects the interests of that country's financial community, or more broad elites. The interaction enhances the strength of the finance ministry— which is often already out of proportion. Critics are labeled as populists, and other members of government are told that if they resist the demands of the finance ministry, it will jeopardize the Fund program, forcing the country's budget into disarray, and risking the country's standing in international financial markets. Since

typically only the finance ministry deals directly with the IMF, and the dealings
are in secret, other ministries have to take the threats seriously: the IMF, in effect,
enlarges the bargaining power of the finance ministry. . . . It is more than likely
that the IMF would have been more concerned about the effects of its policies on
unemployment and wages if it reported directly to labor ministers!

In all this there is a danger in oversimplifying what is going on. Many
critics of structural adjustment talk as if the international financial
institutions are solely responsible for imposing structural adjustment
from outside on a passive Latin America. In many ways, this view
resembles the oversimplifications of the "dependency school" of development economics of the 1960s and 1970s, which tended to place all of
Latin America's economic ills at the door of the rich metropolitan
countries of the North, blaming them for having locked the region into
an endless cycle of commodity dependence and poverty.

Adjustment also had powerful allies within Latin America, not least
among the business groups who have made fortunes out of privatization and deregulation. Even among those who do not stand directly to
gain, the collapse of the import substitution model, and the failure in
the mid-1980s of many of the attempts to find a less painful "heterodox" way of stabilizing the economy, led to the widespread adoption of
the "there is no alternative" attitude. In 1988, even the Sandinistas in
Nicaragua turned to a more or less neoliberal package to stabilize an
economy riven by hyperinflation. There was also a much higher level of
consensus over the need for longer-term export-led growth than over
how to stabilize the economy in the first years of the silent revolution.
Furthermore, those doing the adjusting found the IMF an ideal scape-
goat for policies that they may well have wanted to introduce anyway.
For any Latin American politician, an IMF riot is infinitely preferable to
an anti-government revolution.

Yet while many Latin American governments may agree with much
of the neoliberal recipe, the wider issue of sovereignty is at stake. With
each new twist and turn in Fund and Bank policy, further conditions
have been placed on the recipient governments. First the IMF's broad
macroeconomic targets, then the World Bank's more detailed
demands—privatization, public sector redundancies, and sectoral
adjustment. Now a new layer of second-generation issues is being
added. Many of these changes, such as signing regional trade agree-

ments, or dollarization, are in practice almost impossible to reverse, should future governments wish to do so. The steady encroachment by the multilateral organizations and their rich sponsors on the sovereignty of the indebted nations of the South seems inexorable.

## THE IMF IN 2003

Despite its tattered self-confidence, the crises in the Andes and the Southern Cone in 2002–2003 showed how little has changed. In return for new lending to Ecuador, the Fund was demanding mass layoffs in the public sector, international administrators for the state-run electricity and telecoms companies, and a cut in the subsidy on domestic cooking gas.[69]

In Brazil, the Fund approved a $30 billion loan during the middle of the election campaign that ultimately led to the victory of the left-wing Workers' Party candidate, Lula. First, however, it sent representatives to Brazil for pre-election discussions with the candidates, tying the hands of the future leaders to its terms (including serious spending cuts) before agreeing to the loan. Critics objected to this level of political interference, arguing that it ignored Brazil's political process, under which the Senate must approve foreign loans.[70]

In Argentina, when crisis hit, the Fund made matters worse by pressuring Argentina to apply its standard, and heavily criticized, pro-cyclical recipe of trying to balance budgets during a recession by cutting public spending. In January 2003, the Fund's agreement with the Duhalde government included the requirement to generate a $13 billion surplus in 2003. To achieve this, public sector wages and pensions will be frozen in nominal terms, despite the government's own prediction of 35 percent inflation over the year. VAT and utility charges were also increased.[71]

Joseph Stiglitz, from his vantage point as former chief economist at the Bank and chair of the U.S. Council of Economic Advisers who guided President Clinton, is in no doubt that beneath the change in tone, what is going on remains a form of colonial control:[72]

> Though different from 19th-century colonialism, the new economic colonialism is perhaps equally insidious: the nascent democracies have economic policies dictated to them by the international organizations, whose policies in turn are largely driven by the G-7, and some would say by the financial interests of the "G-1."

# 3—The Lost Decade
## Latin America 1982-1991

The tiny adobe house is crammed with gnarled *pailliris* (mining women) in patched shawls and battered felt hats whose calloused hands break up rocks on the surface in search of scraps of tin ore. Outside, the scene is one of high-altitude poverty, all grays and browns in the thin Bolivian air. The paths between the miners' huts are strewn with plastic bags and human excrement, dried black in the unforgiving *altiplano* sun. Rising beyond the squalid settlement, the barren hills and gray slag heaps of the tin mines complete the bleak panorama. The litany of poor women's woes begins, gathering momentum as it goes:

> Before, it was not too bad, but now we never have a good month. We're mainly widows or abandoned. My husband left to look for work and never came back. Now I have to look after four kids—I can't pay for their schoolbooks and clothes. I've been doing this work for seven years now and my lungs are finished. I've vomited blood for weeks at a time and still had to keep working.

> In the old days, women used to stay at home because the men had work. Now, with the recession, we've had to go out to work. Many of our children have been abandoned. Their fathers have left and there's no love left in us when we get home late from work. We leave food for them, they play in the streets—there are always accidents, and no doctors. I feel like a slave in my own country—we get up at 4 A.M. and at 11 at night we are still mending and patching.

The speaker, Josefina Muruchi, breaks down in a coughing fit. Suddenly, in a mixture of Spanish and Quechua, all the other women burst into speech, unleashing a torrent of pain and suffering. In the gloom, most of the women are sobbing.

This is *doloroso* for us. We have nothing. Nothing. Only coca [a stimulant leaf chewed to suppress hunger] to keep us going. It's the children, we want them to study, but they're so malnourished and the price of tin is so low. Our kids say, "Mami, I want to help," and don't do their homework, but then they fail their exams and have to repeat the year and the teachers are always asking for money and we haven't got it, and because our children are so ashamed they drop out of school. If I start vomiting blood again, what's going to happen to my children?

This was life below the poverty line in 1991, at the end of Latin America's "lost decade." Moreover, it was happening in the country that was the golden boy of neoliberal reform through much of the 1980s.

"No other area in the world is taking so many initiatives to open and integrate its economies with world markets," enthused Shahid Hussain, the World Bank's vice president for Latin America and the Caribbean.[1] In mid-1985 a new government took power at a time of acute economic crisis. Inflation, driven by a massive fiscal deficit, was running at an almost inconceivable annualized rate of over 23,000 percent, the national economy had been shrinking for five consecutive years[2] and real wages had fallen by 30 percent since 1981.[3] The country had been unable to keep up with the repayments on its foreign debt since March 1984.[4]

The foundations of what was christened the New Economic Policy were laid by presidential decree 21060 in August 1985. The decree was drawn up by Harvard professor Jeffrey Sachs following discussions with the IMF and World Bank and was designed to win IMF approval, which in turn would enable Bolivia to reschedule its debt payments to Western governments and commercial banks. In Bolivia the decree is known merely by its number—one enterprising radio taxi company in Cochabamba had the brainstorm of buying a 21060 telephone line, guaranteeing that its customers would never forget it.

The main measures contained in the decree were:[5]

- removal of restrictions on imports and exports;
- establishment of a single, flexible exchange rate;
- public sector wages frozen for four months (later reduced to three);
- an end to fixed prices on most goods and services;
- state companies given one month to present programs for "rationalizing" (i.e., sacking) staff;
- "free contracting" introduced in all firms, allowing management to hire and fire at will.

After the initial stabilization, subsequent decrees tried to reactivate the economy by stimulating exports and encouraging both foreign and local investment.

The harsh medicine duly won approval from the IMF, which in June 1986 announced $57 million in new credits, while the World Bank started lending again after a three-year gap and creditor nations agreed to reschedule debt repayments on favorable terms.[6] Further IMF aid for structural adjustment followed in the years to come.

Professor Sachs has since exported the model to Poland and other Eastern European economies, but as he himself admits, there are severe limitations to the Bolivian "miracle." "I always told the Bolivians, from the very beginning, that what you have here is a miserable, poor economy with hyperinflation; if you are brave, if you are gutsy, if you do everything right, you will end up with a miserable, poor economy with stable prices."[7]

Which is a pretty accurate description of what has happened. On the positive side, the shock therapy rapidly stabilized the economy, as inflation fell to 66 percent in 1986, and just 11 percent in 1987.[8] Moreover, the stabilization was achieved without a severe recession; after 1987 the economy returned to growth, albeit at low levels in per capita terms. Despite the near collapse of the world market for Bolivia's main export, tin, total exports increased steadily, largely thanks to new non-traditional crops such as soy beans and coffee. A tax reform greatly increased government revenues.

But the bad news outweighed the good. The shock therapy contained more shock than therapy, exacting a tragic human cost discernible in the statistics of falling wages and rising inequality, but more powerfully apparent to any casual observer of Bolivia's streets and farms.

In 1992, seven years into the Bolivian miracle, at regular intervals along the empty country roads, children stood all day holding out imploring cupped hands in the vain hope of a coin or two tossed from the occasional passing car. According to local aid workers, the practice only started in the late 1980s. One study by the UN's International Fund for Agricultural Development revealed that 97 percent of the rural population lived below the poverty line—the highest level of rural poverty in the world.[9] Structural adjustment had worsened the crisis in peasant agriculture by giving the lion's share of credit and investment to big agribusiness farms producing for export, while lowering barriers to cheap food imports. As a result, Bolivian peasants found themselves unable to sell their crops.

"I've seen far more serious malnutrition in children since '85," said Dr. Ana María Aguilar of the Children's Hospital in La Paz. Tuberculosis, a poverty-related disease, was also on the rise. In the early years of structural adjustment, from 1987 to 1991, government figures showed the percentage of Bolivian families below the poverty line rising from 74.6 percent to 80.1 percent.[10] In El Alto, the slum city on the outskirts of La Paz, 96 percent of babies had birth weights of less than the international standard for low birth weight, 5_ pounds.[11] By way of comparison, the figure for Ethiopia in 1990 was just 16 percent.[12] In one of Dr. Aguilar's wards, a thirteen-year-old boy stood protectively over the motionless form of his sister, whose brain was being attacked by TB-meningitis. "She can't say anything, but she knows I'm here," he whispered.

In the cities the fearful euphemism "rationalization" spawned wave upon wave of redundancy notices. Often the managers used the "shake-out" to get rid of the troublemakers first. The man shining tourists' shoes at his little stall on La Paz's main street was Selvestre Hiladi, age fifty-one. Until 1988 he was the trade union general secretary in a factory making plastic shoes. Thereafter, his working week went from 40 to about 65 hours, and his wife had to go out selling clothes on the street. He had no choice, he said. "We old ones have to do whatever we can, you have to swallow your pride. The customers treat you like shit and you just have to take it." For ten minutes' work, he charged the equivalent of 18 cents. Meanwhile, Selvestre added, the factory owners were doing fine. After they broke the union, they sacked the whole workforce and hired new people at lower wages.[13]

As protection was stripped away, cheap imports bankrupted over 120 of Bolivia's factories, reversing decades of gradual industrialization.[14] Many of those let go had no option but to join the "informal sector," where over 60 percent of Bolivia's urban population now scrape a living as best they can among the overcrowded ranks of street sellers, self-employed artisans, and others engaged in desperate forms of hand-to-mouth existence.[15] A man in the prime of life spends his entire day trying to hawk a handful of wooden coat hangers to indifferent passers-by; Indian women sit motionless in shawls and bowler hats, guarding tiny heaps of shrunken fruit. Too many sellers, not enough customers to go round. According to social scientist Silvia Escobar, by 1991 there was a street seller for every three families in Bolivia's cities.[16]

For the rich and powerful, Bolivia's silent revolution may have seemed a stunning success. But not for workers. Richard Ardaya, a textile worker sacked as a result of decree 21060, was even more damning about the stabilization program than Professor Sachs: "What's stabilized here is poverty—it's permanent."[17]

The *pailliris* of Bolivia are a human reminder of the importance of the shifting tides of economic "common sense" in the corridors of power in Washington and finance ministries across the region. The region's "lost decade" actually began in 1982, when the Mexican government defaulted on its foreign debts. This marked the end of the era of import substitution in Latin America and sent Washington's financiers into panic, as they realized that the top thirteen U.S. banks were owed $16.5 billion—almost half their capital—by Mexico.[18] A former president of Citibank described the state of mind at the annual IMF-World Bank meeting in Toronto, a few weeks later: "150-odd finance ministers, 50-odd central bankers, 1,000 journalists, 1,000 commercial bankers, a large supply of whisky and a reasonably small city produced an enormous head of steam driving an engine called 'the end of the world is coming.'"[19] If Mexico defaulted and other major debtors joined in, a bank crash on the scale of the 1930s seemed inevitable. The debt crisis was under way, bringing in its wake the silent revolution of neoliberalism.

Latin America's economic roller coaster during the lost decade can be roughly divided into three periods:

1982–83    Deep recession caused by the immediate response to the debt crisis.

1984–87    A false dawn, led by Brazil and Argentina's "heterodox"
           stabilization programs.

1988–91    Stagnation while structural adjustment gathers pace, paving the way
           for renewed capital inflows and the short-lived optimism of the early 1990s
           (the 1990s are discussed in chapter 4).

TABLE 3.1. Latin America and Caribbean: Regional Economic Performance 1981–1991[20]

|      | GDP GROWTH | EXPORTS | IMPORTS | N.R.T. | DEBT | INF  | GDI[21] |
|------|------------|---------|---------|--------|------|------|---------|
| 1981 | 0.7        | 96      | 98      | 11.3   | 288  | 57   | 220     |
| 1982 | -1.2       | 88      | 78      | -18.7  | 331  | 85   | 191     |
| 1983 | -2.6       | 88      | 56      | -31.6  | 353  | 131  | 144     |
| 1984 | 3.7        | 98      | 58      | -26.8  | 367  | 188  | 150     |
| 1985 | 3.4        | 92      | 59      | -32.2  | 377  | 280  | 158     |
| 1986 | 3.7        | 78      | 60      | -22.5  | 393  | 64   | 171     |
| 1987 | 3.2        | 88      | 67      | -16.2  | 428  | 209  | 180     |
| 1988 | 0.8        | 101     | 77      | -28.8  | 420  | 774  | 180     |
| 1989 | 1.0        | 111     | 82      | -28.0  | 423  | 1206 | 169     |
| 1990 | 0.3        | 122     | 95      | -15.4  | 442  | 1185 | 163     |
| 1991 | 3.5        | 121     | 112     | 6.6    | 456  | 200  | 176     |

GDP GROWTH: % change in regional Gross Domestic Product

EXPORTS: value of regional exports of goods FOB (US$ billions)

IMPORTS: value of regional imports of goods FOB (US$ billions)

NRT (Net Resource Transfer): overall flow of resources into/out of the region;
    a positive figure indicates a net inflow, a negative figure a net outflow (US$ billions)

DEBT: total external debt (US$ billions)

INF: change in consumer price index (inflation)

GDI: Gross Domestic Investment (millions of 1988 US dollars)

## DEEP RECESSION: 1982–1983

The slump in Latin America's economy that followed the Mexican collapse contributed to one war and several bloody "IMF riots." Argentina's military leaders invaded the Falklands to divert attention from a collapsing economy, while riots, protests and looting afflicted cities across the continent.

Before the 1980s, Latin Americans were accustomed to a growing economy. In every year between 1964 and 1980, the regional economy grew by more than 4 percent, making the recession that hit in 1982 all the more painful.[22] In 1982 Latin America's economy shrank in real terms for the first time since the Second World War. Chile was the worst hit, with per capita GDP falling by 14.5 percent in a single year, as the regional slump was exacerbated by the collapse of the initial

"Chicago Boys'" policies of financial liberalization, combined with an overvalued exchange rate.[23] The despair of Chile's unemployed workforce was captured in the lyrics of one of its top rock bands in the late 1980s, *Los Prisioneros*:

> They're idle, waiting for the hands
> that decide to make them run again
> The mist surrounds and rusts them. . . .
> I drag myself along the damp cement,
> remembering a thousand laments.
> Of when the misery came, when they said
> don't come back, don't come back, don't come back
> The factories, all the factories have gone.[24]

The immediate cause of the recession was the sudden end to lending by foreign banks, which had sustained the Latin American economy throughout the 1970s, combined with rising world oil prices after the second oil "shock" of 1979 and a sharp rise in debt interest payments as world interest rates rose. Recession in the North also hit world commodity prices. From 1979 to 1981 capital flowed into Latin America at an average of $13 billion a year.[25] By 1983, Latin America had started to *export* capital for the first time in decades. The transfer of wealth from the poor countries of Latin America to the institutions of the rich first world went on until 1991, a net flow of $218.6 billion, or $534 for every man, woman and child in the continent.[26] Even debt service payments on this scale failed to keep up with the interest falling due, and the bizarre logic of the debt game ensured that the region's total external debt rose from $243 billion in 1980 to $456 billion in 1991.[27]

Yet even these figures for Latin America's capital hemorrhage may be underestimates, since they exclude capital flight, which does not appear in the official statistics, as the nervous elites of the region used every dodge they knew to convert their wealth into dollars and spirit it to a safe haven in Zurich, New York, or the Cayman Islands. By one estimate, in 1983 capital flight from the five largest Latin American economies came to a further $12.1 billion.[28] As one former World Bank executive director commented at the end of the 1980s, "Not since the *conquistadores* plundered Latin America has the world seen a [financial] flow in the direction we see today."[29]

When Mexico crashed, the banks stopped lending, leaving Latin American governments to look elsewhere for the dollars with which to keep up their debt repayments. Aside from limited inflows from the international financial institutions (with all the strings attached), they had two stark choices: either declare a moratorium on their debts and become an international financial pariah or generate a trade surplus and use the excess hard currency to pay the banks. They chose trade.

At the time of the Mexican default, Latin America's trade was roughly in balance. It therefore had either to increase exports or cut imports. Since it had neglected exports for decades under import substitution, and the world in the early 1980s was in the grip of recession, import suppression was the only realistic option. Furthermore, import suppression can usually be achieved much faster, since it is invariably easier and quicker for a government to force its citizens to stop consuming than to persuade the citizens of other countries to buy Latin American exports. Only Brazil bucked the trend, building on export promotion policies dating back to the 1960s to expand export volume by half between 1982 and 1985.[30] The IMF's recipe, accepted willingly or otherwise by fourteen Latin American countries between 1982 and 1983, drove country after country into devaluation (to make exporting more profitable and increase the cost of imports) and recession (to suppress domestic demand for imported goods and curb inflation).[31] The IMF even encouraged Latin American governments to wheel out and strengthen the region's traditional barrage of import controls (supposedly anathema to the neoliberals) in the effort to generate dollars. The results were extraordinary: Latin America's imports halved in volume between 1981 and 1983.[32]

Initially, Latin America's exports failed to grow significantly, due partly to the recession going on in the industrialized nations, but the import collapse turned roughly balanced trade into a mighty trade surplus, rising from $9 billion in 1982 to $31.5 billion a year later.[33] By the time the trade balance swung back into the red again in 1992, Latin America had generated a total trade surplus of $242.9 billion.[34]

Although financial commentators and governments generally sing the praises of exports, and worry about rising imports, it is worth bearing in mind that their social impact is exactly the opposite, at least in the short term. Imports are goods and services consumed by the population; exports are those forgone in pursuit of foreign exchange earnings. Those hard-earned dollars might themselves be used to buy imports, but in Latin America in the 1980s, they went instead to servicing the debt. Almost all the trade surplus generated by the sacrifices of the lost decade left the region as the $218.6 billion in capital outflows, mostly for debt service payments.

This extraction of wealth from the region left a large hole in the economy, in the form of an investment collapse. Governments forced to adopt IMF austerity measures found it less politically costly to cut public investment than to sack employees in the middle of a recession (although many did that as well), while the private sector was deterred from investing both by the impossibility of borrowing abroad and the recession and high interest rates at home, as governments lifted interest rates to fight inflation. Foreign investors also took fright. Bank loans dried up and annual foreign direct investment fell from $8 billion in 1981 to $3 billion in 1983, as recession and fears of instability frightened off the executives of the transnational corporations.[35] Across the region, gross domestic investment (which includes both local and foreign investment) collapsed from $213 billion in 1980 to just $136 billion in 1983.[36] The level of investment is crucial to any economy's prospects; Latin America was mortgaging its people's future to pay its debts.

Falling investment and the domestic recession brought about by austerity programs provoked an industrial collapse. By 1983, the degree of industrial development in Latin America had regressed to the levels of 1966. In Argentina and Peru it was back to 1960 levels, while in Chile and Uruguay it was more like 1950.[37]

Governments faced a further problem in turning the trade surplus into debt service payments. Except in the few countries where state enterprises earned a large slice of export income (copper in Chile, oil in Venezuela and Mexico), export dollars lay in the hands of the private sector within each economy. Yet most of the debt repayments were the government's responsibility, forcing it to find a way to buy the private sector's dollars in order to then send them abroad to the banks. At the same time, devaluation made the dollars needed for debt service more expensive in terms of local currency. Most governments were already running deficits when the debt crisis broke, and the ensuing recession and import collapse hit revenues from taxes on sales, income, and imports. Despite IMF-decreed cuts in spending, few were able to generate a surplus with which to buy dollars from the private sector.

Many governments were left no option but to turn to the printing press, churning out local currency with which to buy dollars, and triggering a new bout of inflation. The largest economies (Argentina, Brazil, and Mexico) managed to imitate governments in Washington and London, using exceptionally high interest rates to persuade reluctant private investors to buy government bonds. This avoided immediate recourse to the printing press, but only at the cost of running up a large domestic debt to rival the foreign debt, and at much higher interest rates. In Mexico interest payments as a percentage of central government expenditure rose from 10 percent in 1980 to 50 percent in 1987.[38]

The spiraling internal debt and rising cost (in local currency) of servicing the foreign debt after devaluation ensured that, despite the cuts in public investment, government expenditure went up, in Brazil reaching 51 percent of GDP by 1985.[39] Fiscal deficits grew, forcing even the largest governments to print currency, and the inevitable upsurge in inflation ensued. In the early years of the debt crisis, the North's thirst for debt dollars took clear precedence over its neoliberal zeal for a low-spending, non-inflationary public sector. The IMF's insistence on devaluation to generate a trade surplus further boosted inflation by triggering an immediate increase in the prices of imported goods. Between 1981 and 1983 inflation rose from 131 to 434 percent in Argentina, from 91 to 179 percent in Brazil, and from 58 to 131 percent in Latin America as a whole.[40] The debt crisis and the IMF's stabilization programs were producing a high-inflation, recession-hit economy—the exact opposite of the Fund's stated intentions.

## THE FALSE DAWN: 1984–1987

In the early years of the debt crisis bankers and government officials from all sides saw it as a short-term liquidity problem in which the main goal was to keep Latin America from defaulting, while the continent's economy recovered its former dynamism. In 1984 their optimism seemed about to be proved right as the region returned to positive per capita growth, and a brief and sluggish recovery began that continued until 1987. Most of the recovery was accounted for by Brazil, which in 1984 responded to a resurgent first world economy by increasing its manufactured exports by 37 percent in a single year.[41]

Thereafter, however, Brazil's short-lived success followed a distinctly unneoliberal path. In 1985 the country returned to civilian government after twenty-one years of military rule. The incoming president, José Sarney, promptly raised wages in pursuit of a growth-first policy that bounced the economy up to an annual growth rate of over 8 percent. Brazil also defied the international financial community by announcing a unilateral restriction on its debt service payments. The Brazilian economy was single-handedly responsible for turning a negative per capita growth figure for the rest of Latin America into a positive figure of 1 percent for the region as a whole.

By early 1985, doubts over the wisdom of IMF-style stabilization programs had become widespread in the region, prompting policy makers to look for alternative ways to end inflation without provoking a huge recession. The result was a series of so-called heterodox stabilization programs in the mid-1980s. These used temporary government freezes on wages, prices, and exchange rates and introduced a series of new currencies to symbolize a new start and to break "inflationary expectations," whereby producers and employers constantly raise prices and wages in a self-fulfilling inflationary spiral. Heterodox programs are designed to give the economy a cooling-off period while the government takes steps to remedy the underlying causes of inflation, such as the orthodox measure of cutting the fiscal deficit (hence the "heterodox" nature of the formula).

Such programs showed mixed results in achieving stabilization, registering a significant success in Mexico in 1988. But in the best-known cases—the *Austral* plan in Argentina (June 1985), the *Cruzado* plan in Brazil (February 1986)—and the *Inti* plan in Peru (July 1985), the governments failed to deal with their spending deficits and merely succeeded in temporarily suppressing inflation through price controls. When the controls were finally removed, the underlying imbalances drove inflation even higher than before the programs were introduced.

In terms of growth, the failed plans produced a short-lived boom, as stable prices without accompanying austerity led to a brief surge in consumption. In the anchor economy of Brazil, the Cruzado plan led to an 8.1 percent growth rate in 1986, while the Austral plan produced a 1986 growth figure of 5.8 percent in Argentina.[42] The consumption boom in Brazil diverted attention from the export drive; even though manufacturing production rose by a further 11.3 percent in 1986, exports actually declined and the trade surplus started to fall.[43]

The domestic booms in Argentina, Brazil, and Peru all petered out in 1987 as the initial growth could not be sustained, and inflation made a fierce comeback. In Brazil, inflation dropped from 228 percent in 1985 to just 58 percent in 1986, but was back to almost 1,000 percent by 1988. Argentina and Peru followed a similar path. The false dawn was over.

In trading terms, 1984 to 1987 saw the beginnings of a long-term shift to the model of export-led growth and trade liberalization that was to emerge triumphant at the end of the "lost decade" of the 1980s. In 1984, Chile and Ecuador began cutting trade tariffs and eliminating import quotas, and Mexico, Bolivia, and Costa Rica followed suit a year later. However, such changes were initially masked by the impact of the heterodox programs. After the 1984 export boom in Mexico and Brazil, the region's overall trade performance deteriorated rapidly, from the peak trade surplus of $40 billion that year down to around $20 billion in 1986 and 1987.[44] Heterodox booms diverted export goods to the domestic market, and the terms of trade (the price received for Latin America's exports - largely raw materials - compared to the price it had to pay for its mainly manufactured imports) continued to deteriorate. Exports fell in value and did not recover their 1984 value until 1988.[45] Moreover, trade liberalization opened the door to a rapid growth in imports which from 1986 started to bounce back from the effects of import suppression in the first days of the debt crisis.

While growth made a fleeting recovery, investment became, in the words of the Inter-American Development Bank, "the great casualty of the debt crisis."[46] Annual investment in the period 1984–1987 never rose above $180 billion, compared with $220 billion in the year before the debt crisis began, and the slight rise during these years was almost entirely accounted for by investment during Brazil's heterodox experiment.[47] Foreign direct investment stayed below $6 billion a year, as Latin America remained a basket case in the eyes of international investors.

Meanwhile, the debt hemorrhage continued. Between 1984 and 1987, debt service payments flowed out of the region at over $30 billion a year, while the total foreign debt rose past $400 billion.[48] Latin America's governments continued to put debt repayments and current spending before investment, and a backlog of what became known as the "social debt" built up—a disintegrating education and health service and an economy dogged by crumbling infrastructure—potholed

roads, intermittent electricity supplies, and millions of families without access to drinking water or mains drainage. The social and economic fabric of Latin America was falling apart.

An official statement from the Peruvian government summed up
the state of much of the region at the end of the lost decade:

> Between 1985 and 1990 prices increased 20,000 times. The economy underwent
> the second longest-running hyperinflation recorded for any country in this cen-
> tury....The country was isolated from the international financial community...
> [debt] arrears were above $14bn (70 percent of total debt). Peru has been declared
> ineligible by the World Bank and the IADB. Export figures were 40 percent lower
> than in the previous decade....In July 1990 international reserves were a negative
> $50m. The state was broke.[49]

## NEOLIBERALISM RISING: 1988–1991

The collapse of heterodox programs in Brazil, Argentina, and Peru led
Latin America back into slump. Per capita GDP fell steadily from 1988
to 1990, before beginning a patchy recovery. Once "easy" heterodox
solutions had been discredited, neoliberalism spread rapidly across the
region; these were the years when the longer-term structural adjustment of Latin America's economy gathered pace. Trade liberalization,
government cutbacks, privatization, and deregulation became the
norm in almost every country.

The increase in world interest rates in 1988 led to a sharp increase in
the rate of Latin America's capital going overseas in 1988 and 1989. The
announcement in March 1989 of the new Brady Plan, masterminded by
U.S. Treasury Secretary Nicholas Brady, did little to correct the outflow.
The Brady Plan allowed Latin American governments to reduce their
debts by indulging in the kind of financial jiggery-pokery beloved of the
international capital markets. Governments exchanged their debt for
"Brady bonds" at a lower face value or supposedly below-market fixed
interest rate. They could also use their foreign reserves or new loans to
buy back their own debt at a discount, or encourage foreign investors to
swap debt for national currency with which to invest or buy up privatized companies, a practice known as "debt-for-equity swaps." Loans
from the international financial institutions were almost always
involved to finance debt buybacks or otherwise underwrite the deals.

The direct impact of the Brady Plan on the debt burden was limited. According to an evaluation for Oxfam by David Woodward of the six countries that had Brady Plans in place by mid-1994 (Mexico, Costa Rica, Venezuela, Uruguay, Argentina, and Brazil), overall effective debt reduction came to less than 6 percent of the countries' debts.[50] Only Costa Rica received an effective reduction of more than 7 percent (its debt was reduced by 21 percent) and Venezuela actually faced higher debt service payments over the long term, since its repayments on Brady bonds were fixed at rates higher than current global interest rates.

Debt-for-equity swaps, which went on outside the remit of the Brady Plan and were often linked to privatization programs, had a larger impact, according to Woodward, cutting about a quarter off the total debt of Argentina and Chile between 1984 and 1992. These two countries accounted for more than half of all debt-for-equity swaps worldwide, and Mexico and Brazil for a further quarter. However, this was achieved only at the cost of the governments losing national control over large parts of the "family silver" built up under import substitution.

Despite its limited immediate impact on debt service payments, the Brady Plan provided an exit for Latin American economies from the quagmire of the lost decade. It marked a turning point in investor confidence. A Brady Plan deal came to be seen, like an IMF Stand-by Arrangement, as a bill of good economic health, opening the door to foreign investment, which played a dominant role in the region's recovery after 1990. After squeezing nearly $220 billion out of Latin America from 1982 to 1990, the international capital markets suddenly began pouring money back into the region, and by 1991 the capital tide had turned. Debt service payments came to $31 billion that year, but capital inflows more than doubled in one year to reach $38 billion, leaving a net inflow of $7 billion.[51]

## SOCIAL IMPACT OF THE LOST DECADE

Throughout the region, after decades in which the percentage of Latin Americans living in poverty had been falling (though not their actual number) poverty once again began to rise. The 1980s saw 64 million new names join the grim roll call of the poor, leaving 46 per cent of the population, 200 million people, living in poverty in 1990, almost half of them barely surviving on incomes of less than a dollar a day.[52]

Shrinking wages, rising prices for food and other essentials, increased unemployment or "underemployment" and collapsing government services. The human cost mounted inexorably, exacting a toll of hunger, disease, and despair. At the dawn of the 1990s, according to the director of the UN International Fund for Agricultural Development, "chronic and persistent hunger" was killing 40,000 people a day. Some 55 million people suffered from undernourishment in the region, while the mortality rate due to "chronic non-infectious diseases" typical of malnutrition had doubled in the past few years.[53] Neglected sewage and water systems, victims of the investment collapse of the 1980s, played an important role in allowing cholera to return to the continent in 1991 after a gap of over sixty years. Within two years, nearly a million people had been infected, of whom 8,793 had died.[54] Malaria and tuberculosis were also making a comeback in the new, structurally adjusted Latin America.

## HOME AND FAMILY

At the eye of the social and economic storm unleashed by the silent revolution lay the family. Home is where future generations are born, grow up, and become citizens; it can be a sanctuary in troubled times, or a torment, or sometimes both. The central figure in the Latin American family is the mother. Traditionally, her main role may have been childbearing, child rearing, and housework, but economic and social change had added new tasks to her workload. Women formed an increasing percentage of the workforce, rising from 22 percent in 1980 to 38 percent by 1990.[55] Many of the new, low-waged or part-time "informal sector" jobs generated by adjustment went to women, while many men lost their role as family breadwinner as full-time waged jobs disappeared, or wages fell so far that a single income became insufficient to feed a family.

On top of this "double day" of work and running the home, the deterioration of social services, especially in urban areas, forced women into a third role, taking responsibility for running their communities, fighting or substituting for inadequate state services in schools, health, drainage, water supply, or roads.

Adjustment made all these tasks more vital to the family's survival and more exhausting: "flexibilization" often meant lower wages, longer hours, and greater insecurity, just as cuts in state subsidies have brought steep price rises in basics like food and public transport. Television became accessible to most poor homes in the region's shantytowns. In a cruel widening of the "frustration gap," the number of television sets per thousand homes rose by 40 percent in the 1980s and real wages fell by the same amount.[56] Teenagers, out of work or out of school, or fed up with dead-end jobs, were taunted by the racy lifestyles they saw in the daily diet of imported US TV shows or local soap operas. They wanted Nikes and Ray-Bans and on a good day they got rice and beans. Losing their jobs and status as breadwinners, men turned to alcohol and rage, while grown-up children had neither the money nor the opportunity to leave home. Houses filled up with frustrated, hungry people, with predictable results: family breakdown, alcoholism, domestic violence, drug abuse and crime spread through the region, creating a state of near panic and social disintegration. In the slums of Brazil the fear of street crime became so great that many poor people actually welcomed the "social cleansing" of the death squads, making their nightly cull of street children.

A study by Caroline Moser offers a unique glimpse of how adjustment and the debt crisis affected the women of one poor community in Guayaquil, Ecuador's largest city.[57] From 1978 to 1988, Moser regularly visited and studied the community of Indio Guayas, a swamp area of shantytown which in 1978 had about 3,000 residents. She was therefore able to take a series of socioeconomic snapshots of the community as the Ecuadorean government adopted eight different stabilization/adjustment packages between 1982 and 1988. Her findings are a microcosm of the human cost of adjustment, above all on women:

WOMEN'S JOBS: The proportion of women working rose from 40 percent to 52 percent over the period, most of the increase being in the informal sector or domestic work. Women identified rising prices and the increased cost of sending their children to school as the main reasons for going out to work. Wages for domestic workers fell by a third over the period. Whereas women had cleaned or laundered for one or sometimes two families in 1978, ten years later they were forced to work for at least two families, working as long as 60 hours a week just to keep earning at the same level. Many of those interviewed had to leave the house at 6 A.M. to travel across the city to their jobs, returning home at 8 or 9 P.M. Women were also now forced to go out to work when their children were younger, often having no choice but to leave small children locked up in the home while they were away.

MEN'S JOBS: The number of men with fixed-term contracts fell, as more and more were forced to find work on a day-by-day basis. Many men were forced to leave home to find work on the shrimp farms that became one of Ecuador's prime export sectors during the 1980s.

HOUSEHOLDS: The number of homes with only one wage-earner fell from 49 percent to 34 percent over the period, while the number with three or more members working rose from 19 percent to 32 percent. The number of households headed by women rose from 12 percent to 19 percent, often as a result of men leaving to work on the shrimp farms and never coming back. There was an increase in the number of married sons and daughters still living with their parents despite starting families of their own.

CONSUMPTION: Successive adjustment packages led to large price rises and falling real incomes. By July 1988, those families who could still afford milk had cut their consumption from 4.6 liters a week to 1.4. People ate fish less than two times a week instead of three and drank powdered fruit drink instead of fresh fruit juice. At first, families ate smaller meals, then cut out supper, then cut out breakfast. By 1988, one-quarter of households ate only one meal a day, and 79 percent of the children attending the local health center showed some degree of malnutrition. Women fed themselves last and least, and many were suffering from anemia.

SELF-HELP: Women had taken the lead in organizing schemes such as a savings club to help pay for school fees and new clothes at Christmas. They had also set up a scheme whereby forty families paid weekly quotas into a rotating fund used exclusively for buying housing materials.

EDUCATION: Although state schools were technically "free," a number of fees were imposed on parents during the course of the decade. By 1988, the cost of keeping a child at school, including a uniform, books, and bus fares, came to between one and two minimum salaries.

HOUSEWORK: Despite women's growing role outside the home, men took on no new housework. Instead, as mothers were forced to leave home for longer and longer periods to earn a living, they got up at 4 A.M. or 5 A.M. to cook food for the family to eat during the day. As eldest daughters reached ten or eleven years old, they were expected to take over cooking and housework, neglecting their school homework and falling behind the boys in their studies. Instead of getting more rest, women simply worked longer hours once their daughters had freed them from some of the housework.

CHILDREN: With mothers out all day, the rate of truancy among children increased. Mothers were also not present to ensure a fair distribution of food, so the smallest children often lost out to their hungry elder brothers and sisters. One of the greatest concerns expressed by women forced out to work was that they could no longer keep an eye on their sons, who were increasingly prone to drop out of school, get involved in street gangs, and start taking drugs. During the research, the community's first ever suicide occurred; a young male cocaine addict killed himself in despair after an argument with his wife about using their money to pay for his habit instead of feeding their three small children.

DOMESTIC VIOLENCE: Almost half the women said that there had been an increase in domestic violence. Trouble nearly always started when the women had to ask the men for more money—men either grew angry and ashamed at not earning enough to feed the family or wanted to spend what they had on themselves. However, adjustment also worked in the other direction. One in five women reported an improvement, putting it down to their increased independence once they had been forced to go out to work.

Moser found that women reacted in three different ways to the impact of structural adjustment on their lives. About 30 percent of the women were coping, juggling the competing demands of their three roles in the workplace, home, and community. They were more likely to be in stable relationships with partners who had steady jobs. Another group, about 15 percent of the women, were simply "burned out," no longer able to be superwomen 24 hours a day. They were most likely to be single mothers or the main breadwinners and were often older women, physically and mentally exhausted after the effort of bringing up a family against such heavy odds. They tried to hand over all household responsibilities to their oldest daughter, while their younger children frequently dropped out of school and roamed the streets. The remaining group, about 55 percent, Moser described as simply "hanging on," sacrificing their families by sending sons out to work or keeping daughters home from school to help with the housework. If nothing was done to change the impact of adjustment policies, Moser feared that many of these women would burn out, swelling the number of families broken by the impact of Latin America's silent revolution.

The lost decade was a profound trauma for Latin America, sweeping aside the assumptions of progress that had grown up since the Second World War. But, after a decade of turbulence and failure, Latin America entered the 1990s clutching the promise of good times to come. If the gurus of the IMF and other bastions of neoliberalism were to be believed, the pain of stabilization and adjustment had been a necessary sacrifice. The region could now step forward and claim its reward—entry into a brave new world of globalization, modernity, and export-led growth, bringing prosperity to all.

# 4—Silent Revolution
## Latin America 1991-2003

Everyone smoked in the Mexican stock exchange, a beautiful new twenty-story mirror-glass building shaped like a Stanley knife, cutting into the smog of downtown Mexico City. It was 1992, and on a roundabout in the street below, a grimy statue of some Aztec emperor cut a forlorn figure, marooned in the traffic. Inside, away from the glare of the sun, the disciples of the new order rushed to and fro; well-groomed men shouting orders to shoulder-padded and stilettoed peroxide-haired women. On the trading floor, green computer screens were the only color to break the gray and silver monochrome of business suits and stainless steel fittings. Young men's voices shouted out offers, echoing in the vast glass-domed chamber.

Efraín Caro was the Exchange's Director of International Affairs. He was thirty-three, but looked younger. On the wall of his office a *Wall Street Journal* cartoon showed an executive being told by his boss, "It has come to my attention that you're not under enough stress." The following week, Efraín was hosting a worldwide conference for representatives from sixty stock markets—he had stress to spare. Chain-smoking, grabbing phones, shouting out orders to subordinates even younger than himself, he spared ten minutes to rattle off figures in perfect English, albeit a largely unintelligible brand of investment-babble. In 1992 the Mexican stock market was booming, pulling in a total of $22 billion in foreign investment, 80 percent of it raised on Wall Street. That day's papers carried vital news from the presidential campaign going on in the United States, "Clinton says yes to NAFTA;" Efraín believed the dollars would keep on coming forever.

TABLE 4.1. Latin America and Caribbean: Regional Economic Performance 1991–2002[1]

|      | GDP  | Exports | Imports | NRT   | Debt | FDI  | Inflation | GFC |
|------|------|---------|---------|-------|------|------|-----------|-----|
| 1991 | 3.5  | 121     | 112     | 6.6   | 456  | 11.1 | 200       | 264 |
| 1992 | 3.0  | 127     | 138     | 26.6  | 479  | 12.5 | 414       | 221 |
| 1993 | 3.5  | 134     | 149     | 31.5  | 527  | 10.4 | 877       | 302 |
| 1994 | 5.2  | 153     | 171     | 10.1  | 562  | 24.2 | 333       | 337 |
| 1995 | 1.1  | 264     | 273     | 19.2  | 617  | 25.3 | 26        | 322 |
| 1996 | 3.7  | 296     | 304     | 22.6  | 639  | 40.0 | 18        | 338 |
| 1997 | 5.2  | 327     | 359     | 32.3  | 663  | 55.9 | 10        | 383 |
| 1998 | 2.2  | 326     | 379     | 27.2  | 745  | 60.9 | 10        | 394 |
| 1999 | 0.4  | 341     | 363     | -3.1  | 762  | 79.7 | 10        | 372 |
| 2000 | 3.8  | 407     | 421     | -0.2  | 740  | 67.7 | 9         | 387 |
| 2001 | 0.3  | 392     | 412     | -4.6  | 726  | 68.1 | 8         | 378 |
| 2002 | -0.5 | 393     | 382     | -39.1 | 725  | 39.0 | 11        | 354 |

GDP GROWTH: % change in regional Gross Domestic Product

EXPORTS: value of regional exports of goods FOB (US$ billions)

IMPORTS: value of regional imports of goods FOB (US$ billions)

NRT (Net Resource Transfer): overall flow of resources into/out of the region;
a positive figure indicates a net inflow, a negative figure a net outflow (US$ billions)

DEBT: total external debt (US$ billions)

FDI: Foreign Direct Investment (US$ billions)

INFLATION: weighted average 12-month increase in consumer price index
(initial high figures largely caused by Brazil)

GFC: Gross Fixed Capital Formation (US$ billions, constant 1995 prices)

Ten years later, his optimism looks misplaced. Capital inflows to Latin America resumed in 1991, bringing with them the promise of a return to growth, but they proved a fickle friend. In 1994, the investment-driven boom of the early 1990s ended, as did the dance of the millions of the 1970s, with a crash in Mexico that reverberated across the other major Latin American economies in the so-called tequila effect. No sooner was the region back on its feet than a series of crashes in Asia and Russia led to a crisis in Brazil and effectively ended the era of easy access to capital. A further recovery, and another slump, this time driven by spectacular implosion in Argentina, and a global recession. Latin America's growth and investment curves looked like a roller coaster, as short-lived boom gave way to slump and back again with bewildering speed. According to economist Dani Rodrik, Mr. Caro and his capital markets bear much of the blame:

> For the 1990s, the evidence suggests that the instability in private capital flows has been perhaps the most important single determinant of macroeconomic volatility.... Some of the smaller countries of the region with little access to private capital flows (Bolivia and Guatemala) have experienced the lowest levels of macroeconomic volatility. Argentina and Venezuela are at the other extreme, with very high levels of exposure to volatility in private capital flows and correspondingly high levels of macro-volatility. Countries like Brazil, Chile, and Colombia, which have managed private capital flows, are somewhere in between.[2]

Capital comes in several guises, and the inflows diversified during the 1990s, as the bank loans to governments, which had led to the debt crisis of the 1980s, gave way to other forms of lending:

- Purchases of equities (stocks and shares) in companies on Latin America's stock markets
- Purchases of bonds issued by Latin American governments
- Bank loans to Latin American companies
- Foreign direct investment (FDI) in farms, factories, and service industries

As Latin Americans have learned to their cost, these different sources of capital behave in radically different ways, in terms of their potential social benefits and their degree of unreliability. Capital flows can come in the form of "hot money," which can disappear overnight, or enter in less volatile "stickier" varieties, such as foreign direct investment, which is both more stable and produces more benefits in the form of jobs and improved infrastructure. This chapter explores the different aspects of capital flows, investment and industry.

## EQUITIES

In the early 1990s, stock markets like Mexico's sprang up around the continent (even little Nicaragua tried to join the club in 1994) to absorb the incoming dollars, initially becoming an essential part of international fund managers' portfolios—a titillating, high-risk/high-profit addition to their more sober investments at home. In the pages of *The Economist*, the most lucrative areas of the third world and Eastern Europe were renamed "emerging markets," with an entire page devoted to weekly stock market reports from Buenos Aires to Bangkok.

One such was Singer and Friedlander's "Aztec Fund," launched in 1994 with glossy brochures promising painless profits (albeit with the usual caveat that "you may not get back the amount you originally invest"), and a free, and evidently low-budget, video in which a series of uncomfortable-looking young fund managers sang the praises of the silent revolution in capitals from Santiago to Mexico City. The language was standard marketese—franchises, market shares, and profit growth; the delivery astonishingly wooden. A potbellied chief executive appeared at the end to praise the "all-pervading level of optimism you find at every level of society" in the new Latin America and to conclude, in a "greed is good" vein, by urging on the investors, "*Now* is the time to buy."[3]

In naming the fund, perhaps the PR people overlooked the Aztecs' customary treatment of their victims, but the name proved unexpectedly apposite. Almost as soon as the fund was launched, Latin America's stock markets went into a nosedive, following the assassination of the favorite in Mexico's presidential campaign and the subsequent financial crisis. Across Latin America, stock markets collapsed as portfolio investment slumped from $65 billion in 1994 to a mere $5 billion in 1995.

The euphoria of Mr. Caro's early 1990s boom never returned. Today, the eagerness of even the smallest economies like Nicaragua to open stock markets during the 1990s boom appears like folly. The snake-oil salesmen of the markets have long since moved on, as Latin America's large firms decided to take their custom elsewhere, opting to list on the New York Stock Exchange.

## BONDS

One of the fastest-growing sources of capital has been government bonds, sold abroad by the larger Latin American countries. Borrowings in the bond market shot up from less than a $1 billion in 1989 to peak at $52 billion in 1997, on the eve of the Asia crash. Thereafter, it fell back to just $16.2 billion in 2002.[4] Again, the big countries take the lion's share: Mexico, Brazil, and Argentina accounted for 85 percent of bond sales,[5] leaving the rest of Latin America with the crumbs.

One by-product of the bond boom has been a sharp rise in the total external debt, which includes bonds from both governments and private companies, but excludes stocks and shares. After staying roughly level at around $420 billion from 1987 to 1989, the total debt began to rise again, reaching a peak of $762 billion in 1999, before falling back to $725 billion in 2002, as Mexico and Brazil repaid their bailout loans from the 1995 and 1999 crashes (see below).[6] Even given the sharp growth in exports, this level of repayments accounted for 36 percent of total export income, much the same as in 1980, at the start of the debt crisis.[7] Despite the plaudits accorded to the impact of the Brady Plan and the shift to direct and portfolio investment as the chief source of foreign capital, interest payments on the debt came to $55 billion in 2000, while repayments of the original loans accounted for a further $112 billion.[8]

## INVESTMENT, GROWTH, AND DEVELOPMENT

Although the new influx of foreign investment after 1991 was greeted with fanfare in the world's financial press, it barely took up the slack left by the collapse of public investment caused by the debt crisis and structural adjustment. According to CEPAL, Latin America's economy needed to grow at 4 percent per capita every year to generate sufficient jobs and income to reduce poverty. This in turn required average investment rates of 28 percent of GDP, a figure achieved only by Chile in the late 1990s. By then, out of eight of the largest economies, four (Argentina, Brazil, Colombia, and Mexico) had lower investment rates than in 1980, on the eve of the debt crisis.[9] Investment remains the Achilles' heel of the silent revolution, reaching just 18 percent of GDP in 2002.[10]

Moreover, it was often the wrong kind of investment, concentrated in a relatively small number of sectors. Only one sector (telecommunications) saw dynamic investment in all countries, and only one country (Chile) increased investment in every major sector. Manufacturing investment was particularly dynamic in certain capital-intensive subsectors (for example, cement, steel, petrochemicals, and chemicals), but that did little to create jobs.

Activities that had traditionally produced the largest volume of employment, such as textiles and garments, declined across the board. Only the *maquila* assembly plants, operating under different conditions from the rest of the economy, provided the strong growth in highly labor-intensive activities that the reforms were expected to generate. Commercial agriculture and manufacturing firms in the formal sector underwent important modernization processes, involving more intensive use of capital, stifling job creation in sectors where output grew most strongly, such as natural-resource-based commodities and the automobile industry.[11]

## CAPITAL PUNISHMENT

When Mexico crashed in 1994, Michel Camdessus, the IMF managing director, prophetically described the event as "the first major crisis of our new world of globalized financial markets."[12] Succeeding years rapidly proved him right, with a series of severe national financial crises hitting Thailand, Indonesia, Korea (1997), Russia and Brazil (1998), and Argentina (2002). All of them shared a common cause—the prior liberalization of national capital markets had left them vulnerable to massive capital flight. They also shared a common outcome—it is an iron rule of financial crises that the taxpayer always ends up picking up the bill for bailing out banks and foreign investors alike. As one banker told the Wall Street Journal in 1985, "We foreign bankers are for the free market system when we are out to make a buck, and believe in the state when we're about to lose a buck."[13]

These crises hit what had become known as "emerging markets" (perhaps best rechristened "submerging markets" in numerous cases). In Latin America, the big three, sometimes known as Abramex (Argentina, Brazil, and Mexico), were the middle-income countries that had proved most attractive to Northern investors, who had bought up shares and government bonds, and banks who had lent to local corporations and governments. Most small economies had attracted little interest and benefited little from the capital boom, although many were badly hit by the backwash from the big crises (for example, via falling export demand and commodity prices).

## ROOTS OF THE CRISES

In the first years of the 1980s, countries had both to reduce inflation and generate a massive trade surplus with which to keep up their debt service. The only means to achieve this double objective was to inflict a huge recession at home.

In the early 1990s, however, there was an entirely new option, as foreign capital provided a cushion against the worst effects of adjustment. Leaders such as Mexico's Carlos Salinas, Argentina's Carlos Menem, and Brazil's Fernando Henrique Cardoso found themselves able to get inflation under control without the same degree of austerity, by using capital inflows to keep up debt repayments and fund the restructuring of the economy. Large capital inflows also allowed them to fix their currencies at overvalued rates, which helped suppress inflation by holding down import prices. The cost of this strategy was a loss of export competitiveness and ensuing trade deficit, but this too was covered by capital inflows, as long as they lasted.

The effects were spectacular: Argentina's inflation fell from 4,923 percent in 1989 to 18 percent three years later,[14] and within months of the adjustment package, the economy moved smoothly into four years of record-breaking growth—over 6 percent in every year from 1991 to 1994.[15] Brazil got its adjustment over in 1994, cutting inflation from 930 percent in 1994 to 22 percent the following year, as growth leapt to 6.2 percent in 1994 and 4.2 percent in 1995.[16]

But the strategy left governments at the mercy of external events. In Mexico, rising U.S. interest rates in 1994 meant that investors lost their appetite for Mexican bonds. Mexico also demonstrated unusual signs of political fragility—the Zapatista uprising in January 1994, followed by the assassination of the ruling party's presidential candidate in March and elections in September, increased investors' worries about "political risk." In his last year in office, President Salinas wanted to go down in history as the hero of NAFTA and structural adjustment, not as a devaluer. He chose to use Mexico's reserves to prop up the peso. By December, he had squandered $22 billion, leaving only $7 billion in the kitty for his successor, Ernesto Zedillo.[17] Prior to taking office, Zedillo had twice begged Salinas to devalue, but had been rebuffed.[18]

In Brazil, the trigger for crisis was more distant. Russia's financial crisis of August 1998 led to "contagion," as the markets decided Brazil would be next—a self-fulfilling prophecy as they proceeded to remove their capital. Reserves fell by $30 billion in two months.

Argentina inherited Brazil's problems. Four external shocks hit the currency after 1998: commodity prices (and with them Argentina's export earnings) fell due to the Asia crash, followed in 2001 by the global slowdown; capital inflows dried up after the Asia crash; the U.S. dollar (and therefore the peso) appreciated against other currencies, making Argentine exports even less competitive; and Brazil devalued, hurting Argentine trade within Mercosur.

Argentina's difficulties were compounded by the particularly severe constraints of its fixed exchange rate system. In 1991, the government ended inflation by pegging the peso to the dollar under the "Convertibility Plan." This step, which effectively made devaluation illegal, also said that the government could only issue pesos if they were backed by dollar reserves. In the event of a fiscal deficit, the government's only option was therefore to borrow dollars to cover the gap.

And fiscal deficit there was, but the cause was not so much government profligacy or corruption, as pension privatization. Urged on by the World Bank and IMF, Argentina moved rapidly from a "pay as you go" scheme in which the government used income from those currently working to fund its pension commitments, to a funded scheme, where individuals saved for their own retirement. The problem was the transition period, during which the government no longer received pension contributions but still had to pay out to current pensioners. In the Argentine case, decades of state patronage had led to a massive pension bill, and the switch to funded schemes accounted for 70 to 80 percent of the deficit during the 1990s.

A number of other adjustment measures increased Argentina's vulnerability: bungled and corrupt privatizations led to a high-cost economy, with tariffs for phones and electricity up to ten times international rates. This, plus an overvalued currency and trade liberalization led to a surge of imports that destroyed Argentine industry and inflated the trade deficit. Financial deregulation, the privatization of the banking system and the liberalization of capital flows meant that government effectively lost control over much of the economy.[19]

## THE COST OF THE CRISES

Unable to prop up their currencies, all three governments were forced into sudden devaluations, with varying costs. Argentina suffered the greatest trauma, as government spending cuts and its decision to freeze dollar-denominated bank accounts sparked protests in which twenty-seven people died, and five governments fell in the space of two weeks toward the end of 2001. The political chaos triggered the one of the worst peacetime economic and social collapses in Latin American history, which was far from over at the time of this writing, in 2003.

Brazil suffered zero growth in 1998, combined with high interest rates and government spending cuts, pushing up unemployment by one-quarter. In the words of one nun working in a Brazilian shantytown: "This year, the music's gone from my street— the people have pawned their sound boxes or got behind on their payments. They've lost their music and the life's gone out of them."[20] The government avoided a bank crash and worse recession by restructuring the banking sector in the years prior to the devaluation. Although this cost the public purse the equivalent of 11 percent of GDP, it was a cheaper option than launching a rescue operation in the middle of a crisis.[21]

Urban unemployment in Mexico almost doubled between 1994 and 1995.[22] Real wages fell by 10 percent in a year, and did not recover their 1995 value until 2001.[23] In the two years following the crash, 20,000 small firms declared bankruptcy.[24] The government was saddled with the huge cost of a bank bailout, amounting to $63 billion, or 17 percent of its GDP.[25] The Mexican crash also produced the "tequila effect"—a flight by investors from other emerging markets such as Brazil and Argentina, leading to continent-wide slowdown.

## LESSONS FOR THE FUTURE

Reliance on the fools' gold of fickle capital inflows made the region vulnerable both to events beyond its control, such as the Asia crisis of 1998, and to the received wisdoms of the markets. Governments with competent leadership and a clear mandate were often able to manage the dictates of the market, but if domestic political crisis (for example, a succession struggle, or standoff between president and Congress) should strike, then the impact of capital markets was to amplify the cost—if investors didn't like what was going on, they pulled out their cash, frequently precipitating a much greater crisis. The discipline of the markets was both more claustrophobic, and often less well-informed than that of the IMF, as the *Financial Times* caustically observed shortly after the Mexican crash:

> Because they process the many billions of dollars' worth of investments flowing
> across national borders each day, the markets have become the police, judge and

jury of the world economy—a worrying thought given that they tend to view events and policies through the distorting lenses of fear and greed.[26]

And what of the voters? With the IMF and the markets exerting increasing control, the "customers" of these policy decisions were seeing their ability to influence government policy rapidly eroded. As one Brazilian academic lamented:

> Social policy is held hostage by "business confidence." Citizens' confidence is measured every four years with an election. The market measures business confidence every four seconds.[27]

The successive crises have also prompted much debate on exchange rate regimes. While pegging exchange rates to the dollar produced enormous benefits in curbing inflation, the difficulty appeared to lie in designing a stabilization program with a clear exit strategy, enabling governments to come off a pegged exchange rate once stabilization had been accomplished. No government did so willingly, but in retrospect Brazil's exit from a less rigid pegged currency arrangement in 1999 was more successful than Argentina, which clung to its more draconian currency board system until the very last minute, thereby greatly increasing the economic and social costs of devaluation.

But beyond the technical aspects of the debate, the main lesson is that capital account liberalization is not the answer to Latin America's historical inability to save and invest in sufficient quantities to generate growth and jobs. Moreover, continued dependence on capital inflows will remain costly. In April 1999, Javed Burki, World Bank vice president for Latin America and the Caribbean, told reporters, "My belief is that we should stop talking about crises and start talking about extreme volatility. Essentially, I think we should be preparing ourselves for a perpetual state of volatility rather than a recurring crisis."[28]

## DOLLARIZATION AND THE EXCHANGE RATE DILEMMA

In response to this state of permanent volatility, some of the smaller economies concluded that the luxury of a national currency could no longer be justified, and opted for the U.S. dollar instead. Ecuador (2000) and El Salvador (2001) joined Panama (which has been dollarized since 1903). In so doing, they gave up much of their ability to manage their economies, along with the income that governments gain from printing money, known as *seigniorage*. Without their own exchange rates, their interest rates are effectively determined by the U.S. Federal Reserve, plus whatever risk premium the markets attach to the country in question, leaving only one of the three big "handles" of economic policy (fiscal) still available to the government.[29]

The argument for dollarization is particularly strong for smaller economies, where floating exchange rates have traditionally proved more volatile and currency fluctuations have a more direct effect on inflation. Ecuador, however, also demonstrates the perils. Following dollarization, it proved unable to get inflation down to U.S. rates, leading to a steady loss of competitiveness. Although this was masked by new oil finds, which continued to bring in dollars, the government faced the prospect that, without the option of devaluation, a severe domestic recession would be needed at some point to get prices back in alignment.[30]

Dollarization is just the latest twist in a policy conundrum that has bedeviled third world governments—what to do about the exchange rate. By 2002, the received wisdom in Washington and elsewhere was that floating exchange rates or complete dollarization were the only option. Any attempt to find a middle ground—for example, by pegging currencies temporarily to smooth out fluctuations—merely offered speculators a juicy target, encouraging an attack on the currency, in which market players gamble on being able to force a country to devalue, and make huge sums when it does so. Yet floating currencies too have their drawbacks, condemning exporters to cope with exchange rate gyrations that can make their products uncompetitive overnight.

## STICKY MONEY: FOREIGN DIRECT INVESTMENT

While hot money such as bonds and equities was distinctly unreliable, foreign direct investment (FDI), in which foreign companies invest in or buy farms, factories, and service industries like telephone companies, proved a more stable source of foreign exchange and technology.

Adjustment's torch-bearers generally see FDI as better for development than bonds or equity investment—not only is it less volatile, they argue, but it creates jobs, earns dollars if the investing companies are in the export sector, and introduces the latest technology in vital areas such as telecoms or pharmaceuticals, to a region with few scientists or researchers of its own.

FDI has certainly proved a much more stable form of finance than its more fickle stable mates, taking off from $10 billion in 1993 to reach a peak of $79 billion in 1999, before recession in the United States and concerns over emerging market stability caused it to fall back to $39 billion in 2002.[31] However, there are a number of caveats:

LINKAGES: Foreign companies tend to be less willing to buy inputs from local suppliers, often preferring to source from their own country or parent company. Especially in the case of export industries, this can mean that TNCs come to resemble enclave economies, providing few benefits to the rest of the economy beyond export earnings and jobs. Mexico's maquila belt, which creates a large number of jobs, is one of the better kinds of FDI, yet government figures show that Mexican-produced inputs to their products reached a peak of just 3.1 percent of total value in 2000. If wages are included, national content has actually fallen from 22 percent to 17 percent since the start of NAFTA, due to the falling use of labor as companies upgrade their technology.[32] In some cases, however, linkages have started to develop, for example, in the clusters of car component manufacturers around large car plants in Mexico and Brazil or local software suppliers around Intel's Costa Rican plant.

TECHNOLOGY TRANSFER: Successful developing countries such as Taiwan have in the past ensured that they absorb and adapt technologies that would otherwise have taken them years to develop, for example, through joint ventures with foreign companies. These days, however, companies are less willing to share cutting-edge technology, and find it easier to keep it to themselves through stronger international patenting rules.

CONCENTRATION IN LARGE ECONOMIES: FDI has flowed disproportionately to the big economies, partly because these have the most attractive domestic markets. Of the $58 billion entering Latin America in 2001, 81 percent went to the big three, Argentina, Brazil, and Mexico, although to be fair, these three countries account for 60 percent of the region's people.[33]

JOB CREATION: FDI tended to introduce capital intensive technology that generated few jobs. In a nine-country study of the impact of two decades of adjustment (1980–2000), Barbara Stallings and Wilson Peres concluded:

> The reforms did not solve, and quite probably increased, two problems: invest-
> ment continued to be concentrated among large enterprises that have not shown
> the capacity to develop backward and forward linkages with smaller firms, and
> supplier chains were destroyed by the quest for competitiveness through increas-
> ing imported inputs. Moreover... transnational corporation subsidiaries gained
> ground vis-à-vis large domestic conglomerates. Nonetheless, the large firms con-
> tributed relatively little to the generation of employment since they tended to be
> more capital-intensive.[34]

One extreme example of low-job, high-value investment was Intel's decision to set up a plant in Costa Rica in 1998. Despite employing only some 2,200 people, Intel galvanized the country's growth figures for two years. In 1999, Intel alone accounted for over one-third of Costa Rica's exports, pushing growth figures over 8 percent, before the bursting of the high-tech bubble and U.S. recession led to growth slumping to zero in 2001.[35]

PROFIT REMITTANCES: Corporations are not altruistic, they invest in emerging markets on the expectations of higher profits than they can find at home and expect to be able to use those profits how they see fit. That may involve reinvestment locally, but over time, Latin America has also seen a sharp increase in the outflow of profit remittances. According to CEPAL, the annual outflow of corporate profits rose from $7 billion in 1990 to around $20 billion from 1997 to 2000. Net inflows of FDI peaked at $79 billion in 1999, but then slipped back to $39 billion in 2002, by which time remittances accounted for a half of FDI inflows.[36]

DOWNWARD COMPETITION ON INCENTIVES: Latin American governments desperate for foreign capital and technology go to enormous lengths to outbid their rivals. David Mulford, George Bush's Undersecretary for International Affairs of the Treasury chose a questionable metaphor to describe their lot: "The countries that do not make themselves more attractive will not get investors' attention. This is like a girl trying to get a boyfriend. She has to go out, have her hair done up, wear makeup."[37]

Besides the privatization program, Latin America's "makeup" includes perks such as tax exemptions for incoming investors, easing restrictions on profit remittances, reducing all kinds of red tape and establishing special export processing zones along the lines of Mexico's *maquiladoras*. Governments have also watered down labor legislation and gone out of their way to ensure a compliant labor force for foreign companies. As poorer countries like China and Vietnam have climbed aboard the globalization bandwagon and started to compete for investment, the downward pressure has intensified.

Counterbalancing this has been the demand by investors for a qualified, healthy workforce, which has increased pressure on governments to invest in their countries' "human capital."

GROWING TNC DOMINANCE: The foreign direct investment boom has not always led to an increase in productive capacity, since it has consisted mainly of mergers and acquisitions of existing assets, first public (privatizations) and more recently private. From 1997 to 1999, flows associated with private mergers and acquisitions represented around 40 percent of foreign direct investment. According to *The Economist*, TNC-led consolidation "is becoming the norm in LA, in industries from food to retailing to banking. Once it starts, it often proceeds at great speed. In Brazil's white goods industry, for example, within just two years all three local firms sold out to foreigners which had begun as technological partners with minority shareholdings—Sweden's Electrolux, Germany's Bosch and America's Whirlpool."[38] Transnationals saw their share of the regions' largest 500 firms' sales rise from 27 percent to 38.5 percent during the 1990s.[39]

## PRIVATIZATION

One of the key lures for FDI has been privatization of state-owned companies. While few significant sell-offs occurred in the chaos of the lost decade, in the 1990s, Latin America came to resemble a giant fire sale, as government after government sold off dozens, if not hundreds, of state-owned enterprises. As the chair of one large transnational corporation told his fellow business magnates at an IDB conference on Latin

America's "New Economic Climate," "the race for Latin America has started and the latecomers will lose out."[40]

From 1990 to 1996, Latin America led the developing world in the privatization race, raising over $82 billion during that time.[41] As at any fire sale, there were numerous bargains to be snapped up by the wily dealer, and the wave of privatizations prompted a veritable feeding frenzy among foreign investors and transnational companies. The scale of the sell-off could best be judged by leafing through the pages of the *Financial Times*, where in a kind of international investors' gossip column, paid advertisements announced the value of the latest completed deals, along with the names of buyers and fixers. In just three days in July 1993, these included:

20 JULY    Madeco, a Chilean timber firm. Sold for 3,937,500 American Depositary Shares @ $15 each. Two-thirds of the shares sold in the United States.

20 JULY    MASISA, another Chilean timber firm. Sold for 3,875,000 American Depositary Shares @ $14.125.

21 JULY    "The Republic of Argentina has sold a 59 percent interest in Hidroeléctrica Alicurá SA to a consortium formed by Southern Electric International and the Bemberg Group for an aggregate consideration of US$315,641,771."

22 JULY    The Argentine government has raised $2.66 billion in the form of 140 million shares in the state oil company, YPF. "Joint global coordinators" for the sale were Merrill Lynch and CS First Boston Group; 65 million shares were sold in the United States and 35 million in Argentina, the rest elsewhere. This was a big sale, meriting a full page with all the big names: Salomon Brothers, First Boston Corp,, Credit Suisse, Deutsche Bank, Baring Brothers.

22 JULY    In Argentina, Hidroeléctrica Cerros Colorados SA sold to Dominion Energy Inc and SACEIF Louis Dreyfus y Cía Ltd. for $146,213,232.

The pressures on governments to privatize seemed irresistible. The growing fiscal crisis of the state sector, provoked by both foreign and domestic debt payments, forced governments to increase revenue or cut expenditures; privatization achieved both, shedding loss-making companies while raising substantial amounts of cash. It also enabled governments to attract new investment and technology in critical areas of the economy, such as telecoms. Between 1990 and 1998, privatization earned the Brazilian government $45 billion, while Argentina received $19.5 billion and Peru pulled in $7.1 billion.[42] In Mexico, the family silver raised a total of $13.7 billion in 1990–1991, during which time privatization receipts provided just under one-tenth of government revenues.[43]

Due to the increasing uncertainty generated by the recession in the industrialized world, several privatizations were postponed in 2001, and revenues were expected to fall short of the level posted in 2000 ($18 billion). Some 80 percent of that figure corresponds to Brazil, a late adjuster playing catch-up. Elsewhere, governments that were running out of things to privatize sought to replace the income by auctioning concessions to build infrastructure. CEPAL sees the slump in FDI since 1999 as heralding a permanent fall in inflows, because of these structural issues.[44]

Privatization was also part of the broader ideological shift, since neoliberals believe in cutting back the state and passing ever-larger chunks of the economy over to the private sector. Once privatized, they argue, management will be able to take decisions based on economic efficiency rather than politics and a company's performance is bound to improve. The rhetoric employed was the same as in Mrs. Thatcher's Britain, the only country to surpass the large Latin American economies in its privatizing zeal. In Latin America, privatization also provided a juicy carrot with which to attract foreign investment back into the region after the capital famine of the debt crisis. Overshadowing the internal debate over privatization lay the brooding presence of the international financial institutions, especially the World Bank, which made such sell-offs a condition for its loans.

State airlines and telecommunications companies went on the block throughout the region, but only Argentina and Bolivia have so far allowed their rush to market to sweep away their state oil companies. Despite two decades of neoliberalism, the three largest companies in Latin America remain state-owned oil enterprises.[45] Elsewhere, governments have been reluctant to hand over such strategic or highly profitable companies, preferring instead to encourage joint ventures with transnational corporations to attract technology and investment while retaining some degree of overall control.

The track record of privatizations varied enormously. One analysis of the telecommunications sector concluded that though there was a significant improvement in the quality of services, "in virtually all cases" there was much less progress in bringing down extortionate charges for installing new lines and international calls, because privatization created underregulated private monopolies that set about gouging the customers. [46] In 2002, the United States resorted to taking Mexico to a WTO dispute over Telmex, which it claimed was charging an exorbitant $13.50 per minute for international calls, compared to just four cents a minute for domestic connections.[47]

The telecommunications sector is one of the most suited to privatization in that it requires constant injections of rapidly advancing technology. State companies had long since given up the chase, partly due to the freezing of public investment in the early years of the debt crisis. In Argentina in the early 1980s, houses and apartments were advertised for sale or rent "with telephone"—a major selling point, since the average waiting time for a new telephone line to be installed was six years (it fell to one month after privatization).[48] In Venezuela's pre-privatization system, 80 percent of international calls and 70 percent of domestic calls simply failed to get through.[49]

Other areas of the economy seem to benefit far less from privatization than the high-tech telecoms sector. In 1990 the Argentine government awarded contracts to resurface and repair nearly 10,000 kilometers of roads. "Nine months later," reported the *Miami Herald*, "most concessionaires have done little more than erect tollbooths." The paper continued:

> Other routes have seen even more startling abuses. Contractors in control of a road leading to a popular beach resort sparked protests by building earthen barriers across alternative routes in order to force motorists to pass through their pay booths. And after travelers complained about the rip-off along another highway, contractors parked a fleet of phony squad cars at tollbooths to give the appearance of police backing.[50]

Such dirty tricks paid off handsomely, helping to earn private companies an extraordinary rate of return of 40 percent per year.[51]

One of the most disastrous sell-offs was that of the Argentine airline, Aerolíneas Argentinas, to Spain's Iberia (ironically, itself government-owned). The new-look airline got off to a bad start when it tried to sack a third of its employees, provoking weeks of strikes and demonstrations. At the height of the unrest less than half of its aircraft flew on time.[52] But customers risked more than an irritating delay; shortly after its privatization Aerolíneas scored an international public relations disaster when 65 passengers reported symptoms of cholera (one died) after taking one of its flights to California.[53] Perhaps it was just as well that the Argentine consumer protection law passed in 1995 did not apply to privatized companies.[54] The airline ran up losses of $500 million in its first three years in the private sector.[55] Problems persisted, and as it prepared for its own privatization, Iberia transferred its Aerolineas shares to SEPI, a Spanish government holding company. SEPI holds 92 percent of the shares in Aerolineas, which by 2001 was losing $30 million a month.[56]

In recent years, bank privatizations have been among the most lucrative transactions. In 2001, the U.S. Citigroup's $12.5 billion cash and stock acquisition of Banamex, Mexico's second biggest bank, was the single largest deal ever made in Mexico, equal to a year's FDI. It brought "emerging market" earnings up to 25 percent of Citigroup's total revenue. Mexico's remaining banks are now waiting for offers. As one Banorte executive sees it, "It is as if we are the last Coca-Cola in the desert. The question is, how many thirsty travelers are there?"[57] Chile and Argentina have also largely denationalized their banking sectors, while Brazil's financial system remains largely in national hands. Spanish banks, which were among the most active in Latin America, got their fingers badly burned in the Argentine crisis of 2002, when the government's decision to devalue the peso threatened the viability of the whole Spanish banking sector.

Like transnationals in industry, foreign-owned banks behave differently and sometimes worse (from a development perspective) than domestic ones. According to the economist Stephanie Griffith-Jones, foreign banks in Latin America typically lend less to small and medium-sized companies, adding to the credit squeeze already faced by such businesses.[58]

The combination of big money, privatization, and deregulation proved irresistible to the region's grafters, and privatization and corruption soon became indelibly linked in the minds of many voters. Occasionally someone got caught, for example Angel ''The Divine'' Rodriguez, who fled Mexico in 1995 after his bank, Banpais (the country's eighth-largest bank, privatized in 1991), and his insurance company, Asemex, were seized by the government. Charged with $200 million in fraud, Rodriguez was arrested on his yacht off the Spanish island of Ibiza in 1996. A year after his extradition in 1998, he had not so much as set foot in a Mexican prison and was living comfortably at his home in a Mexico City suburb.[59] Foreign banks, too, were not averse to cashing in. Citibank, for example, helped transfer $90–$100 million out of Mexico for Raúl Salinas, the notorious brother of neoliberal crusader Carlos Salinas. Raúl Salinas was subsequently arrested on corruption charges.[60]

Privatization also played an important political role, enabling leaders such as Peru's Alberto Fujimori and Argentina's Carlos Menem to attack the power of the trade unions, which are traditionally strongest in the state sector. If all this sounds familiar to British readers, it is hardly surprising. British consultants fresh from the experience of *Thatcherismo* back home were highly sought after as advisers for privatizing Latin American governments.

In many sell-offs, governments desperate for cash or keen to reward their cronies merely transformed public monopolies into virtually unregulated private monopolies, which promptly raised prices to consumers and make enormous profits. Telmex's profits shot up 77 percent to $2.3 billion in the year after privatization.[61] Subsequently, an OECD report subsequently showed Telmex to be the most profitable telecom company in the OECD. Unfortunately, that did not help consumers—Mexico also had the lowest number of telephone lines (12 for 100 people).[62] By one estimate, such poor regulation added 16 percent to Argentines' household bills for things like phones and electricity. The big conglomerates that snapped up the best deals duly returned the favor, chipping in for Carlos Menem's reelection campaign in 1995.[63]

When privatization encroached on essential services like water, the results could be explosive. In 1999, following years of pressure, the Bolivian government agreed to privatize the Cochabamba water system. A subsidiary of utilities giant Bechtel was given a forty-year lease. Within weeks of taking over the water supply, the company tripled water rates. Families suddenly faced monthly bills of more than US$20 to be paid from earnings of less than $100 a month. A range of organizations mobilized against the privatization, forcing the Bolivian government to declare martial law in April 2000. Then, following the death of a protestor, the government agreed to renationalize the water system and reduce water rates.

By the end of that year, the government of Bolivia formally canceled Aguas Del Tunari's forty-year contract. Bechtel promptly retaliated by seeking $25 million compensation from the Bolivian government for breach of contract. The case was accepted in February 2002 by the International Center for the Settlement of Investment Disputes (ICSID)—a little-known arm of the World Bank Group.[64]

## CAN THE PRIVATE SECTOR ADAPT?

For Latin America's private sector, the last twenty years have been like a hurricane, sweeping away the old certainties of import substitution, when local companies could rely on the state for protection from outside competition, allowing them to fix prices and skimp on investment. Since 1982, privatization has greatly expanded the size and importance of the private sector while trade liberalization has bankrupted thousands of companies. The survivors have been forced to play by the new rules of the game, investing in new technology and improving productivity to remain competitive. One of the most ferocious industrial shakeouts has been in Mexico, where trade liberalization had a seismic impact even before NAFTA came into force:

> Only birdsong disturbs the silence inside the La Josefina textile factory in the village of Panzacola in the central Mexican state of Tlaxcala. Yards of white cotton cloth still hang from its lines of looms, stopped in mid-weave when the factory shut a year ago and its 100 workers were laid off. The nameplates on the machines explain what happened. They are from a bygone Lancashire: the cast iron looms were made more than a century ago by John M. Summer of Manchester, J. Dugdale & Sons of Blackburn and G. Keighly of Burnley. The spinning machines came from Dobson & Barlow Ltd., Bolton, in 1912, and the carding equipment from Platt Bros. of Oldham in 1920.

> Since 1881, La Josefina had made yarn and cotton cloth for the Mexican market. It closed because its machines, though still in perfect working order, could not compete with modern, electronically controlled rivals. In the past five years, Mexico has become one of the world's most open economies, scrapping import licenses and slashing its maximum external tariff from 100 percent to 20 percent. Consumers have benefited from low-priced imports, but many businesses are struggling. "Yarn came in from India, Korea and Taiwan at half the price we sold at," Valentín Rangel, La Josefina's administrator, says. "We were caught out, technologically backward and without the capital to renew our machinery." La

Josefina is one of thousands of Mexican companies that have fallen victim to a savagely swift process of economic change.[65]

Bankruptcy is commonest among small and medium-sized firms that cannot afford to invest in the necessary improvements, especially when local interest rates have been driven sky high as part of the adjustment process. Larger companies and transnational subsidiaries can borrow abroad at lower interest rates and find it easier to compete.

Companies that can adapt to the new environment stand to benefit from pro-business government policies, improved access to foreign investment and technology, and more opportunities to export their products. Some of Mexico's biggest companies, such as the glass manufacturer Vitro and the cement producer Cemex (see box), are well on the way to becoming Latin America's first genuine transnationals, buying up U.S. companies to ensure they have a commanding position within the North American market under NAFTA.[66]

### CEMEX: A LATIN AMERICAN TRANSNATIONAL

In the 1990s, Mexico's Cemex moved swiftly to become the third-largest cement business in the world, and more profitable than its two larger rivals (from France and Switzerland). In 1991, it was the first Latin American firm to list on the New York Stock Exchange. Like many large Latin American companies, it still has strong connections to its founding family—it was founded by the current chair's grandfather, also called Lorenzo Zambrano, in 1906. Grandson Lorenzo is worth $2.1 billion, according to Forbes, making him the second-richest man in Mexico. Aggressive expansion in the 1990s has given the company subsidiaries in the United States, Philippines, Egypt, Spain, and Thailand, as well as numerous Latin American countries.

Key to its success has been introducing pioneering high technology into a traditionally low-tech business. Computer and global positioning satellite systems in every truck enable the company to cut costs for its quick-drying cement. Average delivery times have fallen from 3 hours to 20 minutes—a miraculous achievement in the traffic-clogged nightmare of Mexico City. Cemex has even spun off a highly profitable IT consultancy.

At home, meanwhile, the prospects look rosy—Mexico's president Vicente Fox has promised that every peasant shack in the country will have a cement floor before he leaves office in 2006.[67]

In Mexico, many of the success stories have been in services, rather than manufacturing. The largest national retailer, Cifra, saw profits boom after it went into a joint venture with the U.S. chain Wal-Mart and other large Mexican chain stores rapidly followed suit.[68]

Almost without exception, successful companies have had to lay off large parts of their workforce in the drive for greater productivity. Some of the most successful companies also adopted more modern management methods. At the Brazilian company of Acesita, privatized in 1992, management sacked a quarter of the workforce, then turned years of heavy losses into growing turnover and profits by abolishing time clocks, improving training, and cutting three out of seven management layers as well as looking for a more specialist, high-profit market niche and investing heavily in new technology. Those who kept their jobs saw real wages rise by 11 percent.[69]

In many cases, however, Latin American companies have responded to globalization by behaving more like multinationals, and reducing domestic linkages. Studies of the business strategies of forty medium and large garment firms in Chile, Mexico, and Venezuela in the mid-1990s showed that successful firms reacted to competitive pressures by using increasing amounts of imported inputs. Some even decided to outsource all their manufacturing to Asia, concentrating, à la Nike, on design, distribution, and marketing, with disastrous consequences in a high-employment sector like textiles.[70]

## PENSION FUNDS

One new source of domestic investment has been the introduction of private pension funds in Latin America.[71] As so often, the pioneer of this facet of the silent revolution was Pinochet's Chile, which introduced a compulsory private scheme in 1981 to replace the traditional Latin American pay-as-you-go system, under which the state pays out pensions and takes in contributions from current employees. Over the next fifteen years, Peru, Colombia, Argentina, Uruguay, Mexico, Bolivia, and El Salvador introduced similar schemes.

The Chilean pension system is both the most sweeping, and has accumulated the most capital to date, totaling $30 billion, or 40 percent of GDP. Private pension funds are restricted in their ability to invest overseas, helping to create a pool of investment capital in the

Chilean economy that has reduced its dependence on foreign inflows.

Whatever its contribution to the economy as a whole, however, there are serious concerns over the system's high administration costs. These can eat up 20 to 30 percent of contributions, and are pushed up by the armies of salesmen employed to poach clients from rival pension funds. In Chile, 50 percent of all contributors switch providers every year.

In Argentina and Bolivia, rapid pension fund reform loaded new costs onto governments, since they ceased to generate income from contributors, while continuing to have to pay pensions to existing beneficiaries. Some observers see this as a major course of the fiscal problems that precipitated Argentina's economic meltdown in 2002, while the burden on the Bolivian exchequer was estimated at $300 million a year.[72]

## INFLATION

By disposing of loss-making companies and pulling in one-off windfalls, the privatization bonanza has, however, played a crucial part in curbing governments' spending deficits and getting inflation down in many Latin American countries in the early 1990s.

Inflation in the region as a whole peaked at around 1,200 percent in 1989 and 1990, largely as a result of the collapse of the heterodox programs in Argentina, Brazil and Peru.[73] Thereafter, privatizations, further government cutbacks in spending and investment, and improved tax collection all helped to get fiscal deficits down. Furthermore, privatization and the Brady Plan deals contributed to the general rehabilitation of Latin America in the eyes of the world's investors. The capital inflow took off in 1991, allowing governments to cover their deficits in a non-inflationary manner by borrowing abroad, rather than printing money and enabling them to run overvalued exchange rates as an anti-inflation tactic, as discussed previously.

Given Brazil's disproportionate weight in regional indices, the turning point came with Brazil's 1994 *Real* plan, which brought Latin America's annual inflation rate down from 877 percent in 1993 to 26 percent in 1995. From then on, inflation fell steadily to an estimated 7 percent in 2001, apparently unaffected either by the growing instability of the region's economies or the rise in fiscal deficits in the capital drought of the late 1990s.[74]

## VARIATIONS BETWEEN COUNTRIES

Regional averages are deceptive, concealing individual booms and slumps, and the strong performance of some economies relative to others. (For a country-by-country economic summary, see appendix A.) Moreover, the regional statistics are disproportionately influenced by Brazil, which accounts for over a third of Latin America's GDP. Such complications can make unraveling Latin America's economic performance a difficult exercise, not least for the reader, but it is important to move beyond regional generalizations to get some idea of how the different countries fared during the silent revolution.

Countries vary in terms of both policy and performance. No one country has implemented the full neoliberal recipe. Several supposedly exemplary neoliberal regimes have clung to lucrative and strategically important state enterprises in copper (Chile) and oil (Mexico). Elsewhere, political opposition has forced governments to abandon or water down their privatization programs (Uruguay, Colombia, Brazil, Bolivia, Nicaragua, Ecuador). Several of the most successful countries have mixed orthodox neoliberal adjustment with heterodox government controls.

The most comprehensive attempt to date to differentiate between country performance has been carried out by CEPAL's Growth, Equity and Employment project, a series of studies carried out at the end of the 1990s seeking to answer the question, "Was it worth it?"[75]

Rather than a comparison with the chaos of the 1980s, CEPAL's team chose to compare the 1990s with the three postwar decades. Their results highlighted the variety of country experiences—for some, the 1990s represented their best postwar decade, while for others it was their worst (see table 4.2).

Only four out of 18 countries (Uruguay, Bolivia, Argentina, and Chile) grew faster in 1991–2000 than in 1945–1980. The pattern of economic activity also showed a marked dependency on the ups and downs of foreign financing, leading to two very different growth phases in the last decade. The first was characterized by a notable increase of capital inflows to the region, which facilitated the application of successful anti-inflationary programs in several countries and the implementation of structural reforms.

The rapid growth experienced by some countries during the first years of the 1990s then slowed down. This is the case with Argentina,

TABLE 4.2. Ranking of the Seventeen Latin American and Caribbean Economies on the Basis of the Growth Rates in the Base Period and the 1990s

| COUNTRY GDP GROWTH (1951–1980) | | COUNTRY GDP GROWTH (1991–2000) | |
| --- | --- | --- | --- |
| 1. Brazil | 7.2 | 1. Chile | 6.0 |
| 2. Mexico | 6.6 | 2. Dom. Republic | 5.2 |
| 3. Costa Rica | 6.5 | 3. Peru | 4.7 |
| 4. Ecuador | 6.2 | 4. Argentina | 4.6 |
| 5. Dom. Republic | 6.1 | 5. Costa Rica | 4.4 |
| 6. Paraguay | 5.4 | 6. El Salvador | 4.4 |
| 7. Venezuela | 5.2 | 7. Guatemala | 4.2 |
| 8. Colombia | 5.1 | 8. Bolivia | 3.8 |
| 9. Guatemala | 5.0 | 9. *Latin America/Caribbean* | 3.4 |
| 10. *Latin America/Caribbean* | 4.9 | 10. Mexico | 3.3 |
| 11. Peru | 4.8 | 11. Uruguay | 3.2 |
| 12. Honduras | 4.6 | 12. Honduras | 3.2 |
| 13. El Salvador | 4.4 | 13. Colombia | 2.6 |
| 14. Jamaica | 3.9 | 14. Brazil | 2.6 |
| 15. Chile | 3.7 | 15. Venezuela | 2.1 |
| 16. Argentina | 3.4 | 16. Paraguay | 2.0 |
| 17. Bolivia | 3.4 | 17. Ecuador | 1.8 |
| 18. Uruguay | 2.3 | 18. Jamaica | 0.0 |

Chile, El Salvador, Panama, and Peru, the five countries that had posted growth rates of over 5 percent between 1990 and 1994. After the "tequila effect" crisis of 1995, only Chile maintained the pace.[76]

The CEPAL study found that the economies that were most successful during the first three postwar decades were noticeably unsuccessful in the 1990s. Brazil, Mexico, Ecuador, Paraguay, and Venezuela were star performers and occupied the top of the list of the Latin American economies from 1951 to 1980. In the 1990s, however, they fell to the bottom of the list. Chile, Peru, and Argentina, on the other hand, behaved in the opposite fashion. Perhaps not surprisingly, the most chaotic and underperforming economies seemed to have most to gain from adjustment, while those that had done well under import substitution had most to lose from reform. This issue is intimately connected with the politics of adjustment, discussed in chapter 6.

When the CEPAL results are cross-referenced with an IDB study attempting to rank countries according to their degree of neoliberal reform, a complex picture emerges that suggests that the measures pushed so assiduously by the IMF and World Bank are only loosely connected with actual economic performance.[77] The three countries identified by the IDB as the most vigorous reformers are Bolivia, Jamaica, and Peru, yet Jamaica emerges from the CEPAL study as the *worst* performer in terms of GDP, while Bolivia is halfway up the table. A similar picture emerges with slow reformers (Venezuela, Mexico, and Uruguay). It appears that economic success depends on factors other than faithful application of the neoliberal recipe.

## LATIN AMERICA IN 2003

Neoliberals prefer to think and act in terms of macroeconomic variables like growth and inflation, paying less attention to other issues such as income distribution, quality of life, or job security. It is therefore to be expected that the silent revolution is more likely to register success at the macroeconomic level than in the lives of the poor. Even so, the macroeconomic record of recent years is decidedly mixed.

The one single, unmitigated success has probably been to have got the region's inflation under control. Low inflation is good for business and good for the poor, and conquering it is, by any standards, a triumph. However, taming inflation was mainly a one-off gain, and now that inflation is down to single figures across much of the region, it should not remain a major source of concern.

While the region's gross domestic product has grown since 1980, so has the population. In per capita terms, Latin Americans did not get past the 1980 figure until 1996, just when the region entered the late-1990s era of crisis and uncertainty. Latin Americans have gone through a recession and a recovery that has got them back to where they started.[78] This partial recovery was promptly reversed by the "lost half-decade'" of 1997–2002, during which GDP per capita fell back 2 percent, as capital flows dried up in the wake of the 1997–1998 Asia crisis.[79] All this stands in marked contrast to the steady growth of the region's economy in the postwar decades.

Investment performance is similarly discouraging, for gross fixed capital formation slumped during the 1980s, and as a share of GDP or in per capita terms, it had still not recovered by 2000.[80]

The record on the region's foreign debt is also mixed. Despite twenty years of debt rescheduling and other measures, the region's total debt is now hovering around $725 billion, double its level at the start of the debt crisis. According to the World Bank, total debt service takes up one-third of the income from booming exports, the same figure as in 1980. The debt itself is more diverse than in the 1970s, both in terms of the kind of debt and the type of creditor, which means that debt crises such as those in Argentina and Mexico in the late 1990s have become more complex than the 1980s versions.

For a time, reform rehabilitated the region in the eyes of foreign investors, but Latin America's extreme dependence on foreign capital has always been a mixed blessing. The availability of easy money in the world's capital markets precipitated a series of crashes, creating a new and anxious world of chronic financial volatility and impending crisis. Moreover, the constant imperative of currying favor with the markets diverted governments from trying to chart a path of long-term development based on the region's own resources.

While recognizing gains in terms of exports, reduced fiscal deficits and getting inflation under control, CEPAL concluded:

> Efforts to boost economic growth and productivity met with disappointing results in the 1990s. The "destructive" factors at work in some of the sectors and firms that have been unable to adjust to the new scheme of economic incentives have predominated over the "creative" effects associated with the development of competitive sectors and firms.

> Today, the region has more "world-class" firms (many of which are subsidiaries of transnational corporations), but it also has many other firms, especially small and medium-sized enterprises, that have been unable to adapt to the new policy environment.[81]

What appears to be emerging in the early years of the new century is a Latin America of increasing fragmentation and differentiation. Countries differ in policy regimes (exchange rates, industrial policies, public spending) and performance (trade, growth, investment) to a seemingly unprecedented extent. National economic crises are affecting some countries (Argentina, Ecuador, Venezuela) and not others (Mexico, Chile); some elements of the Washington Consensus package are under sustained political attack (privatization, capital market liberalization) while others retain a degree of consensus among decision makers (such as fiscal discipline, controlling inflation, and promoting exports).

If history is any guide, when a movement that has shaped the "common sense" of its time (such as neoliberalism in much of the 1980s and 1990s) suffers this kind of dispersion and fragmentation, it heralds a shift to a new common sense, much as neoliberalism itself replaced the school of thought that underpinned import substitution. However, that process appears a long way off—there is no obvious new "big idea" waiting in the wings or the university corridors for future generations of politicians to seize and run with. Instead, the region's leaders seem to be taking a kind of "mix and match" approach to the neoliberal package amid a growing sense of confusion and uncertainty.

# 5—Export or Die
## Export-Led Growth and Regional Trade

It hits you from hundreds of yards away, the rich sweet smell of fermenting wood floating through the crisp air of a Chilean night. The scent emanates from several huge mounds of wood chip, silhouetted against the dockside floodlights. Dwarfing the wooden houses and shops of the southern port of Puerto Montt, the mounds steam gently as they await loading onto the Japanese ship that rides at anchor in the bay. Each pile contains the remnants of a different species of Chilean tree, hauled from the country's dwindling native forest.

Along the southern coast, the wire-mesh tanks of innumerable salmon farms dot the picturesque fjords and inlets. On the beaches, the black strings of *pelillo* seaweed lie drying, before being sent to Japan for processing into food preservative. In the ports, the fishmeal factories grind mackerel into animal fodder. All these products will be shipped overseas as part of the Chilean export boom, a vast enterprise that has turned the country into the fastest-growing economy in Latin America and the flagship of the neoliberal model.

The phenomenon is being repeated across the region. On the runway at Guatemala City airport, a forklift truck loads boxes of leaves into a cargo plane. Within hours the lush tropical foliage will arrive in Miami, for use in the next day's flower arrangements throughout Florida. In Colombia thousands of women toil, drenched in pesticides and fertilizers, among extraordinary swathes of color. They are growing carnations for sale by the florists of Europe. Other, less palatable entrepreneurs have also got in on the act; one drug kingpin of Colombia's Cali cartel was convicted after 22 tons of cocaine was found hidden in consignments of frozen broccoli bound for the United States.[1]

These burgeoning "nontraditional exports" are part of Latin America's new thrust for export-led growth, cashing in on improved transport and packing technologies to diversify the kind of primary products that have traditionally dominated Latin American exports. The other side of the export drive is an attempt to increase the exports of manufactured goods, usually low-tech products such as shoes or textiles, or the output of assembly plants, such as the *maquiladoras* strung along the U.S.–Mexican border, where imported components are assembled by cheap Latin American labor.

Diversification lowers a country's vulnerability to sudden swings in world prices for a single, all-important export product. By moving into fruit, timber, and fisheries, Chile reduced the preponderance of copper in its exports from 79 percent in 1970 to 40 percent in 2000.[2] The more exotic nontraditional exports, such as fresh salmon or strawberries (or cocaine) also carry a higher profit margin than tanker loads of copper ore or soya beans.

The record on export-led growth has been mixed—Latin America achieved the exports, but not the growth. In the 1990s, the region had one of the world's highest growth rates for merchandise trade, with income from exports booming at an average 9 percent a year, but growth did not recover to pre-debt crisis levels.[3]

Moreover, Latin America's attempt to get in on the ground floor of the global economy as a purveyor of raw materials risks confining it to one of the most sluggish areas of world trade, continuing its traditional reliance on the fickle prices of the commodity markets. In the 1990s, the recovery in its exports was swamped by a flood of imports, following blanket trade liberalization, bankrupting potentially competitive local producers and raising fears that the "opening" had undermined the region's industrial future. Furthermore, the boom in nontraditional exports has been achieved at a high social cost, exacerbating inequality and undermining the region's food security, while both assembly plants and pesticide-intensive agriculture have damaged the environment.

It is worth noting that several of the most dynamic sources of foreign exchange do not show up in the region's export figures. One of the region's most successful exports is people, and Latin American migrant workers, mainly in the United States, sent home $17 billion in 2000, much of it going straight into the pockets of the poor.[4] Tourism is similarly absent from the export figures.

## COMPARATIVE ADVANTAGE

The theoretical underpinnings of neoliberal attitudes to trade predate both Marx and Keynes. The great thinkers of liberal economics believed that free trade would benefit all parties through the mechanism of what they termed "comparative advantage." The Scottish economist David Ricardo established comparative advantage as the logical basis for free trade as long ago as 1817. He showed that everyone would enjoy higher incomes and a better standard of living if every producer, be they country, company, or individual, concentrated their activity in areas where they had the greatest cost advantage (or the smallest cost disadvantage) over their competitors.

To illustrate his theory, he took the example of two countries, Britain and Portugal, and two products, wine and cloth. In the early nineteenth century Britain was the most technologically advanced economy in the world, but Portugal has a much better climate for grapes, so Ricardo argued that the welfare of both would be maximized if Britain stuck to making cloth and imported Portuguese wine. Any other arrangement would be a waste of time and money.

There are numerous objections to the modern application of this theory[5] (George Bernard Shaw once described free trade as "heart-breaking nonsense")[6] and its application to Latin America. It ignores the key question of how Britain came to be technologically advanced in the first place. To frame the discussion in terms of a comparative advantage that is static and, by implication, permanent, ignores the way a government or other agents can change the nature of a country's strengths. In Ricardo's example, Portugal could decide to compete with Britain by sending some engineers to learn the secrets of the British textile industry, then set up its own textile sector by importing some British looms or learning how to make them in Portugal. At that point the lower wages in Portugal would make its cloth cheaper than the British variety and it could export cloth *and* wine.

In that situation, the British textile industry could survive if the government imposed tariffs against Portuguese cloth or drove down wages to Portuguese levels, but a more positive solution would be for British companies to pursue a *dynamic* comparative advantage in textile production, seeking to maintain a sufficient technological edge over their Portuguese competitors to compensate for the difference in wages. This requires a commitment to invest in research and development (R&D).

In recent years, rapidly industrializing Asian economies such as Japan or South Korea have built their success on the basis of this kind of dynamic comparative advantage. If Korea had followed the World Bank's current advice, it might still be exporting wigs, its principal export in the 1950s.[7]

Moreover, experience has shown that the economies that rely on exporting raw materials fare worse than those that have managed to industrialize. The "terms of trade"—the amount of raw materials a third world country must export to pay for a particular range of manufactured goods—have historically tended to deteriorate, obliging the commodity producer to "run just to stand still," exporting ever greater quantities of primary products to buy the same amount of industrial goods. One reason is that technological advance has reduced the amount of raw materials required by the advanced economies; in 1984, for instance, Japan used only 60 percent of the raw materials it needed in 1973 to manufacture an equivalent industrial product.[8] Tin cans use less and less tin as production processes improve, bad news for Bolivia; fiber-optic cables replace copper wire in telecommunications, hitting Chile's main export.

Raw material exports also suffer from abrupt price swings and are subject to substitution by other products. Biotechnology now allows U.S. companies to use corn syrup in soft drinks, and prices have plummeted for the cane sugar grown in the Caribbean. World trade in manufactured goods in the 1980s grew eight times faster than that in commodities.[9] Commodity exports are becoming a less and less important part of world trade, so, argue the critics, why back a loser?

Changes in the world economy in recent years challenge some of Ricardo's underlying assumptions. The whole idea that trade takes place between independent nations is looking increasingly outdated. According to the U.S. Department of Commerce, in 1997 so-called intra-firm trade, where different subsidiaries of the same transnational company trade with each other, accounted for around two-thirds of global trade.[10] The spectacular rise in size and power of the transnational companies is increasingly making national borders irrelevant, and provides the driving force behind the worldwide spread of free trade agreements.

Ricardo believed that British technology and capital would always prefer to stay in Britain. In a passage that sounds wonderfully innocent in the age of the footloose transnational investor, he wrote of the "natural disinclination which every man has to quit the country of his birth and connections" and argued that "most men of property" would be "satisfied with a low rate of profits in their own country, rather than seek a more advantageous employment for their wealth in foreign nations."[11] Today's Lancashire mill owner would be far more likely to relocate his factory in Lisbon to cut his costs and boost his profits.

Yet despite the arguments against applying the concept of static comparative advantage in the late twentieth century, it remains central to the neoliberal gospel. The apostles of the silent revolution are convinced that everyone will benefit if each country sticks to what it is "naturally" good at and removes trade barriers to unleash the efficiency of open markets. Chilean citizens will be best off if their country exports kiwi fruit and imports computers. If Chile tries to develop a computer industry, it will mean trade barriers, higher prices for computers, and second-rate products.

Although the arguments are usually carried on in technical, abstract terms, self-interest is never far from the surface. First world industries clearly stand to gain from keeping third world countries in their place as suppliers of raw materials and cheap labor. Instead of allowing local firms to become industrial competitors, transnational corporations build local factories in third world countries, enabling them to take advantage of their low local wage levels and to use the threat of such relocation to hold down wages in their remaining plants in the North.

Besides the pressure exerted via the international financial institutions, the major economies use import tariffs to discourage developing countries from trying to process their own primary products. In a phenomenon known as "tariff escalation," the EU and Japan's tariffs on processed food are twice as high as on unprocessed goods, while the United States imposes 30 percent tariffs on orange juice and 132 percent tariffs on peanut butter to protect its own growers.[12]

In historical terms, the United States is a relatively recent convert to the merits of free trade. In a prophetic speech, U.S. President Ulysses S. Grant once said:

For centuries England has relied on protection, has carried it to extremes and has obtained satisfactory results from it. There is no doubt that it is to this system that it owes its present strength. After two centuries, England has found it convenient to adopt free trade because it thinks that protection can no longer offer it anything. Very well then, Gentlemen, my knowledge of our country leads me to believe that within 200 years, when America has gotten out of protection all that it can offer, it too will adopt free trade.[13]

President Grant apparently underestimated the speed of history—the United States became the world's foremost economic power and its most determined advocate of free trade within seventy years of his death.

## NONTRADITIONAL AGRICULTURE

Orchards filled the Aconcagua Valley northeast of Santiago de Chile. Parallel rows of peach trees stretched off to infinity, playing tricks on the eye. The monotony was punctuated by the occasional fat-trunked palm tree or weeping willow, shining with new leaf on a cold and dusty spring day.

Carlos Vidal was a union leader, president of the local *temporeros*, the temporary farm laborers who plant, pick, and pack the peaches, kiwi fruit, and grapes for the tables of Europe, Asia, and North America. A shock of black curls streaked with gray fringed his round, gap-toothed face. A freezing wind off the nearby Andes blew across the vineyards as Carlos told his story:

On this land there were 48 families who got land under [former President] Allende. We grew vegetables, maize and beans together, as an *asentamiento* [farming cooperative]. There were a few fruit farms then, but we planned them. After the coup the land was divided up between 38 families—the others had to leave. Then it started to get difficult, we got the land but nothing else—the military auctioned off the machinery.

Then the *empresarios* started to arrive, especially an Argentine guy called Melitón Moreno. The bank started taking people's land—foreclosing on loans—and Moreno bought it up. Three *compañeros* committed suicide here because they lost their farms. Melitón got bank loans and bought yet more land and machinery. He planted nothing but fruit—grapes at first, then others.

My father was a leader of the *asentamiento*. The first year after the coup we were hungry, lunch was a sad time. We began to sell everything in the house, then we looked for a *patrón* to sell us seeds and plough our land for us, and we paid him with part of the harvest. Next year we got a bank loan and managed to pay it off, but the following year they sold us bad seed. We lost all the maize and the whole thing collapsed. We had to sell the land and Melitón Moreno bought it.

Of the 38 families, most are now *temporeros*. We all sold our land but kept our houses and a small garden to grow food. Trouble is, even the gardens are no good, the water's full of pesticides from the fruit. This area used to be famous for water melons and now they don't grow properly anymore. They chuck fertilizer and pesticide everywhere, it doesn't matter that the earth is dead because the fruit trees live artificially. No one grows potatoes or maize any more—it's cheaper to buy the imported ones from Argentina.

Life is hard for Chile's 400,000 *temporeros*, most of them women. "They work you like a slave here, squeeze you dry then throw you out," said Roxana, a smartly dressed thirty-year-old. She could only find work during the harvest and packing seasons, seven months in the year. The few permanent jobs all went to men, she complained. Roxana's house was a wooden hut with a tin roof, a few sticks of furniture, no heating and no glass in the windows. The family baked in summer and freezes in winter. Cold poverty is not as blatant or exotic as the tropical poverty of Haiti or Nicaragua, but the runny-nosed children were pale and bronchitic and the cold cut to the bone. A fruit picker typically takes home about one dollar an hour.[14]

Carlos's allegations about pesticides were confirmed by a series of horrific birth defects. In the regional hospital at Rancagua, investigations showed that every one of ninety babies born with a range of neural tube defects in the first nine months of 1993 was the child of a *temporera* working on the fruit farms. The Rancagua figure was three times the national average. Pesticide poisoning is a feature of nontraditional agriculture throughout the region. Women in the Colombian flower industry report miscarriages, premature births, and respiratory and neurological problems,[15] while in Ecuador 62 percent of workers in one survey said they had suffered health disorders from exposure to pesticides at work.[16]

The ownership of farms producing nontraditional exports varies widely. In Chile or Colombia, many are in the hands of wealthy local growers, while foreign ownership is widespread in Costa Rica. Of the fourteen largest flower growers there, only two are Costa Rican. The degree of foreign control also varies according to the crop; Del Monte in Costa Rica and Dole in Honduras produce the majority of pineapples and bananas, respectively, and control virtually all the transport and marketing (often the most lucrative parts of the production chain).

Ownership tends to be in the hands of rich farmers, whether local or foreign. Peasant farmers rarely have the access to technology or capital required; flower plantations, for example, require a capital investment of $80,000 per acre and few banks are prepared to lend such sums to poor farmers.[17] When small farmers try to climb aboard the export bandwagon, they run serious risks. Costa Rica's countryside is littered with failures like Norberto Fernández, a small farmer in the North. Norberto received a loan in 1990 to switch from growing corn for the domestic market to red peppers for export. He says that a non-traditional promoter passed through his village "promising riches, a new car, a better house, education for my children" if he switched crops. When his crop of red peppers came in, Norberto was told they did not meet export quality-control standards. He had to sell his thirty cows to repay the loans.[18]

Elsewhere in Central America, small farmers have overcome some of the obstacles by forming cooperatives. In Guatemala, some 20,000 mainly Indian peasant farmers produce nontraditionals including broccoli and mange-tout, often on plots of less than two acres. But such cooperatives are usually unable to export their crops themselves, forcing them to sell at lower prices to exporters.

Across Latin America, governments have neglected food crops in the rush for exports. In the early 1980s, about 90 percent of the money spent in Latin America on agricultural research went on food crops, especially beans, which contribute about 30 percent of the protein consumed by the region's 200 million low-income families. A decade later, only about 20 percent of research money went to food crops, as scientists and spending were redirected into the export drive. Every Latin American country apart from Argentina, Chile, and Ecuador had become a net importer of beans.[19]

At first sight, this is not necessarily a bad thing; if Chinese-grown beans are cheaper than the domestic variety, consumers should benefit from switching to cheap imports. In 1988, the then-president of Costa Rica's Central Bank, Eduardo Lizano, confided that he saw no reason why his country should grow *any* food if it could all be imported more cheaply.[20] But what is at stake is known as "food security." When it is lost, market forces acquire control over the very stomachs of the poor.

If a country switches from growing to importing its food, access to food becomes dependent on income; poor peasants with a piece of land can grow maize or beans to survive, but once they have been ousted by export-oriented agribusiness growing fruit, vegetables, or acres of carnations, they are far more likely to go hungry. More generally, reliance on food imports make a country more vulnerable to sanctions and trade disputes, while a sudden devaluation or removal of subsidies can raise prices overnight beyond the reach of the poor.

As a development strategy, there are serious limitations to the nontraditional craze. As more and more developing countries leap aboard the bandwagon, the increased competition floods the market. As one author asked, "How many macadamia nuts or mangoes can North Americans be expected to eat, even at lower prices?"[21] In the Aconcagua Valley, growers were hacking down hectares of kiwi fruit trees because of a world glut. Chile's apple growers have also suffered from first world protectionism—importers such as the EU often respond to a bumper apple crop at home by virtually closing their doors to Chilean apples.

Chile's salmon boom meant that by 2001, it was about to overtake Norway as the world's largest producer, earning about $1 billion a year, but as supplies rose, prices collapsed. The country's income from salmon and trout exports in 2001 rose only 4 percent, despite a massive 52 percent increase in volume.[22] This is little more than a new twist to Latin America's historical travails with the terms of trade. With the exception of Mexico, which is discussed separately, the silent revolution has done little to reduce the region's traditional reliance on the commodity trade; almost half of Latin America's exports still stem from agriculture or mining.[23] With each passing year the region has had to export more and more raw materials to import the same amount of manufactured goods. One study showed that some $75 billion out of the $179 billion of debt accumulated by Latin America between 1980 and 1988, or 42 percent of the total, was accounted for by the deteriorating terms of trade.[24] Commodity prices fell a further 17 percent over the course of the 1990s.[25]

The neoliberal response to falling prices resembles a hamster on a treadmill, churning out ever greater quantities of raw materials to compensate. Consumers in the Northern countries reap the benefits of cheaper broccoli, fresh strawberries at Christmas, or exotic tropical leaves for their winter flower arrangements, but in developmental terms it is a strategy with severe limitations.

In Chile, government economists acknowledge these limitations, and argue for a new kind of industrialization, based on natural resources and destined for export rather than import-substitution. Chile should export wine, not grapes, and furniture instead of wood chip. By processing natural resources before selling them, Chile would capture more of the final selling price of the finished product, made up of the price of the original commodity, plus the "value added" in turning it into something fit to stock on a supermarket shelf. In the longer term, it should try to mimic Finland, which successfully found a niche in the world market when it developed timber-processing and paper machinery on the foundations of its forestry sector.[26]

To date, however, the Chilean government has failed to shake off its neoliberal inferiority complex, believing that the state can only harm the economy by stepping in to protect and nurture this process. Without a concerted government industrial policy, the leap to a broader resource-based industrialization will never happen, even in a country as uniquely endowed with natural riches as Chile.

In February 2002, Adolfo Zaldivar, the newly elected leader of Chile's Christian Democrats and a likely future president, raised hopes that this might indeed happen when he announced his intention to ditch neoliberal dogma, saying, "We must resist the temptation of adopting models, schools of thought and economic theories as if they were absolute truths." He began assembling a team of economists known for disagreeing with the canons of neoliberalism, including prominent CEPAL figures such as chief economist Ricardo Ffrench-Davis.[27]

## CHEAP LABOR

It's 36 minutes after midnight when the factory bell rings, and José González emerges from the air-conditioned world of the Zenith television assembly plant in Reynosa, Mexico. Gonzalez's pay for eight hours of work comes to $8.50. He counts off 50 cents for the bus and heads home to the shantytown known as Voluntad y Trabajo—Will and Work—and his one-room, scrap-board shack that lacks running water, electricity, and sewer lines.

Up north, in the Chicago suburb of Melrose Park, Pedro Camacho's eight hours of work at the Zenith picture-tube plant earn him $60 in take-home pay. When his shift ends at 3 P.M., he hops in his car and drives home to a recently purchased three-bedroom, wood-frame house nearby. Dinner is pizza, heated in his microwave.

Both men are Mexican by birth, about the same age and quit school in Mexico in sixth grade. Both are married, both have two children.[28]

A step across the 2,000-mile U.S.-Mexican border takes U.S. companies into a corporate paradise of cheap labor, compliant unions, and lax environmental, health, and safety regulations. Hundreds of factories have moved there from the United States since the border strip was turned into a long snaking free trade zone in 1965. These were the advanced guard of what became the second element in the silent revolution's export drive—a boom in labor-intensive manufactured exports which have spread through Mexico, Central America, and the Caribbean in recent years.

The Border Industrialization Program allowed export-oriented assembly plants to set up within 12.5 miles of the border. The plants paid no duties on imported parts, which they then assembled into the finished product, packaged and sold back to the United States. The result by 2001 was a chain of nearly 4,000 factories employing 1.4 million people, over half of them women, and a massive boost in "Mexican" manufactured exports.[29]

The 1982 debt crisis was a watershed for the *maquila* industry. When Mexico was forced to devalue the peso in 1982, the dollar value of wages fell from $1.69 an hour in 1982 to just 60 cents by 1986. This was one-third of Taiwanese wage levels, and foreign investment flooded in.[30] The 40 percent devaluation of the Mexican peso in early 1995 provided another boom for the *maquiladoras*. But hitching the Mexican wagon to the U.S. economy had its downside; the U.S. slump of 2001 meant that, for the first time in its thirty-five-year history, Mexico's export processing sector shrank significantly, with more than 230,000 workers dismissed in the twelve months to November.[31]

The North American Free Trade Agreement (NAFTA) effectively extended the rules of the maquila zone south to the rest of Mexico, and once the political turmoil of the 1990s was out of the way, small Central American economies also found themselves pulled along in the slipstream, with a proliferation of factories in countries such as Honduras and Guatemala.

The arguments over who wins and loses from the *maquiladoras* are heated, and central to the debate over NAFTA and the rapid spread of free trade zones (also known as export processing zones) elsewhere in the developing world. Jobs in the zones, which usually resemble indus-trial parks, include everything from making clothes and assembling TVs and computers to data input (doing the keyboard drudgery for U.S. supermarket chains and credit card companies). In return for setting up there, companies are allowed to import goods for final assembly and then re-export them free of taxes or restrictions on profit repatriation. The only value that accrues to the host country is that of the jobs gen-erated in the zone and the usually low level of "linkage" with the local economy in the form of local materials or services.

Local residents have complained at the pollution created by *maquiladoras*, which are often run by "dirty industries" fleeing the Unit-ed States to avoid its expensive environmental protection legislation. Individual workers complain at the low wages, ailments stemming from overwork and poor health and safety standards, minimal job security, and frequent industrial injuries. Some of the injuries have been particularly horrific:

The director of the Matamoros School for Special Education, Isabel de la O Alon-so, first began to notice them in 1982. Dr. de la O worked with about 200 young-sters with physical and mental handicaps, the majority of them children of working-class parents. But one small group stood out. Their disabilities ranged from severe retardation to slow learning. Physically they bore similar character-istics, such as broad noses, thin lips, bushy eyebrows, and webbed hands and feet. A few were deaf. Yet the children did not fit any of the categories of birth defects that she had previously studied or observed. Dr. de la O decided to com-pile a clinical history and soon found that all the children had one thing in com-mon—their mothers, while pregnant, had worked in the same Matamoros *maquiladora*. It had been called Mallory Capacitors, and the children became known as the Mallory Children.

The Mallory workers had to handle a range of toxic chemicals in the plant, but one in particular seemed the most likely cause for such severe birth defects. The capac-itors—small devices for television sets which store an electrical charge—were washed in a product the workers only knew as *electrolito*. Dr. de la O believes that this liquid might well have contained PCBs, as her research indicated some similarities in the women's descriptions of the effects of the fluid and studies already carried out in the United States. PCBs, or polychlorinated biphenyls, have been banned in the U.S. because of their links to cancer. They are also believed to affect the body's chromosomes. The women recalled that working with *electrolito* caused their fingernails to turn black, a classic reaction to PCB exposure.

They are growing up now, leaving their teenage years and entering young adulthood, but they will always be the Mallory Children. Together they represent the most obvious legacy of the perilous conditions under which thousands of Mexicans toil for their minimum wage.[32]

But protests over such abuses have been largely ineffective, since most trade unions are in the pocket of the Mexican government, which is determined to avoid rocking the *maquiladora* boat by enforcing environmental legislation or antagonizing employers. In any case, most unemployed Mexicans would jump at a job in a *maquiladora*, where conditions, although bad by first world standards, are often better than those in nationally owned factories.

In the United States, the *maquiladoras* have been used by U.S. business to depress wages and cut costs, either by relocating to Mexico, or threatening to do so during negotiations with U.S. employees.[33] In the mid-1980s, General Motors' Packard Electric Division gave its employees in Cleveland, Ohio, a taste of things to come when it threatened to move their jobs to Mexico unless they accepted a 62 percent pay cut for all future employees. Since GM already had tens of thousands of workers in Mexico, it was no idle threat. Negotiations eventually reduced the cut to 43 percent. In Centralia, Ontario, Fleck Manufacturing's employees refused to be bullied by similar threats and went on strike; hours later the plant shut down and moved to Ciudad Juárez, Mexico.[34]

Wages in free trade zones elsewhere in the region are even lower. In Nicaragua's free zones are $100 a month or less, which only covers a quarter of the national "basket of goods" deemed necessary for a family.[35]

Like nontraditional agriculture, the *maquiladora* route to development has serious limitations, but at least it creates jobs. Employment in Mexico, Central America, and the Caribbean grew at 3.7 percent a year during the 1990s, compared to 2.9 percent in South America, where agriculture and mining provided the bulk of export growth.[36]

## THE RACE TO THE BOTTOM

But even these wage rates were cheap compared to the ultra low-cost producers of Asia, where this author interviewed Indonesian garment workers who in 1998 were earning 50 cents *a day* making clothes for high-profile U.S. brands.[37]

One casualty has been the Brazilian shoe industry, concentrated in the southern state of Rio Grande do Sul. Brazil's shoe companies broke into exports as far back as the early 1970s, when U.S. manufacturers switched from producing shoes themselves to importing and selling them. At the same time the Brazilian government introduced export incentives to encourage local firms to earn hard currency. Initially, Brazil benefited from this reshaping of the world footwear industry in spectacular fashion. In 1969, Brazil exported just over a million pairs of shoes per year; over the next 15 years, that rose to almost 150 million pairs.[38] From 1970 to 1990 Brazil's share of world exports rose from 0.5 percent to 12.3 percent, making it the world's third-largest exporter after Italy and South Korea. By 1990, shoes were earning Brazil more hard currency than its most famous export, coffee.[39]

In the late 1980s, however, a new generation of even lower-wage countries entered the fray, battling to undercut each other in an increasingly competitive world economy. Most of these are in Asia, notably the vast labor pools of China and Indonesia. Low wages and often deplorable working conditions in shoe factories in these countries represent an increasing threat to middle-income producers such as Brazil, which finds itself squeezed between the low-wage economies of Asia and the high-tech producers of Europe. According to Raúl Martini, the president of Abicalçados, the Brazilian shoe manufacturers' association, "China is today doing to Brazil what Brazil did to Italy in the 1970s."

The human impact of the resulting crisis is most stark in Novo Hamburgo, the capital of the shoe industry, set up by German emigrants in the nineteenth century. The streets of this town of 200,000 people are dotted with Bavarian-style churches and abandoned shoe factories. Shoe workers can point them out, left and right, as you drive through the city. On a typical day in July 1997, the office of the shoe workers' trade union is packed with people—when a shoe factory closes down, the first port of call is the union, to begin the lengthy legal process of claiming redundancy payments that unscrupulous factory owners try to withhold.

A circle of glum-looking women stand listening to a union lawyer explain the legal system, seeing their money recede into the impenetrable bureaucratic fog that hangs over industrial relations in Brazil.

Lourdes is a tough, battle hardened veteran of the shoe industry. She has come to the union office to pursue her case against a former employer:

> The Haas factory sacked 400 of us two years ago—September 1995. There are only 200 left there now. They didn't pay us any of the holidays or wages owing to us— nothing. We'd been on strike—about a hundred of us—demanding wages which hadn't been paid. We'd paid our national insurance, but the factory just kept it for themselves, so there was nothing for us. There are hardly any factory jobs anymore, and those there are pay next to nothing. Out there by the motorway there's a sign which calls this city "the capital of shoes." I want to cross it out and put "the capital of unemployment," instead.[40]

## LATIN AMERICAN TRADE PERFORMANCE SINCE 1982

TABLE 5.1. Latin American Trade: 1973–2002

| YEAR | EXPORTS (FOB,US$ billions) | IMPORTS (FOB,US$ billions) | YEAR | EXPORTS (FOB,US$ billions) | IMPORTS (FOB,US$ billions) |
|------|------|------|------|------|------|
| 1973 | 25 | 23 | 1988 | 101 | 77 |
| 1974 | 39 | 39 | 1989 | 111 | 82 |
| 1975 | 36 | 42 | 1990 | 122 | 95 |
| 1976 | 42 | 43 | 1991 | 121 | 112 |
| 1977 | 49 | 49 | 1992 | 127 | 137 |
| 1978 | 53 | 56 | 1993 | 134 | 149 |
| 1979 | 71 | 70 | 1994 | 153 | 171 |
| 1980 | 92 | 93 | 1995 | 264 | 273 |
| 1981 | 96 | 98 | 1996 | 296 | 304 |
| 1982 | 88 | 78 | 1997 | 327 | 359 |
| 1983 | 88 | 56 | 1998 | 326 | 379 |
| 1984 | 98 | 58 | 1999 | 341 | 363 |
| 1985 | 92 | 59 | 2000 | 406 | 419 |
| 1986 | 78 | 60 | 2001 | 392 | 412 |
| 1987 | 88 | 67 | 2002* | 393 | 382 |

* Preliminary estimate Source: CEPAL preliminary overview, various years

Since the onset of the debt crisis in 1982, the twin paths of primary products and *maquiladora*-produced manufactured goods have led the drive for the neoliberal goal of export-led growth. According to CEPAL:

> Trade liberalization led to two different patterns of export growth in the 1990s: integration with the North American market through manufactured exports in Mexico, Central America and the Caribbean, versus a concentration on natural resource–based commodities in South America.[41]

Mexico's trade performance has indeed been striking. Between 1995 and 2000, the value of its exports soared by 250 percent, at which point it accounted for almost a half of Latin America's total exports (compared to just over a quarter in 1990).[42] This was the result of the country's virtual assimilation into the U.S. economy as a cheap labor production platform. By 1999, 88 percent of its exports were heading for the United States, and 90 percent of them were manufactured goods, up from only half in 1990.[43] It now accounts for 11 percent of U.S. imports. The rest of Latin America and the Caribbean put together manages only another 6 percent.[44] Mexico has come a long way from its days as an oil exporter. However, this level of dependence on the United States cuts both ways, and the U.S. recession in the first years of the new century led to a fall in exports in 2001 and 2002, which in turn prompted a fall in Mexico's per capita GDP.[45]

Elsewhere, modest trade growth did little to generate growth or change the structure of Latin American trade, or move it away from commodities into more dynamic sectors. Excluding Mexico, commodities still accounted for nearly 40 percent of exports at the end of the century.[46]

Overall, Mexico's trade boom at least appeared to have halted the long-term decline in Latin America's position in world trade, raising it to 5.2 percent of global exports in 1999, compared to a low of 4.3 percent in 1993. But the region is still nowhere near the 12.3 percent global market share it enjoyed after the Second World War.[47]

The relative performance of exports and imports changed between the two decades of the silent revolution. Exports grew steadily from the mid-1980s, but the wild gyrations of imports led to successive trade surpluses and deficits. In the gloomy years of debt crisis and stabilization, the IMF's standard recipe of severe devaluation and import controls in Mexico and Brazil (hardly part of the neoliberal panacea, but sins to which the IMF turned a blind eye) not only made Latin American goods more competitive on the world market, but also made imports from abroad prohibitively expensive.[48] The result was a slump in imports and a large trade surplus, used to pay off vast sums in debt service rather than in productive investment. The results can be seen in table 5.1.

From the late 1980s, under pressure from the international financial institutions, Latin America began to liberalize imports at a breakneck pace. The average tariff on imports fell from 45 percent in the mid-1980s to 13 percent in 2000.[49] At the same time, renewed capital inflows allowed governments to finance the escalating import bill.

Neoliberals argue that liberalizing imports improves economic efficiency and benefits everyone. Local factories can import the best available machinery and other inputs to improve their productivity, while consumers can shop around, rather than be forced to buy shoddy home-produced goods. Competition from abroad will force local factories either to close or to improve their products until they become competitive with other countries' goods, paving the way for increased manufactured exports.

In practice, import liberalization unleashed a consumer boom, as Latin Americans flocked to snap up imported goods at bargain prices, with a drastic impact on the region's trade balance. Mexico and later Argentina quickly ran up huge trade deficits as import bills skyrocketed—in Argentina imports quintupled between 1990 and 1994. Latin America's regional trade balance swung back into the red in 1992 and stayed there throughout the 1990s, although it fell when the Asia crisis ended capital inflows and forced governments to cut their import bills. In 2001 only Argentina and Venezuela (both forced to cut imports to cope with capital outflows) and Chile had a trade surplus. The rest of the continent was in deficit.

Two respected CEPAL economists, Ricardo Ffrench-Davis and Manuel Agosín, have laid out some clear conditions for a successful trade reform: the value created by new activities must exceed that lost due to the number of factories destroyed by competition from cheap imports; export industries must be sufficiently linked to the rest of the national economy to spread the benefits of improved exports throughout the country; and increased competitiveness must be achieved by continuous gains in productivity rather than through low wages or ever-greater subsidies or tax breaks.[50] The authors do not believe these conditions have been met in the recent Latin American trade reforms and point out numerous serious failings:

- Countries have unilaterally opened up their economies in a protectionist and stagnant world economy, allowing other regions to increase their imports to Latin America without having to reciprocate by buying the region's exports.
- Countries have liberalized far too rapidly, not allowing local firms sufficient time to make the necessary changes and investments to adapt to the new rules and improve their productivity before the import floodgates open. This has wiped out numerous potentially competitive companies in a wholly avoidable manner.
- Latin America has fallen back into relying on its static comparative advantage, which has led it to concentrate its efforts in the least dynamic areas of the world economy, such as commodity exports.
- The deregulation of Latin America's financial markets and influx of foreign capital, which has coincided with trade liberalization, has led to overvalued exchange rates and high interest rates (set by governments to attract foreign currency). Overvalued currencies have made the region's exports less competitive, while high interest rates have discouraged exporters from borrowing to invest in increasing production.

Moreover, some influential bodies in development thinking are becoming increasingly skeptical about the wisdom of the *maquiladora* strategy. UNCTAD's 2002 *Trade and Development Report* pointed out that booming global trade figures in fact mask a high degree of "double counting." If a television set is assembled in eight different countries, the components from the first producer country are counted each time they cross a border to the next point in the global assembly line, artificially inflating overall both import and export figures for each country in the chain. By looking instead at the value added in each country, UNCTAD found that developing countries' share of global manufacturing has actually fallen in recent years.

UNCTAD concludes, "Few of the countries which pursued rapid liberalization of trade and investment and experienced a rapid growth in manufacturing exports over the past two decades achieved a significant increase in their shares of world manufacturing income."[51] This is because the TNCs that control the production chains tend to keep the most lucrative sections of the chain, such as design, in the North. Instead, UNCTAD believes governments should look again at "domestic sources of growth" rather than relying purely on exports, as well as upgrading their technology.[52]

## TRADE PATTERNS

TABLE 5.2. Main Trading Partners for Largest Latin American Economies, 2000 (as % of total trade)[53]

| Exports to: | Argentina | Brazil | Mexico* | Venezuela |
|---|---|---|---|---|
| U.S. | 12 | 26 | 81 | 55 |
| Japan | 2 | 5 | 2 | 1 |
| EC/EU | 19 | 30 | 4 | 4 |
| Lat. Am. | 50 | 26 | 4 | 34 |

| Imports to: | Argentina | Brazil | Mexico | Venezuela |
|---|---|---|---|---|
| U.S. | 18 | 27 | 62 | 38 |
| Japan | 3 | 4 | 3 | 3 |
| EC/EU | 22 | 27 | 8 | 20 |
| Lat. Am. | 32 | 20 | 2 | 25 |

* Includes *maquiladora* trade.

SOURCE: IMF, *Direction of Trade Statistics Yearbook*, Washington, 1990 and 1994.

Table 5.2 shows the wide variations between different Latin American countries' trading patterns. Some of the most outstanding points are:

• The southernmost economies such as Argentina and Brazil have a much more even spread of trade between Latin America, the United States, Europe, and Japan, whereas Mexico, Central America, and the Caribbean are highly dependent on the U.S. economy.

- Over the course of the silent revolution, these differences became more pronounced as the *maquila* boom brought growing de facto integration between Mexico and the United States.
- With the exception of Mexico, recent years have brought a boom in trade between Latin American countries, especially in the Southern Cone, where trade between Argentina and Brazil took off following the Mercosur agreement (discussed below).
- The United States increased its dominance over Latin American trade as a whole, although a large part of this was due to the U.S.–Mexican trade boom. U.S. exports to the region came to $167 billion by 2000, accounting for 21 percent of the total.

## AGREEING TO TRADE

### MAIN CURRENT REGIONAL TRADE AGREEMENTS
### IN LATIN AMERICA AND THE CARIBBEAN
(excluding NAFTA and the WTO)

*Andean Community*: founded as the Andean Pact in 1969 by Bolivia, Colombia, Chile, Ecuador, and Peru. Venezuela joined in 1973 and Chile left in 1976. Went into decline during 1980s, but revived in early 1990s when Venezuela, Colombia, Ecuador, and Bolivia agreed on a common external tariff that came into force in 1995, but only for Ecuador, Colombia, and Venezuela. Regular disagreements between member states have impeded the integration process.

*Caribbean Common Market (CARICOM)*: formed in 1973 by Barbados, Guyana, Jamaica, and Trinidad, later joined by the rest of the English-speaking Caribbean. In 1988 the original members (except the Bahamas) started to remove controls on trade that had sprung up during the debt crisis. In 1992 eight member states agreed on a common external tariff that would be reduced over time. The following year, the group also announced plans to move toward a single currency. In 1995 Suriname became the first non-Commonwealth country to join, followed by Haiti in 1997.

*Central American Common Market (CACM)*: created in 1960 by Guatemala, Nicaragua, Honduras, and El Salvador. Costa Rica subsequently joined in 1963. Honduras withdrew in 1970 when it became clear that the larger economies were benefiting at the expense of the weaker ones. In 1980s escalating regional tension forced it further into crisis. Revived in the 1990s, the five members and Panama agreed to a gradual reduction in trade barriers and the introduction of a common external tariff. However, subsequent disputes have slowed up the integration process. In 2003 the United States began talks with the five CACM members on a U.S.–Central American Free Trade Agreement (U.S.–CAFTA).

*Group of Three (G3)*: In 1993 the presidents of Colombia, Venezuela, and Mexico signed a free trade agreement to come into force in 1994 for an initial ten-year period.

*Organization of Eastern Caribbean States (OECS)*: Existing within CARICOM, the OECS is a group of small island economies that currently operates the only true common market in Latin America and the Caribbean. It has continued uninterrupted since its foundation in 1968. The OECS operates a single currency, the EC dollar.

*Southern Cone Common Market (Mercosur/Mercosul)*: Signed in 1991 by Argentina, Brazil, Paraguay, and Uruguay. Formed common market January 1, 1995, although protection in some sectors (cars, computers) will be phased out over a longer period of time. Bolivia (1997) and Chile (1996) joined as "associates" meaning that they are part of the free trade agreement but have not adopted Mercosur's common external tariff regime. Tensions between the two main players, Argentina and Brazil, have dogged Mercosur, but may ease following Argentina's devaluation in 2002.

In addition to these main groupings, there are numerous bilateral accords.

Source: Europa Publications, *South America, Central America and the Caribbean 2001*; CEPAL, "Desarrollo reciente de los procesos de integración en América Latina y el Caribe" (unpublished paper, 1994); David Woodward, "Regional Trade Agreements in Latin America and the Caribbean," (unpublished paper, 1993).

Everybody's doing it. Since the late 1980s, Latin America's trade negotiators have been spending a large slice of their waking hours concocting a bewildering variety of regional trade agreements (RTAs). By 2002, Latin America could boast dozens of bilateral accords and several subregional pacts, but the best known (and most controversial) is the only RTA between first and third worlds. NAFTA came into force in 1994 despite fierce opposition and marked a watershed in the neoliberal approach to trade integration. In U.S. eyes, at least, it was the prototype for an even more ambitious project, the proposed Free Trade Area of the Americas (FTAA) for the whole hemisphere (minus Cuba).

RTAs enshrine comparative advantage at the heart of the economic relationship between nations. If each country sticks to what it does best, goes the argument, and imports everything else it needs, everyone will be better off. In the case of NAFTA, Mexican and U.S. exporters and investors will obtain guaranteed access to each other's economies; Mexican consumers can enjoy the benefits of cheap food imports, the latest computer technology, and even experience the dubious delights of an invasion of U.S. fast food chains. Elsewhere, RTAs between more equal players such as the Central American republics allow members to pool know-how and achieve economies of scale unavailable to single small nations. According to the comparative advantage school of thought, the best option would be a free trade world, as espoused by the WTO, but an RTA can be a step toward it.

Some economists point out that there is one significant specter at this free trade feast:

> In the last great wave of globalization, before the First World War, labor migration was a crucial part of the story. A globalization process in which one factor of production (capital) is free, but not the other (labor) is like Hamlet without the prince. It has no justification in economic theory.[54]

When signing RTAs, governments typically agree to phase out, or drastically reduce, tariff barriers between RTA members and eliminate nontariff barriers such as import quotas. Over time, RTAs may lead to deeper forms of integration such as a customs union, which charges a common external tariff on imports from outside the RTA, a common market, which allows free movement of labor and capital between members, or even a monetary union as agreed by the European Union in the Maastricht Treaty.[55]

Within Latin America, the upsurge in RTAs has involved reviving and strengthening moribund agreements from the previous round of free trade areas in the 1960s and 1970s. These include the Andean Community (originally made up of Bolivia, Chile, Colombia, Ecuador, Peru, and Venezuela); the Central American Common Market (Nicaragua, El Salvador, Honduras, Guatemala, Costa Rica); and the Caribbean Common Market (CARICOM), which covers the English-speaking Caribbean.

The first generation of agreements sprang up in the 1960s in response to the difficulties experienced under import substitution, principally the limited size of domestic markets for locally produced goods. The aim was to nurture import substitution's "fledgling industries" by providing a large captive market for their goods (in essence an extension of import substitution's protectionism to a wider geographical area).

The early RTAs floundered and eventually collapsed at the onset of the debt crisis. Such organizations never solved import substitution's basic problem of the shortage of hard currency; Peru needed dollars, not Bolivian pesos, to buy manufactured goods and pay its debt service. In addition, within each RTA the stronger economies tended to swamp the weak; El Salvador's industry boomed as it exported to the more backward Honduran and Nicaraguan economies, which ran up large and unpaid debts.

So why have Latin Americans turned again to RTAs as part of the solution to their troubles? Supporters of the new RTAs argue that they share a fundamentally different purpose from their forebears. The new generation of agreements aims to reap the benefits of an expanded domestic market in order to increase exports to the world outside. Where once they were primarily a defensive laager of uncompetitive nations, RTAs are now portrayed as an "export platform" from which to sell goods to outside markets, principally the United States. In 1994, CEPAL coined the term "open regionalism" to describe the new approach.[56]

RTAs had other advantages. The outside world's main interest in trading with Latin America is to gain access to its raw materials, but when Latin American countries trade with one another, a much higher proportion of manufactured goods is usually involved. Excluding Mexico, in 1999, 77 percent of Latin America's intra-regional trade was in manufactured goods, compared to only 55 percent of its trade with the outside world.[57] RTAs can therefore help stimulate the industrialization process.

In addition to reviving existing, but moribund, RTAs, new ones have been created, notably the giant of Latin American integration, Mercosur (El Mercado Común del Sur), bringing together two big fish—Brazil and Argentina—and two minnows—Uruguay and Paraguay. Chile and Bolivia subsequently joined with associate status. Established by the Treaty of Asunción in March 1991, the early years of Mercosur saw intra-block trade boom. Total intra-Mercosur imports rose from $4.1 billion in 1990 to $20.7 billion in 1997.

Since Brazil's devaluation and switch to a floating exchange rate in January 1999, Mercosur has been dogged by escalating tensions between its two main partners, which at some points threatened its very existence. As a result, trade stagnated and then fell back: intra-Mercosur exports totaled $17.6 billion in 2000. According to a preliminary estimate, they fell further in 2001, to $16 billion.

In Latin America as a whole, a combination of RTAs and the recovering regional economy more than doubled intra-regional trade between 1987 and 1992, reaching $24.5 billion, or 15 percent of the region's total trade.[58] It then rose further to reach a peak of 20.3 percent, before Mercosur's troubles sent it tumbling back down to 15 percent in 1999.[59] As a proportion of total trade, this brought intra-regional trade back to the same levels Latin America had enjoyed on the eve of the debt crisis.

## NAFTA

The border at night is a battle of lights. On the Mexican side, the feeble yellow glow of countless single bulbs marks Tijuana's shantytowns. They are dwarfed in intensity, if not in number, by the neon billboards of the motels and burger bars that light up the night on the U.S. side.

By day, the contrast is even starker. Tijuana's dusty sprawl covers every square inch of the hillsides, right up to the border fence. From their backyards, the shantytown residents look out on the bare, scrub-covered hills of Southern California. Separating the two worlds is *la linea*, the frontier.

Tijuana on the U.S.–Mexican border is a unique eyeball-to-eyeball confrontation between first and third worlds, a town where dollar and peso are interchangeable, a brothel and booze resort built during the prohibition years to service U.S. marines from the San Diego naval base. It also served as a prototype for the future relationship between the two countries, enshrined in the North American Free Trade Agreement signed by the presidents of the United States, Mexico, and Canada in October 1992. Some critics believe NAFTA is turning the whole of Mexico into a giant Tijuana.

On New Year's Day 1994, NAFTA came in with a bang. Unfortunately for the Mexican government's public relations team, it was the sound of gunfire in the southern state of Chiapas, as 2,000 fighters of the previously unknown Zapatista National Liberation Army rose in rebellion against the oldest one-party state in the world. The uprising was an extraordinary hybrid of ancient and modern. Exhausted Indian fighters speaking little Spanish slumped next to their barricades in San Cristobal de las Casas while a few yards away, tourists queued up to take cash out of the automatic teller machine. The largely indigenous rebels were protesting age-old grievances such as the discrimination against Mexico's large Indian minority, but the trigger for the uprising was the silent revolution: the government's reversal of their constitutional right to communal land, and NAFTA, which they described as a "death certificate for the indigenous peoples."[60]

NAFTA is a very different entity from the proliferating Latin American RTAs. It is the first ever RTA between a first world and a third world economy and, in the words of one writer, "a crucible in which advanced technology, subsistence farming, global finance capital, massive under-employment, and contrasting legal and political systems are mixed for the first time."[61] Whereas Latin American RTAs are, at least to some degree, a marriage between equals, the disparities within NAFTA are stark. The U.S. economy is almost twenty-five times larger than Mexico's and the social and developmental gulf is arguably even wider.[62]

---

### WHAT IS NAFTA?

The North American Free Trade Agreement gradually eliminates almost all trade and investment restrictions between the United States, Canada, and Mexico over fifteen years. Side agreements, concluded in August 1993, require the enforcement of some environmental and labor laws, under penalty of fines or sanctions.

The United States and Canada entered an RTA in 1989, and the pact thus mainly affects their trade and investment with Mexico. NAFTA came into effect on January 1, 1994.

#### GENERAL PROVISIONS

- Tariffs to be reduced over fifteen years, depending on sector.
- Foreign investment restrictions to be lifted in most sectors, with the exception of oil in Mexico, culture in Canada, and airlines and radio communications in the United States.
- Immigration is excluded, although restrictions on the movement of white collar workers are to be eased.

- Any country can leave the treaty with six months' notice.
- Treaty allows for the inclusion of any additional country.
- Government procurement to be opened up over ten years, mainly affecting Mexico, which reserves some contracts for Mexican companies.
- Dispute resolution panels of independent arbitrators to resolve disagreements arising out of treaty.
- Some tariffs to be allowed if a surge of imports hurts a domestic industry.

### SECTORAL PROVISIONS

- Agriculture: most tariffs between the United States and Mexico to be removed immediately. Tariffs on 6 percent of products—maize, sugar, and some fruit and vegetables —to be fully eliminated only after fifteen years.
- Automobiles: tariffs to be removed over ten years. Mexico's quotas on imports will be lifted over the same period; cars eventually have to meet a 62.5 percent local content rule to be free of tariffs.
- Energy: Mexico's ban on private-sector exploration continues, but procurement by Pemex, the state oil company, to be opened up to the United States and Canada.
- Financial services: Mexico to gradually open its financial sector to U.S. and Canadian investment, eliminating barriers by 2007.
- Textiles: eliminates Mexican, U.S., and Canadian tariffs over ten years. Clothes eligible for tariff breaks must be sewn with fabric woven in North America.
- Trucking: North American trucks can drive anywhere in the three countries by the year 2000.

### SIDE AGREEMENTS

- Environment: the three countries are liable to fines, and Mexico and the United States to sanctions, if a panel finds repeated nonenforcement of environment laws.
- Labor: countries are liable for penalties for nonenforcement of child, minimum wage and health and safety laws.

### OTHER DEALS

- United States and Mexico to set up a North American Development Bank to help finance the cleanup of pollution along the U.S.–Mexican border.

SOURCE: *Financial Times*, November 17, 1993.

At the heart of NAFTA lies the growing incompatibility between nation-states and the workings of international companies. In many ways NAFTA is a misnomer, since the bulk of the text concerns investment rather than trade, and in almost every case, it concerns Mexico, rather than the United States or Canada.[63] NAFTA opens up formerly protect-ed areas such as mining and (partially) petroleum; it binds Mexico into strict new patent rules for pharmaceuticals and computer software and prevents Mexico from trying to delay or obstruct the repatriation of profits by transnational companies. Mexican law must now treat U.S. and Canadian businesses exactly like Mexican companies. The 2,000-mile border with the United States ceases to exist for corporations, though not for Mexico's would-be migrant workers.

In addition to its growing role as a cheap labor "export platform" from which transnational corporations can export their products back to the United States, Mexico also constitutes an attractively large and willing market for U.S. companies. This includes both U.S.-based exporters, and investors such as Wal-Mart, which by 2002 dominated Mexico's retail sector with 520 stores generating annual sales of $9 bil-lion. Like other firms, linkages with the rest of the Mexican economy were minimal. Wal-Mart's shelves were almost entirely devoid of Mexi-can-produced goods. Even its best-selling popcorn brand was made from U.S. rather than Mexican maize.[64]

Critics see NAFTA's investment provisions as one of its most alarm-ing features. Chapter 11 of the treaty allows foreign investors to sue governments in an international arbitration system that overrides national legal codes. Article 1110 of the treaty allows companies to seek compensation for "expropriation," both direct and "indirect." This could be held to cover any government action or changes to regulations that reduce corporate profits. U.S. toxic waste company Metalclad used the new rules when it sued the Mexican government in 1997, demand-ing compensation under Chapter 11 for being denied planning permis-sion by local authorities in San Luis Potosi. In August 2000, it won, and Mexico was ordered to pay $16 million in compensation.[65]

NAFTA also served a long-term purpose. Although Mexico's President Carlos Salinas (in office when the NAFTA treaty was negotiated) and his predecessor Miguel de la Madrid had pushed through a free market/free trade transformation of the Mexican economy since the debt crisis hit in 1982, there was as yet nothing to stop future presidents from reversing the process. Now, NAFTA has "locked in" Mexico to an agreement with the United States by making it much more costly to revert to statist or protectionist models. It also locked in the United States at a time of rising protectionist sentiment in Washington, thereby ensuring that Mexico would be inside the fold should the United States ever return to its isolationist past. With each year that passes under NAFTA, the three economies will become more integrated, and the economic and political price of prising them loose will rise ever higher.

Locking in neoliberal reforms via NAFTA makes Mexico a far safer prospect for foreign investors deciding where to locate their factories and banks, or whether to make loans or buy shares in Mexican companies. When the U.S. banking giant Citigroup paid $12.5 billion in cash and stocks for Mexico's second-largest bank, Banamex, Victor Menezes, Citigroup's head of Emerging Markets, explained, "We view the acquisition as a North American play. Mexico has broken away from the rest of Latin America."[66]

## NAFTA AND MAIZE

The village of Los Cerritos, two hours' drive from Mexico City, exemplifies the impact of NAFTA on the Mexican countryside.[67]

Ernesto Olivera Rezendes, thirty-six, is a maize farmer. In cowboy hat, jeans, and boots, standing in a dirt road, by his battered pick up, he berates NAFTA, and the adjustment programs that have accompanied it:

> The free market benefits the big farmers, but it's finished us off. The 1970s and '80s were good; when you got your harvest in you went out and got drunk—now you just think about paying off your debts. We had the luxury of going out to buy clothes or going out for a meal. Now we don't go hungry (God is great) but since the 1980s we just think about debts and problems. Since 1980 it's been *puros lamentos*.

Ernesto says the old communal lands in the village have been divided up, and the big farmers are buying out the small ones, as they get into debt. Mexico's historic land reform is being reversed by the market.

In the center of the village, in a church-owned barn, another aspect of NAFTA is on display. There, 350 women are making Tommy Hilfiger sweaters. The price labels they attach to the garments show that they must work for a week to earn the price of one sweater, but even so, the factory has helped stop the exodus of young women from the village, and the workers have just won union recognition, so wages may start to improve.

Maize cultivation is the main livelihood for some 3 million farmers in Mexico, accounting for 40 percent of the agricultural sector. During the NAFTA negotiations, attention focused on the fundamental structural differences between U.S. and Mexican maize farming. U.S. maize is grown on large farms at an average of 40 percent of the cost of production in Mexico, with average yields per hectare between 4 and 5 times higher and heavy subsidies from the U.S. government. Moreover, they grow different varieties. Some 60 percent of Mexican farmers use locally adapted varieties, leading to a rich genetic resource-base for maize farming. Mexican farmers in general grow white maize in contrast to the nutritionally inferior yellow maize grown in the United States.

Given the social sensitivity of the maize issue, NAFTA allowed a fifteen-year phase-in period for free trade in maize. In practice, however, the Mexican government waived this right and the maize trade was effectively freed within thirty months of the start of NAFTA. A massive influx of U.S. maize ensued, leading to a sharp reduction in the price paid to Mexican producers. By August 1996, prices had fallen by 48 percent. The government's apparently paradoxical decision to ignore the safeguards it had negotiated for itself led to protests by farmers, including road blockades, which the government violently suppressed. Mexican producers argue that the pressure to import came from some government institutions and large grain companies and food processors in Mexico, many of them with headquarters in the United States, including Purina, Continental Grain, and Cargill. Many of these companies are exporting the grain from the United States, with the help of export credits from the U.S. government.

At the same time as prices have fallen, farmers have been hit by other adjustment measures, including cuts in state subsidies and the abolition of the state purchasing and supply agency, CONASUPO. Contrary to expectations, all this has not led to mass emigration from the countryside or a decline in maize production in Mexico, which has held remarkably steady. Mexican farmers have stubbornly continued to plant maize, often more for symbolic/cultural reasons than for any hope of profit. They cross-subsidize the activity through a complex series of family survival strategies, including sending children to the *maquiladoras* or the United States, doing daywork in construction, selling craftwork, and growing food for family consumption. However, such survival strategies are undoubtedly a struggle, and could wear farmers down over the long term, leading to increased emigration.

From the point of view of consumers, cheap maize was expected to lead to lower prices for Mexico's staple food, tortillas. However, a combination of reduced government subsidies and monopolistic practices by food-processing cartels has meant that tortilla prices actually rose as maize prices fell.

## THE FREE TRADE AREA OF THE AMERICAS

With 800 million people, a third of global economic output, and more than a quarter of the world's exports, the Free Trade Area of the Americas (FTAA) would be the world's largest trade grouping.[68] When Washington initially proposed negotiations, it envisaged a "NAFTA plus" approach, absorbing countries through accession into NAFTA. However, it rapidly became clear that the South Americans, and in particular Brazil, would not accept what they saw as a NAFTA agreement skewed toward U.S. interests. Instead the FTAA negotiations have emerged as a process of bargaining between the different blocs, in particular, NAFTA and Mercosur, led by the United States and Brazil. The FTAA process, which is due for completion by January 2005, should keep the trade negotiators busy, as the WTO negotiations launched in Doha in November 2001 are supposed to reach their conclusion in the same month.

One major difference with the NAFTA negotiations is the degree of transparency involved—following protests from a range of civil society organizations, the draft agreement was published in July 2001 and is available on the FTAA website.[69] Those same civil society organizations, grouped together in the "Hemispheric Social Alliance," are following the negotiations closely and publishing well-argued critiques on their own websites.[70] One of those best-placed to discuss the proposal is RMALC, the Mexican Network on Free Trade, which has charted the impact of NAFTA on Mexico. Its conclusion is clear: "NAFTA in no way should be considered the basis for a continent-wide negotiation.... [It has led to] job losses, falling wages, the closure of an important part of small and medium industry, and has ruined or impoverished small-scale farmers." [71] As well as critiquing NAFTA and the current FTAA draft, NGOs in the alliance have developed a proposal, "Alternatives for the Americas," which is discussed in chapter 8.

The outcome of the FTAA negotiations will largely be decided by the battle between the United States and Brazil, the giants of North and South America, respectively. Both will be aiming to gain maximum access to other countries' markets while protecting their own. According to one analysis, Brazil is likely to be very competitive in textiles, beef, soy, steel, and ceramics, but likely to suffer on machinery and electronics. "Brazil's greatest fear is that the U.S. is plotting to stop it from becoming a big exporter of high-value manufactured goods and to make it return to its historic role of churning out low-value commodities."[72] Other authors point out that the real prizes for the United States do not have to do with merchandise trade, but with guaranteeing markets for its service industries (finance, telecoms, etc.), protecting intellectual property rights, and opening up government procurement.[73]

Lula's election in 2002 raised hopes among the FTAA's opponents that Brazil would take a much more active role in confronting the inequities of the FTAA proposal. Opposition in Brazil is well organized—a plebiscite under the auspices of Brazil's grassroots organizations in 2002 recorded an extraordinary 10 million votes against the FTAA, with only 113,000 in favor. Although Lula described the FTAA as an "annexation project" rather than an "integration project" during his election campaign, he moderated his tone thereafter, as he sought to balance the views of his party with Brazil's acute need for export dollars with which to service its debts.[74]

George W. Bush, too, faces domestic opposition—U.S. trade lobbyists are concerned about import surges harming citrus and sugar growers, and unions and NGOs fear that the FTAA will merely magnify the problems of NAFTA. Both governments have other options, should FTAA talks founder. The United States may opt for bilateral agreements with individual Latin American countries, while in Brazil, according to Lula's predecessor, President Cardoso, "Mercosur is a destiny for us, while the FTAA is an option."

## MIXED RESULTS

Latin America's twenty-year march toward free trade and export-led growth has yielded mixed results. Based on the twin tracks of primary commodities (including nontraditional agriculture) and labor-intensive manufactures, exports and imports have indeed boomed. Yet they have only generated limited growth and improvements in the lives of Latin American consumers. Commodities continue to suffer from declining terms of trade and fail to generate enough jobs, while labor-intensive manufacturing faces intense competition from even poorer countries in Asia.

The trade drive has been indiscriminate, failing to push the kinds of products that create jobs and reduce poverty and too often ignoring the impact of modernization on social inequality or the environment.

Governments' excessive faith in the wisdom of the market has led them to neglect the kind of industrial and social policies that could have corrected these shortcomings, allowing transnational corporations to extend their grip into every corner of Latin America's economy and reducing the chances of repeating the kind of growth with equity achieved in Southeast Asia.

The nature of the silent revolution's model of trade and the growth it has driven have ratcheted up inequality and exacerbated the region's historical blight of social exclusion and political instability. Perhaps most worrying of all, the regional and global trade agreements signed and still being negotiated by governments make it far harder for any future leader to change the region's direction toward a more equitable model of development. It is imperative that Latin America's leaders learn the lessons of successful development models in Asia and elsewhere (discussed in chapter 8), if they are to reorient their trade strategy to achieve real benefits for their peoples.

# 6—Silences of the Revolution
## The Human and Environmental
## Costs of Adjustment

If you believe the World Bank, structural adjustment bears no trace of blame for the region's current social travails. On the contrary, "without adjustment, the condition of the poor would undoubtedly have been worse."[1] Unfortunately, there is no scientifically watertight means of proving whether the World Bank is right or not. Economists are faced with several unsatisfactory options. They can compare a country's economy after adjustment with its condition before adjustment began, but that ignores changes in the world economy in the meantime. They can compare a country's performance with that of countries that have not adjusted, but factors other than adjustment can cloud the issue. They can compare a country's current performance with its own earlier performance or with the international financial institutions' stated targets, but the targets may well have been unrealistic in the first place.

Back in real life, the link between neoliberalism and Latin America's increased poverty and inequality can be all too obvious. In Bolivia the redundancy notices issued to thousands of factory workers when the government began its structural adjustment with the infamous Decree 21060 made their neoliberal origins brutally clear: "The Company has found it necessary to rationalize the workforce," went the notice to Richard Ardaya, a trade union activist, from his employers at the La Modelo textile plant, "therefore with recourse to Article 55 of Decree 21060 of 1985, I regret to inform you that your services are no longer required." The letterhead notepaper is bordered with the logos of La Modelo's fashionable customers: Pierre Cardin, Playboy, and Van Heusen.

In other cases, however, the connection is less direct and harder to prove or disentangle from all the other influences on Latin America's economy—international commodity prices, the end of commercial bank lending to the region after 1982, world recession, international interest rates, and domestic influences such as political instability and the effectiveness (or otherwise) of government. The suffering in Bolivia's tin mines is a good example; critics blame it on structural adjustment, yet the government's supporters point out, with considerable justification, that it would be unfair to blame adjustment for the collapse in world tin prices that occurred just two months after decree 21060 was issued.

One way to try to reach some firmer ground beyond the war of words is to look at adjustment's impact on each of the main elements that determine the daily fate of poor Latin Americans. There are many ways that economic changes can affect people's quality of life: incomes, taxes, working conditions, prices, health and education, social security, the impact on home life and the family, and the broader impact on the community and the environment. Adjustment and stabilization measures affect all of these. This chapter will first look at the silent revolution's record to date on poverty and inequality, and then drill down into some of these contributory factors.

## POVERTY

TABLE 6.1. Latin America: Poor and Indigent Individuals, 1980–1999

| | POOR | | | | | | INDIGENT | | | | | |
|---|---|---|---|---|---|---|---|---|---|---|---|---|
| | Total | | Urban | | Rural | | Total | | Urban | | Rural | |
| | Mn | % | Mn | % | Mn | % | Mn | % | Mn | % | Mn | % |
| 1980 | 136 | 41 | 63 | 30 | 73 | 60 | 62 | 19 | 22 | 10 | 40 | 32 |
| 1990 | 200 | 48 | 122 | 41 | 79 | 65 | 93 | 23 | 45 | 15 | 48 | 40 |
| 1994 | 202 | 46 | 126 | 39 | 76 | 65 | 92 | 21 | 44 | 14 | 47 | 41 |
| 1997 | 204 | 44 | 126 | 37 | 78 | 63 | 89 | 19 | 42 | 12 | 47 | 38 |
| 1999 | 211 | 44 | 134 | 37 | 77 | 64 | 89 | 19 | 43 | 12 | 46 | 38 |

POOR: Insufficient income to meet basic food and non-food needs (e.g., housing, clothing, education)

INDIGENT: Even if all income is spent on food, it is insufficient to meet nutritional needs.

SOURCE: CEPAL, Social Panorama of Latin America 2000-2001, p. 2, on the basis of special tabulations of data from household surveys conducted in the relevant countries.

As table 6.1 shows, at the end of the 1990s, approximately 44 percent of Latin America's people (211 million individuals) were poor and 19 percent were extremely poor, or indigent, meaning they were unable to feed themselves properly. The economic turmoil of 2001 is likely to have increased these numbers. The pattern of poverty over the two decades of the silent revolution was one of a massive increase in the 1980s, followed by only minimal change in the absolute numbers of the poor in the 1990s. Due to a growing population this meant that the proportion of poor people fell back from a high of 48 percent in 1990 to 44 percent in 1999. Latin America ended the two decades of turmoil reform with a greater proportion of poor people than in 1980. One in five Latin Americans did not earn enough to feed themselves properly.

Traditionally in Latin America, the poor are concentrated in rural areas, but the impact of neoliberalism shifted poverty to the cities, more than doubling the number of poor people in urban areas. Indigence, sometimes known as absolute or extreme poverty, remains mainly a rural blight.

Certain groups were disproportionately affected. Cuts in state spending mean that in Bolivia, Ecuador, Honduras, the Dominican Republic, and Venezuela, between 20 and 40 percent of public officials are now below the poverty threshold.[2] Because poor families tend to have more children, over half of Latin America's children and adolescents are poor. The total number of those aged under twenty living in poverty rose from 110 million in 1990 to 114 million in 1999.[3] As always, Latin America's 40 million indigenous people languish at the bottom of the social heap.

## INEQUALITY

Total GDP grew by 52 percent between 1980 and 2000, so why has poverty increased, both in absolute and percentage terms?[4] The answer lies both in population growth of 44 percent and in inequality, a traditional Latin American malaise exacerbated by the reforms, which ensured that even the paltry 8 percent difference in per capita GDP growth failed to reach the poor.[5] The World Bank concluded that in the 1980s "the wealthy were better able to protect themselves from the impact of the recession than were the poor."[6] *The Economist* put it more bluntly, commenting that "stabilization and structural adjustment have brought magnificent returns to the rich."[7]

The link between inequality and poverty reduction is best illustrated by comparing Chile, one of the region's most unequal countries, with Uruguay, one of its most equitable. In Chile, the 52 percent increase in per capita GDP between 1990 and 1998 translated into a 46 percent decline in poverty. In Uruguay, a much smaller increase in per capita output (26 percent) gave rise in a similar period to a somewhat larger relative fall in poverty than in Chile. Because the cake was shared more fairly, more people benefited from less growth.[8]

One study of a group of nine countries between 1986 and 1997 revealed that inequality in urban income distribution increased in four of them; there was practically no change in four others; and in only one (Uruguay) did inequality decline to any appreciable degree. Countries with high growth rates (for more or less extended periods) after the recovery that followed the crisis did not become more equitable. Income distribution deteriorated markedly in Argentina, Mexico, Panama, and Venezuela.[9]

CEPAL concluded that stabilization and adjustment programs have created three parallel societies in Latin America: higher, intermediate and lower:

> Higher-income occupations (e.g. executives, managers, high-ranking officials) account for just over 9 percent of the labor force; workers in this category earn considerably more than those in other categories and thus clearly stand apart from them. Only 14 percent of the employed population is now in the intermediate category (professionals with lower level of education, technicians and admin employees), which had grown enough in the postwar era to become a symbol of increasing social mobility in some countries of the region. Finally, the lower-income category comprises a large and diverse mass of workers (manual and unskilled nonmanual)—three-quarters of the total—whose average earnings in most countries are not enough by themselves to enable a typical family (in terms of size and composition) to rise above poverty.[10]

Various aspects of the silent revolution have contributed to this:

- The decline in small and medium enterprises, squeezed out by government policies and large companies and transnationals, which create fewer jobs.

- Land concentration in some countries (e.g. Mexico) following market reforms in the countryside.
- Increased private provision of health and education, available only to the better off.
- Changes in the labor market, making work more insecure, reducing workers' rights and increasing the size of the informal sector.
- The "hollowing out" of the middle class, as state employees are laid off, or their wages are cut.

Some of the more zealous neoliberals argue that inequality is a necessary evil, providing workers and managers alike with the incentive to work hard and generate economic growth. Such arguments conveniently ignore the extraordinary track record of the Southeast Asian economies, where Taiwan, for example, has one of the most impressive growth records in the world over the last thirty years, yet also enjoys the world's fairest distribution of income.[11] Most observers now agree that the extreme levels of inequality occurring in Latin America are an obstacle to development, depressing the domestic market and generating political instability and repression in the continuing war between the haves and the have-nots. CEPAL believes that these issues should form the basis for a "third generation" of reforms designed to put equity at the heart of the region's development.[12]

And there *is* enough money to go round. Latin American inequality is on such a scale that a comparatively minor move toward a fairer distribution of income could eradicate poverty overnight, according to the World Bank's 1990 *World Development Report*: "Raising all the poor in the continent to just above the poverty line would cost only 0.7 percent of regional GDP—the approximate equivalent of a 2 percent income tax on the wealthiest fifth of the population."[13]

Top of Latin America's inequality league table comes Brazil, one of the most unequal nations on earth, where the richest 10 percent of the population earns 49 times the income of the poorest 10 percent (by comparison, the figures for the United States and Britain are 17 and 10 respectively).[14] Brazil has been scathingly rechristened "Belindia"—a hybrid where the middle class enjoy the European lifestyle of a Belgian, surrounded by the impoverished masses of an India. Mexico has also gained ground rapidly in the inequality stakes since structural adjustment accelerated in the late 1980s.

At the other end of the spectrum is Cuba, which has maintained the most equitable income distribution in the region, despite the tensions created by the serious economic crisis it experienced in the early 1990s and the subsequent restructuring process, although it was not able to prevent significant drops in per capita consumption.[15]

## A LIVING WAGE

The rural poor sometimes have a plot of land on which to grow food, but the urban poor have few assets beyond their labor, so their well-being depends to a large extent on what they can earn. Structural adjustment affects wages in numerous ways. There is an undeniable link between macroeconomic performance and wages. If the economy is shrinking, people lose their jobs and wages fall. The recession unleashed by stabilization programs in the early 1980s led to a sudden deterioration in living standards. From the mid-1980s open unemployment began to fall in most countries and growth resumed in some, but wages only rose in a few cases, as the changes to the labor market wrought by structural adjustment took a further toll. From 1980 to 1990 real wages fell in Venezuela and Argentina by 53 percent and 26 percent respectively.[16]

In the 1980s, government cutbacks led to numerous redundancies, but their main impact has been a sharp fall in wages among remaining public employees, the sector hit worst by adjustment. Public sector pay packets shrank by 24 percent in Costa Rica (1981–1988)[17] and 56 percent in Venezuela (1981–1990).[18] Many of those worst affected were middle class, thousands of whom end up joining the ranks of the "new poor" created by adjustment policies. At a regional level, from 1980 to 1986, wages fell faster for those with more than nine years of schooling than for any other sector of the workforce, and many professionals were forced to take second or even third jobs to make ends meet.[19]

In the 1990s, average real wages recovered in most countries, although they suffered a temporary setback with the "tequila crisis" of 1995. The best performers over the decade were Bolivia, Chile, and Costa Rica. Only in Peru were wages in 2001 lower than in 1991.[20] But even as real wages recovered, unemployment rose by a third over the course of the decade to reach 8.4 percent in 2001, representing another 10 million people out of work. Even this grossly underestimates the problem, as it does not include the army of informal sector and "under-employed"; in Latin America, regular waged work was rapidly becoming a luxury denied the majority of the population. Worst hit were Argentina, Colombia, Panama, the Dominican Republic, and Uruguay, all of which had rates over 15 percent.[21] One *Economist* headline summed up the puzzlement of the neoliberals: "Great reforms, nice growth, but where are the jobs?"[22]

## CHANGES TO THE LABOR MARKET

One answer to *The Economist*'s question was the traditional neoliberal response to poor results—the problem was not too much adjustment, but not enough. In particular, the World Bank and others drew attention to the need to "flexibilize" labor.

The Bank believes that labor must be made more flexible to increase productivity and attract investment for the kind of labor-intensive industry that import substitution never managed to create. Since jobs are the main source of income for the poor, the argument goes, labor deregulation will relieve poverty, at least in the long term. It seems a particularly twisted form of economic logic to argue that the pay of the poor must be forced down and their working conditions deteriorate in order to reduce their poverty.

In practice, this has meant cracking down on trade unions and making it easier for managers to hire and fire employees, shift to part-time work, and to cut costs by subcontracting work to smaller companies, often little more than sweatshops. In El Salvador, legal reforms annulled clauses containing protections for women, such as those outlining special conditions for pregnant women.[23] Overall, economist Dani Rodrik thinks the market has had more impact than legislation:

> There has not been much change in formal legislation on employment protection, despite much talk about the need to render labor markets more "flexible." However, the recession and liberalization have done the job instead. In Argentina, for example, the percentage of the non-agricultural labor force represented by unions has fallen from 49 percent in 1986 to 25 percent in 1995. In Mexico, the corresponding number has gone down (if the statistics are to be believed) from 54 percent to 31 percent in the span of two years (1989 to 1991).[24]

In Chile, the neoliberal tiger, a labor force once accustomed to secure unionized jobs has been turned into a nation of anxious individualists. According to one World Health Organization survey, over half of all visits to Chile's public health system involve psychological ailments, mainly depression.[25] "The repression isn't physical anymore, it's economic—feeding your family, educating your child," says María Peña, who works in a fishmeal factory in Concepción. "I feel real anxiety about the future," she adds. "They can chuck us out at any time. You can't think five years ahead. If you've got money you can get an education and health care; money is everything here now."[26] In Argentina such changes meant that having a job was no longer enough to stave off hunger. By the early 1990s, 23 percent of wage earners in the manufacturing sector were living below the poverty line, whereas before the debt crisis a job in a factory virtually guaranteed a pay packet big enough to keep a family out of poverty.[27]

This atomization and loss of community have also contributed to what opinion polls regularly show to be the number one concern—the region's growing levels of violent crime. CEPAL believes the answer is to "create 'more society.' . . . In all the societies of the region, to a greater or lesser degree, people are losing their sense of belonging to society, of identification with collective goals and of the need to develop ties of solidarity. The outbreak of so much violence in many countries is perhaps the most visible manifestation of this."[28]

Incomes for non–wage earners also took a battering at the hands of adjustment. Government cutbacks whittled away at Latin America's already paltry welfare system, as the elderly in particular saw state pensions dwindle in value. In 1991 Argentina's president, Carlos Menem, decided to stop indexing pension payments to inflation, which reached 84 percent that year. By late 1994, 70 percent of Argentina's pensioners, some 2.2 million elderly people, were stuck on the poverty line earning the minimum pension of $150 a month.[29] As the real value of pensions fell, protests erupted. "OAPs Riot" ran one headline, as a dozen people were wounded in clashes between pensioners and riot police.[30] Pensioners also took to the courts, filing an astonishing 350,000 individual cases by late 1994. Of these, 100,000 had already been settled in the pensioners' favor, pending appeals. Lawyers, it seemed, were one group unlikely to face penury in neoliberal Latin America.[31]

## THE INFORMAL SECTOR

To the visitor, the street traders are the most striking members of the informal economy. In Bolivia's capital city, La Paz, the Avenida Buenos Aires and adjoining streets are the site of the capital's biggest street market. Young men dressed in denims sell the latest line in microwaves or stereos, smuggled in from Brazil, while one street away, Indian women sit patiently in their bowler hats and ponchos, selling dried llama fetuses which are buried under the foundations of most new houses in Bolivia to bring good luck. Herbal remedies, BMX bicycles, imported disposable nappies, toiletries, and pots and pans—the list of available goods is endless.

During the recession of the 1980s and the adjustment of the 1990s, the informal sector has acted as a gigantic sponge, soaking up those who have been laid off, or who are entering the workforce for the first time. As Latin America's streets have become clogged with vendors desperately seeking customers, incomes have fallen. In La Paz, where 60 percent of the workforce is now in the informal sector, there is one street trader for every three families—there are just not enough buyers to go around.[32] By 1989 the income of the average Latin American working in the informal sector had shrunk to just 58 percent of its 1980 figure, harder hit than even the public sector.[33]

In Latin America as a whole, the percentage of informal employment in urban areas has climbed by over five percentage points (nearly 20 million individuals) since 1990. What is more, the percentage of new jobs in the informal sector rose from 67.3 percent in 1990–1994 to 70.7 percent in 1997–1999.[34] Of every ten jobs now being created, seven are in the low-tech, low-wage economy with only the most tenuous connection with the modern world and international markets. Globalization, Latin America–style, is excluding nearly three-quarters of its citizens.

## TAXES

The tax system is important in determining what portion of income actually reaches the home as well as how much the government has to spend on social services. Since the late 1980s, tax reform has also gained increasing importance as a means of balancing government budgets and curbing inflation. However, some of the resulting changes in the tax regime have penalized the poor.

On the positive side, as part of their adjustment program, several countries have improved their level of income tax collection either by closing loopholes (Mexico, Argentina) or in some instances (Chile, Colombia) by increasing taxation rates.[35] Most countries, however, have switched away from income taxes (already among the lowest in the world, since the Latin American elite has always been violently averse to parting with its wealth) toward greater emphasis on sales taxes. Governments argue that this tax is easier to collect, especially where in some cases over half the workforce are in the informal sector and therefore are not registered to pay taxes.

In the 1980s, the average top rate of personal income tax in Latin America fell from 48 percent to 35 percent, and the average rate of corporate tax from 43 percent to 36 percent. Bolivia, darling of the neoliberals, effectively abolished both.[36] Sales taxes, on the other hand, boomed. In Argentina revenues from value-added tax (VAT) rose from 0.6 percent of GDP in 1989 to over 9 percent by the end of 1992.[37] Sales taxes are usually regressive, costing the poor more than the rich, since they spend a larger proportion of their income on buying goods and services. Tax reform thus helped fuel the rising social inequality that has been one of the outstanding features of the silent revolution.


## CREDIT

Since the neoliberal understanding of the economy is essentially monetarist, the belief is that cutting the amount of money circulating in the economy is the best means of curbing inflation. Removing money from the economy means reducing credit. This has been done largely by imposing high interest rates to make borrowing more expensive. The result has been a collapse in demand for credit and a deep recession in many countries, as local industry has suddenly found it impossibly expensive to take out loans for investment.

When many economies returned to growth in the late 1980s, they often relied for their success on continued inflows of foreign capital, which had to be lured in by offering appetizingly high interest rates. The squeeze on borrowers has continued, since only the largest firms have been able to borrow abroad at lower interest rates. Since the late 1980s, privatization has also done away with numerous state banks, some of which targeted at least some of their credit to small and medium-sized farmers and small businesses in the towns. Left to their own instincts, experience shows private banks, especially those in foreign hands, prefer to lend to big business. Just as millions of people have been joining the informal sector, they have seen their attempt at self-help crippled by the scarcity of credit.

## PRICES

Inflation has been aptly described as "a tax on the poor." In a high-inflation economy, the better-off usually find ways to defend their incomes from its erosive effects by investing their money in index-linked bank accounts or turning it into dollars. The poor have no such options, and for them, the sustained fall in inflation in the 1990s was neoliberalism's single greatest achievement.

Different facets of adjustment have different winners and losers. Often the winners from one measure lose from another, creating a complex pattern of costs and benefits. The end of government subsidies and price controls on many basic foods and fuel has hit the urban poor hard. The sudden removal of fuel subsidies, and the subsequent increase in public transport fares, has been one of the commonest causes of anti-IMF rioting in the region, notably in Venezuela in 1989.

Most governments have replaced general subsidies with attempts to "target" subsidies at the poorest. Although the neoliberal argument (that general subsidies are a waste of money and often end up subsidizing the wealthy middle-class consumer) is at first sight convincing, talk of targeting is in practice often little more than a smokescreen for government cuts, while the logistical difficulties of identifying the poor and getting subsidies to them often mean that many slip through the extremely tattered safety net. When Jamaica replaced a general subsidy with a targeted subsidy, it managed to reach only 49 percent of those identified as the target group. Those it reached were much better off than under the general subsidy, but the remainder were faced with a jump in food prices and no help from the state.[38]

Trade liberalization can benefit the urban poor, bringing cheaper food imports. Removing protective tariffs on imports often means lowers prices and higher quality for the consumer. Often, however, such gains are captured by the food-processing companies (often themselves multinationals) that import the food. Moreover, simultaneous adjustment measures such as the removal of food subsidies often undo any potential benefits to the poor. In reality, the main beneficiaries of this kind of economic integration are often the middle class, from buyers of computers to those in need of a Big Mac or state-of-the-art disposable nappies.

In the countryside, the effects have been different. An end to controlled prices has in some cases allowed farmers to sell their crops at a better price, but trade liberalization has swamped markets with cheap imported food, which has had the opposite effect.

The combined impact of changes to prices and the labor market under adjustment has shifted poverty away from the rural to urban areas. From 1980 to 1999 the number of poor Latin Americans in rural areas increased from 73 to 77 million, but was overtaken for the first time by the battalions of the urban poor, which jumped from 63 to 134 million people (see table 6.1).

## STATE SERVICES

The health center in Argentina's Ciudad Oculta was in a sorry state. Occupying the ground floor of an abandoned fourteen-floor hospital, the walls were running with damp. In the dark corridors ragged men and women, many of them with the Indian features of migrant workers from Paraguay or Bolivia, held their snot-nosed babies and waited in a depressed silence, punctuated by the coughing of the children. On the walls a handwritten sign read, "The social workers have stopped working because there are no wages. We won't work until it's been sorted out." The notice was dated March 1990; the newly elected president Carlos Menem's "economic miracle" was in its first flush.

Despite the pressures on public spending in the wake of the debt crisis, over the region as a whole health indicators such as infant mortality continued to improve. Infant mortality fell from throughout the 1990s, and maternal mortality fell by 26 percent (from 153 to 114 per 100,000 live births). Access to drinking water improved—those without access fell from 31 to 16 percent.[39] Improvements in health stemmed from the spread of low-cost, effective technology such as vaccinations, which helped counteract the health impact of rising poverty under adjustment.

Decent education and health care are two of the most effective ways of lifting people out of poverty, and from the late 1980s onwards, the

World Bank and other institutions began to urge Latin American governments to increase spending on health and education, the areas of social spending that most benefit the poor.

The World Bank's conversion to the cause of increased social spending looks like a remarkable U-turn. Figures for the share of government spending devoted to education and health between 1981 and 1989 show that the heaviest cuts fell precisely in those countries defined by the World Bank as "intensively adjusting." All of them cut health expenditures, and only one failed to cut spending on education. In part, this was because the intensively adjusting countries also saw the sharpest rise in interest payments on the governments' domestic debts, which doubled to an average of 40 percent of total government spending over the period. As one analyst concluded, "The evidence bears out the view of the international financial institutions as efficient debt collectors."[40]

Average spending on primary education fell from US$164 per child in the early 1980s to US$118 by the end of the decade.[41] An extreme example occurred in Peru, where in August 1990 the newly elected President Alberto Fujimori unleashed a particularly radical adjustment program which became known as "Fujishock." Educational spending which in 1980 had averaged $62.50 per student fell to just $19.80, according to Ministry of Education figures. Teachers' wages fell to one-quarter of their former value, leading to a mass exodus from the profession,[42] while 30 percent of registered students dropped out, as children left school to supplement dwindling family incomes.[43]

Since 1990, the pressure from the Bank, coupled with the growing realization that cutting social spending undermines the region's prospects for growth, has reversed the trend. The greater effort resulted in a sizable increase (around 50 percent) in per capita social spending. From an average of US$360 per capita at the start of the decade, social expenditure climbed to US$540 per capita by its end.

The rise was prompted both by a reactivation of economic growth and a decision to give greater priority to social spending, which climbed from nearly 42 percent to almost 48 percent of total public expenditure during the decade. Evidence also suggests that governments have also become more determined to protect social spending when crises hit: in six countries in which GDP contracted in 1999—Argentina, Chile, Colombia, Honduras, Uruguay, and Venezuela—governments shielded social services from the effects of the downturn.[44]

But total spending is only part of the story. In many Latin American countries, government welfare spending is actually quite high compared to other developing countries at a similar stage of development, but the way the money is spent increases inequality by giving priority to the needs of the better-off.[45] Compared to its per capita GDP, Brazil's education budget is one of the highest in the world, but too much of it goes to fund public universities, which in practice cater to the children of the middle classes.[46] Primary education is far more effective in improving the prospects of the poor than universities that they are unlikely to attend. Similarly preventive medicine and local clinics are more effective than expensive operating theaters in hospitals. Yet historically, Latin American governments have put hospitals and universities first. The evidence here is that the poor have benefited from changes in education spending over the last twenty years, which have placed a priority on primary education, but that there has been a deterioration in their slice of health sector expenditure in all the intensively adjusting countries.[47] Cuts in health spending are all the more painful since the social impact of adjustment has simultaneously undermined people's health. In Lima, the 1990 Fujishock program led to a 30 percent fall in the average protein intake between July and November.[48]

Health and nutritional problems compound the difficulties poor children face in getting a decent education. In Jamaica (a keen adjuster), Alanzo Jones, principal of Bogue Hill All Age School near Montego Bay, saw the impact on his pupils:

> We can see the literacy rate falling and exam results getting poorer. I think attendance patterns have got worse too—we have more problems with sleepy children, children without textbooks. Every year we get worse children to work with, in terms of their reading level and response. The GCSE results are deteriorating. We have seen a resurgence of the diseases we used to know in the 1960s: ringworm is back, along with mumps and measles. They had been kept down for years, but all of a sudden they've come back in the last year or so.

According to Mr. Jones, even though the Jamaican government's education budget stayed ahead of inflation, the impact was undone by the broader impact of adjustment in increasing poverty. "If you don't deal with the people's economics, it won't work," he concluded, "you can't convert a hungry man."[49]

Many governments have followed in the footsteps of Mrs. Thatcher and General Pinochet, encouraging the middle classes to "opt out" of the crumbling state system and put their money into the burgeoning private education and health care sectors. The shiniest new buildings in Santiago's current construction boom are invariably banks or private hospitals. The World Bank concluded that "by targeting the richest segments of Chilean society, the [new health insurance funds] impoverished the rest of the social insurance system. . . . They have 'skimmed' the population for good risks, leaving the public sector to care for the sick and the elderly."[50] Chile's move to a two-tier health care system has exacerbated Pinochet's legacy of social inequality. A study for Chile's Ministry of Health in 1993 showed that infant mortality was seven per 1,000 births for the richest fifth of the population, and 40 per 1,000 for the poorest 20 percent, the Chilean underclass.[51]

Although the Bank pushed for increased government spending, it also pressed governments to improve "cost recovery," its euphemism for introducing charges for what used to be free health and education services. Carmen, a sad-faced grandmother from a poor quarter of Mexico City, saw the collapse of the public health system from close up. "They operated on my husband six months ago. He'd paid social security all his life, but they told him he had to buy his medicine privately and provide two liters of blood—my son had to give it. All they give you is penicillin for everything—it's the magic ingredient!"[52] In one Nicaraguan town, a couple of hours from the capital, a notice on a health center's grimy wall reads: "Anyone coming for an injection must bring their own syringe, elastoplast, gauze and bandages. Attention is free. Thank you."[53]

Young people who have acquired a full education leave school to find that the only jobs available are worse paid and more insecure than in their parents' time. As an exhausted mother in a Chilean shanty town commented, 'why should kids read Neruda or go to the theater if they're just going to end up picking oranges?"[54] One CEPAL study concluded that in the 1990s, "for the young people of Latin America, expectations are being increasingly thwarted."[55]

Moreover, in an increasingly competitive global world, a form of "educational devaluation" is taking place. People have to earn better qualifications just to get the same kind of jobs. On average, 20- to 24-year-olds in Latin America have received three and a half years more schooling than their parents, but that is still not enough to improve their employment opportunities and earning power. From the standpoint of the labor market, this "devaluation" of education has meant that only 47 percent of young people in urban areas, and 28 percent in rural areas, have improved their occupational outlook by increasing their educational level (in comparison with their parents') above the levels required by the job market. This is consistent with survey results, which show that only half of Latin America's youth believe that they have better opportunities than their parents.[56]

One expert on social spending is skeptical on all four of the main changes in Latin America over the last twenty years: decentralization of services has fostered inequality between richer and poorer regions; the increased role for the private sector has led to a two-tier system— "Experience has shown that a service exclusively for the poor is usually a poor service," he argues—the shift from collective to individual insurance has been accompanied by a fall in the number of people with coverage; and the increased emphasis on safety nets has involved only small levels of spending, many of them short-lived with only limited impact.[57]

## SAFETY NETS

Another element in the international financial institutions' growing attention to poverty alleviation since the late 1980s has been the use of special compensatory programs, aimed at softening the impact of adjustment by extending the new vogue of "targeting" to job creation, community improvements, and other areas. The most prominent examples to date have been in Mexico, Bolivia, and Chile. A study by the International Labor Organization of the Bolivian and Chilean cases concluded that "although social funds have been able to take the sting out of the hardships of adjustment," they have mostly benefited "only a small number of people," and that, like targeted food subsidies, such programs often provide a public relations smokescreen for wider cuts in government spending.[58]

CEPAL argues that the time has come for governments to go back to trying to provide universal benefits: "Now that the crisis of the 1980s has been overcome in many respects, it is important to regain some degree of universality in social policies, especially in sensitive areas such as health."[59]

## ADJUSTING THE COUNTRYSIDE

Although structural adjustment's greatest impact has been in the cities, it has also exacted a high human price in the countryside. The halfhearted agrarian reform programs of the 1960s and 1970s have been swept aside by the cut and thrust of the "export or die" mentality. Public spending cuts and the determination to leave everything to the market have meant the end for a range of institutions that at least gave some limited support to peasant farmers. State development banks, state marketing boards, technical support services, and guaranteed prices for their crops have all been curtailed (although in some cases this has allowed farmers to charge higher prices). Import liberalization has produced floods of cheap imports, undercutting peasant crops like potatoes and maize. NAFTA prised open doors to cheap U.S. maize, halving the prices received by some three million Mexican peasant farmers, while Peru, the country where potatoes were first cultivated, now eats potatoes imported from Belgium.

As elsewhere, in rural areas the deregulated market has increased inequality. Banks lend to big landowners and transnationals with collateral and ignore small peasants with nothing to pledge. Peasants get squeezed off the land by bankruptcy or offers they cannot refuse and end up becoming paid workers on their former lands.

## ADJUSTING THE ENVIRONMENT

According to a World Wide Fund for Nature study of the environmental impact of adjustment lending by organizations like the World Bank, such loans "have had, at best, a random impact on the environment and, without qualification [have] failed in placing adjusting countries on a sustainable development path."[60] Such conclusions are hardly surprising, since when drawing up a structural adjustment program the Bank's economists prefer to ignore its impact on a country's "natural capital." Like women's work in the home, environmental damage is one of those "externalities" that is missing from indicators such as GDP used to measure progress, neoliberal style. Former top Bank economist Larry Summers best summarized the astonishingly blinkered views of the people branded by Susan George as "techno-cultists":[61]

> There are no ... limits to the carrying capacity of the earth that are likely to bind
> any time in the foreseeable future. There isn't a risk of an apocalypse due to glob-
> al warming or anything else. The idea that we should put limits to growth,
> because of some natural limit, is a profound error.[62]

Latin American leaders often seem to share his views. One short-lived Ecuadorean president, Gustavo Noboa, dismissed opposition to a $1.1 billion pipeline through one of the world's few intact cloud forests as "four birdwatchers and a couple of mayors."[63]

But environmental issues can be all too immediate for the poor: "Twelve years ago we came to live here," recalled Maurilio Sánchez Pachuca, the stout president of the local residents' committee in a dingy *colonia* just outside Tijuana, Mexico. "We thought we'd be in glory because it was an ecological reserve—lots of vegetation, animals, birds. Two years later the *maquiladoras* started to arrive up there." A fat thumb gestured up at the plateau overlooking the *colonia*, with its clean blue and white *maquiladora* assembly plants. "Now many of us have skin problems—rashes, hair falling out, we get eye pains, fevers. My kids' legs are really bad— all the kids have nervous problems and on the way to school the dust and streams are all polluted. We've tried to stop them playing in the streams, but kids are kids."[64] He flicked despairingly through a treasured folder full of blurred photocopies of the hand-typed letters he had written to the authorities and their replies, a nine-year Kafkaesque exercise in futility. "The first thing [the *maquiladoras*] do is to buy the local officials. There are too many vested interests—dark interests, dollars. I have so many lovely letters from the government—but they aren't real."

Up on the plateau, huge container trucks were at the loading bays, gorging themselves on the products of the 189 factories—Maxell cassettes from a crisp new Sanyo plant, Tabuchi Electric de México. A security guard ushered unwelcome visitors from the site. A black and pink slag heap of battery casings was piled up by the fence surrounding the factories, where truckloads of old batteries from the United States were being broken up to recycle the lead and acid. By law, the remnants should have been returned to the United States, but they were just dumped here on the edge of the plateau.

Beyond the world of home and workplace, school and hospital, adjustment is leaving its mark on the earth, air and water of Latin America. Since the days of the *conquistadores*, Latin America has seemed condemned to a development model based on plunder, but neoliberal-ism has greatly increased the pressure on an already fragile ecosystem. In the rush to export, the region turned to its natural resources, sacrificing long-term sustainability for short-term gains.

One of adjustment's most immediate impacts has been on Latin America's rain forests—the largest remaining reserve of trees in the world. In Costa Rica, the World Bank's push for increased beef exports drives the "hamburger connection," whereby forests are felled to make way for cattle that are subsequently sold to the U.S. fast-food industry. By one calculation, Costa Rica loses 2.5 tons of topsoil for every kilo-gram of beef it exports.[65] Governments have also encouraged logging as a further export earner. The leader of Brazil's Workers Party (PT), Luís Inácio da Silva (Lula) put it better than most: "If the Amazon is the lungs of the world, then debt is its pneumonia."[66] Brazil is both the third world's top debtor and the globe's top deforester.

The soybean agribusiness boom in southern Brazil drove vast num-bers of peasant farmers from their land, forcing them to head for the "agricultural frontier" of the Amazon in search of farmland, cutting down forest in slash-and-burn agriculture. They made the trek along the new roads built with World Bank and international bank loans in the 1970s and 1980s, the very loans that drove up Brazil's debt and cre-ated the hunger for export dollars in the first place. By 1987 "satellite photographs showed 6,000 forest fires burning across the entire Ama-zon Basin—every one of them deliberately started by land clearers. Many of the fires were burning close to the [World Bank–funded] High-way BR-364."[67] Thousands of the hungry migrants also found work turning mile upon mile of rain forest into charcoal to feed the smelters of the Amazon's giant Carajas development. Carajas turns huge deposits of iron ore and bauxite (the raw material for aluminum) into export dollars (which then promptly leave the country as debt service).

In neighboring Guyana, largely untouched forests came under the hammer as part of an adjustment program made with the IMF in the late 1980s. Guyana duly parceled out its forests and rivers to an unholy alliance of Brazilian and Asian mining and logging companies. In return for a fifty-year license on a 4.13 million–acre concession, the notorious Sarawak-based logger, Samling Timbers, promised to export 1.2 million cubic feet of Guyanese timber a year (compared to national exports of just 94,000 cubic feet in 1989).

Guyana is also sitting on substantial gold reserves, which were opened up to foreign investment as part of the adjustment program. In August 1995 disaster struck at the Omai gold mine in Guyana, jointly owned by two Canadian multinational mining companies. A huge pit, into which were piped cyanide liquids and other waste products from the gold extraction process, ruptured and over the next three days spewed three million cubic meters of cyanide-laced toxic waste into the Essequibo, Guyana's largest river. Guyana's president, who only years before had sung praises of the mine, was forced to declare the area an "environmental disaster zone." Indians, traders, and miners living along the riverbank reported dead fish and wild hogs floating belly up, and for two months suffered skin rashes and blistering after using river water.[68]

Elsewhere, the growth of nontraditional agricultural exports has also had some disastrous side effects. In targeting the luxury fruit and vegetable market, Latin American farmers have to ensure unblemished products to satisfy finicky Western consumers, while the trend toward monocultures like soybeans in Brazil offers ideal breeding grounds for pests. In both cases farmers have responded with massive doses of pesticides and fungicides, poisoning workers and local communities. In Jacona, Mexico, farmworkers pay a high price for getting 4.5 million kilograms of strawberries a year to U.S. tables in the middle of winter. According to his death certificate, Blas López Vásquez, thirty-six, died in December 1992 from a respiratory insufficiency" caused by "intoxication from organophosphates" after backpack-spraying a strawberry field.[69] Three other workers died that year in Jacona and fourteen others were hospitalized.

While governments, the public, and the Bretton Woods institutions have become more aware of the importance of environmental issues, the logic of adjustment still often runs in the opposite direction. Nicaragua signed an ESAF loan with the IMF in 1994. As part of the stabilization and adjustment program, credit to the agricultural sector was cut by 62 percent. Small and medium-sized farmers hit hard by these cuts were forced to slash-and-burn forested areas to clear space for subsistence crops, further reducing the country's forests. The environmental result of this economic strategy of increased logging and agricultural expansion has been severe deforestation that has left the country with only a few productive forests. These forests may not last more than the next ten to fifteen years if logging continues at existing rates.

The human tragedy of deforestation was highlighted when Hurricane Mitch struck Central America in 1998. Central America's worst natural disaster of the twentieth century, the hurricane's effects were exacerbated by widespread deforestation, which left the landscape susceptible to rapid rainfall runoff and increased rates of erosion. The results were tremendous mudslides and flooding, causing billions of dollars in damage, over 10,000 dead with a another 9,000 missing, presumed dead and 2.5 million Central Americans left homeless.[70] According to the World Bank, deforestation caused by human development and agricultural expansion increased the devastating effects of Hurricane Mitch.[71]

In Brazil, the financial crisis of 1998–1999 led to harsh budget restrictions as part of the IMF rescue package. As of July 1999, funding for the enforcement of environmental regulations and supervision programs was reduced by over 50 percent. For example, one of the leading and most effective government-run environmental protection programs, the Pilot Program for the Protection of Tropical Rainforests, created after the 1992 Earth Summit in Rio de Janeiro, had its government funding cut from $61 million to $6.3 million in November 1998, at the time the IMF agreement was being signed. Following international pressure, the government restored the budget to $20 million, less than one-third of the originally budgeted amount.[72]

## A PAINFUL WAIT

By 2003, after twenty years of debt crisis, adjustment, and undoubted pain, most Latin Americans are still waiting for the long-promised benefits of structural adjustment to "trickle down" to their neighborhoods. Although the rich have had a vintage two decades, most of the region's people are poorer and more insecure: their homes, communities, schools, and hospitals are collapsing around them, and their cities, towns and villages are increasingly polluted. Latin America is left trying to find its way in a cut-throat global economy, saddled with a population weakened by poverty and ignorance. Politicians have moderated their tone, and some governments are much more committed to reducing poverty and improving public services, but often their basic economic model remains unchanged. Small wonder that so many doubt their good faith, and that disillusion with politicians of all hues grows daily.

# 7—For and Against

## The Politics of Neoliberalism

By 2002, twenty years after Mexico's default on its foreign debts precipitated the continent's debt crisis and the deeper market restructuring that this book terms a "silent revolution," the interplay between economic policy and the region's politics had produced an extraordinary variety of outcomes.

In Mexico, NAFTA took some of the credit for loosening the erstwhile stranglehold of the PRI party after seventy-one years in power. Argentina was enduring the worst peacetime economic crash in Latin American history, during which popular protests overthrew five presidents in the space of two weeks. Riots had derailed government austerity and privatization plans in Uruguay, Peru, and Paraguay. In Brazil, Lula, an avowed leftist and lifelong opponent of the neoliberals, was on the road to victory with a program that tried to achieve a new balance between fiscal conservatism and deep social reform.

Consensus, collapse, or a new political synthesis, the contrasts of the region after two decades of adjustment exemplify the range of political models and processes that have accompanied the silent revolution.

In the 1970s, when General Pinochet was ruling Chile, it was commonly believed that his brand of radical free-market reforms could only be achieved through dictatorship and repression to quell the fierce public resistance that was bound to occur. Yet in June 1993, twenty years after the coup that brought Pinochet to power, the people of neighboring Bolivia elected the architect of the country's structural adjustment to be the new president. Gonzalo Sánchez de Lozada, "Goni," a mining entrepreneur whose U.S. upbringing has left him speaking Spanish with a gringo accent, took the helm promising privatization and business efficiency instead of the corruption and incompetence of "the politicians." How had free-market ideology become electable in the intervening decades?

The roots of this political turnaround lay in the collapse of the previous economic system, import substitution, the perceived failure of the attempt to find less painful "heterodox" forms of adjustment in the mid-1980s and the broader ideological impact of the disintegration of state-run economies in Eastern Europe. The Cuban system's survival of the collapse of communism at least offered some possibility of an alternative development path, but its severe economic difficulties, and partial embrace of dollar tourism lessened its attraction as a model.

The traumas of the debt crisis and hyperinflation increased voters' readiness to grapple with the market, while renewed capital inflows in the early 1990s allowed politicians to pursue less painful forms of structural adjustment. They were backed not just by the IMF and World Bank, but by powerful Latin American business groups that had previously benefited from import substitution but now believed their future prosperity depended on a full engagement with the rapidly globalizing economy. Moreover, voters were rarely offered a clear choice. In the late 1980s and early 1990s, numerous presidents were elected on anti-neoliberal platforms, only to perform abrupt U-turns upon taking office.

As the traumatic memories of hyperinflation faded, the capital flows dried up, and the promised fruits of adjustment failed to materialize, the political star of neoliberalism began to wane. Many erstwhile neoliberal crusaders turned out to be crooks, leading to a rash of impeachments and arrests. Former presidents from Mexico, Ecuador, and Peru ended up fleeing their accusers and the continent for exile in unlikely spots such as Ireland or Japan. By the early years of the new millennium, pollsters were detecting serious signs of "adjustment fatigue," but so far this had affected political rhetoric more than practice. Economic policy remained largely hostage to the market and the harsh dogmas of the silent revolution.

## MILITARY AND MARKETS

The Chilean military espoused a particularly brutal form of economic Darwinism. When asked about the high bankruptcy rate caused by the government's adjustment policies, Pinochet's colleague in the junta,

Admiral Merino, replied, "Let fall those who must fall. Such is the jungle of . . . economic life. A jungle of savage beasts, where he who can kill the one next to him, kills him. That is reality."[1]

Faced by a labor force accustomed to secure, unionized jobs, Pinochet's bloody repression of the trade union movement played an essential part in the "adjustment" process. "If he hadn't killed all those people, the economy wouldn't be where it is today," admits Luz Santibañez, a former exile in Scotland who now runs her own clothing workshop in Santiago.[2] Over 3,000 people were slaughtered to clear the way for the new Chile.[3]

Elsewhere, however, the military has never been an automatic ally of the market (Pinochet himself hesitated for almost two years before finally adopting the neoliberal creed). In Brazil, the military government that took power in 1964 ran up the third world's largest foreign debt by its massive support for infrastructure and state companies, while also opening up key sectors of the economy to investment by transnational corporations. In Argentina, the juntas after 1976 destroyed much of the country's industry by abandoning all protection for local producers, but never considered privatizing the military's mighty industrial complex. In Paraguay, the Generalísimo, Alfredo Stroessner, built his thirty-five-year rule on a combination of brutality and graft, buying the army's support with the proceeds from smuggling goods into Paraguay from neighboring Brazil and Argentina.

Nor, for that matter, has big business invariably been a supporter of deregulation. Import substitution enjoyed considerable support from both transnational corporations and local manufacturers, both of which produced goods for the local market. Safe from the competition of better, cheaper goods produced elsewhere, they were able to foist shoddy, overpriced products on generations of Latin American consumers. In most countries, the market was controlled by a few large companies that were able to avoid internal competition by fixing prices among themselves. However, as the globalization of the world economy got under way, other groups of entrepreneurs became increasingly determined that Latin America should redirect its economies towards exports and foreign investment. The two groups have often come into conflict (often via their political proxies), but the debt crisis, increased influence of outside forces like the IMF, and the collapse of import substitution decisively weakened the hand of the older generation of industrialists.

Military government in Latin America carried the seeds of its own destruction. Power politicized and fragmented the military institution itself, and the population's anger at the generals' authoritarian ways grew as the military failed to deliver on its initial promises of efficient management and economic boom. In the late 1970s and early 1980s this process coincided with the death throes of import substitution and the onset of the debt crisis. Latin America in the early 1980s therefore experienced a historical anomaly; whereas in the past, economic recession has provoked military unrest and seizures of power, when the debt crisis hit in 1982, the military were already in full retreat to the barracks. A new generation of civilian governments took office as their economies were collapsing around them. The suffering of the "lost decade" had a profoundly negative impact on the continent's return to democracy, but did not lead to a swift return to military rule.

In the immediate aftermath of the Mexican crisis of August 1982, government after government accepted IMF tutelage and applied its standard shock treatment to stabilize the economy. However, when it became clear that the result was often *destabilization* of the economy through a lethal combination of inflation and recession, several governments broke ranks and began looking for an alternative and less painful means of stabilizing the economy. The resulting heterodox packages led to a brief recovery, before most of them collapsed in a welter of hyperinflation.

The failure of the heterodox shock programs left neoliberal structural adjustment as the undisputed orthodoxy, and from the late 1980s political parties of all stripes, from Nicaragua's leftist Sandinistas to El Salvador's right-wing, death squad–linked ARENA party, signed up for the treatment. Initially, they faced an acute political quandary: how could a party hope to be elected (still less reelected) if its policies were guaranteed to inflict an instant and devastating blow to the standard of living for the population? Peru's Fujimori explained his dilemma, saying, "It's very difficult and terribly unpopular to apply stabilization measures in an impoverished country like Peru, but it would be even harder to lead the country toward social and national disintegration through economic ruin."4

Whether through bad faith or the recognition upon taking office that the external forces pressing for adjustment were overwhelming, some of the men who subsequently became the darlings of the neolib-

erals won the presidency by campaigning on an anti-neoliberal platform, then performing a policy somersault on coming to power. Taking
office in 1989 and 1990, Peru's Alberto Fujimori, Argentina's Carlos
Menem, Brazil's Fernando Collor de Mello, and Venezuela's Carlos
Andrés Pérez all performed sharp economic U-turns immediately after
being elected on anti-austerity platforms.

To do so, they were forced to ride roughshod over democratic institutions, using the traditional Latin American technique of governing
by decree in order to bypass congressional opposition. Argentina's President Menem announced over three hundred "decrees of necessity and
urgency" from 1990 to 1994, compared to just twenty-five instances of
their use from 1853 until he came to power.[5] Civil rights also took a battering. In Bolivia, the government attempted to defuse union opposition to the 1985 structural adjustment decree by declaring a state of
siege and imprisoning 143 strike leaders in Amazonian internment
camps.[6] In Colombia, the government used anti-terrorist legislation in
1993 to try fifteen trade union leaders opposing the privatization of the
state telecommunications company.[7] In the most extreme example,
Peru's Alberto Fujimori dealt with a troublesome Congress by simply
dissolving it in April 1992 (with army support) and seizing emergency
powers in what was billed a "self-coup."

The four U-turn specialists achieved mixed results, though all
ended up in differing degrees of public disgrace. Menem and Fujimori both led their countries swiftly from stabilization to renewed
growth and were rewarded by reelection in 1995. However the growth
could not be sustained, and the autocratic and corrupt tendencies of
both presidents eroded public support. In the end, they both over-
stayed their welcome and were publicly humiliated with house arrest
(Menem) and exile and an international arrest warrant (Fujimori). In
Brazil and Venezuela, Collor and Pérez's even more blatant economic
failure and corruption ensured they were both publicly vilified and
impeached when only halfway through their terms in office. One
neoliberal crusader who had no trouble winning the election was
Mexico's Carlos Salinas, who used the corporatist controls of the
world's longest-lived one-party state to come to power in 1988. However he, like so many of his colleagues, ended up in exile (in Ireland)
after leaving office.

## WINNING SUPPORT FOR NEOLIBERALISM

The real extent of public support for neoliberal reforms is still hard to gauge precisely because so few presidential candidates have stood on an openly neoliberal ticket. The fact that they have not suggests that at least politicians believe that open support for the market remains an electoral liability. In one of the few cases when voters were asked specifically to endorse a neoliberal program, the Uruguayan government held a referendum in 1992 that it expected to rubber-stamp its plans to privatize five state companies. Instead, to the neoliberals' dismay, the Uruguayan public voted overwhelmingly (72 percent) against privatization. In Uruguay, as the *Financial Times* commented, "slogans like 'solidarity' and 'unity' still carry real weight," although the *FT* took this as a sign of the Uruguayan people's "unyielding conservatism" rather than anything more positive.[8]

Support, or at least acquiescence, was easier to obtain in countries that had been through the trauma of hyperinflation, as in Nicaragua, Peru, Bolivia, and Argentina. Where a government was able to stabilize the economy and eradicate inflation, the population was often willing to support it, even at the cost of recession and increased poverty, as in Peru under Fujimori.

The 1994 elections in Brazil gave a graphic demonstration of the importance attached by the poor to ending inflation. With four months left before polling, the candidate of the left-wing Workers Party (PT) was over twenty points in the lead in the opinion polls and looked certain for victory. In July the *Real* Plan, a new economic package drawn up by then Finance Minister Fernando Henrique Cardoso, was introduced, cutting inflation from 50 percent a month to 1 percent in the space of three months.[9] Cardoso then went on to run for president in October. He clearly recognized the devastating impact of inflation on the lives of the poor, commenting during the campaign, "If I were the devil and wanted to invent a tool to punish the poor, that tool would be inflation."[10] The poor multitudes of the shantytowns proved him right, electing Cardoso by a landslide. Four years later, he duly got a second term in recognition of his achievements. Equally, the fact that Venezuela had *not* undergone the ravages of hyperinflation could explain the lack of support for Carlos Andrés Pérez's adjustment program following his election in 1988, which led to the bloody protests and repression of the

*Caracazo*. Venezuelans had not suffered enough to convince them of the need to swallow the neoliberal medicine.

The degree of political opposition to a stabilization and structural adjustment program is also affected by the degree of pain involved, since some adjustments are more painful than others. One of the key factors in determining the pain level is the availability of international capital. Countries that stabilized in the mid-1980s did so in an international climate where virtually no one was interested in lending to Latin America. But by the end of the decade, Latin America was back in the good books of international lenders, and pickings were thin back in the United States and Europe. In the early 1990s, countries like Argentina led the boom in investor interest in "emerging markets" and were able to count on massive international capital inflows to ease the pain of adjustment, especially if they went on privatization sprees to attract foreign investment. In Argentina, large capital inflows paid for imported machinery to upgrade productivity in the factories, while also creating an overvalued peso that has depressed the price of imports, keeping inflation down without the need to provoke a recession. President Menem was able to stabilize the economy in 1990 without going into recession, then move swiftly toward high economic growth.

In Brazil, Fernando Henrique Cardoso followed much the same path, allowing him just enough time to win a second term in 1998 before the capital inflows dried up, and Brazil succumbed to a financial crisis.

As subsequent events proved, economic growth based on a massive trade deficit and capital inflows was not sustainable in the long term (except, perhaps, in the case of the United States), but it made the initial phase of adjustment much less painful and politically costly than the kind of recession that adjustment brought to Chile in 1975, when GDP fell by 13 percent in a single year and unemployment rose to 20 percent.[11] No government other than a dictatorship could have survived that kind of disaster, as Argentina showed in 2002.

The political conditions for successful stabilization differed from those needed for longer-term structural adjustment and a return to export-led growth. Stabilization required little more than the absence of effective opposition as the government axed public spending, clamped down on consumption, and brought inflation under control. The best time for such steps was usually in the honeymoon period immediately after an election victory, while the new president's prestige was at its highest, the opposition was demoralized, and there was still plenty of time to get the most painful part of the stabilization over with before the next election.

Adjustment and an eventual return to growth were altogether more complex tasks, as a former Venezuelan industry minister explained:

> Stabilization programs are difficult and politically costly to launch, but their technical and administrative requirements are much simpler than those of structural reforms. In most countries, the executive branch of government has the power to cut public budgets unilaterally, liberalize prices, devalue the local currency, and tighten the money supply. In contrast to those "decree-driven" measures, structural changes like privatization, the restructuring of social security systems, tax reform, and the institutional transformation of industry, agriculture and higher education require more than the stroke of a pen and are immensely more complex. The public bureaucracy, Congress, the courts, state and local governments, political parties, labor unions, private sector organizations, and other interest groups all get involved in the process ... the debate ... can seem endless.[12]

Touting for private-sector investment, whether domestic or foreign, meant building business confidence in the government's plans. This, in turn, meant guaranteeing efficient government and political and social stability. Political and social unrest caused by the stabilization effort, combined with the level of incompetence and corruption in government, deterred foreign investors and left some economies struggling to recover from the ravages of stabilization.

To avoid such unrest and instability, a degree of social consensus on the need for market reform seemed essential, which called for a very different approach to that taken by General Pinochet. In Mexico, it was achieved by the ruling PRI, a corporatist chameleon which in the 1980s metamorphosed from the nationalist tub-thumper that brought oil nationalization and import substitution to Mexico in the mid-twentieth century into a neoliberal cheerleader, dragging the country into the GATT, NAFTA, and a profound adjustment program within the space of ten years.

## REVERSING THE REVOLUTION

Diego Zapata looked nothing like his grandfather, General Emiliano Zapata, Mexico's revolutionary icon. The portraits that lined the grandson's grimy front room showed a solemn, handsome young man sporting the famous droopy moustache, bandoliers, sombrero, and sword. Diego, on the other hand, was a sixty-three-year-old peasant with an unshaven, lived-in face, who was clearly annoyed at being woken from his siesta. He lived in the village of Anenecuilco, birthplace to his famous forebear. It was 1992, and thanks to the PRI, the tide of neoliberalism was in full spate.

He talked fondly of his grandfather, "El General," but Diego's face hardened at the mention of the then president of Mexico, Carlos Salinas. He was unimpressed when Salinas dropped in to inaugurate the new Zapata museum, even though the president had bought the village a new statue of its most famous son, which now stood in the neat palm-lined village square, opposite the Zapata pharmacy and the Zapata kindergarten. "They come here and talk marvels about Zapata but it's just politics. The General wanted to give land to the peasants, now Salinas is doing the exact opposite," he said.

Everyone is a Zapatista in Mexico, where the old guerrilla hero is revered as the spiritual leader of the chaotic Mexican Revolution of 1910–1917. Much like Sandino in nearby Nicaragua, Zapata mobilized the masses for revolution and was then assassinated before his image could be tarnished by compromise or old age. Zapata's death in 1919 is seen as part of the wider betrayal of the revolution's ideals, which left Mexico in the hands of the aptly named Institutional Revolutionary Party, or PRI. The PRI turned Mexico into the world's oldest one-party state, keeping a tight grip on power for seventy years, through a blend of fraud, bribery, violence, and appeals to revolutionary nationalism.

Zapata's cry of "Land and Liberty" still strikes a chord with Mexico's dispossessed. In the decades after the revolution, many large ranches were handed over to the peasants, but the cream of the agricultural land stayed in the hands of the wealthy. In the 1990s, the PRI reversed even that land reform, allowing in market forces to demolish the communal landowning structures put in place by the revolution. "The ones with the money will end up with the land, just like before," grumbled Diego. Along the way the government's claim to be the true inheritors of the revolution became increasingly untenable. In 1994, his name was taken by the Zapatista insurgents in Chiapas, led by the pipe-smoking intellectual Subcomandante Marcos. Like their eponymous hero, the largely indigenous fighters of the Zapatista National Liberation Army (EZLN) demanded land reform and equal rights for Mexico's indigenous peoples.

The PRI's octopus-like control over every aspect of society enabled the PRI successfully to coerce, co-opt, and divide potential opposition after President Salinas embarked on his sweeping structural adjustment program in the late 1980s. One critic of the ruling party acerbically observed, "The PRI's *raison d'être* is to help the government avoid the irritations of democracy."[13]

As leader of what the Peruvian novelist Mario Vargas Llosa famously described as "the perfect dictatorship," Salinas could rely on the ruling PRI's control of trade unions, peasant organizations, the media, and just about everything else to smooth the way for privatization, government cutbacks, and free trade. Nicholas Scheele, director of Ford Motor Company's Mexican operations, was very appreciative. "It's very easy to look at this in simplistic terms and say [union corruption] is wrong, but is there any other country in the world where the working class took a hit in their purchasing power of in excess of 50 percent over an eight-year period and you didn't have a revolution?"[14]

Salinas understood the breadth of the undertaking, and even attempted to rewrite the historical iconography of the Mexican Revolution. In 1992, the then education secretary Ernesto Zedillo caused a national furor by trying to revise Mexico's primary school textbooks.[15] Overnight, prerevolutionary dictator Porfirio Díaz was transformed from archetypal bloated plutocrat to misunderstood modernizer and Zapata's revolutionary agrarian reform plan suddenly disappeared from the pages. So blatant was the effort that Zedillo was forced to withdraw the texts, although his blunder did not prevent him from taking over the presidency from Salinas when the PRI won its final election in 1994. Zedillo promptly named a cabinet stuffed with young foreign-educated economists to continue Salinas's market crusade.

At the heart of the crusade lay an abrupt change of policy toward the United States, traditionally depicted as the bogeyman of the Mexican Revolution. In the days before PRI rule, one Mexican president had coined the famous epigram "Poor Mexico: so far from God; so near the United States." Now the PRI energetically pursued a free trade agreement with the United States, and near total absorption into the U.S. economy. According to Richard Lapper, Latin America editor of the *Financial Times*, the PRI was prepared for "a Faustian bargain—they've sacrificed their sense of separateness to become part of the U.S. market. It's fundamental—it defines who they are."[16]

Salinas watched events in Russia and drew a simple conclusion; Gorbachev's mistake had been to put political reform (*glasnost*) before economic restructuring (*perestroika*). The PRI opted instead to pursue the path adopted by the Chinese Communist Party, pursuing radical economic adjustment, while keeping the lid on protest and deferring political reform. Roberta Lajous, the PRI's Secretary of International Relations, may have looked modern, in her office-wear of black leather trousers and blond bouffant, but her politics were definitely in the PRI tradition: "We are not going to throw away the corporatist structure as long as it's useful. Not for votes, but to help the government implement policy. We'd never have been able to carry out the reforms without pyramidal structures."[17]

In the end, the PRI's fate was much the same as that of the Soviet Communist Party. In cutting back on the role of the state and opening up the economy to market forces, it eroded its ability to maintain political control. In the past, its power has been based on massive state spending through a corporatist network of state-sponsored trade unions, peasant associations, and other groups. The party's ideological U-turn provoked severe internal divisions between the neoliberals and those they labeled the "dinosaurs": old-style politicians who feared the loss of party power implicit in the reforms. In 2000, their fears were confirmed when the population finally got rid of the PRI but replaced it not with Cuauhtémoc Cárdenas, the remote and charismatically challenged leader of the Left, but with Vicente Fox, a glad-handing former Coca-Cola executive from the pro-business National Action Party.

Elsewhere in the region, other governments tried to emulate the PRI. In Argentina, the Peronist party (Partido Justicialista) went through a striking U-turn in the 1990s under Carlos Menem's leadership. Historically a champion of import substititution, nationalization, and state activism (including an important element of wealth redistribution), Peronism became the party of deregulation, privatization, and neoliberalism. Within the space of a decade, it presided over the boom and bust of the Argentine economy.

The Peronists left power in 2001, ensuring that the collapse of the Convertibility Plan could be blamed on Menem's successor, the hapless Fernando de la Rua and his left-of-center Alliance coalition. Out of the chaos of early 2002 emerged a caretaker government under Eduardo Duhalde, a Peronist.

The Peronists' network of local bosses played a crucial part in co-opting or corrupting attempts at grassroots organization and preventing it from developing into a national alternative. To do this it used both political skill and cash (for example, through its control of the distribution of the World Bank–funded Heads of Household scheme).

The favorite slogan of the protestors during the chaos of 2001–2002 was *"Que se vayan todos"* (roughly, "Let's get rid of the lot of them"), reflecting their disgust with the political system as a whole. But whatever the energy shown in the grassroots movement, national change required a corresponding new political project. Some observers felt that, by discouraging new actors from engaging in politics, *"que se vayan todos"* played into the Peronists' hands, perpetuating the status quo. The Peronist victory in the 2003 elections confirmed their right to the PRI's title of Latin America's most dogged political survivors.

As leaders used up the political capital accrued from import substitution and the taming of hyperinflation, and wealth showed no signs of trickling down to the poor, politics itself became increasingly tarnished. When Fernando de la Rua attempted to salvage Argentina's crumbling economy by bringing back Domingo Cavallo, the architect of the 1991 stabilization program, Cavallo's new rescue attempt left him a hate figure needing police protection. Bolivia's adjustment czar, Gonzalo Sánchez de Lozada, described the mood as "anti-party and anti-system," adding: "Everybody is saying political parties are done for. There is really little time left before the political class is completely discredited."[18]

Public contempt for politics has seen many of the region's established political parties slide into decline. Into the political vacuum created have stepped some exotic new breeds of politician. Some are more modern versions of Latin America's traditional *caudillo* strongmen— providential leaders on horseback or, these days, more likely to be driving a Ferrari. Men like Bolivia's brewing magnate Max Fernández or media star "Compadre" Carlos Palenque used their wealth and radio and TV chat shows to reach out directly to the battered and disoriented communities of the shantytowns. Politicians like Peru's Alejandro

Toledo or Mexico's Vicente Fox tried to appeal to the electorate by saying they were not really politicians at all, but political outsiders
untainted by the corruption of the political elite, businessmen or technocrats who just wanted to "get things done." Toledo's predecessor,
Alberto Fujimori, described the nature of modern *caudillismo*, saying,
"One of my goals is total independence—from political parties, from
institutions—so I don't have any obligations. This distancing has
helped me get closer to the people."[19]

Occasionally, electorates opted for more traditional *caudillos* like
Venezuela's Hugo Chavez. The leader of a failed military coup in 1992,
he built up a political movement from scratch, promising radical political reform and an economic "third way" (but nothing like the Tony
Blair version). He won a landslide victory in the elections of 1998 and
embarked on a series of political reforms, many of which seemed to be
aimed at consolidating his own personal power and moving Venezuela
back to the region's corporatist past (for example, by trying to replace
the trade union movement, which rapidly became the main focus of
opposition to his presidency, with a single pro-Chavez body).

On taking office, Chavez initially followed a "prudent" economic
policy, trying to keep a check on spending and raise both sales and
income taxes. But once the constitutional reform process was completed in late 1999, he turned on the taps. With income from booming oil
prices and increased debt through bond issues, he raised government
spending by 46 percent in the space of a year.

Chavez's heterodox policy mix included a partial return to import
substitution, raising tariffs on imports and seeking to diversify out of
oil, and steps to oblige banks to lend 15 percent of their money to agriculture. These measures, along with inserting clauses favoring workers
and small producers in the new constitution, provoked capital flight
and political opposition. Capital flight forced him to float the Bolívar
in February 2002, while his autocratic tendencies led to rising opposition, leaving him increasingly isolated, despite successfully seeing off a
clumsy coup attempt by an alliance of businessmen and military leaders in April 2002 and a widely supported strike by oil workers in early
2003. The conflict was costing Venezuela dearly, as GDP fell by an estimated 7 percent in 2002.[20]

In Ecuador, another former army officer and coup leader, Lucio
Gutiérrez, won the presidency in 2003 but appeared to be following a

more traditional route, heading immediately for Washington to sign an IMF agreement and promise budget cuts and price rises. It remained to be seen if he could sell this package to Ecuador's turbulent popular movements.

Through all the politicians' twists, turns, and reinventions, the Latin American public's disenchantment with them and their adjustment programs has grown steadily. According to the InterAmerican Development Bank, by 2002 "popular disillusionment with reforms and disenchantment with democracy are both increasing, while many countries are mired in economic stagnation or outright recession."[21] Privatization has become particularly unpopular, due both to the opposition of state trade unions and the increasing evidence that leaders have lined the pockets of themselves and their friends, while the population at large have lost out.

Annual public opinion surveys by the polling organization Latinobarometro have charted the growing disenchantment. By 2001, 63 percent of Latin Americans said privatization had not benefited their countries, up from 43 percent in 1998; 45 percent disagreed with the principle that lies at the heart of the silent revolution, "The State should leave productive activities to the private sector," up from 28 percent the previous year. Even more worrying, only one in two believed that democracy was the best form of government.[22] The threadbare political and social consensus behind neoliberal reforms was unraveling, and threatening to take democracy with it.

Though weakened, Latin America's democratic transition proved resilient. Corrupt politicians were eventually overthrown, and the military generally stayed in the barracks. The overthrow of Fujimori, the end of the PRI, and the impeachment of Collor and Pérez were signs that those in power must at least take note of the opinions of their people. But this is hardly the vibrant democracy for which thousands of men and women laid down their lives in the 1970s in their fight to rid the continent of military dictatorship. Increasingly, ordinary Latin Americans turned to grassroots movements to fill the gap.

## OPPOSITION AND PROTEST

The roadblock was a couple of tree trunks and a few boulders, cutting off the dirt road to Potosí where it passed through the scattered huts of another bleak Bolivian *altiplano* village. In the dusty school hall a young man read out a communiqué to the growing number of trapped truck and bus drivers. The local peasants union was cutting the roads in protest at the government's deal with Lithco, a U.S. transnational mining company, which would allow it to exploit Potosí's vast salt lake for virtually nothing in return. A woman warns, "They're stoning people at the next *bloqueo*. People are drunk. You must go back to Sucre." Potosí, the poorest department of the poorest nation in South America, has watched its mineral wealth drain away for five hundred years. "We don't want the same thing to happen with lithium as happened with our tin and silver," said one leader of the protest, "whatever transnational comes will rob us, we just want them to rob a little and not take everything."[23]

Two decades after the Mexican debt crisis paved the way for the silent revolution, there are relatively few islands of political calm in Latin America. In many countries, opposition to the impact of structural adjustment has sputtered and occasionally ignited in sporadic riots, strikes, rural uprisings, land takeovers, and, increasingly, street protests against corrupt or unpopular governments. These have claimed some notable scalps in ousting presidents in Peru, Ecuador, and Argentina within the first two years of the new century.

In general, however, the opposition is scattered and incoherent, dogged by its lack of a coherent alternative. Grassroots political leaders and intellectuals alike bemoan the opposition's inability to move from *protesta* (protest) to *propuesta* (proposal).

Turning opposition into a serious political force has been hampered by the very impact of the adjustment process, which has weakened many of its natural opponents. In the shantytowns, women who led the grassroots social movements that were instrumental in driving the military from power now exhaust themselves in the struggle to feed and clothe their families in increasingly hostile conditions, leaving little time for community activism beyond that strictly necessary to their "survival strategies." Government cuts have targeted the most unionized sector of the workforce, public employees, while overall casualization policies have drastically weakened the bargaining power of industrial unions. On the positive side, the decline in government backing for "official" trade unions has encouraged a resurgence of more democratic and independent unions such as those involved in founding Brazil's Workers Party.

In Chile, adjustment has created an atomized society, where increased stress and individualism have damaged its traditionally strong and caring community life. According to press reports, suicides increased threefold between 1970 and 1991. According to Betty Biza-mar, a twenty-six-year-old trade union leader, "Relationships are chang-ing. People use each other, spend less time with their family. All they talk about is money, things. True friendship is difficult now. You have to be a Quixote to be a union leader these days!"[24]

With political parties battered by their lack of prestige and frequent irrelevance to national politics, as well as their lack of an alternative to the neoliberal recipe, much of the real opposition to adjustment has taken place elsewhere. In the cities riots and strikes have punctuated the adjustment process; in the countryside land takeovers and occa-sional uprisings have occurred in countries such as Ecuador and Mexi-co, while at an organizational level a plethora of institutions including non-governmental organizations (NGOs), trade unions, peasant, Indian and women's organizations, and Latin America's ever-active intellectu-als have stubbornly opposed the neoliberal crusade.

Argentina's political crisis in 2002 produced an extraordinary degree of "social effervescence" in a plethora of new popular movements. In the barrios, local people spontaneously set up "popular assemblies" to deal with the crisis confronting their communities, setting up soup kitchens and barter clubs to help people survive. Laid-off workers seized factories and restarted production, while groups of "piqueteros" marched and blocked traffic on an almost daily basis, demanding food and work. Many of these people were new to social activism.

Those protesting at the social costs of adjustment have received strong backing from the radical wing of the Catholic Church, which has repeatedly attacked the social injustice of the market. At the meet-ing of the Conference of Latin American Bishops in Caracas in March 1993, the Bishop of Cali in Colombia, reflected, "In Latin America the economy is doing well, but the peoples are doing badly: you must not worship neoliberalism because it is inhumane, unacceptable, because it cares only about economic success and does not put human beings at the center of things."[25]

During the unrest, hundreds of protesters have been killed and thousands arrested in a continent-wide tide of protest. Typically the measures leading to unrest are those most directly affecting the poor:

cuts in government food subsidies, price rises on public transport or basic services, the firing of state employees. In the protests in Argentina in late 2001, which brought down a succession of presidents over the course of a few weeks and left twenty-seven people dead, the final straw was the freezing of bank accounts, leaving the people cashless and at the mercy of the government. In a telling symbol, the people of Buenos Aires banged their pots and pans in nighttime *"cacerolazos,"* the same expression of protest used against Pinochet's tanks almost thirty years earlier.

The bloodiest of the riots occurred in the Venezuelan capital of Caracas in 1989, when the incoming president Carlos Andrés Pérez doubled the price of petrol:

> As people flagged down buses, the drama began. Bus drivers angrily insisted that they had had to double fares over the weekend because Pérez had doubled the price of petrol. Students were told that their discount cards were no longer valid. The first violence erupted at the Nuevo Circo bus station in the city centre. Rocks and bricks were thrown, roadblocks went up, buses were set on fire.

> Within hours Caracas was gripped by insurrection. People streamed down from the slums to help themselves to food, clothes, and anything else from the shops whose windows they smashed. Some police and troops tried to intervene. Others actively helped the looters. Fabricio Ojeda, a journalist from El Nacional, reported that grateful slum-dwellers passed soldiers presents through the smashed-in shop windows. People careered along the main streets of Caracas, pushing supermarket trolleys crammed with loot or dragging entire beef carcasses from butchers' shops. As news of the caracazo reached other towns in Venezuela, similar riots broke out.

> Eventually, on Wednesday, a massive military presence retook control of Caracas. By then, many shops and entire streets were in ruins. The army arrested thousands of people as they swept through the shantytowns searching for stolen goods. In the course of the following week, perhaps 1,500 people died at the hands of the military, although the government admitted to only 287. Soldiers opened fire without warning in poor barrios, people who appeared suddenly at windows were shot dead by nervous troops. Many bodies were later found in unmarked graves. Caracas, said El Nacional, had become Beirut, an urban killing field.[26]

In the countryside, opposition has been less frequent, perhaps not surprising since it is the urban poor who have been worst hit by adjustment. When rural protests do erupt, however, they are often spectacular, especially when combined with the burgeoning indigenous movement.

The impact of neoliberalism has played an important role as a catalyst for the continent-wide resurgence of the indigenous protest movement in recent years. In Ecuador, where indigenous organizations have several times closed down large parts of the country in protest at the government's adjustment packages, Jamil Mahuad followed his election as president in 1998 by trying to push through an orthodox neoliberal program. He was overthrown by a novel alliance between 10,000 indigenous activists who seized the center of Quito, and discontented middle-ranking officers. Together they launched what was probably Latin America's first indigenous-military junta since the Conquest, but within days the army high command regained control, enabling former Vice President Gustavo Noboa to take office.[27]

The reversal of previous government commitments to indigenous forms of communal land ownership has been particularly explosive. The Mexican government's decision to alter the constitutional commitment to communal *ejido* landownership precipitated the Zapatista uprising in the southern state of Chiapas in 1994, while a similar decision in Ecuador in June of the same year also provoked nationwide protests in a well-organized "Uprising for Life," which paralyzed large parts of the country.

With its focus on individualism and the market, the silent revolution stands diametrically opposed to the indigenous traditions of community, subsistence agriculture, and reciprocal aid. One such culture clash took place in Bolivia in 2000, when the logic of privatization came up against Bolivia's indigenous traditions.

Outside the run-down offices of the Coordinating Committee for Water and Life in Cochabamba, evidence of Bolivia's biggest political protest in more than a decade is still fresh. Graffiti calling for cuts in water rates and the expulsion of the British-led consortium that imposed them are visible on every wall. Inside, against a background of faded portraits of Che Guevara and Fidel Castro, Wilfredo Portugal still sounds surprised by the scale of popular revolt. "It is the first time that so many people got together. People thought that water should not be a business because it is a blessing from God," says Mr. Portugal, a trade unionist. "It grew like a snowball." [28]

## FROM BARRICADES TO BALLOT BOX?

Two decades of sporadic protests against the impact of neoliberalism have achieved mixed results. In countries such as Uruguay, Bolivia, El Salvador, Colombia, Nicaragua, Brazil, and Venezuela, protests have managed to stall the privatization program and other parts of adjustment packages. In Ecuador, Brazil, Peru, and Argentina, protesters have overthrown presidents, but not always with any major impact on economic policies. When an uprising in Ecuador overthrew President Mahuad, it did not prevent his successor Gustavo Noboa implementing Mahuad's original plan to dollarize the economy.

Individuals and organizations protesting against adjustment have been handicapped by their lack of a concrete alternative to the neoliberal recipe, which means that successful protest tends to produce a policy vacuum and economic stagnation, rather than anything more positive. The damage caused was compounded by the intense pressures from the market, foreign governments, and the Bretton Woods institutions, which could all too easily undermine leaders' willingness to challenge the neoliberal paradigm. Such failures risked undermining the validity of the protesters' criticisms and eventually laying the basis for another round of adjustment measures.

At least until Lula's 2002 triumph in Brazil, one of the protesters' chief failures had been to turn opposition into victory at the ballot box. Throughout the silent revolution, Latin American elections have exhibited what one Mexican author described as "apparent schizophrenia. Right-of-center, pro-business regimes are voted in at national level, while left-of-center, socially oriented adminstrations are elected at a municipal one."29 In Brazil, the Workers Party achieved some notable successes in local government after winning control of the town halls of massive cities such as Sao Paulo, Santos, and Porto Alegre. By 2002 it had extended its control to six major cities and many smaller towns. Since 1988, the Uruguayan capital of Montevideo has been in the hands of the *Frente Amplio* (Broad Front) of left-wing parties and other organizations. Similar victories have since occurred in Asunción, Mexico City, and Caracas. In Argentina in 1994, in the midst of Carlos Menem's neoliberal boom, the population of Buenos Aires chose the left-wing *Frente Grande* (Big Front) coalition to run their city of ten million people.

The Left thus won a degree of local power, without gaining corresponding control of resources, since neoliberal central governments
were in charge of taxation and setting national budgets. Within these
constraints, however, the Left has been able to lay the basis for a new
kind of participatory politics, encouraging the explosion in grassroots
movements and, along the way, acquiring an invaluable reputation for
honesty and efficiency in local government. In the case of the southern
Brazilian town of Porto Alegre, the reputation has spread worldwide.
After more than a decade in Workers Party hands, during which the
administration has pioneered public involvement in setting the municipal budget, Porto Alegre in 2001 became the venue for the first World
Social Forum, a gathering of the world's anti-globalization activists,
timed to coincide with the Davos World Economic Forum of global
business leaders.[30]

Instead of a clean break in which neoliberal policies were replaced
by some new model, the "savage neoliberalism" of the 1980s evolved
into a more complex and nuanced set of ideas. In part, this was a
response to the economic failure and growing political unpopularity of
hardline adjustment policies, along with the debate in Washington on
the need for a "second generation" of reforms to enable adjustment
finally to deliver the long-promised benefits. Brazil's Fernando Henrique Cardoso, an erstwhile sociology professor and leading thinker of
the social democratic Left, explained, on coming to power in Latin
America's largest economy in 1994, "If you leave it to the markets to
resolve social problems, it won't work. The market solves some problems, but not that of poverty. You have to have a state and an effective
reform of the apparatus of that state."[31]

In governments like Cardoso's, this osmosis between neoliberalism
and its critics increasingly blurred the boundaries. While promoting
privatization and liberalizing capital flows, Cardoso increased real
public spending (excluding debt service payments) at an impressive 6
percent a year during his eight years in power and settled 600,000 families as part of his land reform program. School enrollment soared.[32]

By 2003, the region's rich political ecology included leaders such as
Chile's Ricardo Lagos and Brazil's Lula, struggling for a shotgun marriage between social justice and neoliberalism. Within the constraints
imposed by fiscal discipline and placating the international capital markets, they sought to redistribute wealth and increase social spending.

The slow loss of coherence within the neoliberal camp was matched by confusion and doubt among its opponents. The increasingly blurred boundaries between neoliberalism and other economic models left politicians faced with a baffling smorgasbord of options, from which they mixed and matched policies according to the national situation, economic moment, and the demands of their political power base. What was lacking was a new "common sense" with the power and clarity of either import substitution or neoliberalism in their early glory.

# 8—Other Paths

## The Search for Alternatives

Despite the ornamental lake, graced by a pair of Chilean black-necked swans, the squat gray concrete bunker is probably the ugliest building in Santiago. It houses the UN's Economic Commission on Latin America and the Caribbean (CEPAL, better known by its Spanish acronym CEPAL), and hundreds of economists stroll its corridors, chatting and arguing in a bewildering range of languages.

The bunker design is appropriate, for CEPAL has been one of the few intellectual redoubts against the neoliberal tide that has swept across Latin America over the last twenty years.[1] If by the early years of the new century, the neoliberal model was still very much the regional orthodoxy, its shortcomings were becoming increasingly obvious. As grassroots rejection of the neoliberal crusade has grown, it has become ever more necessary to find a credible alternative that can both channel protest into positive action and attract new support. If not, the opposition movement runs the risk of being branded as dinosaurs, clinging to the vested interests of the old order. Now CEPAL is leading the effort to define a new economic model that will put the continent on a path to long-term sustainable development. Other sources of inspiration have come from the study of Asian economies such as South Korea or Taiwan, which have succeeded in industrializing with a relatively high degree of social equity. At the grass roots, Latin America's burgeoning network of social movements and non-governmental organizations (NGOs) have been active in criticizing the neoliberal model and searching for sustainable alternatives at the community level. Some of the most economics-savvy of these have banded together to challenge the logic underlying the Free Trade Area of the Americas (FTAA) negotiations, in many cases building on their experiences with NAFTA.

Any discussion of "alternatives to neoliberalism" must first clearly identify the enemy. Although the core of neoliberal thinking is largely unvarying, the theory has acquired many different practical forms during its implementation in Latin America. Geography (for example, proximity to the United States), the state of the world economy at the time of adjustment, the size of the domestic market, the availability of natural resources or a skilled workforce, the capacity of the civil service, and the prior existence (or absence) of a dynamic local private sector, besides the political preferences of different presidents, all influence the way neoliberal ideas are put into practice.

Furthermore, neoliberalism has evolved over time, passing from its "savage capitalism" phase at the start of the debt crisis, in the heyday of Ronald Reagan and Margaret Thatcher, to the "kinder, gentler" neoliberalism of the 1990s, at least in its attitude to civil and political freedoms. To varying extents, neoliberals have rediscovered the issue of poverty and the need to educate their citizens. At least at the level of rhetoric, few politicians would now publicly admit to being neoliberals.

The combination of change and continuity is best illustrated by Chile, where the savagery of the Pinochet dictatorship was replaced by the consensus of the Aylwin, Frei, and Lagos governments, which achieved a measure of tax reform and impressive degrees of poverty reduction. Nevertheless, the underlying economic model hardly changed; despite the superficial variations, there is clearly an ideological and intellectual core to the silent revolution.

Over the continent as a whole, the rhetoric has changed far more than the reality. Poverty is still on the rise (Chile is the exception), market forces are boosting inequality in an already hugely unequal society and in most cases the "social market" boils down to little more than improved regulation of *laissez-faire* capitalism with greater attention to reducing poverty and improving health and education services.

Although those proposing alternatives faced governments who were energetically stealing their rhetoric, as the 1990s wore on, a growing chorus of individuals, parties, grassroots organizations, and institutions started to challenge the ideological dominance that enshrined neoliberalism as the economic "common sense'"of the 1980s. It was fast becoming what one veteran British Marxist termed "yesterday's truth," although which, if any, "big idea" was to replace it was still far from clear.[2] Neoliberalism may have many faces, but so also do the sources of alternatives. Here too, generalization is dangerous, not least in identifying any source of ideas as coming from "the Left," which in Latin America, as elsewhere, is an increasingly elusive and amorphous entity.

The search for alternatives within Latin America responded in part to the shifting tides of political opinion in the North, and above all in the United States. The Clinton presidency of the 1990s explicitly rejected Reaganomics and argued for a new enhanced role for the state. In Europe the revival of social democratic parties in Britain and German espousing the slippery concept of the "third way" fed the public policy debate in Latin America. Brazil's Fernando Henrique Cardoso was even anointed as an international third way leader, when he was invited to a summit of its chief architects, including Bill Clinton and Tony Blair, in Florence in 1999. However, George W. Bush's victory in the 2000 U.S. elections and the subsequent spate of neoliberal initiatives in the United States made clear the limits of any anti-neoliberal backlash in the North, as did the timidity of the U.K. government in addressing the failures of market forces in areas such as public transport.

Even when advocating a retreat from the extremes of neoliberalism, Northern governments have largely failed to practice what they preach. The United States and EU subsidize their farmers to the tune of $21,000 and $16,000 per farmer per year, respectively, use import tariffs to protect major industries such as steel, and demand "managed trade" agreements with competitors such as Japan, but they are singularly reluctant to countenance such activities from the South, for which they continue to prescribe large doses of free trade and deregulation through vehicles such as the WTO and the FTAA.[3] The flow of ideas from the North has nourished the debate, but the political pressures from Washington and Europe have simultaneously closed it down.

Furthermore, the international financial institutions continue to use their power as the gatekeepers of world capital to force an outdated and damaging doctrine onto countries in the South. The debate over reform of the IMF, World Bank, and other multilateral institutions is central to the discussion on reforming development models within Latin America, since the large lenders are now the chief intellectual repository of neoliberal beliefs and currently enjoy a virtual right of veto over economic policy in many countries in the region.

## STATE VS. MARKET: THE LESSONS OF ASIA

In the search for the elusive goal of long-term, sustainable economic development, the Newly Industrializing Countries (NICs) of East Asia, such as South Korea, Taiwan, Singapore, and Hong Kong, have acquired iconic status. Study and analysis of their achievement of rapid and socially equitable growth has become a thriving academic industry, but have failed to yield much in the way of a consensus on the most basic question—is the triumph of the NICs down to their adoption of neoliberal policies, or exactly the opposite?

According to the World Bank, the NICs' sustained growth and industrialization based on exports, rather than protectionism and import substitution, proves once and for all what the market can achieve once the state gets off its back. In its report on East Asia's spectacular achievements in poverty reduction, the World Bank attributes the successes to "sound macroeconomic management . . . improving the business-enabling framework, and liberalizing markets and prices," measures that the Bank says provide "powerful incentives to private-sector led growth," along with other cherished Bank policies such as targeting health and education spending at the poorest groups.[4]

But a closer examination reveals that, far from demonstrating the virtues of liberalization and government noninterference, the East Asian NICs' successes have been based on a high level of state intervention in the economy, a fascinating duet between state and private sector, and many more restrictions on foreign capital than ever existed under import substitution in Latin America. Many of the lessons to be learned are anathema to the neoliberal orthodoxy and could instead play a valuable part in the search for alternatives to the dogma of the silent revolution.

## SOUTH KOREA AND TAIWAN

The two countries that allow the best comparisons with Latin America are Taiwan and South Korea, since the other two Asian "tigers" (Singapore and Hong Kong) are too small to have much in common with economies the size of Mexico or Brazil.[5] In recent decades, other countries such as Malaysia and Thailand have given further insights into what governments can and can't achieve in the modern era.

After the Second World War, Taiwan and South Korea emerged from prolonged periods of Japanese occupation with classic colonial economies restricted to exporting raw materials. After war and independence had shattered their former colonial ties, with an impact on their trade balance similar to the effect of the depression on Latin America, the two countries had little choice but to opt for an initial period of import substitution (although in the case of Korea, this was delayed until after the end of the Korean war). When this showed signs of running out of steam, the two countries switched to an all-out export drive based on manufactured goods. The results were extraordinary. Taiwan's exports rose a hundredfold between 1965 and 1987, while South Korea's multiplied by two-hundred-fifty times over that period.[6] In 1965 South Korea and Argentina both had about 0.1 percent of the world market in engineering products. Two decades later Argentina still had 0.1 percent, but South Korea's share had gone up twenty times.[7] Taiwan, in many ways the star performer, can boast negligible unemployment, virtually 100 percent literacy and the fairest income distribution in the world.[8] Furthermore, until 2001 it had achieved all this without ever being a member of GATT/WTO—portrayed by the powerful nations as the prerequisite of trading success.

The lessons to be learned from the successes of the Asian NICs challenge the received wisdom on both sides of the state-versus-market debate in Latin America.

### FOREIGN CAPITAL

Whereas policy makers in Latin America have veered between blanket hostility to an uncritical infatuation with foreign capital, at least until the 1990s, the NICs proved able to work with foreign capital, while subordinating it to their national interests. Initially, foreign capital inflows in East Asia were largely in the form of government loans, which entered in large amounts immediately after the Korean War, but fell thereafter. Since government loans usually went to the recipient state, they were easy to control and direct toward priority export industries. In South Korea the government allowed transnationals to invest only through joint ventures with Korean companies, while Taiwan was slightly more open to foreign investment (though not as much as Brazil and Mexico), but directed it to the benefit of the national economy, using a system of tax incentives that varied according to what the company was producing, how much it exported, and what proportion of local products it used. There are no transnationals among the top ten largest companies in either country.

In Latin America, on the other hand, governments have encouraged transnationals to play a leading role in many economies, and they have acquired enormous influence over policy direction in pursuing their own rather than the national interests. Behind the transnational corporations stand powerful supporters, not least the U.S. government and the international financial institutions, like the IMF and World Bank, as well as the transnationals' local employees and managers. All of them share and promote the transnationals' agenda on issues like free trade and deregulation.

In the 1990s, East Asian governments threw caution to the winds, as they adopted the Washington Consensus view and opened up their economies to short-term capital flows. This led to a sudden influx of capital, sowing the seeds of the financial collapse of 1997–1998.[9] It remains to be seen whether the long-term impact of the crash will be a reversion to the previous model of caution, or whether financial and other reforms can reduce the region's vulnerability to "hot money" through a more deregulated "Anglo-Saxon" economic model.

In Latin America, however, foreign capital inflows rose inexorably until the onset of the debt crisis. After the capital famine of the 1980s, when Latin America exported much-needed capital to pay the interest on its foreign debt, renewed inflows of foreign capital led to a pattern of stop-start surges and crashes in the late 1990s. Nevertheless, renewed inflows were frequently hailed as one of the proofs that Latin America's economy was on the mend. The East Asian experience suggests that Latin America's continued dependence on foreign capital is a sign of weakness, not strength, and is a serious obstacle to charting a path to sustained economic growth.

## INVESTMENT AND SAVINGS

Over the years, the Achilles' heel of Latin America's economy has been its inability to generate domestic savings and investment, a weakness that has been exacerbated by the investment famine of the silent revolution. An impoverished majority with nothing to spare and a small, rich elite addicted to a U.S. consumer lifestyle, unwilling to pay even minimal taxes and always ready to slip its capital overseas has meant that the region has always skimped on investment, much of which has had to be funded by foreign, rather than domestic, capital. South Korea and Taiwan, on the other hand, have inexorably increased their levels of domestic savings over the years, thereby reducing their dependence on foreign capital. Taiwan has been so successful in accumulating capital that it now has the third-largest foreign currency reserves in the world, after Japan and China.[10]

## EQUALITY

One of the reasons for the NICs' success is distinctly unpopular with the neoliberals—agrarian reform. Before industrialization began, sweeping land reforms in Taiwan (1949–1951) and South Korea (1952–1954) established an initial distribution of wealth and income far fairer than anything achieved in Latin America. One of the driving forces behind the reforms was the United States, desperate to head off the threat of communist revolt in the aftermath of the Chinese revolution and the Korean civil war. By comparison, the kind of reforms enacted in Latin America following the Cuban revolution ten years later were timid, systematically watered down by a stubborn landowning aristocracy despite Washington's pressure for land reform.

For the United States, the geopolitical stakes were much higher in Asia, where the Chinese revolution was swiftly followed by wars in Korea and Vietnam. Washington was therefore far more ready to provide large quantities of aid with few strings attached, and accept defiance on policy issues from the Asians; for example, Taiwan has systematically rebuffed U.S. pressure to privatize state firms.

In Asia, agrarian reform created nations of small farmers who constituted a market for the initial phase of import substitution. Between 1952 and 1954 owner occupation of land in South Korea went up from 50 to 94 percent.[11] By contrast the gulf that has always divided rich landowners and landless peasants in Latin America is not only unjust, but greatly reduced the size of the internal market for the products of import substitution. Frances Stewart of Oxford University argues that initial asset redistribution is important because

it influences the rest of the development strategy in a variety of ways; for example, more equality leads to more widely spread education, and it may lead to mass
markets for labor-intensive consumer goods rather than elite goods. The consequent political economy tends to favor more pro-poor economic decisions.[12]

Later on, when the Asian countries switched to export-oriented industrialization, they gave priority to labor-intensive industry, while always
planning to upgrade subsequently to more high tech sectors. This
meant that the benefits of industrialization spread to the whole of society, and the region has maintained its equal distribution of income
throughout its period of extraordinary growth. In Latin America, the
decision to deepen import substitution based on capital-intensive
industry, frequently owned by transnationals, created far fewer jobs,
further skewing income distribution.

Conditions in the Korean and Taiwanese factories were often harsh.
Even until the 1980s, many Korean factory owners banned the drinking
of water, or even soup, by their workers because they did not want
them to take toilet breaks, and workers were routinely hit by the fore-
men.[13] In time, however, wages and conditions improved. Unfortunately, when the NICs' new entrepreneurs moved abroad, they kept the
abusive practices. Taiwanese factories in southern China are every bit
as exploitative as U.S. factories in Mexico, and Korean textile *maquiladoras* in Mexico and Central America have become notorious for their
harsh working conditions.

## STATE AND PRIVATE SECTOR

In both Taiwan and South Korea, the state played a leading role in
directing national economic development, using the finance sector to
guide investment. In South Korea, the state wielded its financial mus-
cle to push and prod the giant conglomerates, known as *chaebols*, along
its chosen course. In Taiwan, the government used its many state-
owned companies and public research and service organizations to
direct the economy. Taiwan proved that state ownership is not automatically an obstacle to success. At the end of the 1970s, state-owned
enterprises accounted for a third of domestic investment, more than
their counterparts in Brazil or Mexico.[14] When the Taiwanese government decided to encourage a new industry that either needed lots of

capital (e.g. steel) or new technology (e.g. semiconductors) state-owned companies moved in and set it up, but then withdrew, handing it over to the private sector.

## PROTECTION FOR INDUSTRY

Both regions have periodically protected local industries from foreign competition as part of their strategy for industrialization. However, the nature of Asian protection is very different from the Latin American variety. Whereas Latin America during import substitution opted for blanket protection across the whole of industry on a permanent basis, Taiwan and South Korea used selective protection for key industries. They also made it clear from the beginning that protection was not permanent, but would be phased out according to a predetermined timescale, by which time the industry would have to be internationally competitive to survive in the world market. In Latin America, only Brazil opted for this model with some success in establishing a domestic microelectronics industry, using selective and temporary protection along Asian lines.[15]

## SOCIAL ROLE OF BUSINESS

The private sector in Asian economies has different social and economic functions to its Western equivalent. According to Ajit Singh these include:

- a close relationship between government and business
- government interventions carried out informally, rather than through legislation
- a long-term relationship between finance and business, compared with the short-term imperatives of a stock market-based system
- cooperative relations between managers and employees, e.g., lifetime employment.[16]

In Latin America, on the other hand, such relationships may have partially described jobs in the public sector, but the private sector has behaved in a much more traditionally Anglo-Saxon fashion towards it employees and financial relationships.

## POLITICS AND CULTURE

One point of similarity rarely mentioned by the neoliberals is the undemocratic political systems in the four countries. South Korea's drive for
industrialization was launched following a military coup in 1961, just
as Brazil's economic miracle followed the military coup of 1964. South
Korea is if anything the most brutal of the four regimes, and still regularly uses its Darth Vader-like riot police to crush protesters. Taiwan's
one-party state, ruled by the Kuomintang (KMT) since 1947, bears a
remarkable resemblance to Mexico's Institutional Revolutionary Party
(PRI), which clung doggedly to power from 1929 to 2000. Both regimes
even finally succumbed in 2000 to complete the transitions to more
representative democratic regimes, which had started with Brazil
(1985) and South Korea (1989).

However, the East Asian states have a far greater degree of autonomy
than their Latin American equivalents. Japanese occupation conveniently destroyed the old landed oligarchy and allowed the post-inde-
pendence governments' technocrats to chart a new course, leading to
the kind of economic success story associated with other war-flattened
economies like Germany and Japan. In Latin America, the traditionally
conservative class of large landlords retains enormous political influence, as do foreign capital, new generations of financiers and industrialists, and the trade union movement built up under populism. All of
these groups consistently challenge governments, forcing them into a
higher degree of political and economic compromise than has been
necessary in East Asia.

This raises uncomfortable questions for those seeking a more democratic alternative to neoliberalism in Latin America—how is it that the
most economically egalitarian and successful third world economies
are so authoritarian and undemocratic? Can long-term development
along Asian lines be achieved only by shutting out the voices of the
majority of the people, at least in the initial takeoff phase of growth?
How can a more participatory model in Latin America avoid the pent-
up demands of the poor from immediately forcing the government
into overspending and a rerun of the collapse of import substitution?

The commonplace cultural stereotypes of meek, hardworking Asians
and lazy Latins conveniently ignore the Chinese revolution or the right
to rebellion enshrined in Confucian thought, not to mention the

extraordinary degree of effort involved in so many Latin American households' daily struggle to survive in the era of adjustment. Until the 1980s, East Asia was arguably the most conflict-ridden part of the world, while in the 1950s and early 1960s, Japan lost more working days per worker in industrial strikes than did Britain or France. High levels of violence persist in countries such as Indonesia and the Philippines.[17]

Nevertheless, cultural differences are significant in explaining the differences between the two regions' experiences. The Latin American elite idolizes the North American way of life with its emphasis on consumerism and short-term rewards, whereas the East Asians are influenced by the more austere Confucian tradition. The Latin American elite's affinity to U.S. values is such that it is often hard even to describe them as a "national bourgeoisie" whose first allegiance is to their own country's development. They speak English, send their sons and daughters to U.S. colleges, work for or in partnership with local transnational corporation subsidiaries, move their dollars around the world, and even do their shopping in Miami.

## IMPORTS VS. EXPORTS

Although neoliberals claim that Taiwan and South Korea are exemplars of "export-led growth" and would never dream of indulging in import substitution, the truth is more complex. Both countries simultaneously juggled selective import substitution *and* export drives, in the process steadily developing their economies.

What *is* true is that both Asian economies concentrated on promoting exports while keeping a number of controls on imports. Under import substitution Latin America largely neglected exports and controlled imports. After the onset of the debt crisis, under heavy pressure from Washington and the international financial institutions, it switched to wholesale liberalization of both imports and exports, allowing an influx of imported goods to undo many of the benefits of its improved export performance.

There is a sharp contrast between East Asia, where governments encouraged foreign trade but until the 1990s maintained strict controls on foreign investment, and Latin America, where trade has been controlled but foreign investment allowed to go almost unchecked, acquiring enormous political influence. This is one lesson the neoliberals have not learned. The main significance of the NAFTA and the FTAA is not their commitment to free trade, but that they sweep away almost all controls on U.S. investment in Mexico and the rest of Latin America respectively.

TABLE 8.1. Paths of Industrialization in Latin America and East Asia

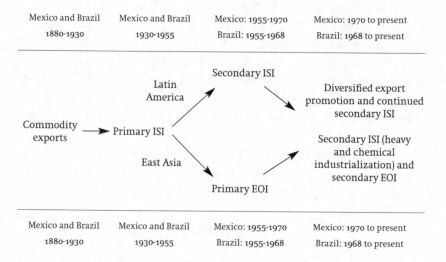

| Mexico and Brazil 1880-1930 | Mexico and Brazil 1930-1955 | Mexico: 1955-1970 Brazil: 1955-1968 | Mexico: 1970 to present Brazil: 1968 to present |
|---|---|---|---|

KEY : EOI = Export Oriented Industrialization; ISI = Import Substituting Industrialization

SOURCE: Gary Gereffi and Donald L. Wyman, eds., *Manufacturing Miracles: Paths of Industrialization in Latin America and East Asia* (Princeton, NJ, 1990), p. 18.

The parting of the ways between the Asians and Latin Americans came in the late 1950s when both regions had come to the end of the first phase of "easy" import substitution (see table 8.1). At this point they were able to produce less complex manufactured goods like televisions and refrigerators, but had to confront their continued dependence on imported capital goods like turbines and cranes and intermediate inputs like iron and steel or chemicals. The Latin Americans chose to deepen import substitution by investing in industries to produce capital and intermediate goods. In doing so they believed they could generate sufficient foreign exchange to pay for essential imports by exporting abundant natural resources such as oil, minerals, or agricultural commodities. Repeatedly in Latin American history this so-called curse of wealth has allowed governments to go on plundering natural resources rather than undertaking long-term and equitable industrialization.[18] Although Mexico and Central America have moved into manufacturing for the U.S. economy, by the early 2000s, some 40 percent of Latin America's exports still consisted of raw materials, [19] which in contrast make up only 8 percent of South Korean exports.[20] The paradoxical legacy of Latin America's natural riches has been chronically underdeveloped and unequal societies.

East Asia had neither the internal market to justify further import substitution nor the natural resources to pay for it, and therefore quickly opted to switch its emphasis to manufactured exports. It chose to rely on the intensive use of labor rather than the huge inputs of capital required for deepening import substitution, and thus did not require massive inputs of foreign exchange. The resulting exports further improved the trade balance.

In the early years after East Asia and Latin America parted company, both prospered. From 1965 to 1973 Latin America's GDP grew by 7.4 percent a year, and East Asia's growth reached 8.3 percent.[21] It took the sudden oil price rise of 1973 to expose the underlying vulnerability of the Latin American model and the resilience of the Asian export-led path.

The first stage of export-led growth came to an end in the early 1970s, by which time the NICs' rapid industrialization had soaked up all available labor and wage levels were starting to rise, damaging the competitiveness of the labor-intensive export industries that had flourished in the first phase. Furthermore, recession and protectionism in the West in the wake of the OPEC oil price rise of 1973 hit the NICs' major export markets. Now that export-led growth had enormously enlarged the size of the internal market, the NICs were able to turn inward for a further phase of import substitution aimed at building up heavy industries such as shipbuilding and chemicals. Korea ran up a large foreign debt in the process, but was able to service it throughout the 1980s because of its export strength. Later the NICs combined this second-stage import substitution with moving into new export fields, involving more capital and skills to produce more complex goods such as electrical equipment or cars, where know-how matters more than cheap labor. Wage levels were thus able to rise without unduly hitting competitiveness.

As long as foreign loans were plentiful in the 1970s, Brazil and Mexico could go ever deeper into debt to keep the creaking wheels of import substitution turning, but when the loans dried up, the model collapsed. Their partial attempt in the 1970s at turning outward and

building up manufactured exports failed to produce the kind of transformation required to stave off the debt crisis.

East Asia's astute alternation between building up its export industries and promoting import substitution enabled it to develop an ever
more complex and complete industrial apparatus, largely under
national control. In contrast, Latin America during its import substitution period gave too much priority to imports, let itself be dominated
by the demands of foreign capital, both creditors and transnational
investors, and seemed to operate out of synch with the world economy.
It tried to shift to exports when the world economy was in recession,
and turned inward when export markets were booming, whereas the
policy changes of the Asian NICs expertly coincided with the ups and
downs of the world economy.

But could Latin America follow in the footsteps of the Asian NICs,
even if it tried to adopt their development models tomorrow? In the
1950s Taiwan and South Korea were of enormous geopolitical importance to the United States in the wake of the Chinese revolution and
Korean War. With Washington at the height of its power, aid flowed in
abundance, and the governments had plenty of leverage in negotiations over its use. Forty years on, the United States is the world's largest
debtor, with an intractable trade deficit and little money available for
aid. Apart from Mexico, Latin America carries little political weight in
Washington, ranking well below Eastern Europe and the Middle East in
the geo-strategic pecking order.

The United States' escalating trade deficit has also led to growing
protectionism against manufactured imports and heightened vigilance
against attempts by third world governments to regulate trade and foreign investment. The WTO, NAFTA, and other regional free-trade
treaties all reduce the ability of Latin American governments to use
selective state controls and subsidies to direct their economies in the
manner of the Asian NICs. Some writers even see the primary purpose
of the WTO and Washington's increased insistence on free trade as part
of a strategy of "kicking away the ladder," preventing developing countries from pursuing the policies that the rich countries employed in
order to develop, and attempting to prise open their economies to
Northern exports and investment.[22]

Other authors see the danger not so much in the new rules and institutions, but in the "tendency of developing country political leadership

toward overconformity with global rules rather than toward challenging them."23 Alice Amsden believes the restrictions on developing country economic sovereignty are overstated, concluding, "All in all, the liberal bark of the WTO appears to be worse than its bite, and 'neo-developmental States' in 'the rest' have taken advantage of this, where necessary."24 She finds that the WTO leaves sufficient elbow room for developmental states to use performance requirements to industrialize and holds out examples such as Taiwan's provision of science parks for chosen companies, or Korean promotion of science and technology through large national research projects, a model later followed by China. However, this relatively benign picture may change as the ever-growing web of constraints formed by the WTO, regional trade agreements, bilateral trade and investment treaties, and agreements with the IMF and World Bank further close down governments' room to maneuver.

Asia's success in recent years has in large part been built on its ability to absorb, adapt, and improve the latest technology. This requires a skilled workforce, high levels of public and private spending on R&D, and the ability to identify emerging new technologies and assimilate them early enough to compete with rivals. As the pace of technological innovation accelerates, it will become increasingly hard for Latin America, which spends little on R&D and is chronically short of technical expertise, to jump aboard the accelerating high-tech train.

The Asian model's extraordinary ability to generate growth *with equity* shows little sign of being repeated in Latin America, where inequality has increased remorselessly both under import substitution and during structural adjustment. Agrarian reforms are being put into reverse in countries like Mexico, Ecuador, and Nicaragua, leading to greater inequality, not less. In any case, now that Latin America is so overwhelmingly urban, agrarian reform can no longer alter radically the distribution of income in much of society. It remains to be seen whether the increasing emphasis on labor-intensive export industries demonstrated by the *maquiladoras* in Mexico and Central America leads to long-term improvements in living conditions, given that the pool of unemployed workers to be soaked up before wages will rise is far larger than in the Asian case.

In addition, the *maquiladoras* are under foreign, not Latin American control, have minimal linkages with the domestic economy in terms of suppliers, and are more likely to leave the country should wage levels eventually start to rise. Nevertheless, there is evidence that levels of technology are starting to rise in the *maquiladoras* (for example, as auto parts and electronics factories start to eclipse the traditional garment assembly lines), and that some of the low-tech, low-wage factories are starting to move in search of the even cheaper labor of Southern Mexico and Central America. If true, this holds out the prospect of repeating Asia's "flying geese" phenomenon where, as one country moved upmarket the factories moved on to poorer Asian neighbors and began the industrialization process all over again.

More generally, there is a so-called fallacy of composition involved, both in terms of the market and the environment, in suggesting that all developing countries follow the NIC path. First, the market for NIC products is limited to the economies of the North, and the more NICs there are, the more cut-throat the competition will be (and the greater protectionist pressures are likely to become in the importing countries). Taiwan and South Korea are both relatively small countries, but when a goliath like China embarks on the NIC path, it is questionable whether the market is sufficient to allow it to achieve full NIC status, let alone whether any room is left for other countries to join in. By 1996, two out of every three pairs of shoes traded worldwide were made in China.[25] It was similarly dominant in the garment trade. Given the poor environmental record of the NICs, and the increased use of fossil fuels and other nonreplaceable inputs that their industrialization involves, there is also serious doubt that the planet could sustain the impact of another hundred NICs.

Despite these misgivings, the rapid rise in recent years of a second tier of Asian NICs such as China, Malaysia, and Thailand has shown that there is still room for maneuver. Many of the measures used by the Asian NICs are still open to Latin America. In order to use them, however, the region's governments will have to shrug off the defeatism of the neoliberals and start managing the economy again.

## CEPALISMO

Within Latin America, the debates over alternatives to neoliberalism range across the political spectrum, from detailed technocratic tinkering to improve its efficiency and reduce its social cost to clarion calls for a new utopia, junking the whole doctrine and starting from scratch to build a new "popular economic alternative."

Occupying the center ground is CEPAL. In the 1960s, CEPAL was seen as the chief theoretician of import substitution, and its influence went into eclipse as the model collapsed. In the late 1980s, CEPAL's economists embarked on the long road back from the intellectual wilderness, pioneering the discussion on "reforming the reforms." The CEPAL website is crammed with a prolific output of high-quality research and policy proposals covering issues such as foreign investment, trade, the role of the state, poverty reduction, and improving social services.[26] Since the original CEPAL model was termed "structuralism" due to its emphasis on the structural impediments to development, the new body of thinking was dubbed "neostructuralism." According to one analysis, the main changes involved neostructuralists "giving more importance to market forces, private enterprise, and FDI as compared to Structuralism . . . in neostructuralist thinking the state no longer plays the pivotal developmental role that it did under structuralist import substitution. The imperative of achieving and maintaining macroeconomic balances is recognized. Another key element of neostructuralism is its greater concern with equity and poverty reduction.'[27]

CEPAL agrees with the neoliberals on the need for radical economic adjustment in Latin America, arguing that the continent missed the chance to adjust in the 1970s when plentiful supplies of foreign capital could have eased the pain. It accepts the need for avoiding giant deficits, whether in government accounts or in trade. However, it disagrees with the orthodox neoliberal recipe on just about everything else.

The heart of the *cepalismo* alternative, laid out in more detail in appendix B, is a redefinition of the goal of the economic model. Instead of neoliberalism's single-minded pursuit of growth at any cost (which in any case it has signally failed to achieve), CEPAL argues for the twin goal of combining growth with equity, a feat never achieved by any Latin American country, but a central characteristic of successful newly industrialized economies in Asia and Europe.[28] In the past, what can be loosely described as Latin America's populist Left (led by men such as Venezuela's Hugo Chavez or Argentina's Juan Domingo Perón in his earlier years) has seemed almost exclusively concerned with redistributing wealth, omitting to say how it would generate it in the first place. The more clearly Marxist Left, such as Nicaragua's Sandinista Front or the Cuban Communist Party, was seduced by the "fetishism of the state," building unwieldy state-owned enterprises to drag backward countries into the industrial age. The statist behemoths usually disappointed their creators (and their customers), rarely becoming the hoped-for "engine of growth" for the rest of the economy.

At the other extreme lies neoliberalism's trickle-down philosophy, which argues that the benefits of growth will eventually "trickle down" to the poor, conveniently absolving planners of any responsibility for ensuring social and economic justice in their all-out rush for growth. In contrast, CEPAL believes that the promotion of equity is a precondition for sustainable growth, and believes "social equity can be seen as the basis for a call for a third generation of reforms that will place equity at the very core of the policy agenda."[29] CEPAL believes this step lays the basis for a radical overhaul of Latin America's political system:

> If the construction of more equitable societies is defined as the essential aim of development, then the primary focus becomes the populace's civil and political rights. . . . The value of economic, social, and cultural rights lies in the fact that they establish a legal and institutional regime that helps to inculcate ethical perspectives which then are mainstreamed into collective objectives and, hence, into economic and political decision-making processes that will make it possible to meet the citizenry's needs and diminish inequalities.[30]

According to CEPAL, growth with equity can only be achieved if trade, investment, and growth are harnessed to further social well-being through a radically enhanced role for "public policy," which it sees as involving much more than simply increasing the role of the state. As part of its commitment to greater citizenship, public policy should also involve local government and a range of civil society organizations in building a society "in which a wide range of social actors participate actively and which is accountable to the citizenry."[31]

This vision is very different from a return to the octopus state of the 1960s, owning large chunks of the nation's industries and running a massive and inefficient state bureaucracy. CEPAL accepts that production should, wherever possible, be left in the hands of the private sector. Instead, it argues for a managerial state, in alliance with civil society, regulating the private sector, intervening in the economy to move it toward higher levels of technology and industrialization, training, and caring for its population.

CEPAL's program does not convince all those looking for an alternative to neoliberalism. For one thing, *cepalismo* is a decidedly broad church described by one think tank as a "widely dispersed current of thought with no clear center."[32] Fernando Leiva, a radical Chilean economist, believes that it only "comes onto the scene once the dirty work has been done by neoliberals."[33] In his view, *cepalismo* is a logical and necessary second phase to follow the "savage capitalism" of the Pinochet school, rebuilding consensus around a largely unchanged model of export-led growth.

Although this view of *cepalismo* as merely "neoliberalism with a human face," rather than a true alternative, may ring true in Chile, CEPAL's policy framework goes further than the Chilean government on crucial issues like the need for proactive industrial policies, wealth redistribution, agrarian reform, and increased rates of income tax. As a recipe for a fairer and more effective path to development, *cepalismo* is an impressive body of thought, drawing on the lessons of successful economies elsewhere and rejecting the dogma of both import substitution and the silent revolution.

The CEPAL model's main weakness is political—how to make it happen. At the global level, opponents of neoliberalism must convince the IMF, World Bank, Washington, World Trade Organization, and international markets that such a new approach can work (and works for them). Unless these external forces can at least be persuaded to give an alternative development model a chance, the international obstacles to any move to a new model will be great and perhaps insuperable.

Over the course of the 1990s, the Northern powers appeared ready to accept and promote "second-generation" reforms to rebuild the regulatory role of the state, but only when these were confined to issues such as transparency, competition policy, and other steps seen as improving the workings of the market. They were more hostile to any suggestion that governments should go further, for example, in treating foreign investors differently from local ones by requiring them to use inputs produced locally or export a certain proportion of their output. They also showed few signs of accepting the importance of wealth redistribution, preferring to talk in terms of reducing poverty, rather than inequality.

CEPAL is also unconvincing on the issue of democratization. Its economic recipe calls both for enhanced participation by a range of civil society organizations, and for an efficient state run along East Asian lines by highly qualified and impartial technocrats, free from political pressures. In countries such as Taiwan and South Korea, this was achieved through repression, as authoritarian regimes kept the work-force at arm's (or truncheon's) length from the decision-making process, yet CEPAL argues for increased participation and decentraliza-tion. But it does not explain how to prevent the acute needs and frus-trations built up under neoliberalism forcing the government into addressing immediate demands rather than the technocrats' long-term development objectives.

As the silent revolution has ground on, and awareness of its short-comings has risen among both the public and decision makers, ele-ments of the CEPAL agenda have started to be adopted in a cross-fertilization between the neostructuralist and neoliberal schools. Some authors see a "convergence" under way in the policies of more social democrat leaders like Brazil's Fernando Henrique Cardoso, or Ricardo Lagos in Chile.[34] This effort is crucial since, in their eyes, "despite the shortcomings of neostructuralism, it is the only feasible and credible alternative to neoliberalism in the present historical cir-cumstances."[35]

## IS THERE A LEFT ALTERNATIVE?

When discussing these issues, what can loosely be termed the political left tends to fall into two camps: those concerned with short-term improvements within the existing global and national economic frameworks, and those who think in the longer term and believe the existing order must be swept away and a new society built from scratch in order to achieve any lasting improvement in the lives of ordinary Latin Americans. Not surprisingly, short-term concerns are most in evi-dence among those parties and individuals with at least some interest in, and a real possibility of, coming to power in the near future. Simi-larly, short-termists are more likely to believe that achieving state power is the essential first step to any social transformation, whereas many of the proponents of grassroots alternatives remain suspicious of the state whatever its political leadership, and look instead to a strate-gy of local organization and mobilization. Among the party political Left, differences also emerge between their more rigorous intellectual supporters and professional politicians, who often seem trapped in the rhetoric of the past, appearing nonplussed when asked to propose alternatives to neoliberalism.

These debates have been played out in fairly public view in the heart of the region's largest left-wing party, Brazil's Workers Party (PT). Born out of the independent trade union movement's struggle against the military government, the PT initially adopted a strongly socialist message, declaring "A Workers' Party means a party without employers . . . we do not want to create just another party. We want a party deeply committed to eliminate one man's exploitation by another."[36]

As time wore on, and the party proved unable to build on its local victories to win power at national level, it underwent a "modernizing process" along the lines of the British Labor Party, modifying its socialist policies and toning down its rhetoric. Tarso Genro, ex-mayor of the city of Porto Alegre, a PT stronghold in the far south of Brazil, proposed a "moratorium on utopias," adding that "the Left must have the humility to realize that it lacks a socialist project capable of winning over a broad majority, of achieving hegemony over them." Other major figures in the party now refer with embarrassment to previous wish lists in which total spending proposals added up to a figure far higher than Brazil's GDP. Lula himself seems to have acknowledged the argument that Brazil's state bureaucracy is often inefficient, and that the problem of the sizable public deficit must be addressed. He recently said that he is no longer against privatization on principle, but suggested it should only be carried out where absolutely necessary.

As for the thorny question of Brazil's debt to foreign financial institutions, whereas in the 1980s Lula used to declare that it should not be paid, he now appeals to a wider audience by saying, "There are some contracts that simply must be complied with, though that doesn't mean we agree with them." Despite the change in tone, the party continues to call for radical land reform and has shown itself both radical and innovative in local government. The result is a confused public position, mixing elements of pro-market "new labor" policies with more traditionally statist policies on distributional issues such as land and social services. In 2002, Lula finally triumphed, winning the chance to put this hybrid agenda into action.

Brazil is also home to the Movimento Sem Terra (MST), or landless movement, one of the most powerful popular movements in the world.[37] Since its creation in the early 1980s, the MST has focused on the problem of landlessness, exacerbated by the rise of agro-exports under neoliberalism. It organizes the landless, whether in shantytowns or rural villages, to occupy land, and claim it under Brazil's often ignored agrarian reform laws. The MST's achievements have been extraordinary: today it has about a million members, and its actions have won nearly 50,000 square kilometers of land for its members, equivalent to half the state of Ohio or three-quarters of Ireland. Over 100,000 children now study in MST schools. The struggle for land has often been bloody—several hundred MST members have died at the hands of gunmen hired by the large landowners or local politicians.

The MST's achievements extend far beyond the acquisition of land. It has been able to recruit "hopeless cases"—drug addicts, emotionally disturbed street children, and violent criminals, and has often managed to turn them into productive, fulfilled citizens. MST settlements have become a kind of social and political laboratory, exploring alternative methods of agriculture, education, and health care that give greater priority to community involvement and the environment.

Unwilling to compromise and skeptical of electoral politics, the MST has remained fiercely independent of political parties and opted to go it alone, in the face of fierce opposition from governments, even including the relatively enlightened administration of Fernando Henrique Cardoso. It is independent from, but close to, the PT, and a PT federal government brings both opportunities and threats to the movement.

### FIGHTING FOR LAND:
### MARIA JOAQUINA DE NASCIMENTO (NAZINHA)

I'm 57 years old. I was born in Água Branca in Ceará. My father had a small plot of land. We were lucky because it had a spring, so we always had water. I was the only girl, but I had five brothers. I went to school for a short while. I had to get up, cook lunch for my parents, and then walk the four kilometres to school. I really only learned to sign my name. When I was 22 years old, I married. My husband didn't have land of his own so he worked with my father.

We all left Ceará because my father got ill. One of my brothers lived in Petrolina, so we went there. We had to buy everything, even gas for cooking. Before that we'd always used wood from the countryside. We found it strange to have to buy fuel to cook. It was difficult. I went hungry for the first time in my life in Petrolina. My husband got a job on a building site. I had seven children, but three died. My first-born died when he was eleven months old. Then I had twins, who were born dead. But the other four—three girls and a boy—survived.

We were living in Petrolina with all these problems when some lads came to the door and invited us to a meeting. They said they were from the MST and they could help us win land. We were so pleased! So we all took part in the occupation of Safra estate. We spent five months in this camp. But there wasn't enough land in Safra for all the families. So on 5 January 1996 we went with 105 other families to occupy Ouro Verde estate and that's where we won land. We were evicted once from here, on 31 January 1996. The police came and it was really frightening. But we reoccupied again, on 18 February 1996, and in the end we won the land. Everything is fine now. I've got a nice house, with a veranda. We sit out here in the evenings. It was my dream, to have a house like this. My parents had a house with a veranda. It was better than the one I've got, but I'm going to make this one as good as theirs one day. I've planted lots of trees in the garden and I've got flowers in pots. It looks like a real home.

We can grow all our food now. That's so much better. The only bill we have to pay is for the electricity—for the house and for the water pump for the grapes. We only have two crops to sell on the market—grapes and *azerola* [a tropical fruit]. They don't really bring in enough money. We still suffer, but life is so much better.

SOURCE: Sue Branford and Jan Rocha, *Cutting the Wire: The Story of the Landless Movement in Brazil*, (London, 2002), p. 100.

The MST is no utopia—some members cannot stand the harsh conditions in the settlements, and there are ideological and personal differences as in any other movement, but its impact on the lives of its members has been profound, and it has provided a different way of seeing the world to those seeking alternatives to the conventional nostra of market reform in Brazil and beyond.

The MST's approach is the antithesis of the way in which the silent revolution has been conceived and implemented: it has been developed with the participants' involvement; it has family needs as the starting point; the farmers themselves are implementers; a local market is actively being sought, and sustainability is a vital consideration in the project. Such approaches lie at the heart of many of the more radical proposals for a new Latin American development model to replace neoliberalism.

Some of the cooperative movements' thinkers see Latin America's vast network of associations as the core of a "social sector," a third force to work alongside state and private sector in humanizing the market. One such visionary is Leonidas Avila, of ICADE, a Honduran NGO working with peasant families around the country.[38] According to Avila, Honduras is particularly rich in such associations, boasting 1,600 cooperatives, with about 600,000 people (a tenth of the total population). There are also a range of community banks, trade union-based and consumer cooperatives, community shops, and mutual aid funds.

Such movements receive some help from abroad, for example, in funding from Northern NGOs committed to grassroots development or from the fair trade movement, which helps small producers of crops such as coffee and bananas by paying stable, above-market prices and contributing to community development projects.[39] In Mexico, a Latin American equivalent, *Comercio Justo*, has been launched as the first Southern-based project to certify fair trade producers.[40]

All this amounts to a rich web of economic associations—the "social economy," involving a majority of its people, whether as owners, investors, beneficiaries, or workers. It is based on the principles of cooperation, fairness, democratic participation and justice. Economically, it is almost invisible on a national scale, but it forms a "third sector" alongside the private and state sectors. "ICADE's dream is to take this very divided sector and give it political identity and voice," says Avila. "In the '70s, we demonized business—anyone who talked about it was a traitor. But we'd forgotten that the workers are also businessmen, part of the private sector." Avila's vision of *"homo gregarius"*—people immersed in (and defined by) a network of social and economic relationships—stands in sharp contrast to *homo economicus*, the lonely consumer of orthodox economic thinking, and poses a profound challenge to the guiding logic of neoliberalism.

Activists like Avila and groups like the MST are undoubtedly courageous and inspiring, but are they just utopian follies that ignore the global economic realities that must shape any national economic program? How can they scale up their ideas to a continental or global proposal? What kind of approach on crucial macroeconomic issues such as exchange rate policy, FDI, and taxation would be required for their vision to flourish and what obstacles, internal and external, would need to be overcome? What compromises need to be made with other parties or political movements in order to win backing in legislatures? Government necessarily brings hard decisions and trade-offs, which social movements or their political leaders used to being in opposition could find difficult to resolve—a PT presidency in Brazil is probably the most likely place for such a struggle to be fought out.

One of the places where activists have come together to discuss such questions is the World Social Forum, a global gathering held in the southern Brazilian city of Porto Alegre in successive Januaries from 2001 to 2003, as a radical rival to the World Economic Forum of the global business elite, normally held in Davos, Switzerland. The 2003 WSF brought together an estimated 100,000 people for a chaotic but often inspiring three days of workshops, rallies, a triumphant appearance of the newly elected Lula and (in the face of the escalating U.S.–Iraq conflict) antiwar protests. Under its general slogan of "Another world is possible," participants explored five main themes: democratic sustainable development; principles and values, human rights, diversity, and equality; media, culture, and counter-hegemony; political power, civil society, and democracy; democratic world order, the fight against militarism, and promoting peace.[41]

Participants at the WSF focused on the big picture (rights, justice, democracy) and on process (participation, citizenship, alliances, institutions, international conventions). They celebrated the vibrancy of grassroots organizations and drew inspiration from one another's stories of struggle and resistance. On economic issues, the focus of discussion was on denouncing present injustices and deciding how wealth should be distributed: there was little on ways of generating wealth in the first place—there was clearly some way to go in putting together a convincing and comprehensive alternative economic model.

In any case, it is arguable that the search for a "big idea" to replace neoliberalism is misconceived. One meeting of NGOs from all over the region concluded, "There is no one alternative for all countries; there are many. One of the reasons for the failure of adjustment is that it was imposed in an undemocratic and secret manner, without taking into account the diversity of natural and human resources in different countries."[42]

Moreover, recent research suggests that grand visions and sweeping changes can be counterproductive. Successful economies have avoided such "knock down and rebuild" approaches to the complex world of social and economic institutions. According to economist Dani Rodrik, when it comes to policy change, it seems that small is often beautiful:

> The experience with development during the last half-century reveals another striking fact: the best performing countries are those that liberalized partially and gradually. . . . All these countries unleashed the energies of their private sectors, but did so in a cautious, controlled manner. An important reason why gradualist strategies worked in the cases mentioned is that they were better tailored to preexisting institutions at home.[43]

Unfortunately, this is the exact opposite of the kind of institutional scorched-earth tactics espoused by neoliberals over the last twenty years.

## ALTERNATIVES FOR THE AMERICAS

The most ambitious attempt at creating a pan-Latin American alternative proposal has been triggered by the negotiations to set up an FTAA. Known as the Hemispheric Social Alliance, it was established at the first "People's Summit" in Santiago in 1998, which ran parallel to the official Summit of the Americas.[44] Its steering committee comprises NGO representatives from Canada, Central America, the United States, Brazil, and Mexico, as well as regional organizations such as ORIT (the Interamerican Regional Workers Organisation) and CLOC (the Latin American Peasant Congress). For the following meeting in Quebec in April 2001, the HSA published an eighty-page document (expanded and updated in December 2002), "Alternatives for the Americas," setting out a detailed *"propuesta"* for progressive reforms across the whole spectrum of economic, political, and social issues.

Two key themes run through the document: the need to subordinate economic policies to broader social and environmental goals, and to defend national sovereignty against encroachment by unaccountable bodies, be they large foreign corporations or international institutions dominated by the North.

In addition to the FTAA negotiating areas, the document covers more familiar NGO territory such as process and politics (civil society participation, respect for human rights, taking gender properly into account), opposition (to most aspects of structural adjustment), and defense of sovereignty.

The alliance of prominent Latin American movements, such as Mexico's RMALC (a national network of trade unions, peasant and environmental movements. and NGOs) with U.S. and Canadian activist groups is perhaps a mixed blessing. Although this has given the alliance access to some of the U.S. and Canadian organizations' work on issues such as investment and patent rules, it means that the document has a somewhat North American feel to it. Compared to CEPAL's work on alternative development proposals, Alternatives for the Americas underplays poverty reduction and development issues and defers to a more Northern agenda on issues such as the environment and labor rights.

However, the detail of the document shows how much thinking has moved on from the pure oppositionalism of the early 1990s. In the chapter on the role of the state, for example:

> We propose a fully democratic state, economically and socially accountable to its citizens, which radically challenges corruption at every level; a state with a qualitatively new role within the economy. We are not proposing an oversized state burdened by huge, inefficient enterprises. The number and size of public corporations is less important than the role they fulfill. Society, not only governments, should make decisions relating to industries in the public realm. . . . The goal should not be traditional protectionism, but building a state accountable to society that can implement a democratically established national development plan.[45]

The tone on foreign investment has also evolved noticeably from the anti-TNC language of earlier decades:

> Foreign investment is welcome in our countries, provided that it adheres to regulations that enforce the economic and social rights of citizens and environmental sustainability.[46]

Compared to the kinds of documents put out by Northern NGOs (which often seem to lay the blame all the world's ills at the IMF's door), Alternatives for the Americas also strikes an excellent balance between the need for reform at national and international levels. The neoliberals within Latin American finance and trade ministries must change their ways, as well as their colleagues (and often former employers) in Washington.

At times, the text is disappointingly vague in terms of providing an alternative development model it. For example, it offers little clue about where jobs, growth, and poverty reduction are likely to come from. In part this may be because it is responding to the main themes of the FTAA negotiations, such as the regulation of investment and trade, rather than broader development issues such as what kinds of jobs are needed. For example, one of the main drivers behind the alliance, Mexico's RMALC, goes a good deal further in its own documents, stressing that two key elements of any alternative economic strategy are the need to integrate or connect national production chains and strengthen the internal market.[47]

Overall, however, the work of the HSA is an important sign of the kind of serious thinking going on among civil society organizations, as they face up to the challenges posed by the failures of the silent revolution. *Alternatives for the Americas* is an evolving document, reflecting the process of debate and consensus between NGOs, unions, academics, and grassroots movements across the region that is one of its greatest strengths. As the debate over the FTAA and its economic underpinnings gathers steam, the alliance and its members are likely to forge the most coherent civil society alternative to the vision of CEPAL or the World Bank, pulling new organizations and sectors into an expanding public debate over the future direction of the continent.

## COMPARING THE ALTERNATIVES

Although the various proposals share much common ground (for example, distrust of unregulated market forces, determination to revamp the international financial institutions, the need for an enhanced role for the state, support for tax reform, and a degree of wealth distribution), there are several contentious issues that divide them:

- Some are hostile to the market as a means of organizing society while others seek to harness the creative energy of the market for society's benefit.
- Some see growth as essential to human development while others see it as evidence of excessive materialism which could destroy the environment.
- Some are hostile to foreign investment, portraying it as little more than

a continuation of the plunder begun five hundred years ago by the *conquistadores*, while others see it as an essential source of new technology and foreign exchange.

- The CEPAL model clearly commits Latin America to free trade with the North, while promoting regional integration as a platform from which to export to the rest of the world. The more radical programs also support regional integration, but more as an alternative to trade with the North, rather than as a stepping-stone. Some grassroots organizations maintain that the domestic market is what matters to the poor, and that international trade is of secondary importance.

- Some see representative democracy as an essential element, while others believe such structures will always be captured by the elites, and argue either for democracy based on grassroots organizations or for Cuban-style socialism.

Such differences partly stem from a very real dilemma for proponents of alternative economic models. How much can realistically be achieved within the current economic and political constraints in Latin America? The power of international capital, the international financial institutions, the industrialized nations, and the local business community is genuinely great, but has also been exaggerated by a Left that too often has dwelt on its own powerlessness. One of the more destructive legacies of the cruder interpretations of dependency theory is a fatalistic attitude that "nothing can change until everything changes." "In Latin America we were better at establishing the way our action had been historically limited by outside forces, than in establishing our own abilities to run our own lives," admitted one group of radical economists.[48] The challenge is to determine what margin for maneuver truly exists, avoiding the twin pitfalls of defeatism and utopianism that have historically plagued the Left.

# 9—Conclusions

When trying to assess neoliberalism's record, it is essential to set out clear criteria for judging success or failure. The central question must be: success for whom? Most coverage of the issue is strangely impersonal, remaining in the safe world of national economic variables such as inflation or GDP growth, where aspects of the neoliberal record can look more positive. Its luster rapidly dims once real people are made the focus of attention, for although the silent revolution has clearly created both winners and losers within each country and between different countries, the balance is overwhelmingly negative. A minority of the population in each country, comprising the economic and social elite, has benefited from being drawn into the global economy through the structural adjustment process, but the costs for the majority of poor Latin Americans have been extreme. In the eyes of the élite (at least until the post–Asian Crisis slump) adjustment has been a rip-roaring success; in the eyes of the poor, a disaster. As Susan George puts it:

> Some critics make the mistake of proclaiming that development has failed. It hasn't. Development as historically conceived and officially practiced has been a huge success. It sought to integrate the upper echelons, say ten to forty percent, of a given third world population into the international, westernized, consuming classes and the global market economy. This it has accomplished brilliantly.[2]

Another common feature of coverage of the silent revolution is its failure to differentiate between ends and means. The defenders of structural adjustment frequently confuse the two, arguing that a reform program is successful simply because a dozen firms have been privatized or a free trade agreement has been signed. Yet these can only be counted as successes if they further an expressed aim of adjustment, such as improving the quality of life of ordinary Latin Americans.

For both macroeconomists and poor Latin Americans, the single greatest achievement of the silent revolution has been to get inflation under control. The region's average inflation rate fell to 11 percent in 2001, from a peak of 1200 percent in the late 1980s.[3]

Despite the turmoil in world markets, inflows of foreign direct investment have proved reasonably stable, bringing in both foreign exchange and new technology in unprecedented quantities. For the region's consumers, at least those of them still with money to spend, privatization has in some cases brought about improvements in services, while trade liberalization has brought in its wake cheaper, better-quality products, both imported and produced by newly competitive local factories.

Export growth in the 1990s was unprecedented, even approaching Asian levels. Furthermore, the rising trend of regional integration is helping to diversify the region's exports away from an exclusive reliance on a limited range of natural resources.

Other changes are harder to quantify, but no less far-reaching. Driven by the breakneck pace of trade liberalization, the region's industrial culture is well on the way to abandoning its protectionist past, where success depended as much on a firm's skill in lobbying (and bribing) government officials as on the quality or price of the product.

Governments themselves have also shown some healthy changes, in many cases giving up their former penchant for acting as job creation schemes for political supporters. With the acknowledgment of the destructiveness of high inflation levels has come a newfound commitment to balancing the books. Most governments have increased their efforts to reduce their fiscal deficits, although in many cases such efforts are undermined by massive levels of debt repayments.

After gouging public spending in the 1980s, most governments have made serious efforts to increase health and education spending, leading to improvements in enrollment levels and some health indicators such as infant mortality.

Inefficient, loss-making state-run companies have been sold off (along with some perfectly good ones which could have continued to generate revenues for social spending and other purposes).

So much for the good news, for such limited gains have been achieved at enormous social and environmental cost. Latin America's growth path over the course of the twenty years of the silent revolution consists of a modest boom (1991–1997) sandwiched between two large slumps, falling far short of the growth performance under import substitution.

Structural adjustment has aggravated Latin America's existing economic failings. Just like import substitution, neoliberalism has increased inequality in the region. However, import substitution at least managed to lower the proportion of the population living below the poverty line, even as it enlarged the rich minority's slice of the cake. Structural adjustment has not even achieved this. Instead, Adam Smith's benign market forces have in practice become an "invisible fist," inflicting terrible damage on the poor. Just as during the Industrial Revolution, which spawned the classical school of economics, the unregulated play of market forces has favored the rich and squeezed the poor, sweeping away many of the limited gains of job security and a threadbare welfare state achieved by fifty years of import substitution and political pressure.

The growth promised by neoliberalism has never reached high enough levels to help the poor. The economy grew by 52 percent between 1980 and 2000,[4] but population grew by 44 percent,[5] and even that small per capita rise was wiped out by increasing inequality. By 1999, 75 million more Latin Americans had slipped below the poverty line since 1980, bringing the total to 44 percent of the population, over 200 million people.[6]

The deterioration in the quality of life is as much psychological as material, but no less painful for that. Adjustment-driven policies of "flexibilization" have brought new levels of anxiety into millions of lives by generating more insecure, part-time or informal sector jobs, yet neoliberal pundits from Buenos Aires to Washington are still arguing that "labor deregulation" holds the key to growth and poverty reduction.

Changes in the labor market have placed even greater burdens on women, who now have to juggle the increased demands of workplace and home, while a process of disintegration is threatening their families and communities and jeopardizing the well-being and productive potential of the next generation. Crime and social disintegration have become the principal cause for public concern in many Latin American societies.

In the countryside, peasant farmers find credit unobtainable and agrarian reform thrown into reverse, as trade liberalization floods local markets with cheap food imports. Millions of farmers will in time be forced off the land to swell the ranks of the dispossessed in the shantytowns. The advent of adjustment has ratcheted up Latin America's rate of deforestation and other pressures on an increasingly fragile environment.

Investment has been the chief casualty of the silent revolution, as governments have abandoned fifty years of development based on public investment and the local private sector has refused to pick up the slack. Even with the boom in FDI, by the late 1990s, the largest economies in the region all had lower levels of investment than in 1980.[7] The slump of the 1980s in particular took a large bite out of Latin America's stock of investment, leaving a backlog of crumbling infrastructure and battered people that will take decades to repair.

In the 1990s, Latin America's thirst for short-term foreign capital inflows with which to ease the pain of adjustment proved disastrous. Increased reliance on "hot money" created new levels of instability, whereby external events such as the Asia crisis of 1997/8, or changes in U.S. interest rates, or internal events such as political division, could start a financial panic and produce sudden and deep crises, often threatening the collapse of entire banking systems. Crises in Mexico (1995), Brazil (1999), and Argentina (2002) each ratcheted up the social cost of adjustment and added new burdens as governments bailed out the banks or took on new loans to prevent the economy from coming to a complete standstill. Stock markets—flavor of the month in the early 1990s—also proved a fickle source of finance, much of which dried up after 1995.

Overall, renewed net inflows of capital from 1991 had seemed to signal a change in the region's fortunes, but they sank to zero in 1999–2001 and then went negative in 2002, suggesting that, even as it paid the price in terms of increased economic instability, Latin America was failing to reap the promised rewards of financial globalization.

Between them, the international financial institutions, Western governments, commercial banks, and foreign investors, in alliance with local policy makers, have driven the region at high speed down a developmental blind alley. Abundant natural resources and cheap labor are no longer enough to guarantee sustained export-led growth in today's world (if indeed these ever were). Successfully industrializing countries like Taiwan and South Korea break into computers, not kiwi fruit, yet neoliberalism has ignored the lessons offered by the Asian tigers. Governments show little interest in R&D and have failed to develop national industries and know-how through a more discriminating and strategic engagement with foreign companies.

The early 1990s seemed to mark the high point of the silent revolution. Successful attacks on inflation, the "end of history" psychology engendered by the fall of the Communist bloc and the start of the export boom promised a brighter future for the region and made free market presidents electable. By the early years of the new century, the neoliberal tide appeared to be on the wane. After two decades of poor economic performance, politicians who claimed that the promised land of export-led growth and trickle down economics still lay just around the corner were fast losing credibility. Popular opposition to the excesses of bungled and corrupt privatization processes was growing.

The pure draught of Washington Consensus deregulation became increasingly laced with doses of CEPAL-style thinking, as some governments sought to rebuild institutions, take poverty and inequality seriously, and sought to involve civil society in economic planning. Some observers even argued that the differences on economic policy between different governments had become so great that one could barely speak any longer of the existence of a single coherent "silent revolution." Sharp-eyed readers will have noticed the change in this book's subtitle from the first edition: it now reads "The Rise *and Crisis* of Market Economics in Latin America."

The time was ripe for a paradigm shift, but there were good reasons for caution. Many Latin American governments continued to insist on more or less unreconstructed versions of the neoliberal handbook of liberalization, deregulation, and austerity. Just as important, while both the weight of evidence and intellectual momentum may lay with the critics of the silent revolution, Latin America's hegemonic battles do not take place in isolation. When the simple model of the Washington Consensus was seen to fail, the World Bank and others added layer upon layer of new conditions and reforms—property rights, judicial reform, anti-corruption, corporate governance, environmental protection, administrative decentralization, and much more.

This increasingly cumbersome and incoherent vision may seem ripe for the intellectual scaffold, but the danger is that the straitjacket of external constraints imposed by the institutions and processes of globalization will prevent Latin American policy makers from seeking new, more successful paths to development. The baleful influence of the IMF and World Bank will continue to promote policies long since abandoned by their rich sponsors. Any attempt to depart from the neoliberal road will be made more difficult by the growing globalization of the world economy. NAFTA and the WTO agreements greatly reduce the ability of signatory governments to pursue a national industrial or development policy, obliging them to give "equal treatment" to supremely unequal players—local industries and giant transnational corporations.

Such pressures could help explain why there is as yet no new model waiting in the wings, as there has been when other economic orthodoxies entered into periods of self-doubt and disintegration. As the battle over the heresies of the World Development Report in 2000 demonstrated, the "intellectual-financial complex" of the financial institutions acts as a powerful obstacle to new thinking.

Barring a sea change in the world economic order, policy makers in Latin America will have to work within the constraints imposed by the global economy. The current rounds of negotiations at both the WTO and the FTAA will be the test of which is winning the political battle— the logic of a humanized, people-centered approach to the market, or the economic Darwinism of the silent revolution. Only then will it become clear if the rising public concern at the negative impacts of globalization expressed through the Jubilee 2000 movement, the successful campaign against the proposed Multilateral Agreement on Investment in 1998, the street protests at the 1999 WTO ministerial in Seattle and the U.K.'s burgeoning "trade justice movement" are winning the struggle for politicians' minds as well as activists' hearts.[8]

## THE WAY FORWARD

Ever since independence, Latin American governments and planners have veered between state and market in search of the elusive path to long-term development. The transformation of the world economy in the last thirty years may have destroyed full-blown central planning as a viable economic model, but the crude recipes of the free-marketeers have failed to create the foundations for long-term success in the new world order. Rather, neoliberalism is in danger of locking Latin America into a model of export-led growth based on raw materials and cheap labor, leading to growing impoverishment and irrelevance within the global economy.

If neoliberalism has failed most Latin Americans, what realistic alternatives are there? Although supporters of the silent revolution routinely dismiss their critics as economic dinosaurs bereft of alternative ideas, there is already a rich debate over the ingredients for building a better economic model for the region. A clear-sighted study of the policies behind the success of the Asian NICs; the work of CEPAL and the spectrum of ideas grouped together under the heading "neostructuralism"; and the calls for a more visionary approach from grassroots organizations throughout the continent provide good initial starting points for debating and constructing a more effective and just development model. Such a model would need to move away from the silent revolution's overreliance on exports as panacea and focus on the domestic economy, building linkages between sectors, upgrading skills and technology and building on Latin America's rich web of associative structures such as cooperatives to ensure that growth benefits the poor.

A new model should also recognize that Latin America's traditional preference for "slash and burn" shifts in policy making may not be the best approach. As Dani Rodrik argues, partial and gradual reforms have often worked better because they are sensitive to the institutional and political peculiarities of particular countries.[9]

There seems little doubt that if the region is to achieve long-term development, it must find a way of combining economic growth with a far higher degree of social and economic equality. This combination of "growth with equity" has always eluded Latin America, but other countries have shown not only that it is possible, but that the two are mutually reinforcing: equal societies tend to grow faster than unequal ones.[10] Growth with inequality leads to political instability, social breakdown, and a substandard workforce, while seeking equity without ensuring growth is a recipe for political conflict and eventual collapse.

The Achilles' heel of all attempts to transform the neoliberal model into one that works for growth with equity is the difficulty of building a sufficiently powerful political coalition behind the movement for change. Latin America's silent revolution required the catastrophe of the debt crisis and the unceasing arm-twisting of the international financial institutions to bring it about, and history suggests that another such trauma will be required to achieve the degree of change in economic and political thinking that is of life and death importance to the poor of Latin America. For them, the trauma is already happening, but they may have to wait until it touches the elites within the region and powerful interests abroad before a definitive shift can take place. But is it really too much to ask that those currently in charge of the region's destiny, whether they be Latin American, North American, European, or Japanese, learn from history and make the necessary changes before the next disaster occurs?

# Country-by-Country Guide to the Latin American Economy, 1982-2002

SOURCES FOR STATISTICAL TABLES: CEPAL (various publications and years); Economist Intelligence Unit

SOURCES FOR COUNTRY PROFILES: CEPAL, Economist Intelligence Unit Country Profiles and Country Reports, *Silent Revolution* text.

| ARGENTINA | | GROSS (%) | EXPORTS | IMPORTS | NRT | INF | WAGES |
|---|---|---|---|---|---|---|---|
| POPULATION (1999): | 1982 | -6.8 | 7622 | 4859 | -3030 | 210 | 80 |
| 36.6 million | 83 | 0.7 | 7838 | 4120 | -5429 | 434 | 101 |
| GDP PER CAPITA | 84 | 0.7 | 8101 | 4119 | -3050 | 688 | 127 |
| (2000): $7,303 | 85 | -6.1 | 8396 | 3518 | -3321 | 385 | 108 |
| | 86 | 6.2 | 6852 | 4406 | -2448 | 82 | 108 |
| MAIN EXPORTS: | 87 | 1.3 | 6360 | 5343 | -2162 | 175 | 97 |
| oil, cereals, oilseeds, | 88 | -3.3 | 9134 | 4892 | -1697 | 388 | 94 |
| motor vehicles | 89 | -7.4 | 9573 | 3864 | -6465 | 4923 | 76 |
| KEY: GDP per capita (1980 US$); | 90 | -1.3 | 12354 | 3726 | -5573 | 1344 | 79 |
| Growth of GDP per capita (%); | 91 | 7.6 | 11972 | 7400 | -959 | 84 | 81 |
| Exports FOB (US$ millions); | 92 | 8.2 | 12235 | 13795 | 6402 | 18 | 102[1] |
| Imports FOB (US$ millions); | 93 | 4.5 | 13269 | 15633 | 9416 | 7 | 100 |
| Annual inflation (%); | 94 | 4.4 | 16023 | 20162 | 8145 | 4 | 101 |
| Index of average real wages | 95 | -4.1 | 21161 | 18804 | 447 | 2 | 100 |
| in manufacturing industry | 96 | 4.1 | 24034 | 22283 | 5259 | 0 | 100 |
| (1980 = 100 from 1982–91; | 97 | 6.6 | 26431 | 28554 | 9392 | 0 | 99 |
| 1995 = 100 from 1992–2001). | 98 | 2.5 | 26434 | 29448 | 10653 | 1 | 99 |
| | 99 | -4.6 | 27751 | 32698 | 5768 | -2 | 100 |
| | 00 | -2.0 | 31092 | 32822 | 1055 | -1 | 102 |
| * estimate | 01 | -5.6 | 30846 | 27360 | -15749 | -2 | 100 |
| | 02* | -12.1 | 29322 | 13742 | -19780 | 41 | 85 |

ARGENTINA: In 2003, Argentina entered its fifth consecutive year of recession and one of the worst peacetime economic collapses in recorded history. The latest collapse marked the low point in the continent's most spectacular economic roller-coaster ride, which over the previous twenty years had taken it through war, hyperinflation, and spectacular growth rates in the early 1990s—a time when Argentina was portrayed as the poster child of the silent revolution.

The onset of the debt crisis in 1982 coincided with the Falklands/Malvinas war and the subsequent fall of the military junta that had ruled the country since 1976. The military's version of free market reform had already devastated the economy. The civilian government of Raúl Alfonsín tried to avoid giving in to IMF pressure by launching the heterodox "*Austral* plan." Its subsequent hyperinflationary collapse drove Alfonsín back to negotiations with the Fund and World Bank, eventually resulting in substantial loans in 1992 and 1993.

In 1989 the Peronist candidate Carlos Saúl Menem won the presidency and undertook a profound neoliberal adjustment program involving privatization, trade liberalization, and binding the currency rigidly to the U.S. dollar in the so-called currency board system. Public utilities and state-owned enterprises were largely sold off, and much of the banking and manufacturing sectors passed into foreign ownership. The program succeeded in virtually eradicating inflation, and led to an economic boom in the first years of the 1990s. Argentina's membership of the

| **BOLIVIA** | | GROSS (%) | EXPORTS | IMPORTS | NRT | INF | WAGES |
|---|---|---|---|---|---|---|---|
| **POPULATION (1999):** | 1982 | -5.4 | 828 | 496 | -181 | 297 | - |
| | 1983 | -9.0 | 755 | 496 | -117 | 329 | 55 |
| **8.1 million** | 1984 | -3.5 | 724 | 412 | -56 | 2177 | 46 |
| **GDP PER CAPITA** | 1985 | -4.4 | 623 | 463 | -66 | 8171 | 18 |
| **(2000): $951** | 1986 | -5.5 | 546 | 597 | 274 | 66 | 17 |
| **MAIN EXPORTS:** | 1987 | 0.1 | 519 | 646 | 201 | 11 | 20 |
| **soy, zinc, gold** | 1988 | 0.5 | 543 | 591 | 120 | 22 | 21 |
| | 1989 | 0.7 | 724 | 730 | 40 | 17 | 19 |
| KEY: GDP per capita (1980 US$); | 1990 | 2.1 | 831 | 776 | 111 | 18 | 17 |
| Growth of GDP per capita (%); | 1991 | 2.1 | 760 | 804 | 202 | 15 | 27 |
| Exports FOB (US$ millions); | 1992 | -0.7 | 608 | 1041 | 377 | 11 | 86[2] |
| Imports FOB (US$ millions); Net | 1993 | 1.7 | 716 | 1112 | 200 | 9 | 91 |
| Resource Transfers (negative | 1994 | 2.3 | 985 | 1122 | 46 | 9 | 99 |
| figures indicate net outflows) | 1995 | 2.2 | 1041 | 1224 | 250 | 13 | 100 |
| (US$ millions); Annual inflation | 1996 | 2.0 | 1132 | 1368 | 459 | 8 | 99 |
| (%); Real urban minimum wage | 1997 | 2.4 | 1166 | 1645 | 433 | 7 | 105 |
| (1980 = 100 from 1982–91; | 1998 | 2.6 | 1104 | 1759 | 638 | 4 | 108 |
| 1995 = 100 from 1992–2001). | 1999 | -2.0 | 1310 | 1989 | 324 | 3 | 114 |
| | 2000 | 0.1 | 1470 | 2078 | 182 | 3 | 115 |
| * estimate | 2001 | -0.9 | 1521 | 1996 | 49 | 1 | 119 |
| | 2002* | -0.2 | 1463 | 2051 | 98 | 2 | 122 |

Mercosur Regional Trade Agreement with Brazil, Uruguay, and Paraguay has been an important source of export growth, especially of manufactured goods to the large Brazilian market.

A Brady Plan debt restructuring in 1993 restored Argentina's access to foreign loans, and the foreign debt once again began to rise, but low domestic savings rates, a deteriorating fiscal position (caused in part by the mounting costs of pension reform and debt service), and the straitjacket of the currency board system left the country highly vulnerable to the changing moods of the international capital markets. Fallout from the Mexican crisis of 1994 and Brazil's devaluation in 1999 prompted sharp recessions in 1995 and 1999.

In 1999 the Peronists lost the election to a new center-left Alliance coalition, led by Fernando de la Rúa. While stressing the need to pay more attention to social issues, the new president tried to stick with the fixed exchange rate. However, the deteriorating fiscal situation, the overvalued dollar, and backhanded efforts to tinker with the currency board led to a meltdown in 2001. De la Rua resigned after street protests in which twenty-seven people died. After an interim government defaulted on external debts, the incoming government of Eduardo Duhalde scrapped the currency board and devalued. By late 2002, 58 percent (21 million) of the population were living below the official poverty line, while 28 percent (10 million) are classified as "indigent," earning too little even to cover their families' food requirements. In January 2003, the IMF agreed a stopgap loan in exchange for promises of further spending cuts from the Duhalde government.

BOLIVIA: After a century and a half of almost continuous political unrest and a record number of coups, Bolivia has had an elected government since 1982. The new civilian government came to power just as the debt crisis broke, presiding over a spectacular economic collapse from 1982 to 1985. In 1985 a new government took power and launched the "New Economic Policy," a fierce structural adjustment program (the first introduced in Latin America by a democratic government) to combat hyperinflation (over 8,000 percent in 1985) designed with World Bank support. The NEP reduced inflation to 11 percent within two years. The architect of the NEP, Planning Minister Gonzalo Sánchez de Lozada, was subsequently elected president in 1993, and introduced further adjustment measures. Under an innovative privatization program from 1995 to 1997, a 50 percent stake in state companies was given to private companies in exchange for promises of new investment worth $1.67 billion, rather than cash; the remaining 50 percent was used to pump prime the new private pension fund system. The state oil company YPFB was fully privatized by 2000, leading to new funds for investment, attracted by new finds, especially of gas. A new 3000-kilomer gas pipeline built to take gas to Brazil should quadruple gas exports by 2004.

The human cost of the NEP was deepened when the tin market crashed in October 1985. Tin had historically been Bolivia's main export. With state protection removed, the tin mines were largely shut down, causing great hardship in the towns of the Bolivian *altiplano*. Bolivia now suffers from a dual economy, with most growth and innovation taking place in the eastern lowlands, rather than the abandoned and poverty-stricken highlands. Public sector employment fell from 26 percent of the workforce in 1985 to 12 percent in 1996.

Trade with Mercosur countries increased when Bolivia became an associate member in 1997. Mercosur now accounts for half of Bolivia's trade deficit as goods from Brazil and Argentina have flooded in,

while export growth remained sluggish. GDP stagnated from 1999 to 2002. As a result, Bolivia remains addicted to foreign borrowing, and indebtedness remains a major burden on the economy. In 1998 and 2000, Bolivia won two debt relief deals under the World Bank's Heavily Indebted Poor Country (HIPC) initiative.

| BRAZIL | | GROSS (%) | EXPORTS | IMPORTS | NRT | INF | WAGES |
|---|---|---|---|---|---|---|---|
| POPULATION (1999): | 1982 | -1.4 | 20172 | 19395 | -2376 | 98 | 107 |
| 163.9 million | 1983 | -4.5 | 21906 | 15434 | -6060 | 179 | 94 |
| GDP PER CAPITA | 1984 | 3.4 | 27001 | 13915 | -6133 | 203 | 97 |
| (2000): $4,348 | 1985 | 5.9 | 25634 | 13168 | -11414 | 239 | 120 |
| | 1986 | 5.9 | 22348 | 14044 | -9056 | 59 | 137 |
| MAIN EXPORTS: | 1987 | 1.6 | 26210 | 15052 | -6747 | 395 | 128 |
| transport equipment, | 1988 | -2.0 | 33773 | 14605 | -14545 | 993 | 138 |
| metallurgical products, | 1989 | 1.4 | 34375 | 18263 | -11854 | 1864 | 149 |
| soy products | 1990 | -6.1 | 31408 | 20661 | -6559 | 1585 | 131 |
| | 1991 | -0.8 | 31620 | 21041 | -8012 | 475 | 125 |
| KEY: GDP per capita (1980 US$); | 1992 | -1.8 | 35793 | 20554 | 584 | 1149 | 87[3] |
| Growth of GDP per capita (%); | 1993 | 3.0 | 39630 | 25301 | -1714 | 2489 | 96 |
| Exports FOB (US$ millions); | 1994 | 4.7 | 44102 | 33241 | -896 | 929 | 96 |
| Imports FOB (US$ millions); Net | 1995 | 2.7 | 46506 | 49663 | 19599 | 22 | 100 |
| Resource Transfers (negative | 1996 | 1.1 | 47852 | 53304 | 19743 | 10 | 108 |
| figures indicate net outflows) | 1997 | 1.7 | 53187 | 59842 | 7664 | 5 | 111 |
| (US$ millions); Annual inflation | 1998 | -1.2 | 51140 | 57733 | 7291 | 2 | 111 |
| (%); Index of average real wages | 1999 | -0.3 | 55205 | 63443 | -1250 | 9 | 106 |
| in manufacturing in Sao Paulo | 2000 | 2.6 | 64469 | 72774 | 4522 | 6 | 105 |
| (1980 = 100 from 1982–91; | 2001 | 0.2 | 67545 | 72652 | 6776 | 8 | 100 |
| 1995 = 100 from 1992–2001). | 2002* | 0.2 | 69567 | 62138 | -9956 | 11 | 97 |
| * estimate | | | | | | | |

BRAZIL: Brazil is the economic giant of Latin America, with one-third of its people and GDP. It has the third world's largest foreign debt ($230 billion in 2001) and is the most unequal society in Latin America.

As the main winner under import substitution, perhaps it is not surprising that Brazil was initially reluctant to join the neoliberal party. Import substitution had given Brazil a large and diversified indus-

trial sector that was also a powerful exporter. It therefore had more to lose from blanket trade liberalization and was more determined to find alternative ways out of the 1980s malaise. From 1986 to 1991, it tried five stabilization plans, involving the introduction of four new currencies, without success.

The 1990s saw successive governments attempt to pursue market reforms. Trade liberalization was introduced by Fernando Collor de Melo in 1990, but a fuller attempt at structural adjustment had to wait until Fernando Henrique Cardoso's *Real* plan of 1994. The plan, which repeated Argentina's trick of running an overvalued currency to curb inflation while trying to cut back on the fiscal deficit, had a spectacular initial success, winning international acclaim (and investment) by bringing inflation down from 50 percent a month to less than 2 percent. It also won Cardoso the presidency in October 1994, followed by a second term in 1998. As president, Cardoso pushed for further deregulation and privatization.

However, Cardoso's plans for deregulation of the economy faced stiff resistance at home, and his powers to impose his program were constrained by the new decentralizing constitution of 1988. The fierce domestic debate, along with Cardoso's ability as a late entrant to learn some of the lessons from other countries' experiences, led to a more cautious brand of reform, with greater emphasis on state regulation of the private sector and a more prominent role for Brazil's sizeable private sector. For example, whereas banks passed entirely into foreign hands in many other countries, by 2002 Brazil's banking sector was 40 percent state-owned, 40 percent in the hands of domestic capital, and only a fifth was controlled by overseas interests.

Stabilization brought relief from hyperinflation, but relatively poor results in terms of growth, which averaged 2.4 percent from 1995 to 2001. Exports also remained sluggish, hit by problems such as high labor costs and red tape, low productivity and prices, and Brazil's historical inability to educate its workforce. Other underlying problems also weakened the economy, notably a stubbornly low savings rate (Brazil's elite is particularly averse to paying taxes) and the difficulty of curbing state spending, for example, through reform of Brazil's lopsided state pensions system.

Slow progress on reform, coupled with this continued reliance on international capital markets, left the country vulnerable during the crisis of confidence in "emerging markets" that began in Asia in 1997, spreading to Russia and then Brazil in 1998. A massive $42 billion IMF rescue package served only to delay the day of reckoning, and in January 1999, Brazil was forced into a large devaluation of the Real. While unemployment rose and wages fell, the feared relapse into hyperinflation failed to materialize, and Brazil returned to low positive growth rates faster than expected.

In 2002, the IMF stepped in with a further $30 billion loan, as markets grew nervous at the prospect of a victory for the Workers Party candidate, Lula, in the presidential elections. Lula won, but promised to keep up debt service payments, which accounted for over 90 percent of the country's exports, and to stick to strict IMF spending targets. Observers predicted a rocky ride for his attempt to satisfy both the markets and the pent up demands for social and economic justice from his supporters.

CHILE: Chile, which became the jewel in neoliberalism's crown, began the 1980s with Latin America's most spectacular collapse. Per capita GDP fell by over 14 percent in 1982, precipitating a bank crash and forcing General Pinochet to renationalize a large part of the financial sector.

Thereafter it became a model IMF customer, successfully completing numerous Fund and World Bank structural adjustment programs in the 1980s. After the crash of 1982, the regime moderated the extreme monetarism of the "Chicago Boys" in favor of a more pragmatic pursuit of export-led growth. Trade liberalization, a high level of internal savings and investment and Chile's abundant natural wealth have enabled it to increase exports rapidly since 1985, diversifying away from its dependence on copper to a range of natural-resource based exports such as fishmeal, fresh fruit, and forestry products. Chile bucked the neoliberal trend on capital flows, opting for a more cautious opening up to foreign investment and using capital controls to deter short-term speculative flows in favor of longer term direct investment. High levels of per capita growth from 1984 onward have made

Chile into the envy of other Latin American governments.

Chile was also one of the last Latin American countries to return to democracy. After seventeen years of the Pinochet dictatorship, a Christian Democrat/Socialist Party coalition took office in 1990, and has been in power ever since. It largely continued the previous economic program, but used the level of anti-Pinochet consensus and impressive growth rates to persuade the elite (which had become massively wealthy under Pinochet) to accept a limited increase in taxation.

This enabled the governments of Patricio Aylwin, Eduardo Frei, and Ricardo Lagos to run a fiscal surplus while increasing social spending on health, education, and poverty relief with impressive results.

| CHILE | | GROSS (%) | EXPORTS | IMPORTS | NRT | INF | WAGES |
|---|---|---|---|---|---|---|---|
| POPULATION (1999): | 1982 | -14.5 | 3706 | 3643 | -889 | 21 | 109 |
| 15.1 million | 1983 | -2.2 | 3831 | 2845 | -1117 | 24 | 97 |
| GDP PER CAPITA | 1984 | 4.3 | 3651 | 3288 | 240 | 23 | 97 |
| (2000): $5,309 | 1985 | 0.7 | 3804 | 2920 | -661 | 26 | 94 |
| | 1986 | 3.7 | 4191 | 3099 | -958 | 17 | 95 |
| MAIN EXPORTS: | 1987 | 3.9 | 5224 | 3994 | -696 | 21 | 95 |
| copper, fruits and | 1988 | 5.7 | 7052 | 4833 | -811 | 13 | 101 |
| vegetables, fish, | 1989 | 8.0 | 8080 | 6502 | -432 | 21 | 103 |
| wood products | 1990 | 0.3 | 8373 | 7089 | 1264 | 27 | 105 |
| | 1991 | 4.1 | 8929 | 7354 | -401 | 19 | 110 |
| KEY: GDP per capita (1980 US$); | 1992 | 9.1 | 10007 | 9285 | 1421 | 13 | 89⁴ |
| Growth of GDP per capita (%); | 1993 | 4.8 | 9196 | 10187 | 1070 | 12 | 92 |
| Exports FOB (US$ millions); | 1994 | 3.4 | 11604 | 10872 | 2004 | 9 | 96 |
| Imports FOB (US$ millions); | 1995 | 7.5 | 16024 | 14642 | -626 | 8 | 100 |
| Net Resource Transfers | 1996 | 5.4 | 15405 | 16496 | 1748 | 7 | 104 |
| (negative figures indicate net | 1997 | 5.3 | 16663 | 18220 | 4374 | 6 | 107 |
| outflows) (US$ millions); Annual | 1998 | 1.9 | 14829 | 17346 | -39 | 5 | 110 |
| inflation (%); Index of average | 1999 | -2.0 | 19406 | 18056 | -2575 | 2 | 112 |
| real non-agricultural wages | 2000 | 3.1 | 22971 | 21702 | -1386 | 5 | 114 |
| (1980 = 100 from 1982–91; | 2001 | 1.6 | 22315 | 21221 | -2112 | 3 | 116 |
| 1995 = 100 from 1992–2001). | | | | | | | |
| ⁎ estimate | 2002⁎ | 0.6 | 21870 | 20721 | -1319 | 3 | 118 |

Education spending doubled in real terms from 1994 to 2000, while the proportion of Chileans living in poverty more than halved between 1987 and 1998, and extreme poverty fell by two-thirds.

In 1996 Chile reached an Association Agreement with Mercosur, phasing out tariffs over a ten year period, but most of its trade continues to be with the United States and Japan. In 2002, Chile signed a long-delayed free trade agreement with the United States, phasing out all tariffs over a twelve-year period.

Average growth fell from 8.7 percent p.a. in 1991–1995, to a still strong 4.6 percent in 1996–2000, with further stagnation in 2001–2002, due largely to less favorable prices for its exports. Chile has generated a higher level of domestic sav-ings than other Latin American countries, making it less dependent on international capital markets.

Despite the macroeconomic and poverty reduction success story, adjustment under Pinochet radically increased inequality, something which the return to democracy has done little to redress. Unemployment remains obstinately high at around 10 percent of the workforce, and wages have failed to keep up with overall growth. Although there are several other long-term weaknesses and numerous hidden costs to the model, Chile is the nearest thing to a Latin American neoliberal success story and appears to have better medium-term prospects than most other countries in the region.

| COLOMBIA | | GROSS (%) | EXPORTS | IMPORTS | NRT | INF | WAGES |
|---|---|---|---|---|---|---|---|
| POPULATION (1999): | 1982 | -1.1 | 3113 | 5358 | 1231 | 24 | 105 |
| 41.6 million | 1983 | -0.3 | 2970 | 4464 | 7 | 17 | 110 |
| GDP PER CAPITA | 1984 | 1.6 | 4273 | 4027 | -480 | 18 | 119 |
| (2000): $2,287 | 1985 | 0.7 | 3650 | 3673 | 387 | 22 | 115 |
| | 1986 | 4.8 | 5331 | 3409 | -847 | 21 | 120 |
| MAIN EXPORTS: | 1987 | 3.7 | 5661 | 3793 | -1910 | 24 | 119 |
| oil and gas, | 1988 | 2.3 | 5343 | 4516 | -1344 | 28 | 118 |
| chemicals, fruits and | 1989 | 1.7 | 6031 | 4557 | -1670 | 26 | 119 |
| vegetables, coffee | 1990 | 2.2 | 7079 | 5108 | -2216 | 32 | 113 |
| | 1991 | 0.2 | 7507 | 4548 | -2527 | 27 | 115 |
| KEY: GDP per capita (1980 US$); | 1992 | 1.7 | 7263 | 6030 | -1648 | 25 | 94[5] |
| Growth of GDP per capita (%); | 1993 | 2.4 | 7429 | 9086 | 784 | 23 | 98 |
| Exports FOB (US$ millions); | | | | | | | |
| Imports FOB (US$ millions); | 1994 | 3.8 | 9059 | 11085 | 2414 | 23 | 97 |
| Net Resource Transfers | 1995 | 2.9 | 10527 | 13166 | 2994 | 20 | 100 |
| (negative figures indicate | 1996 | 0.0 | 10948 | 13091 | 4414 | 22 | 102 |
| net outflows) (US$ millions); | 1997 | 1.4 | 12057 | 14771 | 3805 | 18 | 104 |
| Annual inflation (%); Average | 1998 | -1.1 | 11454 | 14006 | 2070 | 17 | 103 |
| industrial real wages | 1999 | -5.6 | 13895 | 13396 | -2343 | 9 | 109 |
| (1980 = 100 from 1982–91; | 2000 | 0.4 | 15668 | 14399 | -2069 | 9 | 113 |
| 1995 = 100 from 1992–2001). | 2001 | -0.4 | 14971 | 15844 | 6 | 8 | 114 |
| * estimate | 2002* | -0.1 | 14568 | 15540 | -689 | 7 | 118 |

COLOMBIA: The Colombian economy is something of a paradox. Whereas the country is best known for its unstable political cocktail of drugs, guerrilla wars, and human rights abuses, the economy was the most stable in Latin America during the 1980s, avoiding Chile's wild peaks and troughs in achieving a combination of steady per capita growth and low inflation. As the rest of the continent stabilized to some extent in the 1990s, Colombia once again proved the exception, going into serious decline from mid-decade and finally succumbing to the need for an IMF program in December 1999.

Like Chile, Colombia's growth has been based on natural-resource based exports. In recent years its previous dependence on coffee (it is the second-largest world producer

after Brazil) has been reduced thanks to spectacular finds of oil and coal. In 1990 oil replaced coffee as its major export.

Unlike Chile, Colombia also managed to reduce inequality in the 1980s, while pursuing export-led growth. The roots of these achievements lay in its more consistent effort at poverty eradication, involving regular increases in the real minimum wage. However, an accelerated adjustment process in the early 1990s has since reversed this tendency, leading to an increase in both inequality and urban poverty. Unemployment had risen to over 16 percent by the end of the decade (compared to 9 percent in 1994)—one of the highest rates in Latin America.

Colombia, like Brazil, has proved a cautious reformer, opting to defend its local

| COSTA RICA | | GROSS (%) | EXPORTS | IMPORTS | NRT | INF | WAGES |
|---|---|---|---|---|---|---|---|
| POPULATION (1999): | 1982 | -9.7 | 869 | 805 | 26 | 82 | 71 |
| 3.9 million | 1983 | 0.0 | 853 | 896 | 39 | 11 | 79 |
| GDP PER CAPITA | 1984 | 5.1 | 997 | 993 | -108 | 17 | 85 |
| (2000): $3,685 | 1985 | -1.7 | 939 | 1001 | 80 | 11 | 92 |
| | 1986 | 1.8 | 1085 | 1045 | 11 | 15 | 98 |
| MAIN EXPORTS: | 1987 | 1.6 | 1107 | 1245 | 184 | 16 | 89 |
| maquila products, | 1988 | 0.4 | 1181 | 1279 | 284 | 25 | 85 |
| bananas, coffee | 1989 | 2.6 | 1333 | 1572 | 333 | 10 | 85 |
| KEY: GDP per capita (1980 US$); | 1990 | 0.7 | 1354 | 1797 | 119 | 27 | 87 |
| Growth of GDP per capita (%); | 1991 | -0.4 | 1491 | 1698 | 328 | 25 | 83 |
| Exports FOB (US$ millions); | 1992 | 5.4 | 2724 | 2212 | 330 | 17 | 89[6] |
| Imports FOB (US$ millions); | 1993 | 3.8 | 2625 | 3274 | 464 | 9 | 98 |
| Net Resource Transfers | 1994 | 1.5 | 2882 | 3506 | 273 | 20 | 99 |
| (negative figures indicate | 1995 | 1.0 | 3482 | 3804 | 311 | 23 | 100 |
| net outflows) (US$ millions); | 1996 | -1.9 | 3774 | 4023 | 2 | 14 | 98 |
| Annual inflation (%); | 1997 | 2.7 | 4350 | 4703 | 448 | 11 | 99 |
| Average real wages within | 1998 | 5.6 | 5541 | 5937 | -97 | 12 | 104 |
| social se curity System | 1999 | 5.4 | 8205 | 7183 | -660 | 10 | 109 |
| (1980 = 100 from 1982–91; | 2000 | -0.1 | 7748 | 7295 | -698 | 10 | 110 |
| 1995 = 100 from 1992–2001). | 2001 | -1.2 | 6820 | 6911 | -43 | 11 | 112 |
| • estimate | 2002* | 0.7 | 7158 | 7796 | 568 | 10 | 113 |

private sector. Initially wary of trade liberalization, from the early 1990s, it introduced a program of tariff reductions. Privatization, too, has been a more careful affair than in gung-ho exercises in Argentina and Peru, with more of the sales going to local capital.

From the mid-1990s, Colombia's reputation for careful economic management and stability took a battering as political chaos finally took its toll. The fiscal deficit and public debt rose, pushing up interest rates and hitting growth, while the drug trade and political violence sapped confidence.

COSTA RICA: Costa Rica is an island of calm in the turbulent seas of Central American politics. In 1949 it took the inspired step of abolishing the armed forces, opening the way to three decades of peace and growth, accompanied by the creation of the nearest thing to a welfare state in Central America. When it comes to structural adjustment, Costa Rica has gone for a pick-and-mix approach, pursuing trade liberalization and foreign investment, but proving a reluctant privatizer (e.g.. on telecoms and energy) and a defender of a strong state role in economic management.

In the 1970s, heavy government borrowing ran up one of Latin America's largest foreign debts per capita, laying it open to outside pressure when the debt crisis broke in 1982. Costa Rica became one of the IMF and World Bank's most faithful customers, with numerous loans running right through to the mid-1990s, all attempting to push the country along the structural adjustment path of trade liberalization, privatization, and erosion of the welfare state. However, there has been

political and public resistance, most recently the public's rejection of government proposals for energy reform in early 2000. Costa Rica was also one of the first countries to be rewarded with a Brady Plan debt-reduction scheme.

From the mid-1980s, strong government encouragement, allied to political and social stability and an educated workforce, produced an export boom based on nontraditional exports such as fresh fruit and *maquiladora* products, as well as traditional commodities such as bananas and coffee.

Since the mid-1990s, high-tech manufacturing and services (finance and tourism) have eclipsed agriculture. The Figueres government landed a huge fish when it bagged Intel, whose microprocessor plant came on stream in 1998. This created a dual economy of high-tech plus *maquiladora* enclaves, and the "non-Intel economy." The bursting of the high-tech bubble and U.S. recession in 2001, along with the collapse in coffee prices, led to a sharp fall in growth rates in 2000–2002.

CUBA: Cuba's economic travails in the 1980s and 1990s have been dominated far more by geopolitics than by the debt crisis or the IMF. Following the Cuban revolution of 1959, Washington cut links before announcing a trade embargo in 1962 that is still in place as of 2002. Cuba traditionally depended on trade with the United

States and the initial impact was severe. Once isolated from the United States, Cuba relied increasingly on Soviet support, mainly in the form of cheap oil with which to run the economy and earn hard currency—in the mid-1980s Cuban resale of Soviet oil generated 40 percent of export earnings.

The crisis and subsequent collapse of the Soviet Union in the late 1980s devastated the Cuban economy. GDP fell by a third. Exports fell to one-third of their former value between 1990 and 1993. Deprived of Soviet aid to finance the trade deficit, imports have been cut by three-quarters. By 1998, exports were still only a third of their 1990 level, though well up on 1993. The contraction in the economy took its toll on three decades of exemplary social spending on Latin America's only national health service, which started to unravel with food shortages and rising unemployment.

While stopping well short of the full neoliberal recipe, the government has encouraged tourism and allowed dollars to circulate freely in the economy for the first time, making Cuba resemble a typical Caribbean "tourism and remittance economy." It has also reintroduced direct taxation, abolished in 1967. The desperate search for hard currency has even led to the phenomenon of "health tourism," whereby wealthy westerners come to Cuba to buy operations and other medical care.

While these measures helped restore positive growth from 1994 onward, they have carried some social and political costs. Circulating dollars have undermined social solidarity, encouraged prostitution, and created growing frustration. By 2000, GDP was still 13 percent below the 1990 figure, and exports were still a third lower. Tourism now rivals sugar as a source of foreign exchange.

| CUBA | | GROSS (%) | EXPORTS | IMPORTS | DEBT |
|---|---|---|---|---|---|
| POPULATION (1999): | 1982 | 3.3 | 4.9 | 5.5 | 3.2 |
| 11.2 million | 1983 | 4.3 | 5.5 | 6.2 | 3.2 |
| GDP PER CAPITA | 1984 | 6.6 | 5.5 | 7.2 | 3.4 |
| (2000): $1,989 | 1985 | 3.8 | 6.0 | 8.0 | 3.6 |
| | 1986 | 0.3 | 5.3 | 7.6 | 5.0 |
| MAIN EXPORTS: | 1987 | -4.8 | 5.4 | 7.6 | 6.1 |
| nickel, sugar, tobacco | 1988 | 1.2 | 5.5 | 7.6 | 6.5 |
| products | 1989 | -0.2 | 5.4 | 8.1 | 6.2 |
| NOTE: All economic statistics | 1990 | -4.0 | 4.9 | 6.7 | 7.0 |
| for Cuba should be treated | 1991 | -25.7 | 3.6 | 3.7 | 8.4 |
| with caution | 1992 | -14.7 | 2.2 | 2.5 | 10.0 |
| | 1993 | -16.5 | 1.1 | 2.0 | 11.3 |
| KEY: Growth of GDP per capita | 1994 | 1.4 | 1.4 | 2.0 | 11.8 |
| (%); Exports FOB (billions | 1995 | 2.8 | 1.5 | 2.9 | 13.5 |
| of pesos); Imports CIF (billions | 1996 | 8.1 | 1.9 | 3.5 | 11.3 |
| of pesos); Net Resource | 1997 | 2.9 | 1.8 | 4.1 | 11.0 |
| Transfers (negative figures | 1998 | 0.8 | 1.5 | 4.3 | 12.1 |
| indicate net outflows) | 1999 | 6.4 | 1.5 | 4.3 | 12.0 |
| (US$ millions) | 2000 | 4.9 | 1.8 | 5.4 | 12.0 |
| | 2001 | 2.1 | | | |
| • estimate | 2002* | 1.1 | | | |

## DOMINICAN REPUBLIC

POPULATION (1999):
8.3 million

GDP PER CAPITA
(2000): $2,059

MAIN EXPORTS:
free zone, ferro-nickel

KEY: GDP per capita (1980 US$);
Growth of GDP per capita (%);
Exports FOB (US$ millions);
Imports FOB (US$ millions);
Net Resource Transfers
(negative figures indicate
net outflows) (US$ millions);
Annual inflation (%).

• estimate

| | GROSS (%) | EXPORTS | IMPORTS | NRT | INF |
|---|---|---|---|---|---|
| 1982 | -1.1 | 768 | 1257 | 57 | 7 |
| 1983 | 2.5 | 785 | 1279 | 2 | 7 |
| 1984 | -2.0 | 868 | 1257 | 79 | 8 |
| 1985 | -4.6 | 739 | 1286 | 38 | 28 |
| 1986 | -0.5 | 722 | 1352 | 39 | 7 |
| 1987 | 6.3 | 711 | 1592 | 2 | 25 |
| 1988 | -1.4 | 890 | 1608 | -77 | 58 |
| 1989 | 2.2 | 924 | 1964 | 49 | 41 |
| 1990 | -6.9 | 735 | 1793 | -80 | 101 |
| 1991 | -3.0 | 658 | 1729 | 242 | 4 |
| 1992 | 6.1 | 566 | 2178 | 451 | 5 |
| 1993 | 1.2 | 3211⁷ | 4654 | -9 | 3 |
| 1994 | 2.6 | 3453 | 4903 | -785 | 14 |
| 1995 | 2.9 | 3780 | 5170 | -455 | 9 |
| 1996 | 5.3 | 4053 | 5727 | -527 | 4 |
| 1997 | 6.3 | 4614 | 6609 | -593 | 8 |
| 1998 | 5.6 | 5204 | 7597 | -453 | 8 |
| 1999 | 6.0 | 7987 | 9289 | -352 | 5 |
| 2000 | 5.5 | 8964 | 10852 | -84 | 9 |
| 2001 | 1.0 | 8366 | 10056 | 181 | 4 |
| 2002• | 2.3 | 8091 | 9978 | -824 | 9 |

DOMINICAN REPUBLIC: The initial impact of the debt crisis drove the Dominican Republic into the arms of the IMF. Subsequent austerity measures in 1984 provoked some of the bloodiest IMF riots in Latin America, leaving over a hundred dead.

Like many other Caribbean and Central American economies, the country's main foreign exchange earners are tourism, *maquila,* and remittances from Dominicans in the United States. The IMF and World Bank have promoted nontraditional exports to reduce the country's dependence on nickel and sugar, mainly via the free trade zones, using cheap Dominican labor to assemble clothing, shoes, and electrical goods. By 2000, 491 companies were employing 206,000 people in the zones. The government does not include income from the zones, or from tourism, in its export figures. Together, they cover much of the large apparent trade deficit. In 2000, free zone exports came to $4,771 million, but actual value added came to $1,019 million. In contrast, tourism and remittances both bring in about $2 billion a year.

Companies setting up in the zones enjoy a 15- to 20-year tax holiday, duty-free raw material imports and low wage rates. Since 1984 they have also benefited from Washington's Caribbean Basin Initiative, under which a number of nontraditional exports have gained duty-free access to the U.S. market. In 2000, textile manufacturers gained totally tariff-free access to the U.S. market under the Africa-Caribbean trade bill. It was hoped this would help revive export growth in textiles, which had been undercut by cheap

Asian imports in the late 1990s.

In 1994 the government was rewarded for its good behavior with a Brady Plan deal that wiped about 10 percent off its foreign debt. Further adjustment continued throughout the 1990s, with a Bolivian-style partial privatization of heavily indebted state-owned enterprises in the late 1990s.

Since 1994, the Dominican Republic has achieved sustained high growth, based on *maquila* and tourism, averaging 7.9 percent from 1996 to 2000, but the dual economy of high-growth enclaves and dollar flows, surrounded by stagnating agriculture and urban squalor, means that poverty and unemployment remain high. U.S. economic troubles from 2000 led to a sharp slowdown in exports and growth.

| ECUADOR | | GROSS (%) | EXPORTS | IMPORTS | NRT | INF |
|---|---|---|---|---|---|---|
| POPULATION (1999): | 1982 | -1.8 | 2327 | 2187 | 41 | 24 |
| 12.4 million | 1983 | -4.0 | 2348 | 1421 | -561 | 53 |
| GDP PER CAPITA | 1984 | 1.8 | 2622 | 1567 | -777 | 25 |
| (2000): $1,417 | 1985 | 2.0 | 2905 | 1611 | -956 | 24 |
| MAIN EXPORTS: | 1986 | 0.2 | 2186 | 1643 | -470 | 27 |
| fish, bananas, oil | 1987 | -7.0 | 2021 | 2054 | 212 | 33 |
| | 1988 | 6.2 | 2202 | 1583 | -323 | 86 |
| KEY: GDP per capita (1980 US$); | 1989 | -2.2 | 2354 | 1693 | -269 | 54 |
| Growth of GDP per capita (%); | 1990 | -0.4 | 2714 | 1711 | -504 | 50 |
| Exports FOB (US$ millions); | 1991 | 2.4 | 2851 | 2207 | -209 | 49 |
| Imports FOB (US$ millions); | 1992 | 0.7 | 3101 | 2083 | -1002 | 60 |
| Net Resource Transfers | 1993 | -0.1 | 3066 | 2474 | 428 | 31 |
| (negative figures indicate | 1994 | 2.1 | 3843 | 3282 | 543 | 25 |
| net outflows) (US$ millions); | 1995 | 0.8 | 4411 | 4057 | -108 | 23 |
| Annual inflation (%); | 1996 | 0.2 | 4900 | 3680 | -740 | 26 |
| Index of real minimum wages | 1997 | 1.8 | 5264 | 4666 | -318 | 31 |
| (1980 = 100 from 1982-91; | 1998 | -0.9 | 4203 | 5198 | 468 | 43 |
| 1995 = 100 from 1992-2001 | 1999 | -9.7 | 5263 | 4073 | -2717 | 61 |
| • estimate | 2000 | 0.4 | 5987 | 5012 | -2019 | 91 |
| | 2001 | 4.1 | 5774 | 6754 | -670 | 22 |
| | 2002* | 1.6 | 5940 | 7943 | 568 | 10 |

ECUADOR: Like Mexico, Ecuador struck oil in the 1970s and it has proved a mixed blessing. Oil production rapidly replaced bananas, shrimp, and coffee as the main export. Oil is still nationalized and accounted for 43 percent of government revenue in 2000. New oil finds kept the economy afloat through the chaos that led to dollarization in 2000. But as in Mexico, the oil boom helped mask the exhaustion of the import substitution process and led to a steep rise in indebtedness during the 1970s, laying Ecuador open to the full blast of the debt crisis after 1982.

This has involved the usual pattern of austerity and IMF agreements rewarded by new loans and debt rescheduling. However, Ecuador has shown itself more reluctant than most to go in for full-blown structural adjustment, for example, over privatization and import liberalization, which it fears would destroy its heavily protected industrial sector. It has also persistently registered inflation of over 30 percent. This has led to regular run-ins with the IMF and World Bank and periodic inability to keep up with debt service. Nevertheless, the government won a Brady Plan debt reduction deal in 1994, along with plentiful support from the World Bank and IDB.

Ecuador has one of the region's most conservative, self-interested, and corrupt elites, and internal political divisions and a fragmented and chaotic Congress have played a major part in holding up adjustment. Other areas of adjustment, such as changes to the landholding system, have provoked fierce resistance from Ecuador's highly organized indigenous groups, which have also protested at the environmental and cultural impact of the government's efforts to encourage foreign oil companies to drill for oil on traditional Indian lands.

A backlash against the neoliberal government of Sixto Duran Ballen (1992–1996) led to political chaos from 1996 to 2000, as two successive presidents were removed by a combination of popular protest and army intervention. In 1999, Ecuador became the first country to default on its Brady bonds, making it an instant pariah at the IMF meetings that year.

As every attempt at market reforms was blocked, and nothing else was on offer, political and economic meltdown ensued. Real wages in 1999 were just 90 percent of their 1990 figure, and unemployment rose from 9 percent in 1997 to 17 percent by the end of 1999, and the banking system was in a state of collapse. In desperation, Ecuador's government proposed dollarization—giving up the national currency, the *sucre*, and with it a large chunk of national economic and political sovereignty.

Although an uprising by Ecuador's strong indigenous movement and reformist groups in the military overthrew the government, the new president, Gustavo Noboa, seized the initiative with a large neoliberal reform package. The IMF promptly approved a loan, conditional on cuts in fuel subsidies, privatization and opening up to foreign investment. In 2003 Lucio Gutiérrez, a one-time coup leader, won the presidential elections and, true to form, headed for Washington to negotiate yet another IMF loan in return for spending cuts.

EL SALVADOR: The 1980s in El Salvador were dominated by the civil war between the government, backed by the United States, and the guerrillas of the FMLN. Although this led to massive disruption of the economy, Washington's crusade against what it saw as the communist menace in Central America resulted in massive flows of military and economic aid—some $4.3 billion by the time the war ended in 1992. In addition, remittances from Salvadorans living in the United States remains equal to the country's total income from traditional exports.

U.S. aid (in the war years), conservative fiscal management by government, and remittances from Salvadorans in the United States have ensured that El Salvador never acquired the kind of debt burden experienced elsewhere in the region, and made only one visit to the IMF during the 1980s. However, it has received regular IMF and World Bank support in the 1990s.

Even so, its economic trajectory has

followed the regional trend. A slump in 1979–1982 was followed by stagnation during much of the 1980s and a recovery in the first half of the 1990s. As elsewhere, neoliberals have come to dominate the political scene in the shape of the Nationalist Republican Alliance (ARENA) founded by death-squad godfathers such as Major Roberto d'Aubuisson in the early 1980s. ARENA cleaned up its act in the late 1980s and has been in power since 1989.

Arena introduced a standard package of privatization, trade, and investment liberalization and encouragement for *maquiladora* assembly plants operating in free trade zones. By 2000, *maquila* was the largest single export earner, bringing in $1.6 billion, although the actual value added was only a

quarter of that—$456 million; 65,000 people were employed in the factories.

Growth averaged a reasonable 3.6 percent from 1995 to 1999, but remains highly dependent on volatile international coffee prices and the footloose *maquila* industry, constantly under threat from competition from even cheaper producers in Asia and elsewhere in Central America and the Caribbean.

In January 2001, the government dollarized, partly in order to tie the hands of any future FMLN government. By early 2002, the currency in circulation consisted of equal numbers of dollars and *colones*, causing severe headaches for non-mathematicians, since the exchange rate was 1:8.75.

| EL SALVADOR | | GROSS (%) | EXPORTS | IMPORTS | NRT | INF |
|---|---|---|---|---|---|---|
| POPULATION (1999): | | | | | | |
| 6.2 million | 1982 | -6.5 | 704 | 826 | 113 | 14 |
| | 1983 | -0.3 | 758 | 832 | 95 | 16 |
| GDP PER CAPITA | 1984 | 1.3 | 726 | 915 | 116 | 10 |
| (2000): $1,753 | 1985 | 0.5 | 679 | 895 | 153 | 32 |
| MAIN EXPORTS: | 1986 | -0.8 | 778 | 902 | 41 | 30 |
| maquila products, coffee | 1987 | 1.0 | 590 | 939 | 194 | 20 |
| | 1988 | -0.3 | 611 | 967 | 135 | 18 |
| KEY: GDP per capita (1980 US$); | 1989 | -0.8 | 498 | 1090 | 519 | 24 |
| Growth of GDP per capita (%); | 1990 | 1.4 | 580 | 1180 | 411 | 19 |
| Exports FOB (US$ millions); | 1991 | 1.2 | 588 | 1294 | 172 | 10 |
| Imports FOB (US$ millions); | 1992 | 5.1 | 598 | 1561 | 190 | 20 |
| Net Resource Transfers | 1993 | 4.2 | 732 | 1766 | 123 | 12 |
| (negative figures indicate | 1994 | 3.7 | 1252 | 2407 | 36 | 9 |
| net outflows) (US$ millions); | 1995 | 4.0 | 1652 | 3115 | 338 | 11 |
| Annual inflation (%); | 1996 | -0.3 | 1788 | 3031 | 243 | 7 |
| | 1997 | 2.1 | 2416 | 3523 | 297 | 2 |
| • estimate | 1998 | 1.6 | 2452 | 3720 | 231 | 4 |
| | 1999 | 1.3 | 3175 | 4714 | 165 | -1 |
| | 2000 | 0.1 | 3662 | 5636 | 132 | 4 |
| | 2001 | 0.0 | 3977 | 5892 | -267 | 1 |
| | 2002* | 0.4 | 3870 | 5814 | -134 | 1 |

| GUATEMALA | GROSS (%) | EXPORTS | IMPORTS | NRT | INF |
|-----------|-----------|---------|---------|-----|-----|
| POPULATION (1999): | | | | | |
| 11.1 million | 1982 | -6.1 | 1170 | 1284 | 240 | -2 |
| | 1983 | -5.4 | 1092 | 1056 | 162 | 15 |
| GDP PER CAPITA | 1984 | -2.8 | 1132 | 1182 | 186 | 5 |
| (2000): $1,558 | 1985 | -3.3 | 1060 | 1077 | 193 | 28 |
| MAIN EXPORTS: | 1986 | -2.7 | 1044 | 876 | -54 | 21 |
| coffee, bananas, sugar | 1987 | 0.7 | 978 | 1333 | 310 | 9 |
| | 1988 | 1.0 | 1073 | 1413 | 178 | 12 |
| KEY: GDP per capita (1980 US$); | 1989 | 0.8 | 1126 | 1484 | 318 | 20 |
| Growth of GDP per capita (%); | 1990 | 0.0 | 1211 | 1428 | 0 | 60 |
| Exports FOB (US$ millions); | 1991 | 0.6 | 1230 | 1673 | 600 | 10 |
| Imports FOB (US$ millions); | 1992 | 2.2 | 1284 | 2328 | 513 | 14 |
| Net Resource Transfers | 1993 | 1.3 | 1363 | 2384 | 704 | 12 |
| (negative figures indicate | 1994 | 1.4 | 1687 | 2559 | 586 | 12 |
| net outflows) (US$ millions); | 1995 | 2.2 | 2157 | 3033 | 210 | 9 |
| Annual inflation (%); | 1996 | 0.3 | 2232 | 2880 | 356 | 11 |
| | 1997 | 1.7 | 2603 | 3543 | 717 | 7 |
| • estimate | 1998 | 2.4 | 2867 | 4366 | 1100 | 8 |
| | 1999 | 1.1 | 3435 | 4984 | 709 | 5 |
| | 2000 | 0.7 | 3860 | 5568 | 1494 | 5 |
| | 2001 | -0.3 | 3896 | 6040 | 1622 | 9 |
| | 2002* | -0.7 | 3809 | 6441 | 876 | 6 |

GUATEMALA: Guatemala has the largest economy and population in Central America. It has also suffered the longest and bloodiest civil war in the region. A forty-year civil war finally came to an end in 1996, by which time 200,000 people had died, mostly from the country's majority indigenous population. The military oversaw a return to civilian rule in 1986, but still exercises enormous political and economic influence. The barbarism of the military meant that the regime was cut off from Washington in the early 1980s, but unlike in nearby Nicaragua, Washington did not extend the boycott to the IMF, which agreed to standby arrangements in 1981 and 1983.

The return to elected government in 1986 improved access to aid and credits, and helped Guatemala return to steady, if unspectacular, per capita growth.

Guatemalan governments are traditionally averse to raising direct taxes, but they also spend almost nothing on their people, especially the Indians. This allowed governments to avoid extreme indebtedness and inflationary spending in the 1980s, apart from a blip in 1990, and has obviated the need for some of the fierce shocks administered elsewhere. Nevertheless, real wages fell steadily from 1983 to 1991. The end of the war enabled the government to spend some of the "peace dividend" on limited improvements in health and education.

Since 1991, successive governments have implemented a fairly mild brand of structural adjustment, cutting the fiscal deficit through a combination of spending cuts and attempts to improve tax collection, liberalizing trade and privatizing telecommunications and rail.

The government has made some progress in diversifying into nontraditional exports such as textiles produced in free trade zones and fresh vegetables like mange-tout and broccoli, but exports are still dominated by the traditional crops of coffee, bananas, and sugar. *Maquila* growth has been slower than in Honduras or Mexico—the number of jobs rose from 70,000 in 1994 to 93,000 in 2000. Coffee earned $574 million in 2000, considerably less than remittances ($895 million) and about equal to tourism ($535 million).

| GUYANA | Year | GROSS (%) | EXPORTS | IMPORTS | INF |
|---|---|---|---|---|---|
| **POPULATION (1999):** | 1982 | -12.6 | 256 | 284 | 19 |
| 0.8 million | 1983 | -12.0 | 189 | 231 | 13 |
| **GDP PER CAPITA** | 1984 | 3.9 | 210 | 213 | 25 |
| **(2000): $761** | 1985 | -0.1 | 206 | 226 | 15 |
| | 1986 | 0.0 | 214 | 241 | 8 |
| **MAIN EXPORTS:** | 1987 | 1.1 | 242 | 266 | 29 |
| gold, sugar, bauxite | 1988 | -2.3 | 230 | 216 | 40 |
| | 1989 | -4.6 | 238 | 258 | 89 |
| NOTE: All economic statistics | 1990 | -3.1 | 218 | 269 | 65 |
| for Cuba should be treated | 1991 | 4.8 | 266 | 307 | 89 |
| with caution | 1992 | 8.8 | 382 | 443 | 14 |
| | 1993 | 11.0 | 416 | 484 | 8 |
| KEY: GDP per capita (1980 US$); | 1994 | 8.9 | 463 | 504 | 10 |
| Growth of GDP per capita (%); | 1995 | 3.3 | 496 | 537 | |
| Exports FOB (US$ millions); | 1996 | 6.9 | | | |
| Imports CIF (US$ millions); | 1997 | 6.2 | | | |
| Net Resource Transfers | 1998 | -2.7 | | | |
| (negative figures indicate net | 1999 | 4.5 | | | |
| outflows) (US$ millions); | 2000 | -2.7 | | | |
| Annual inflation (%) | 2001 | 1.9 | | | |
| * estimate | 2002* | 1.7 | | | |

**GUYANA:** Formerly a British colony Guyana gained independence in 1966. It entered the 1980s run by Forbes Burnham, who committed the country to a "transition to socialism" and strengthened links with Cuba and the Soviet Union. Large parts of the economy were in state hands.

Unfortunately, Burnham had also maintained sufficient links with the West to run up a large debt. In 1982 Guyana got the worst of both worlds—a debt crisis and no help from Western governments, banks, or the international financial institutions, who objected to Burnham's politics. By 1984 the public sector deficit had reached 60 percent of GDP, Guyana was in arrears on debt repayments and no rescheduling was in sight. Per capita GDP fell by over 12 percent for two years in a row and then stagnated for the rest of the decade.

After Burnham's death in 1985, Desmond Hoyte became president and began to abandon statism and look to neoliberalism for solutions to the country's crisis. In 1986 the government began to court foreign investors, bringing in a new investment code in 1988 that opened up virtually all the economy to private investors, especially foreign logging and mining companies, with disastrous consequences for its ecosystem. Timber exports quadrupled from 1996 to 2000 reaching $41 million.

In 1990 Guyana was duly rewarded with two IMF loans that opened the way to debt rescheduling and new loans from multilateral and bilateral sources. This enabled a swift return to impressive growth rates, averaging 7 percent from 1991 to 1997, before political unrest and adverse weather temporarily hit growth in 1998. However, loans also meant increased debt service.

In 1992 former leftist Cheddi Jagan won the presidency and promptly contin-

ued along the neoliberal lines of his predecessor. When he died, his widow, Janet Jagan, continued on the same path from 1997 to 1979. In 1994 the IMF kept up the pressure for reform with a further three-year loan conditioned on reducing the fiscal deficit, further liberalization and tax reform to reduce direct taxes. In 1997, Guyana signed a further agreement with the IMF, but won some limited debt relief under the World Bank/IMF's Heavily Indebted Poor Country (HIPC) initiative.

The 1990s boom in GDP ended in 1998 through a combination of El Nino, political unrest, and falling commodity prices. The state runs companies producing bauxite and sugar, but by 2001 they were losing money heavily. The IMF had their privatization in its sights in negotiations under way in 2002 over a new PRGF loan.

| HAITI | | GROSS (%) | EXPORTS | IMPORTS | NRT | INF |
|---|---|---|---|---|---|---|
| **POPULATION (1999):** | 1982 | -5.2 | 270 | 324 | 212 | 5 |
| 7.8 million | 1983 | -1.2 | 288 | 324 | 133 | 11 |
| **GDP PER CAPITA** | 1984 | -1.4 | 319 | 338 | 144 | 5 |
| (2000): $357 | 1985 | -1.3 | 223 | 345 | 177 | 17 |
| **MAIN EXPORTS:** | 1986 | -1.3 | 191 | 303 | 154 | -11 |
| maquila products, coffee | 1987 | -2.6 | 210 | 311 | 131 | -4 |
| | 1988 | -1.1 | 180 | 284 | 168 | 9 |
| KEY: GDP per capita (1980 US$); | 1989 | -1.0 | 148 | 259 | 154 | 11 |
| Growth of GDP per capita (%); | 1990 | -2.2 | 160 | 247 | 154 | 26 |
| Exports FOB (US$ millions); | 1991 | -4.9 | 163 | 300 | 127 | 7 |
| Imports FOB (US$ millions); | 1992 | -15.4 | 118 | 257 | 38 | 16 |
| Net Resource Transfers | 1993 | -9.6 | 140 | 312 | 54 | 44 |
| (negative figures indicate | 1994 | -19.0 | 117 | 198 | 22 | 32 |
| net outflows) (US$ millions); | 1995 | 7.5 | 153 | 517 | 158 | 25 |
| Annual inflation (%); | 1996 | 3.7 | 170 | 499 | -13 | 15 |
| | 1997 | 1.3 | 206 | 560 | 99 | 16 |
| * estimate | 1998 | 1.0 | 299 | 641 | 7 | 7 |
| | 1999 | 1.1 | 528 | 1169 | 81 | 10 |
| | 2000 | 0.1 | 503 | 1336 | 5 | 19 |
| | 2001 | -2.5 | 442 | 1300 | 95 | 8 |
| | 2002* | -3.3 | 427 | 1230 | -12 | 10 |

HAITI: Haiti has the worst economic record in the hemisphere; it started the 1980s with the lowest GDP per capita and this then fell every year, reaching a miserable $357 per person by 2000. Only four of the last twenty years have registered positive growth figures.

The government has traditionally run a small public sector, levying only minimal taxes on the Haitian elite. Remittances from Haitians in the United States and elsewhere have traditionally provided vital foreign exchange, but balance of payments crises in the early 1980s forced it to go to the IMF for two one-year loans in 1982 and 1083, and then a longer-term structural adjustment facility in 1986. IMF programs have come and gone ever since, the most recent in 1996, obliging the government to

privatize the state flour mill and lay off 6,000–7,000 civil servants.

The country's plight has been worsened by corruption, political unrest, and the military's willingness to intervene in politics. When free elections were finally held in 1990, leading to the election of a progressive priest, Father Jean-Bertrand Aristide, as president, the military overthrew him within six months. After Aristide's overthrow, the economy was further battered by political unrest and a U.S. trade and aid embargo, and shrank by a third from 1991 to 1994. In 1994, Aristide was restored to office following a bloodless U.S. occupation. In return for Washington's support, he accepted a World Bank structural adjustment program, but later backed off key issues such

| HONDURAS | | GROSS (%) | EXPORTS | IMPORTS | NRT | INF |
|---|---|---|---|---|---|---|
| **POPULATION (1999):** | | | | | | |
| 6.4 million | 1982 | -5.2 | 677 | 681 | 2 | 9 |
| | 1983 | -1.2 | 699 | 756 | 55 | 7 |
| **GDP PER CAPITA** | 1984 | -1.4 | 737 | 885 | 219 | 4 |
| **(2000): $710** | 1985 | -1.3 | 790 | 879 | 113 | 4 |
| **MAIN EXPORTS:** | 1986 | -1.3 | 891 | 874 | 99 | 3 |
| maquila products, cof- | 1987 | 1.7 | 833 | 813 | 166 | 3 |
| fee, shrimp and lobster | 1988 | 1.7 | 875 | 870 | 90 | 7 |
| | 1989 | 1.6 | 883 | 835 | 49 | 11 |
| KEY: GDP per capita (1980 US$); | 1990 | -3.4 | 848 | 870 | 57 | 35 |
| Growth of GDP per capita (%); | 1991 | -0.7 | 808 | 864 | 103 | 25 |
| Exports FOB (US$ millions); | 1992 | 2.7 | 839 | 990 | 108 | 7 |
| Imports FOB (US$ millions); | 1993 | 4.0 | 1002 | 1233 | -4 | 13 |
| Net Resource Transfers | 1994 | -4.7 | 1141 | 1399 | 151 | 29 |
| (negative figures indicate | 1995 | 0.7 | 1460 | 1571 | 51 | 27 |
| net outflows) (US$ millions); | 1996 | 0.8 | 1621 | 1759 | 110 | 25 |
| Annual inflation (%); | 1997 | 2.1 | 1839 | 2039 | 254 | 13 |
| | 1998 | 0.5 | 2093 | 2338 | 150 | 16 |
| * estimate | 1999 | -4.1 | 2281 | 3053 | 551 | 11 |
| | 2000 | 2.1 | 2464 | 3318 | 225 | 10 |
| | 2001 | 0.1 | 2447 | 3498 | 328 | 9 |
| | 2002* | -0.6 | 2371 | 3315 | 443 | 8 |

as privatization, in the face of popular protest over job losses.

His successor as president, René Preval, attempted to revive the adjustment program, but only succeeded in provoking political paralysis as successive prime ministers were vetoed by parliament and elections were postponed. The political crisis meant that little attention was given to the state of the economy, and foreign investment and even aid were deterred by the extent of the chaos. Haiti's rock- bottom wage levels have, however, attracted some investment in *maquiladora* garment processing, most notoriously for the Walt Disney corporation. *Maquila* factories employed 30,000 people in 1998, and earned $296 million in exports, but $261 million of this was accounted for by imported inputs. Political chaos and falling coffee prices forced per capita GDP even lower from 1996t o 2000.

HONDURAS: The original banana republic, Honduras has traditionally been the poorest country in Central America, depending on banana and coffee exports to bring in foreign exchange. In recent years, however, its trade has been transformed by the arrival of the *maquiladoras*, which helped to treble exports between 1992 and 2001. Along with remittances from Hondurans living in the United States, *maquila* has become the mainstay of the economy. By 1999, the *maquiladoras* were generating 120,000 jobs and a net income to the country of $545 million.

As in Nicaragua and El Salvador, Honduras's experiences in the 1980s were shaped by geopolitics. In return for allowing the United States to station Contra rebels on its border with Nicaragua, Washington rewarded the Honduran government with large slices of aid, allowing it to resist the worst of IMF policies. After a standby arrangement in 1982, Honduras had no further IMF agreement until 1990.

From 1986 onward, the Contra war began to decline and pressure for a full structural adjustment program began to grow. In addition, U.S. aid began to tail off, forcing Honduras to turn to the IMF and World Bank. The 1990s saw a series of stop-start adjustment programs, punctuated by regular disputes with the IMF. In 1999, Honduras agreed its latest ESAF agreement with the Fund, in return for renewed commitments to privatization (telecommunications, road, airports, and electricity) and other adjustment measures. This paved the way for a debt relief package the following year.

Honduras's escalating debt burden also forced it to seek regular reschedulings, greatly adding to the leverage of the United States, IMF, and World Bank. In 1998, all economic progress was interrupted by Hurricane Mitch, which killed 7,000 people and did damage equivalent to an entire year's GDP. Mitch led to an influx of aid.

JAMAICA: For most of the 1980s, Jamaica was run by a soul mate of President Reagan. Edward Seaga was elected in 1980, the same year as the U.S. president, and brought to an end eight years of social democratic reform by Michael Manley, who had regularly challenged both Washington and the IMF. Seaga was rewarded with special treatment from Washington. In 1989 a chastened Manley was reelected, but opted to continue with much of Seaga's economic adjustment program.

High interest rates designed to attract capital and help close the government's fiscal deficit have led to short-term capital inflows and an unsustainable financial boom. Throughout the second half of the 1990s, the government has had to bail out banks in a series of financial crises, which cost the government 38 percent of GDP to sort out, with a consequent sharp rise in the government's domestic debt. High interest rates also led to a slump in investment and demand, and GDP per head has fallen by 7 percent since 1991.

Despite the efforts of both government and World Bank to diversify, the Jamaican economy is still based on mining and tourism. Alumina and bauxite (used in making aluminum) still account for around 50 percent of merchandise trade, while tourism is instrumental in generating the dollars to make up the persistent deficit on trade, bringing in over $1.1 billion in 1998, and generating nearly 250,000 jobs. The booms and busts in world bauxite prices combined with periodic application of IMF austerity programs to a large extent explain the behavior of Jamaica's per capita GDP since 1982.

The adjustment process has succeeded in establishing a *maquiladora* sector, mainly based in free trade zones. Garment exports peaked in 1995, but thereafter suffered from competition from lower cost produces, particularly Mexico once NAFTA was introduced. Other factories produce chemicals and electrical equipment, or simply perform data input; Jamaican typists key in endless figures for U.S. companies and the data is then beamed back to the parent organization by satellite.

| JAMAICA | | GROSS (%) | EXPORTS | IMPORTS | INF |
|---|---|---|---|---|---|
| **POPULATION (1999):** | 1982 | -1.5 | 767 | 1209 | 7 |
| 2.6 million | 1983 | -0.2 | 686 | 1124 | 17 |
| **GDP PER CAPITA** | 1984 | -1.4 | 702 | 1037 | 31 |
| (2000): $1987 | 1985 | -6.7 | 569 | 1004 | 23 |
| | 1986 | 0.7 | 590 | 837 | 10 |
| **MAIN EXPORTS:** | 1987 | 5.5 | 709 | 1061 | 8 |
| alumina, sugar, | 1988 | 2.1 | 883 | 1240 | 9 |
| bauxite, bananas | 1989 | 6.1 | 1000 | 1606 | 17 |
| | 1990 | 6.0 | 1158 | 1680 | 30 |
| KEY: GDP per capita (1980 US$); | 1991 | -0.1 | 1145 | 1551 | 77 |
| Growth of GDP per capita (%); | 1992 | 1.7 | 1117 | 1541 | 40 |
| Exports FOB (US$ millions); | 1993 | 1.3 | 1105 | 1921 | 30 |
| Imports FOB (US$ millions); | 1994 | 0.7 | 1551 | 2065 | 27 |
| Net Resource Transfers | 1995 | 1.3 | 1793 | 2606 | 26 |
| (negative figures indicate net | 1996 | -0.9 | 1721 | 2715 | 16 |
| outflows) (US$ millions); | 1997 | -2.6 | 1700 | 2833 | 9 |
| Annual inflation (%) | 1998 | -1.6 | 1613 | 2710 | 8 |
| | 1999 | -0.2 | 1499 | 2686 | 7 |
| • estimate | 2000 | 0.1 | 1555 | 2908 | 6 |
| | 2001 | 0.9 | n.a. | n.a. | 9 |
| | 2002* | 1.1 | n.a. | n.a. | 6 |

| MEXICO | | GROSS (%) | EXPORTS | IMPORTS | NRT | INF | WAGES |
|---|---|---|---|---|---|---|---|
| **POPULATION (1999):** | 1982 | -3.2 | 21230 | 14434 | -9594 | 99 | 104 |
| 95.6 million | 1983 | -6.6 | 22320 | 8553 | -12612 | 81 | 81 |
| GDP PER CAPITA | 1984 | 1.0 | 24196 | 11256 | -12118 | 59 | 75 |
| (2000): $3,685 | 1985 | 0.0 | 21663 | 13212 | -12178 | 64 | 76 |
| | 1986 | -6.3 | 16031 | 11432 | -6127 | 106 | 72 |
| MAIN EXPORTS: | 1987 | -0.4 | 20655 | 12222 | -5325 | 159 | 72 |
| maquiladora goods, oil | 1988 | -1.0 | 20566 | 18898 | -11287 | 52 | 71 |
| KEY: GDP per capita (1980 US$); | 1989 | 1.1 | 22765 | 23410 | -3693 | 20 | 78 |
| Growth of GDP per capita (%); | 1990 | 2.2 | 26838 | 31271 | 2811 | 30 | 79 |
| Exports FOB (US$ millions); | 1991 | 1.4 | 26855 | 38184 | 14113 | 19 | 85 |
| Imports FOB (US$ millions); | 1992 | 1.8 | 46196 | 62130 | 16406 | 12 | 101[8] |
| Net Resource Transfers | 1993 | -0.1 | 51885 | 66366 | 17911 | 8 | 110 |
| (negative figures indicate | 1994 | 2.6 | 60882 | 79346 | -1741 | 7 | 115 |
| net outflows) (US$ millions); | 1995 | -7.8 | 79542 | 72453 | -1464 | 52 | 100 |
| Annual inflation (%); Index | 1996 | 3.7 | 96000 | 89469 | -9659 | 28 | 90 |
| of average real industrial wages | 1997 | 5.1 | 110431 | 109808 | 5387 | 16 | 89 |
| (1980 = 100 from 1982–91; | 1998 | 3.3 | 117460 | 125373 | 4945 | 19 | 92 |
| 1995 = 100 from 1992–2001). | 1999 | 2.1 | 148083 | 155465 | 1661 | 12 | 92 |
| • estimate | 2000 | 5.2 | 180167 | 190494 | 6157 | 9 | 98 |
| | 2001 | -1.9 | 171103 | 184644 | 11498 | 4 | 105 |
| | 2002* | -0.3 | 171700 | 183500 | 6300 | 5 | 106 |

MEXICO: Mexico has been the country in the news during the silent revolution, not always for positive reasons. In August 1982 it was Mexico that precipitated the debt crisis by announcing it could no longer pay its debt service. Tough stabilization policies were demanded in return for being bailed out by the Western nations and the banks. In the 1990s, the country embarked on a breakneck process of integration with the U.S. economy, pausing only for a massive financial crisis halfway through the decade.

After the crash of 1982, Mexico first suppressed imports, generating a multibillion-dollar trade surplus with which to pay off the debt. Then, following the fraudulent election of Carlos Salinas in 1988, the ruling Institutional Revolutionary Party (PRI) embarked on a sweeping market transformation of the traditionally state-dominated Mexican economy.

Salinas privatized hundreds of state enterprises, including the telecommunications companies and national airlines. He deregulated trade (Mexico had joined the GATT in 1986) and began negotiating a free trade treaty with the United States that came into force in 1994 as the North American Free Trade Agreement (NAFTA). NAFTA tied Mexico's future permanently to that of the U.S. economy and generalized the *maquiladora* experience to the whole Mexican economy.

Once the economy had been stabilized, privatization and deregulation attracted billions of dollars in foreign capital, both in investment and loans (in 1993 Mexico overtook India as the World Bank's largest borrower). Simultaneously, Salinas lowered tariffs and removed other barriers to imports. The result was a massive import boom; imports almost quintupled from 1987 to 1994, turning the trade surplus of the early 1980s into a $23 billion deficit. Mexico's attempts to cover the gap with bond issues collapsed when market confidence was shaken by political infighting over the presidential succession in 1994, and a massive run on the peso ensued, followed by a banking crisis. Washington was forced to step in to refloat its neoliberal flagship, putting together a huge $50 billion rescue package.

The rescue plan allowed Mexico to resume growth and the access to the U.S. market conferred by NAFTA led to an astonishing export boom, which led in turn to high growth figures. Mexican exports rocketed from $41 billion in 1990 to $137 billion in 1999, more than the exports of Brazil, Argentina, and Venezuela combined. Nearly 90 percent of these were destined for the United States. Manufacturing exports (mainly from *maquiladoras*) increased its share of total exports from 68 percent to 89 percent of the total over the course of the decade.

The human cost of this transformation was not so rosy. The opening of Mexican markets to cheap U.S. maize spelled misery for small farmers, while real wages persistently lagged behind growth and were badly hit by the 1995 crash. The PRI's decision to reverse its traditional support

| NICARAGUA | | GROSS (%) | EXPORTS | IMPORTS | NRT | INF | WAGES |
|---|---|---|---|---|---|---|---|
| **POPULATION (1999):** | 1982 | -3.2 | 21230 | 14434 | -9594 | 99 | 104 |
| 4.9 million | 1982 | -4.0 | 406 | 723 | 276 | 22 | 96 |
| GDP PER CAPITA | 1983 | 1.2 | 429 | 778 | 390 | 33 | 97 |
| (2000): $482 | 1984 | -4.8 | 386 | 800 | 670 | 50 | 79 |
| | 1985 | -7.3 | 305 | 794 | 582 | 334 | 55 |
| MAIN EXPORTS: | 1986 | -3.7 | 258 | 677 | 338 | 747 | 20 |
| maquila products, coffee | 1987 | -3.0 | 295 | 734 | 577 | 1347 | 14 |
| KEY: GDP per capita (1980 US$); | 1988 | -15.6 | 236 | 718 | 627 | 33548 | 5 |
| Growth of GDP per capita (%); | 1989 | -4.3 | 319 | 547 | 390 | 1689 | 9 |
| Exports FOB (US$ millions); | 1990 | -3.1 | 332 | 570 | 251 | 13490 | 15 |
| Imports FOB (US$ millions); | 1991 | -3.6 | 268 | 688 | 572 | 775 | 15 |
| Net Resource Transfers | 1992 | -2.1 | 223 | 771 | 611 | 4 | 101⁹ |
| (negative figures indicate | 1993 | -3.3 | 267 | 670 | 360 | 20 | 93 |
| net outflows) (US$ millions); | 1994 | 0.9 | 360 | 784 | 524 | 14 | 98 |
| Annual inflation (%); Index | 1995 | 1.5 | 445 | 850 | 402 | 11 | 100 |
| of average real wages of those | 1996 | 2.2 | 485 | 941 | 610 | 12 | 98 |
| enrolled in the social security | 1997 | 2.6 | 687 | 1329 | 836 | 7 | 98 |
| system (1980 = 100 from | 1998 | 1.4 | 642 | 1384 | 604 | 19 | 105 |
| 1982–91; 1995 = 100 | 1999 | 4.6 | 838 | 2034 | 1051 | 7 | 110 |
| from 1992–2001). | 2000 | 3.6 | 956 | 1991 | 699 | 10 | 111 |
| * estimate | 2001 | 0.3 | 919 | 1982 | 613 | 5 | 116 |
| | 2002* | -2.1 | 906 | 1923 | 622 | 4 | 122 |

for communal landownership by Mexico's large indigenous population sparked an Indian rebellion in Chiapas in 1994, souring the advent of NAFTA.

NAFTA led to growing north-south divide within Mexico, with powerful industrial clusters developing around boomtowns like Monterrey and along the U.S. border, in contrast to the rural misery and neglect of much of the South of the country.

In 2000, the PRI finally lost the presidency after seventy-one years in power.

Incoming president Vicente Fox, a former Coca-Cola executive, posed few threats to the PRI's neoliberal model, but was unlucky enough to take over the helm just as the U.S. economy was sliding into recession, taking Mexico in its wake. In the space of twelve years, the PRI had used fraud to fend off a challenge from the Left, and paved the way for a handover to the Right. Opinions differed over the extent to which NAFTA had played a part in persuading Mexicans that political democracy and market forces were the way forward.

NICARAGUA: After Haiti, Nicaragua is Latin America's most tragic economic disaster story. In the 1980s, its fate was determined by its conflict with the United States. Following the Sandinista revolution of 1979, Washington isolated the new government, preventing lending by the IMF and World Bank, ending U.S. aid and in 1985 announcing a total embargo on trade. At the same time it launched a counter-insurgency war against the Sandinistas, building up the Contra army, which launched raids across the borders from Honduras and Costa Rica.

The embargo and war effort undid most of the initial achievements of the revolution, diverting government spending away from health and education and generating an escalating fiscal deficit that brought hyperinflation in its wake. In 1988 Nicaragua recorded a Latin American record of 33,548 percent inflation in a single year.

The Sandinistas launched their own stabilization efforts, but with limited success, and in 1990 were voted out of office. By then real wages were down to less than 15 percent of their 1980 value.

Once the Sandinistas were out, the IMF took over where the United States had left off. The new government of Violeta Chamorro was promptly rewarded with an influx of U.S. aid and the ending of the trade embargo, culminating in a three-year IMF loan in 1994 which in turn opened the way to debt rescheduling and new loans. In return the United States, and subsequently the IMF, demanded the usual measures: privatization, stabilization, cutbacks in state spending, and mass layoffs of public employees.

The government complied with most of the measures, and its March 1991 stabilization package succeeded in bringing inflation down from 13,500 percent to just 4 percent in the space of two years. However, it failed to produce economic recovery. The 1990s saw a succession of privatizations and austerity programs and a further ESAF agreement with the IMF, signed in 1998. As one of the poorest countries in the region, Nicaragua also qualified for debt relief from the Bank and Fund under the Heavily Indebted Poor Countries (HIPC) Initiative.

Sluggish growth returned in the mid-1990s, on the back of improved coffee prices and some progress in diversifying exports. As in the rest of the region, *maquiladoras* and remittances from Nicaraguans in the

United States are now the mainstay of the economy. However, this had little impact on chronic underemployment—according to the Central Bank, 56 percent of the work-force operate in the informal sector, while the number of households below the poverty line remains at about 75 percent. Hurricane Mitch devastated the country in late 1998, killing 3,000 people and doing about $1.5 billion of damage.

| PANAMA | | GROSS (%) | EXPORTS | IMPORTS | NRT | INF |
|---|---|---|---|---|---|---|
| POPULATION (1999): | | | | | | |
| 2.8 million | 1982 | 2.7 | 2411 | 3045 | n.a. | 4 |
| | 1983 | -2.2 | 1676 | 2321 | | 2 |
| GDP PER CAPITA | 1984 | -2.6 | 1686 | 2509 | | 1 |
| (2000): $3,308 | 1985 | 1.9 | 1974 | 2731 | | 0 |
| MAIN EXPORTS: | 1986 | 0.8 | 2366 | 2907 | | 0 |
| bananas, shrimp, sugar | 1987 | 0.2 | 2492 | 3058 | | 1 |
| | 1988 | -17.6 | 2347 | 2531 | | 0 |
| KEY: GDP per capita (1980 US$); | 1989 | -2.2 | 2681 | 3084 | | 0 |
| Growth of GDP per capita (%); | 1990 | 3.1 | 3316 | 3805 | | 1 |
| Exports FOB (US$ millions); | 1991 | 7.2 | 4181 | 4983 | | 1 |
| Imports FOB (US$ millions); | 1992 | 6.2 | 5104 | 5480 | -250 | 2 |
| Net Resource Transfers | 1993 | 3.4 | 5417 | 5751 | -97 | 1 |
| (negative figures indicate | 1994 | 1.3 | 6045 | 6295 | -133 | 1 |
| net outflows) (US$ millions); | 1995 | 0.1 | 6091 | 6680 | 32 | 1 |
| Annual inflation (%); | 1996 | 0.9 | 5823 | 6467 | 181 | 2 |
| | 1997 | 2.9 | 6655 | 7358 | 1119 | -1 |
| * estimate | 1998 | 2.9 | 6325 | 7696 | 402 | 1 |
| | 1999 | 1.9 | 7096 | 7832 | 640 | 2 |
| | 2000 | 1.0 | 7820 | 8099 | -7 | 1 |
| | 2001 | -1.1 | 8010 | 7817 | 88 | 0 |
| | 2002* | -1.1 | 7800 | 7722 | -418 | 2 |

PANAMA: Panama is a special case, its economy dominated by the Canal Zone running through its heart and the fact that its currency is effectively the U.S. dollar, giving the government far less leeway in economic management. Moreover, its reliance on banking, services, and the Canal make trade almost an after-thought—imports in 1998 were almost five times larger than exports.

In the early 1980s, problems with debt service forced Panama to go to the IMF. In exchange, some structural adjustment got under way but rapidly fell victim to the escalating conflict between Washington and Manuel Noriega. The crisis in U.S.–Panamanian relations led to U.S. sanctions, while political instability drove investors away from Panama and the enormous Colón Free Zone, the biggest free zone in the world after Hong Kong. Colón is used to reexport industrial goods all over Latin America and generates large amounts of income for the Panamanian government.

Instability and U.S. actions forced per capita GDP into a 17.6 percent nosedive in 1988, paving the way for the U.S. invasion the following year.

After the installation of Guillermo Endara as president, sanctions were lifted and the economy recovered much of the lost ground, growing rapidly until 1995. An IMF agreement followed in 1992, although Endara rapidly fell out of favor with the Fund over the speed of reform. In 1994 the new government of President Pérez Balladares began a five-year program to open up the economy by liberalizing trade and foreign investment and privatizing ports, telecoms, electricity, and even a racecourse and a casino. Panama joined the WTO in 1997, and its rapid dismantling of tariff barriers led to widespread popular protest and the closures of factories belonging to several multinational companies, which found it more profitable to import products, rather than produce them in Panama. In June 2000, a further standby agreement was reached with the IMF, aimed at reducing the fiscal deficit through a combination of spending cuts and improved tax take.

Following a Brady Plan deal in 1995, the government regained access to international capital markets, and the debt began to rise once again. Debt service absorbed $290 million out of the government's $1.5 billion budget in 1998.

Banking, the Canal, and services generate few jobs, making Panama the second most unequal country in the region after Brazil and producing particularly sharp disparities between town and countryside. A UNDP study in 1997 found that 16 percent of the urban population lived below the poverty line, compared to 63 percent in rural areas. Underemployment and unemployment remain high (12 percent unemployment in 1998).

| PARAGUAY | GROSS (%) | | EXPORTS | IMPORTS | NRT | INF | WAGES |
|---|---|---|---|---|---|---|---|
| **POPULATION (1999):** | 1982 | -4.0 | 396 | 711 | 342 | 4 | 102 |
| 5.4 million | 1983 | -6.0 | 326 | 551 | 158 | 14 | 95 |
| GDP PER CAPITA | 1984 | 0.0 | 361 | 649 | 254 | 30 | 92 |
| (2000): $1,553 | 1985 | 0.9 | 466 | 659 | 63 | 23 | 90 |
| | 1986 | -3.4 | 576 | 864 | 74 | 24 | 86 |
| MAIN EXPORTS: | 1987 | 1.4 | 597 | 919 | 86 | 32 | 97 |
| soybeans, cotton, | 1988 | 3.4 | 871 | 1030 | -30 | 17 | 104 |
| timber, meat | 1989 | 2.7 | 1242 | 1016 | -151 | 29 | 110 |
| KEY: GDP per capita (1980 US$); | 1990 | 0.1 | 1376 | 1473 | 392 | 44 | 104 |
| Growth of GDP per capita (%); | 1991 | -0.6 | 1106 | 1691 | 760 | 12 | 102 |
| Exports FOB (US$ millions); | 1992 | -1.1 | 1997 | 1988 | -335 | 18 | 91[10] |
| Imports FOB (US$ millions); | 1993 | 1.3 | 2859 | 2780 | 84 | 20 | 92 |
| Net Resource Transfers | 1994 | 0.4 | 3360 | 3604 | 734 | 18 | 93 |
| (negative figures indicate net | 1995 | 1.7 | 4296 | 4489 | 262 | 11 | 100 |
| outflows) (US$ millions); | 1996 | -1.6 | 3880 | 4383 | 423 | 8 | 103 |
| Annual inflation (%); Index | 1997 | -0.2 | 3980 | 4187 | 478 | 6 | 103 |
| of average real industrial wages | 1998 | -3.2 | 3784 | 3938 | 189 | 15 | 101 |
| in Asunción (1980 = 100 from | 1999 | -2.6 | 3242 | 3533 | 287 | 5 | 99 |
| 1982–91; 1995 = 100 | 2000 | -3.1 | 2926 | 3335 | 25 | 9 | 100 |
| from 1992–2001). | 2001 | -0.1 | 2907 | 3278 | 147 | 8 | 101 |
| * estimate | 2002* | -5.4 | 2782 | 2938 | -85 | 15 | 96 |

PARAGUAY: When Argentina or Brazil sneeze, Paraguay catches cold. The economic fortunes of the sparsely populated, landlocked South American nation are largely determined by events in its giant neighbors, and successive crises there led to a negative rate of per capita growth for six years in a row from 1996 to 2002. Any economic statistics should be treated with particular caution in the case of Paraguay, since much of its economy involves smuggled goods and other "off the books" actitivies.

Both Brazil and Argentina are more important than the United States or EU as trading partners for Paraguay, something of a rarity in Latin America. That relationship deepened still further when Mercosur came into force in 1995. Paraguay's exports are largely in the form of soy, cot-

ton, and hydroelectric power from the two giant dams of Yacyretá and Itaipú.

In the 1970s the country enjoyed a boom based on the construction of the giant Itaipú hydroelectric dam on the borders of the three countries. Construction ended just as the West went into recession and the debt crisis broke in Argentina and Brazil. The years 1982–1983 were a time of recession in Paraguay.

However, Paraguay's own debt burden was not sufficient to create a foreign exchange crisis, and Paraguay, along with Suriname, is one of the only countries in the region never to have needed an IMF standby arrangement. In 1994, the government successfully broke with debt crisis protocol and renegotiated its debt with the Paris Club nations in the absence of

| PERU | | GROSS (%) | EXPORTS | IMPORTS | NRT | INF | WAGES |
|---|---|---|---|---|---|---|---|
| POPULATION (1999): | 1982 | -2.3 | 3294 | 3721 | 634 | 73 | 101 |
| 25.2 million | 1983 | -14.1 | 3017 | 2723 | -72 | 125 | 84 |
| GDP PER CAPITA | 1984 | 2.1 | 3149 | 2141 | -535 | 112 | 70 |
| (2000): $2,342 | 1985 | -0.1 | 2978 | 1806 | -816 | 158 | 78 |
| | 1986 | 5.3 | 2531 | 2596 | 113 | 63 | 101 |
| MAIN EXPORTS: | 1987 | 5.8 | 2661 | 3182 | 275 | 115 | 109 |
| minerals, fishmeal, oil | 1988 | -10.2 | 2691 | 2790 | 486 | 1723 | 82 |
| KEY: GDP per capita (1980 US$); | 1989 | -13.2 | 3488 | 2291 | -189 | 2775 | 45 |
| Growth of GDP per capita (%); | 1990 | -7.5 | 3231 | 2891 | 360 | 7650 | 39 |
| Exports FOB (US$ millions); | 1991 | 0.6 | 3329 | 3494 | 1504 | 139 | 42 |
| Imports FOB (US$ millions); | 1992 | -2.1 | 3661 | 4002 | 1186 | 57 | 95[11] |
| Net Resource Transfers | 1993 | 3.0 | 3516 | 4123 | 1331 | 40 | 94 |
| (negative figures indicate net | 1994 | 10.9 | 4598 | 5596 | 3729 | 16 | 109 |
| outflows) (US$ millions); | 1995 | 6.8 | 5589 | 7754 | 3045 | 12 | 100 |
| Annual inflation (%); Index | 1996 | 0.7 | 5898 | 7886 | 3722 | 8 | 95 |
| of average real private sector | 1997 | 4.9 | 6832 | 8553 | 3320 | 7 | 95 |
| wages in Lima (1980 = 100 from | 1998 | -2.2 | 5735 | 8200 | 1140 | 6 | 93 |
| 1982–91; 1995 = 100 | 1999 | -0.8 | 7635 | 8851 | -502 | 4 | 91 |
| from 1992–2001). | 2000 | 1.4 | 8614 | 9723 | -73 | 4 | 91 |
| | 2001 | -1.4 | 8597 | 9487 | 340 | 0 | 91 |
| * estimate | 2002* | 2.9 | 9267 | 9809 | 738 | 2 | 94 |

an IMF agreement, although discussions with the IMF took place in 2002 in response to the economic contagion from the Argentine crisis.

In 1989 the old tyrant Alfredo Stroessner was ousted after thrity-five years in power, and economic policy began to change. The new president, General Andrés Rodríguez, moved to begin a privatization program and signed the Mercosur agreement. His successor, Juan Carlos Wasmosy, attempted to introduce a more sweeping neoliberal program, but met fierce resistance, both on the streets and from within his own party. As a result, privatization largely stalled, and most reforms took place in the fields of government austerity and regional trade integration via Mercosur.

PERU: Peru took the full IMF medicine in 1982, signing a three-year IMF loan in exchange for the usual stabilization package. The result was disastrous, with per capita GDP falling 14.1 percent in 1983, and the IMF suspending the loan over missed targets. By then 400,000 jobs had been lost in the recession.

For a brief period in the late 1980s, President Alan García introduced a heterodox stabilization program, known as the *Inti* plan. García publicly defied the banks and IMF, declaring that Peru would unilaterally impose a ceiling on its debt repayments equivalent to 10 percent of export income. Peru was severely punished for its temerity, a virtual financial boycott being used to turn it into an international pariah. The *Inti* plan produced two years of strong growth and rising wages, but then collapsed in a welter of inflation and uncontrollable fiscal deficits. By 1988 economic policy was back on the orthodox straight and narrow.

In 1990 Peruvians elected as president the least neoliberal presidential candidate, Alberto Fujimori, but upon taking office he executed a spectacular U-turn and announced a program that became known as "Fujishock." All subsidies were eliminated—the price of petrol went up 3,000 percent overnight—public spending was cut, a tax reform increased tax revenues, and a longer-term adjustment program of trade liberalization and privatization was introduced. Fujishock had an immediate social impact. In Lima average protein intake fell by 30 percent between July and November. All restrictions on foreign investment and capital flows were removed, giving Peru one of the most liberal economic regimes in Latin America.

In 1993 Fujishock received its reward—a three-year IMF loan. IMF approval, falling inflation, and privatization brought large inflows of foreign capital after 1991, creating a stock market boom and a sudden growth spurt in 1993 and 1994, briefly turning Peru into the region's fastest-growing economy.

President Fujimori found his second term in office (1995–2000) a good deal harder than his first. High growth rates came to a halt following the Asian financial crisis and subsequent fall in capital flows to "emerging markets." The initial rosy glow resulting from his defeat of hyperinflation and the Shining Path guerrillas wore off, and public protest grew over low wages, poverty, and rising inequality, as well as his governments' poor record on human rights and corruption. Real wages continued to fall.

Undeterred, Fujimori attempted to win a third term in office, but following criticism of the election, he resigned while on a trip to Japan, opting to stay and obtain Japanese nationality. This proved a wise move since within months, a Peruvian judge issued an international arrest warrant for him over charges of involvement in human rights atrocities.

The ensuing elections were won by Alejandro Toledo, running on an all-things-to-all-people platform promising to create 2.5 million jobs within five years, boost annual investment in order to achieve 7 percent annual growth, restore economic stability, and double public sector salaries, among

other things. When he failed to deliver on most of this program, his popularity ratings went into freefall within months of the election. In December 2001 Peru signed yet another IMF agreement, this time promising an accelerated program of privatizations and concessions, and tax reform, but a successful June 2002 civic uprising against privatization in Peru's second city, Arequipa, suggested a rocky road lay ahead.

| SURINAME | | GROSS (%) | EXPORTS | IMPORTS | INF |
|---|---|---|---|---|---|
| **POPULATION (1999):** | 1982 | - | 429 | 514 | |
| 0.4 million | 1983 | - | 367 | 472 | 4 |
| GDP PER CAPITA | 1984 | -3.2 | 356 | 346 | 5 |
| (2000): $1,490 | 1985 | 0.7 | 329 | 299 | 16 |
| | 1986 | -0.6 | 335 | 327 | 30 |
| MAIN EXPORTS: | 1987 | -8.0 | 306 | 294 | 52 |
| alumina, shrimp, oil | 1988 | 6.1 | 409 | 351 | 7 |
| | 1989 | 2.2 | 549 | 331 | 15 |
| KEY: Growth of GDP per capita | 1990 | -3.6 | 466 | 374 | 20 |
| (%); Exports FOB (US$ millions); | 1991 | -4.3 | 346 | 347 | 26 |
| Imports CIF (US$ millions); | 1992 | -2.1 | 609 | 487 | 44 |
| Net Resource Transfers | 1993 | -4.4 | 298 | 214 | 144 |
| (negative figures indicate net | 1994 | -0.4 | 294 | 194 | 140 |
| outflows) (US$ millions); | 1995 | -0.3 | 416 | 293 | 232 |
| Annual inflation (%) | 1996 | 4.9 | 397 | 399 | -7 |
| | 1997 | 3.0 | 402 | 366 | -1 |
| • estimate | 1998 | 2.5 | 350 | 377 | 14 |
| | 1999 | -3.9 | 342 | 298 | n.a. |
| | 2000 | -1.7 | 399 | 246 | n.a. |
| | 2001 | n.a. | n.a. | n.a. | n.a. |
| | 2002 | n.a. | | | |

SURINAME: Suriname, formerly Dutch Guiana, is an oddity in many ways. The Dutch government forgave all Suriname's debts at independence in 1975, and then continued to fund most of the public investment program. As a result Suriname has managed to avoid incurring a large foreign debt. Even so, rising government fiscal deficits (reaching 29 percent of GDP in 1986), have driven the country into debt arrears. Suriname's growth is largely determined by a combination of the world bauxite price and the degree of political chaos at home (the country was involved in a civil war in the late 1980s and political conflict appears endemic).

The government employs over half the workforce, runs a persistent fiscal deficit, and most political debate is about its regular attempts to restrain public spending, and protests by public employees to reverse those decisions. Despite this highly unorthodox economy, foreign companies have been lured in by Suriname's mineral wealth, principally bauxite and gold. Bauxite and its processed form, alumina, make up 76 percent of exports.

Suriname resisted IMF-style stabilization and adjustment until 1994, when it adopted an adjustment program with funding from the Dutch government, comprising large spending cuts, devaluation, trade liberalization, the abolition of price controls, and a rise in income taxes. Improving mineral prices led to GDP growth 1995–1997, but after that renewed political instability and price falls led back into slump and resurgent inflation of over 100 percent in 1999. In 2000, the architect of the 1994 adjustment program, Ronald Venetiaan, was returned to the presidency, and promised to have another go at introducing a full adjustment program. Venetiaan's job was not made any easier when he discovered on taking office that 98 percent of the national gold reserves had disappeared.

| TRINIDAD AND TOBAGO | | GROSS (%) | EXPORTS | IMPORTS | INF |
|---|---|---|---|---|---|
| **POPULATION (1999):** | 1982 | -0.5 | 2289 | 2487 | 11 |
| | 1983 | -10.6 | 2027 | 2233 | 15 |
| 1.3 million | 1984 | -7.7 | 2111 | 1705 | 14 |
| **GDP PER CAPITA** | 1985 | -4.2 | 2111 | 1355 | 7 |
| | 1986 | -3.7 | 1363 | 1209 | 10 |
| (2000): $5,350 | 1987 | -5.9 | 1397 | 1058 | 8 |
| MAIN EXPORTS: oil | 1988 | -4.3 | 1453 | 1064 | 12 |
| | 1989 | -1.2 | 1535 | 1045 | 9 |
| KEY: GDP per capita (1980 US$); | 1990 | 0.2 | 1935 | 948 | 10 |
| Growth of GDP per capita (%); | 1991 | 0.7 | 1751 | 1210 | 2 |
| Exports FOB (US$ millions); | 1992 | -1.8 | 1691 | 996 | 9 |
| Imports FOB (US$ millions); | 1993 | -1.9 | 1500 | 953 | 13 |
| Annual inflation (%) | 1994 | 3.4 | 1778 | 1036 | 6 |
| | 1995 | 3.4 | 2456 | 1869 | 4 |
| * estimate | 1996 | 3.8 | 2354 | 1972 | 4 |
| | 1997 | 3.4 | 2448 | 2977 | 4 |
| | 1998 | 7.3 | 2258 | 2999 | 6 |
| | 1999 | 3.9 | n.a. | n.a. | 3 |
| | 2000 | 5.6 | n.a. | n.a. | 6 |
| | 2001 | 2.8 | n.a. | n.a. | 3 |
| | 2002* | 2.2 | n.a. | n.a. | 5 |

TRINIDAD AND TOBAGO: The Trinidadian economy has been built on oil, which replaced its colonial dependence on sugar. By 1980 oil made up 92 percent of exports. The global recession and interest rate surge of the early 1980s coincided with the end of the oil boom as Trinidad's oil fields started to run dry. For most of the decade, the government could rely on the reserves built up in the boom years to finance its deficit and debt repayments. But by 1988 the cupboard was bare, and Trinidad had no choice but to fall into line, approve austerity measures, and approach the IMF for help.

In early 1989 the IMF agreed to a standby arrangement in return for public spending cuts, the removal of protection for local industries, and restrictions on credit. A similar agreement was reached the following year. The government also signed a World Bank structural adjustment loan, commenced a privatization program, and began rescheduling debt repayments to its creditors.

In the longer term, the government set out to move away from oil production to gas and petrochemicals. Tax holidays and other incentives lured a surge of foreign investment in both sectors, amounting to an estimated $5 billion from 1995 to 2000, and Trinidad's economy started to grow again at an annual average of 3.8 percent from 1996 to 2000. Rising profit repatriations from these investments, coupled to persistent trade deficits, constituted the Achilles' heel of the new model, producing a large current account deficit that required further doses of foreign investment to fill the gap. Despite the privatization program, Trinidad retains a sizable state sector.

URUGUAY: Sandwiched between its two giant neighbors, Argentina and Brazil, Uruguay is heavily dependent on their economic fortunes. Both countries are its main trading partners, outweighing the importance of the United States or EU, and this dependence only increased when Mercosur, the Southern Cone Common Market, came into force in 1995. Uruguay suffered heavily from the Argentine recessions prompted by the Mexican "tequila effect" crisis of 1994–1995, and the broader emerging markets crisis of 1998 and in 2002, its economy became largely unnoticed economic "collateral damage" of the Argentine collapse.

Uruguay is highly reliant on its traditional *gaucho* exports of meat, hides, and wool, which still bring in over half of all export income.

Uruguay has been a regular customer of the IMF and World Bank since 1981, but the relationship has not been an easy one. Uruguay is proud of its welfare state, one of the most developed in Latin America, and has resisted IMF pressure to dismantle it. Several IMF loans have been suspended as a result. At the end of the 1990s, Uruguay had the lowest poverty and inequality levels in Latin America. Uruguay reduced its debt and debt service with a Brady Plan agreement with the commercial banks in 1990. The Argentine crisis forced it back into the arms of the IMF in March 2002.

Economic policy since the onset of the debt crisis has largely followed Argentina's. Initial stabilization led to a fierce recession in the early 1980s. In 1985 the new civilian government opted to reflate the economy and produced a short-lived boom, but in 1990 a neoliberal president, Luis Alberto Lacalle, took office and pledged to fight inflation and privatize state companies. However, his plans had to

be shelved when the privatization program was rejected in a referendum in
December 1992. Since then, successive governments have preferred a strategy of
adjustment by stealth, preferring piece-
meal deregulation and liberalization (for

example, through joint ventures and partnerships between state-owned companies
and foreign investors) to outright privatization. Even so, the number of state
employees fell from 25 percent to 15 percent of the workforce from 1985 to 1999.

| URUGUAY | | GROSS (%) | EXPORTS | IMPORTS | NRT | INF | WAGES |
|---|---|---|---|---|---|---|---|
| POPULATION (1999): | 1982 | -10.7 | 1256 | 1038 | -369 | 21 | 107 |
| 3.3 million | 1983 | -6.7 | 1156 | 740 | -283 | 52 | 85 |
| GDP PER CAPITA | 1984 | -1.9 | 925 | 732 | -308 | 66 | 77 |
| (2000): $5,885 | 1985 | -0.9 | 854 | 675 | -154 | 83 | 67 |
| | 1986 | 5.9 | 1088 | 815 | -24 | 71 | 72 |
| MAIN EXPORTS: | 1987 | 7.1 | 1182 | 1080 | -54 | 57 | 75 |
| meat, wool, hides | 1988 | -0.6 | 1405 | 1112 | -286 | 69 | 76 |
| and skins | 1989 | 0.7 | 1599 | 1136 | -346 | 89 | 76 |
| | 1990 | 0.3 | 1693 | 1267 | -202 | 129 | 70 |
| KEY: GDP per capita (1980 US$); | 1991 | 2.6 | 1605 | 1544 | -89 | 81 | 73 |
| Growth of GDP per capita (%); | 1992 | 7.5 | 1801 | 1923 | 8 | 59 | 97[12] |
| Exports FOB (US$ millions); | 1993 | 2.8 | 1732 | 2118 | 230 | 53 | 102 |
| Imports FOB (US$ millions); | 1994 | 6.2 | 1918 | 2624 | 294 | 44 | 103 |
| Net Resource Transfers | 1995 | -3.0 | 2148 | 2711 | 203 | 35 | 100 |
| (negative figures indicate net | 1996 | 4.2 | 2449 | 3135 | 185 | 24 | 101 |
| outflows) (US$ millions); | 1997 | 4.6 | 2793 | 3498 | 485 | 15 | 101 |
| Annual inflation (%); Index | 1998 | 3.6 | 2829 | 3601 | 798 | 9 | 103 |
| of average real wages in Lima | 1999 | -4.1 | 3530 | 3981 | 482 | 4 | 104 |
| (1980 = 100 from 1982–91; | 2000 | -2.6 | 3659 | 4193 | 673 | 5 | 103 |
| 1995 = 100 from 1992–2001). | 2001 | -4.1 | 3276 | 3718 | 695 | 4 | 103 |
| • estimate | 2002* | -11.1 | 2859 | 2672 | -2627 | 25 | 93 |

VENEZUELA: Venezuela is a petroleum
junkie whose economy rises and falls in
line with the international price of oil. Oil
still made up 78 percent of exports in 1999.
In the 1970s, Venezuela borrowed billions
of dollars on the strength of its future oil
wealth, but most of them went out the back
door as capital flight—a Venezuelan special-
ity. The stock of flight capital outside the
country is estimated at some $50 billion.

Throughout the first part of the 1980s,
Venezuela used its trade surplus and

reserves to keep up with debt repayments
and avoid recourse to the IMF. However, by
1988 its reserves were exhausted and it
embarked on a painful adjustment in
1989, backed by loans from the IMF and
World Bank. Real wages collapsed to less
than half their 1980 level, prices rose as
subsidies were cut, and anywhere between
300 and 1,500 people died as IMF riots
broke out in the major cities.

The government has been lukewarm
about privatization of the massive state sec-

tor (which accounts for over 90 percent of exports through the state's oil, aluminium, steel, and other industries). Instead, it has encouraged joint ventures to acquire foreign capital and technology without ceding control. It has also introduced some partial trade liberalization and signed a number of Regional Trade Agreements.

Venezuela has seen several halfhearted U-turns by presidents such as Carlos Andres Perez (1989–93) and Rafael Caldera (1994–98) who ran for office on anti-neoliberal platforms, only to be subsequently driven into the arms of the IMF by financial crises. Their political fortunes were largely determined by the price of oil, which provided over 50 percent of government revenues in 2000. When oil prices are high, the government spreads money around and wins friends. When prices fall, cutbacks lead to surges in unpopularity. Price swings for oil can be extreme— Venezuela earned $26 a barrel in 2000, compared to $10.50 in 1998. This pattern has continued throughout the radical political changes of the last twenty years.

In 1998, political fallout from the adjustment program and yet another oil price collapse, led to a landslide victory for one time military rebel Hugo Chávez. Chávez announced that, like Caldera before him, he intended to buck the regional trend and oppose neoliberalism. As growth slumped by 8 percent in 1999, Chávez oversaw the introduction of a new constitution that guaranteed the right to work, the expropriation of unused property, and the right of the government to use tariffs to protect small producers.

Chávez's heterodox policy mix also

| VENEZUELA | | GROSS (%) | EXPORTS | IMPORTS | NRT | INF |
|---|---|---|---|---|---|---|
| **POPULATION (1999):** | 1982 | -4.1 | 16332 | 13584 | -5474 | 7 |
| 23.4 million | 1983 | -8.2 | 14570 | 6409 | -6232 | 7 |
| **GDP PER CAPITA** | 1984 | -3.7 | 15481 | 7260 | -5095 | 18 |
| (2000): $3,097 | 1985 | -3.2 | 14283 | 7501 | -4287 | 7 |
| **MAIN EXPORTS:** oil | 1986 | 2.6 | 8535 | 7866 | -3694 | 13 |
| | 1987 | 1.3 | 10437 | 8870 | -1597 | 40 |
| KEY: GDP per capita (1980 US$); | 1988 | 3.1 | 10082 | 12080 | 291 | 36 |
| Growth of GDP per capita (%); | 1989 | -10.2 | 12915 | 7283 | -4413 | 81 |
| Exports FOB (US$ millions); | 1990 | 4.2 | 17444 | 6807 | -6126 | 37 |
| Imports FOB (US$ millions); | 1991 | 7.1 | 14892 | 10101 | -136 | 31 |
| Net Resource Transfers | 1992 | 4.6 | 14202 | 12880 | 1158 | 32 |
| (negative figures indicate | 1993 | -2.7 | 14779 | 11504 | 134 | 46 |
| net outflows) (US$ millions); | 1994 | -5.8 | 16110 | 8504 | -5590 | 71 |
| Annual inflation (%); | 1995 | 3.7 | 19082 | 12069 | -5864 | 57 |
| | 1996 | -2.5 | 23707 | 9937 | -4076 | 103 |
| • estimate | 1997 | 5.2 | 23703 | 13678 | -2797 | 38 |
| | 1998 | -1.3 | 17564 | 14816 | -2042 | 30 |
| | 1999 | -7.7 | 22122 | 16985 | -4484 | 20 |
| | 2000 | 1.8 | 34394 | 19868 | -9001 | 13 |
| | 2001 | 1.0 | 28296 | 21775 | -8170 | 12 |
| | 2002* | -8.7 | 28760 | 16628 | -13472 | 31 |

included a partial return to import substitution, raising tariffs on imports and seeking to diversify out of oil. His land reform proposals, along with political meddling in the state oil company and the reversal of liberalization on foreign investments in the oil sector, provoked political opposition and capital flight from the business class, culminating in a failed coup attempt in April 2002.

In late 2002, Chávez's increasingly dictatorial tendencies prompted a strike by oil workers, supported by much of the private sector. Although the president was able to tough it out, and the strike eventually crumbled, the price of victory was a further sharp deterioration in the economy.

1   From 1992, wages are based on 1995 = 100.
2   From 1992, wages are based on 1995 = 100.
3   From 1992, wages are based on 1995 = 100.
4   From 1992, wages are based on 1995 = 100.
5   From 1992, wages are based on 1995 = 100.
6   From 1992, wages are based on 1995 = 100.
7   Includes *maquila* products in export and import figures from 1993.
8   From 1992, wages are based on 1995 = 100.
9   From 1992, wages are based on 1995 = 100.
10  From 1992, wages are based on 1995 = 100.
11  From 1992, wages are based on 1995 = 100.
12  From 1992, wages are based on 1995 = 100.

# Comparison of Import Substitution, Neoliberalism, and Neostructuralism

This appendix necessarily oversimplifies reality. It ignores both variations between countries, and the convergence between neostructuralist and neoliberal ideas in some countries (e.g., Chile, Brazil) in the late 1990s. Moreover, it compares the failure in practice of import substitution and neoliberalism with the *proposals* of a largely untried neostructuralism. Since such proposals are usually overoptimistic, it is hardly surprising if neostructuralism emerges looking like the strongest option.[1]

It should also be said that since the mid-1990s CEPAL has largely stopped using the term "neostructuralism." But its thinking has developed along neostructuralist lines, and no better term has yet emerged.

## MOTORS OF DEVELOPMENT

Imp. Sub.: Domestic market, through buildup of import substituting industries (many of them foreign-owned). Agriculture is largely neglected; its main role is to provide cheap food to the cities. Government should intervene through tariff protection and nationalization of strategic industries.

Neolib.: Countries should be driven by their comparative advantage. In Latin America this is mainly based on natural resources and cheap labor. Government should keep interference to a minimum.

Neostruct.: A strong industrialization drive, built on solid state/business partnerships. This requires an activist state in terms of R&D, training, incentives, and the like, but not state ownership. In this way, governments should aim to create "dynamic comparative advantage," rather than accept whatever nature has bequeathed.

## ROLE OF THE STATE

Imp. Sub.: Overintrusive, especially in production, creating large, inefficient state-owned enterprises (SOEs) that drove up fiscal deficits and inflation. In other areas, state was usually inefficient, bureaucratic, and corrupt.

Neolib.:    In economic terms, the state is part of the problem, not the solution. Market
            mechanisms are seen as always preferable to the state. Assault on state
            involvement throughout the economy involves cuts in spending, deregula-
            tion, and privatization. However, state as *political* actor seen as vital in estab-
            lishing the rules of the game for private investment and in disciplining
            labor. More recently, a "second generation" of institutional reforms has
            sought to enable governments to regulate the market in the interests of eco-
            nomic efficiency (e.g., via competition policy).

CEPAL:      Problem is not one of size, but quality. State must be overhauled, strength-
            ened, and turned into an efficient regulator and manager and be account-
            able to a strengthened civil society. Direct involvement in production
            should be kept to a minimum. Apart from managing macroeconomic policy
            (e.g., to prevent boom-bust cycles), the state's main tasks should be in provid-
            ing basic services (transport, health, and education) and intervening
            through R&D, infrastructure, and infant industry programs, to improve
            competitiveness of economy as a whole.

## POVERTY AND EQUITY

Imp. Sub.:  Welfare state gave only partial coverage, largely to urban working class,
            allowing poverty and inequality to grow, especially in deprived rural areas.

Neolib.:    Growth will eventually "trickle down" to the poor. During adjustment, how-
            ever, the government should actively pursue poverty alleviation through tar-
            geted social compensation programs. Poverty relief is more important than
            equality or changes in income distribution, which can endanger the
            prospects for growth.

CEPAL:      Genuine development requires "a third generation of reforms that will
            place equity at the very core of the policy agenda." The two key areas for gov-
            ernment involvement are education and employment, but government
            should also seek to redistribute assets, for example, by housing for the poor
            and providing credit and land.

## HUMAN RIGHTS AND DEMOCRACY

Imp. Sub.:  Associated with populist regimes like those of Perón (Argentina) and Vargas
            (Brazil), which brought the urban working class into the political fray but
            largely excluded the peasantry. In later years, was also linked to military dic-
            tatorship (Brazil after 1964), but rarely with participatory democracy.

Neolib.:    Supports restricted concept of liberal democracy, individual civil and politi-
            cal rights and the rule of law, but in practice has often been associated with
            authoritarian rule, as in Pinochet's Chile or Fujimori's Peru. The erosion of
            equity resulting from neoliberal adjustment endangers the democratic tran-
            sition by increasing social and political instability. Second-generation
            reforms have brought emphasis on decentralization.

CEPAL:        Participation and consensus building are essential to increase equity, establish the political basis for sustained growth, and "create more society." Citizenship should be a third pillar, along with equity and development. The state should ensure respect for core labor rights.

## PUBLIC FINANCES

Imp. Sub.:    Inefficient SOEs, the commitment to subsidies, large state payroll, a limited welfare state and inability/unwillingness to collect taxes led to regular fiscal deficits and inflationary pressures. Governments prefer milking profitable SOEs (such as oil companies) instead of unpopular tax increases.

Neolib.:      Fiscal deficits cut by sharply reducing public spending, and in some cases boosting income. Subsidies and public employment cut back. Tax collection improved. One-time income from privatizations helps balance books and gets rid of some loss-making companies (but also some profitable ones).

CEPAL:        Governments should make "fiscal covenants" with the public, involving progress in reducing deficits, transparency in public spending, improved efficiency, and a higher priority given to equity in its allocation. Accepts need to avoid fiscal deficits, but argues for increase in revenue through progressive tax reform.

## TAXATION

Imp. Sub.:    Taxes low and largely unpaid. State revenues are largely income from SOEs, import and export tariffs, foreign borrowing or the printing press.

Neolib.:      Tax revenues increased and shifted from income tax to sales taxes, hitting the poor. Collection also improved.

CEPAL:        Tax burden should be increased still further, since it still lags a long way behind other areas of the world. Tax reform should be made progressive by shifting toward direct (income and wealth) taxes and away from sales taxes like VAT.

## TECHNOLOGY AND TRAINING

Imp. Sub.:    Ineffectual level of government support, due to lack of demand. Most modern technology imported by transnational companies.

Neolib.:      State funding for R&D and training schemes cut, technological innovation and training left to private sector/transnational companies.

CEPAL:        Essential area of state activity and key to long-term development. State should fund R&D, national training schemes, and promote awareness of importance of technological innovation in achieving global competitiveness. Key target should be improving technology among small and medium enterprises, and thus reduce "structural heterogeneity" within the region.

## STATE-OWNED VS. PRIVATE-SECTOR ENTERPRISES

Imp. Sub.: Large SOEs and private sector companies created, operating as monopolies/oligopolies in protected markets. Prestige projects of public works given priority over quality of service.

Neolib.: SOEs privatized and competition encouraged by withdrawal of protection. However, small and medium-sized companies decline as unregulated market forces favor monopolies.

CEPAL: Concentrate on reforming remaining SOEs to make them efficient, rather than privatizing them. State should intervene to encourage the creation of new enterprises by the private sector, especially in strategic areas. More support for small and medium-sized enterprises, especially cooperatives.

## NATURAL RESOURCES

Imp. Sub.: Seen as infinitely exploitable, often by SOEs.

Neolib.: Intensified exploitation for export, privatization of SOEs.

CEPAL: Increased state regulation of market to ensure "proper exploitation." Tax and regulate private sector, rather than nationalize. Development should be based on sustainability and not the depletion of "natural capital."

## CAPITAL FORMATION AND THE FINANCIAL SYSTEM

Imp. Sub.: State development banks, massive state projects geared to industrialization for domestic market, financed by overseas borrowing, leading to the debt crisis.

Neolib.: Encourage private commercial banks to take over investment in productive sectors. Capital account liberalization and lack of regulation of private sector leads to numerous banking crises. Lacks strategies to increase domestic savings and capital formation.

CEPAL: Priority is to shift credit to small and medium-sized enterprises. Main focus is on boosting domestic savings, rather than borrowing abroad, e.g. through improved pension fund legislation. Legislate to shift the domestic financial market away from short-term speculation toward long-term, productive investment. State should step in to establish long-term financial services, especially for small producers.

## TRADE AND INTEGRATION

Imp. Sub.: A high degree of permanent protection, both through tariffs and quotas. Anti-export bias, putting domestic market first. Regional integration to expand domestic market.

Neolib.: Trade and financial deregulation and liberalization. Suppress domestic consumption to achieve short-term trade surplus, but otherwise do little on specific export promotion. Free international trade.

CEPAL:      Low levels of protection, temporary protection for new sectors contributing to technical progress. Aim for competitiveness based on productivity, not low wages. State should intervene to promote manufactured exports. Regional integration ("open regionalism") should be a springboard to help Latin America compete in world markets by pooling R&D, marketing, communications, etc.

## FOREIGN CAPITAL FLOWS

Imp. Sub.:  After initial period of hostility toward transnational corporations, foreign capital inflows encouraged both as direct investment and, increasingly, as bank loans during the 1970s. Accumulated debts sparked the Mexican crisis of August 1982 and ensuing capital famine.

Neolib.:    Restrictions on capital movements eliminated. Along with privatization, bond issues by governments and private companies, and stock market expansion, this encourages a renewed inflow of capital. However, this left Latin America at the mercy of market mood swings, leading to a series of crises from 1995 onward.

CEPAL:      Foreign capital, especially booms in inflows, should be managed to prevent it distorting the economy and make it contribute to growth with equity. Long-term investment should be given preferential treatment over short-term "hot money." Reform of the "international financial architecture" is needed to mitigate the negative consequences of ever-expanding global financial flows.

1 SOURCES: CEPAL, *Changing Production Patterns with Social Equity* (Santiago, 1990), pp. 98, 99, 100; O. Sunkel and G. Zuleta, "Neostructuralism vs. Neoliberalism in the 1990s," in *CEPAL Review* no. 42 (December 1990); CEPAL, *Social Equity and Changing Production Patterns: An Integrated Approach* (Santiago, 1992); CEPAL, *Latin America and the Caribbean: Policies to Improve Linkages with the Global Economy* (Santiago, 1994); CEPAL, *Equity Development and Citizenship* (Santiago, 2001); CEPAL, *Rethinking the Development Agenda* (Santiago, 2000); CEPAL, *Globalization and Development* (Santiago, 2002).

# GLOSSARY

AMORTIZATION Repayment of principal
of a loan over a period of years
(as opposed to interest payment).

ASIAN TIGERS The rapidly industrializing economies of East Asia, such as
Taiwan and South Korea, often held
up as an example to other third world
countries. Also known as NICs.

BAKER PLAN Debt initiative announced
by U.S. Secretary of Treasury James
Baker in 1985. The plan unsuccessfully
attempted to force commercial banks
to loan new money, while giving the
World Bank an enhanced role in overseeing the adjustment process.

BALANCE OF PAYMENTS DEFICIT /
SURPLUS A country is said to have
a balance of payments deficit when
its income (credits from exports,
cash inflows, loans, etc.) is less than
its payments (debits such as imports,
cash outflows, debt repayments, etc.).

BRADY BOND Government bonds
issued by debtor countries as part
of the Brady Plan debt reduction
scheme, in exchange for part of their
foreign debt.

BRADY PLAN Debt reduction scheme
launched in March 1989 by U.S.
Treasury Secretary Nicholas Brady.

BRETTON WOODS Town in New
Hampshire, the site of an international conference in 1944 that set up the
World Bank and the IMF to regulate
the international monetary system
after the Second World War.

CAPITAL ACCOUNT LIBERALIZATION
The process of opening up an
economy to foreign loans, short- term
investment. and purchasers of shares
in local companies.

CAPITAL FLIGHT Transfer of money
abroad, usually in dollars; often illegal.

CAPITAL GOODS Heavy machinery such
as turbines, cranes, etc., used by
industry to produce consumer goods.

CAPITAL-INTENSIVE The kind of production that involves a high ratio of
capital investment (e.g., in machinery)
compared to labor costs. Capital-
intensive production generates few
jobs for a given amount of investment.

CAUDILLO Political "strongmen" who
have formed the basis of many
populist political movements in Latin
America's history

CEPAL Spanish acronym for the UN's
Economic Commission for Latin
America and the Caribbean, based in
Santiago, Chile.

CEPALISMO Economic model promoted
by CEPAL in the 1950s and 1960s that
provided the theoretical underpinning for import substitution.

COMPARATIVE ADVANTAGE Argument
developed in the eighteenth century
by David Ricardo that the best way
to increase overall welfare is for each

nation to stick to the activity at which it is best, and to trade with others working on the same principle. Frequently cited as a reason why Latin American countries should stick to exports based on natural resources and cheap labor.

CONTAGION Process by which economic crises are transmitted across borders by denting the financial markets' confidence in other countries' prospects, often without any genuine economic basis.

CURRENT ACCOUNT DEFICIT That part of a country's international balance of payments (including foreign trade, payments of interest, and dividends) that refers to current, rather than capital, transactions.

DEBT SERVICE The payment of interest and repayment of the original loan on national debt, whether domestic or foreign.

DEFAULT Nonpayment of debt service.

DEVALUATION A deliberate reduction of the official exchange rate at which one country's currency is exchanged for others. The short-term effect is to make imports dearer and reduce the dollar value of local currency holdings. In the longer term, it should improve export competitiveness.

DISBURSEMENTS Actual payments of promised loans, debt service, etc.

DIVERSIFICATION Increasing the range of goods produced, usually for export. This reduces a country's vulnerability to sudden price swings for a particular product.

DOLLARIZATION Process in which a country adopts the U.S. dollar as its national currency.

CEPAL The UN's Economic Commission for Latin America and the Caribbean, based in Santiago, Chile.

ECONOMIES OF SCALE Phenomenon by which unit costs for a particular product fall as the total number produced increases, since initial investment in research, technology, machinery, etc., is now spread over a greater quantity of goods.

EMERGING MARKETS Description of third world economies of interest to Northern investors.

EURODOLLARS Dollars held by individuals and institutions outside the United States.

EXPORT-LED GROWTH GDP growth driven by increasing exports, rather than by increasing domestic consumption or investment.

FISCAL DEFICIT Caused when a government's expenditure exceeds its tax income. The government is forced to cover its deficit by borrowing (increasing its debt) or by printing money (increasing inflation).

FOREIGN DIRECT INVESTMENT (FDI) Investment abroad, usually by transnational corporations, involving an element of control by the investor over the corporation in which the investment is made.

FTA Free Trade Agreement, such as NAFTA or GATT.

FTAA Free Trade Area of the Americas (ALCA in Spanish). Hemispheric FTA (minus Cuba) currently being negotiated, theoretically due for completion by 2005.

FUJISHOCK Peruvian stabilization program launched by President Fujimori in 1990.

GATT General Agreement on Tariffs and Trade. The major global forum for negotiations aimed at reducing tariffs and other barriers to free trade, controlled by the industrialized countries; superseded by World Trade Organisation in 1995.

GDP Gross Domestic Product. The total annual value of domestic production of goods and services in a national economy.

GNP Gross National Product. The GDP corrected for the net flow of capital into or out of the country.

GOLD STANDARD A system that prevents exchange rate fluctuations by obliging a country's central bank to give gold, at a fixed exchange rate, in return for its currency.

HETERODOX Name given to a number of Latin American stabilization programs in the mid- and late 1980s. These combined orthodox IMF measures with others involving a higher degree of state intervention, such as price freezes, and often involved the introduction of a new currency.

HIPC Heavily Indebted Poor Country Initiative. A debt-relief program for the poorest countries agreed to by creditor governments and institutions in 1996.

IDB InterAmerican Development Bank. Washington-based regional development bank.

INFLATION The rate of increase (usually measured over a year) in the general level of prices, reflecting the decreasing purchasing power of a national currency.

IMF International Monetary Fund. Established in 1944 at the Bretton Woods conference. Its purpose is to provide short- to medium-term financial assistance to countries with balance of payments problems. In exchange, countries are expected to adopt structural adjustment policies.

IFC International Finance Corporation. Arm of the World Bank that lends to private sector bodies.

IFIS International Financial Institutions, such as the World Bank, International Monetary Fund, or InterAmerican Development Bank.

INFORMAL SECTOR Work without a fixed salary (e.g. street selling).

IPR Intellectual Property Right. Copyright and patent laws applied to designs, inventions, and trademarks. Also known as TRIPs (trade-related intellectual property rights).

KEYNESIANISM Economic doctrine inspired by the British economist John Maynard Keynes. In the aftermath of the Great Depression, Keynes pioneered government intervention in the economy to manage demand and reduce unemployment.

LABOR-INTENSIVE The kind of production that involves a low ratio of capital investment (e.g., in machinery) compared to labor costs. This kind of production generates many jobs for a given amount of investment. One example of labor-intensive investment is the maquiladora sector.

LETTER OF INTENT Document in which a government sets out its policy targets for the IMF as a basis for the IMF agreeing to a standby arrangement or other loan.

MAQUILADORAS Assembly plants set up along the U.S.–Mexican border, using cheap Mexican labor to assemble parts imported from the United States and elsewhere, which are then re-exported to the U.S. market for sale.

MERCOSUR Latin America's largest regional trade agreement, signed in 1991 by Brazil, Argentina, Uruguay, and Paraguay. Came into force in 1995, with longer timescales for protection to be phased out in some sectors, e.g., computers.

MONETARISM Economic theory based on the work of economists such as Milton Friedman that holds that inflation is caused by excessive growth in the money supply.

MORATORIUM Cessation of debt-service payments.

NAFTA North American Free Trade Agreement, between the United States, Mexico, and Canada. Came into force on January 1, 1994.

NEW DEAL U.S. President Franklin D. Roosevelt's economic recovery package, launched to rebuild the U.S. economy after the Great Depression of the 1930s. Involved increased government spending and state intervention in the economy to reduce unemployment and prevent repeats of the 1930s slump.

NGO Non-governmental organization.

NIC Newly Industrialized Country. Third world countries such as South Korea or Taiwan that have successfully industrialized in recent years. The term is sometimes also applied to Latin America's main industrial powers, such as Brazil and Mexico.

OPEC Organization of Petroleum Exporting Countries.

PARIS CLUB An informal gathering of creditor nations that meet to discuss rescheduling requests from debtor nations of the loans outstanding to official agencies and governments.

POST-WASHINGTON CONSENSUS Term for rethink of World Bank/ IMF policies from early 1990s, to extend their standard "structural adjustment" recipe to a new range of institutional issues such as property rights and financial codes and standards

PRI Spanish acronym of Mexico's governing party, the Institutional Revolutionary Party, which has ruled the country since 1929 in what is now the world's oldest one-party state.

PRSP Poverty Reduction Strategy Paper. New basis for lending to poor countries by the IMF and World Bank.

PRINCIPAL The capital sum of a loan, as opposed to interest that is then added on.

PROTECTIONISM Practice whereby a government uses tariff barriers, quotas, or other means to protect domestic producers against competition from cheaper imports.

PT Portuguese acronym for the Brazilian Workers Party, the continent's largest left-wing political group.

R&D Research and Development. Usually applied to government and private-sector spending on developing and adapting new forms of technology to improve productivity or produce new kinds of product. This is increasingly seen as the key to economic success.

REAL PLAN Brazilian stabilization plan announced in 1994 by then Finance Minister Fernando Henrique Cardoso.

RESCHEDULE To revise or postpone dates on which capital or interest payments are due.

RTA Regional Trade Agreement, such as Mercosur or the Andean Pact, involving more than two nations in mutual tariff reductions and other measures.

SDR Special Drawing Right. Created in July 1969 as a form of international reserve asset to replace the dollar as the IMF's official unit of account. The IMF makes loans in SDRs to member countries, which can be used to buy dollars to resolve balance of payments problems.

SECONDARY MARKET A market for the resale of foreign debt, at a discount, outside the official market.

SOE State-owned enterprise.

STABILIZATION PROGRAM Government policy package aimed at curbing inflation and stabilizing the economy. Such programs are seen by neoliberals in the IMF, World Bank, and elsewhere as the first stage in a broader structural adjustment program.

SUPPLY SIDE The forces considered by some economists to determine output, the availability or supply of capital and labor, and the state of technology.

STANDBY ARRANGEMENT The name given to the agreement between a government and the IMF under which funds can be drawn by the government over a period of time subject to the government meeting performance targets agreed on in advance and enshrined in a letter of intent.

STRUCTURAL ADJUSTMENT Set of policies designed to move the economy of a third world country onto the path of export-led growth. This involves deregulating trade and commerce, cutting back the role of the state and encouraging foreign investment. Structural adjustment is the neoliberal panacea for most third world ills.

TEMPOREROS Temporary agricultural workers, often involved in producing nontraditional exports such as grapes or kiwi fruit.

TERMS OF TRADE The ratio of the index of export prices to the index of import prices. If export prices rise more quickly than import prices, the terms of trade improve.

TNC See Transnational Corporation

TRADE DEFICIT Negative balance created when a country imports more than it exports.

TRANSNATIONAL CORPORATIONS International companies that have grown so large that they have effectively ceased to be based in any one country, moving factories and investments around the world according to business criteria such as access to market and local government legislation. Also known as multinational companies.

TRIP See IPR.

UNICEF United Nations Children's Fund.

WORLD BANK Also known as the International Bank for Reconstruction and Development (IBRD). Created in 1944 at the Bretton Woods conference to help with postwar reconstruction in Europe, it later shifted its focus to the third world, where it has taken on an increasingly central role in pushing through neoliberal reforms.

WORLD TRADE ORGANIZATION International body set up by the Uruguay Round of GATT to increase pressure for tariff reductions and other free trade measures. Began operation in 1995.

ZAPATISTA Member of the Zapatista National Liberation Army, a guerrilla group based in the southern Mexican state of Chiapas.

# FURTHER READING

There is a vast and constantly expanding literature on each of the subjects covered in this book. Some of the most useful sources in English are listed here.

## GENERAL INTRODUCTIONS

There is no one easily accessible introduction to the Latin American economy. Economics students should try Victor Bulmer Thomas's excellent and comprehensive *The Economic History of Latin America Since Independence* (Cambridge, U.K., 2d ed., 2003). The books of my own U.K. publisher (and former employer), the Latin America Bureau, offer excellent introductions to a range of economic, political, and social issues in the region—see www.lab.org.uk for a full list. But perhaps the richest source of all is the CEPAL website, www.eclac.cl, which churns out a stream of high-quality analyses of Latin American economic development. The websites of the InterAmerican Development Bank (www.iadb.org) and World Bank (www.worldbank.org) contain a wealth of research, usually from a more free market perspective.

More general political and economic introductions are available from Duncan Green, *Faces of Latin America* (2d ed., London, 1997) and Robert Gwynne and Cristobal Kay (eds.) *Latin America Transformed: Globalization and Modernity* (New York, 1999). For a damning case study of the neoliberals' favorite economy, try Joseph Collins and John Lear, *Chile's Free Market Miracle: A Second Look* (Oakland, CA, 1995).

For those wishing to consult the original neoliberal gurus, there is Friedrich von Hayek's *The Road to Serfdom* (London, 1944) or *Constitution of Liberty* (Chicago, 1960) while Milton Friedman's vast output includes *A Monetary History of the United States* (Princeton, NJ, 1963), *Inflation: Causes and Consequences* (New York, 1963) and *Free to Choose. A Personal Statement* (New York, 1980). Readers looking for an overview of the field could instead browse in John Kenneth Galbraith, *A History of Economics: The Past as the Present* (London, 1987).

To help you keep up to date with Latin America's fast-changing economy, CEPAL publishes a number of annual reports, including *Preliminary Overview of the Economy of Latin America and the Caribbean*, *Latin America and the Caribbean in the World Economy*, and the compendious *Statistical Yearbook for Latin America and the Caribbean*.

## ORIGINS AND CONSEQUENCES OF THE DEBT CRISIS

The debt crisis has spawned a massive literature, largely consisting of highly critical studies of the role of Northern institutions and the harsh social impact of their policies in the South. The most readable and evocative general overviews are those of Susan George, notably *Fate Worse Than Debt* (London, 1988). For particular studies of Latin America, try

Jackie Roddick, *Dance of the Millions: Latin America and the Debt Crisis* (London, 1988) or Sue Branford and Bernardo Kucinski, *The Debt Squads: The U.S., the Banks and Latin America* (London, 1988). For a recent update on the debt story, try George Ann Potter, *Deeper Than Debt: Economic Globalization and the Poor* (London, 2000)

## THE ROLE OF THE WORLD BANK AND IMF

The Asia crisis and the Bretton Woods institutions' fiftieth birthday in 1994 generated a number of critical studies. For an excellent hatchet job on IMF thinking from a Nobel Prize-winning economist and Washington insider, see Joseph Stiglitz, *Globalization and Its Discontents* (New York, 2002). Susan George and Fabrizio Sabelli have written an unbeatable study of the World Bank in *Faith and Credit: The World Bank's Secular Empire* (London, 1994). Also worth reading is Catherine Caulfield, *Masters of Illusion: The World Bank and the Poverty of Nations* (New York, 1997).

A number of websites offer regularly updated critiques of various aspects of the World Bank and IMF's programs. One of the best is that of the Bretton Woods Project, www.brettonwoodsproject.org.

In U.S. academia, Dani Rodrik is one of the most impressive dissident economists, offering trenchant and superbly researched critiques of the Fund, Bank, and the WTO. Most of his work can be found on ksghome.harvard.edu/~.drodrik.academic.ksg/.

For a fascinating and readable debunking of the "post–Washington Consensus" based on the history of just about every economy that has ever developed successfully, see Ha Joon Chang, *Kicking Away the Ladder: Development Strategy in Historical Perspective* (London, 2002).

## SOCIAL AND ENVIRONMENTAL IMPACT OF ADJUSTMENT

Again, this area has generated a substantial literature, often as part of broader studies of the debt crisis and the role of the international institutions. CEPAL's website contains numerous studies of the relationship between growth, equity, and human development; for example, *Growth, Employment, and Equity: The Impact of the Economic Reforms in Latin America and the Caribbean, Economic Survey of Latin America and the Caribbean 1999–2000*, as well as its excellent annual publication, *Social Panorama of Latin America*. For the longer view, try Rosemary Thorp, *Poverty and Exclusion: An Economic History of Latin America in the Twentieth Century* (New York, 1998).

For specific studies of the environmental impact of adjustment, see the Friends of the Earth website (www.foe.org), as well as Morris Miller, *Debt and the Environment: Converging Crises* (New York, 1991) and David Reed, *Structural Adjustment and the Environment* (London, 1992). One example of the World Bank's huge papermill on these issues is George Psachoropoulos et al., *Poverty and Income Distribution in Latin America: The Story of the 1980s* (Washington, 1992). For a more critical look from within the UN, see G. Cornia et al., *Adjustment with a Human Face* (Oxford, U.K., 1987). Dani Rodrik provides an excellent summary of his views in a paper entitled "Why Is There So Much Economic Insecurity in Latin America?" (1999).

Useful annual surveys can be obtained from the UN Development Program, which publishes *The Human Development Report* (New York). The impact of adjustment on the labor force can be followed through the International Labor Organization's annual *World Labor Report* (Geneva).

## FOREIGN INVESTMENT AND CAPITAL MARKETS

The Asian financial crisis of 1997–98 has greatly increased the attention being given to the relationship between financial liberalization, growth, and development. Some of the best work in this area has been produced by CEPAL's executive secretary, the Colombian economist Jose Antonio Ocampo, and can be found on its website—for example, *International Financial Reform: A Slow, Incomplete Process* (2002). The issue is also explored in Duncan Green, *Capital Punishment: Making International Finance Work for the World's Poor* (1999), available on the CAFOD website (www.cafod.org.uk/policy).

On FDI, try CEPAL's annual *Foreign Investment in Latin America and the Caribbean*, or the *World Investment Report* (New York), an annual overview of the role of transnationals published by UNCTAD's Program on Transnational Corporations. For the story of Latin American privatization, full of examples of both good and bad practice, see Luigi Manzetti, *Privatization South American Style* (Oxford, U.K., 1999). The *Economist* and the *Financial Times* chart the roller coaster of investor interest in a daily basis.

## GLOBALIZATION AND TRADE

Books on globalization have become a growth industry in recent years. Recent examples include Kamal Malhotra et al., *Making Global Trade Work for People* (New York, 2003), and the excellent Oxfam report, *Rigged Rules and Double Standards* (Oxford, U.K., 2002). For a top-quality introduction to the WTO see Martin Khor, *Rethinking Globalization: Critical Issues and Policy Choices* (London, 2001).

For the key critiques of the hemispheric integration process and the Free Trade Area of the Americas, see the website of the Hemispheric Social Alliance, www.asc-hsa.org. More technical studies abound on the websites of CEPAL and the Latin American Economic System (www.sela.org).

## ALTERNATIVES TO NEOLIBERALISM

Books on alternatives tend to be restricted to the field of academic debate, since the more popular books often concentrate on condemning the iniquities of the present system while failing to offer convincing alternatives. One exception is the work of the Hemispheric Social Alliance, which has published *Alternatives for the Americas*. For an excellent new attempt to discuss alternatives, see Ha-Joon Chang and Ilene Grabel, *Reclaiming Development: Policy Options for Developing Countries in a Globalizing World* (working title) (London, forthcoming 2003). To date, the most readable overall alternative proposal from Latin Americans remains Jorge Castañeda's *Utopia Unarmed: The Latin American Left After the Cold War* (New York, 1993).

Fernando Fajnzylber has written an excellent analysis of the challenge of industrialization in the off-puttingly titled, *Unavoidable Industrial Restructuring in Latin America* (Durham, NC, 1990), while Dani Rodrik offers some mildly heretical opinions in *The Global Governance of Trade as if Development Really Mattered* (New York, 2001).

## NEWSPAPERS AND PERIODICALS

Numerous weekly and monthly summaries are aimed at foreign investors, such as *Latin American Newsletters* (London) and *Business Latin America* (New York), as well as the excellent country-by-country quarterly reports and annual profiles of *The Economist* Intelligence Unit (London).

More critical coverage can be found in a few periodicals published in the South, such as the fortnightly *Third World Economics* (Penang, Malaysia). CEPAL's biannual *CEPAL Review* is not for the fainthearted, but contains good analytical articles on many issues surrounding the development debate. Of the many academic journals on development and related issues, *World Development* (Oxford, U.K.) is one of the most authoritative.

# NOTES

## INTRODUCTION

1   Duncan Green, "Report on Visit to Argentina" (unpublished paper, 2003).

2   William J. Barber, *A History of Economic Thought* (London, 1967), p. 48.

3   David Ricardo, *On the Principles of Political Economy and Taxation*, in Piero Sraffa, ed., *The Works and Correspondence of David Ricardo*, vol. 1 (Cambridge, 1951), p. 105.

4   David Begg, Stanley Fischer, and Rudiger Dornbusch, *Economics* (Maidenhead, Berks, 1991), p. 498.

5   John Maynard Keynes, *The General Theory of Employment, Interest and Money* (Cambridge, Eng., 1974), p. 383.

## CHAPTER 1

1   *Folha de São Paulo*, November 22, 1993

2   *Financial Times*, August 14, 1990

3   Ibid.

4   *Folha de São Paulo*, November 22, 1993.

5   *NACLA Report on the Americas* (February 1993), p. 16.

6   Victor Bulmer-Thomas, "Life After Debt—The New Economic Trajectory in Latin America" (unpublished paper, London, March 1992), p. 1.

7   World Bank, *Latin America and the Caribbean: A Decade After the Debt Crises* (Washington, 1993), p. 143.

8   Werner Baer, *The Brazilian Economy: Growth and Development* (New York, 1989), p. 36.

9   Author interview, September 1993.

10  Duncan Green, *Faces of Latin America* (London, 1997), p. 74.

11  Eliana Cardoso and Ann Helwege, *Latin America's Economy: Diversity, Trends and Conflicts* (Cambridge, MA, 1992), p. 8.

12  Oxford Analytica, *Latin America in Perspective* (Boston, 1991), p.185.

13  Carlos Fortín, *CEDLA, Eight Essays on the Crisis of Development in Latin America* (Amsterdam, 1991), p. 57.

14  CEPAL, *Anuario estadístico de América Latina y el Caribe 1993* (Santiago, 1994), p. 188.

15  World Bank, *World Development Report 1983* (New York, 1983), p. 161.

16  Cardoso and Helwege, *Latin America's Economy*, p. 95.

17  *Financial Times*, December 30, 1991.

18  Green, *Faces of Latin America*, p. 56.

19  Cardoso and Helwege, *Latin America's Economy*, p. 240.

20  Green, *Faces of Latin America*, p. 73.

21  Oxford Analytica, *Latin America in Perspective*, p. 183.

22 Quoted in Bernard Nossiter, *The Global Struggle for More* (New York, 1987), p. 6.

23 Jackie Roddick, *The Dance of the Millions: Latin America and the Debt Crisis* (London, 1988), p. 138.

24 Fortín, CEDLA, *Eight Essays on the Crisis of Development in Latin America*, p. 65.

25 Green, *Faces of Latin America*, p. 73.

26 Roddick, *Dance of the Millions*, p. 65.

27 Karen Lissakers, "Money in Flight: Bankers Drive the Getaway Cars," *International Herald Tribune*, March 7, 1986.

28 Green, *Faces of Latin America*, p. 74.

29 Kamal Malhotra et al., *Making Global Trade Work for People* (New York, 2003), p. 38.

30 William Ryrie, "Latin America: A Changing Region," IFC Investment Review (Spring 1992), pp. 4–5.

31 John Maynard Keynes, *General Theory of Employment, Interest and Money* (Cambridge, Eng., 1974).

32 *Latinamerica Press*, May 6, 1993, p. 6.

33 Eric Hobsbawm, *CEPAL Review* 67 (April 1999).

34 Joel Samoff, "The Intellectual-Financial Complex of Foreign Aid," *Review of African Political Economy* (March 1992), pp. 60–75.

35 José Antonio Ocampo, *Exchange Rate Regimes and Capital Account Regulations for Emerging Economies*, paper delivered at NSI Conference, October 2000, North South Institute, Canada (www.nsi-ins.ca/ensi/events/).

36 Patricio Silva, "Technocrats and Politics in Chile: From the Chicago Boys to the CIEPLAN Monks," *Journal of Latin American Studies* (May 1991), p. 390.

37 Pamela Constable and Arturo Valenzuela, *A Nation of Enemies: Chile Under Pinochet* (New York, 1991), p. 168.

38 Ibid., p. 20.

39 Patricio Silva, "Technocrats and Politics in Chile," p. 392.

40 Ibid., p. 400.

41 Ha-Joon Chang, *Kicking Away the Ladder: Development Strategy in Historical Perspective* (London, 2002).

42 *The Economist*, May 18, 2002, p. 17.

43 Quoted in Herman E. Daly and John B. Cobb Jr., *For the Common Good* (London, 1990), p. 31.

44 Ibid., p. 32.

45 Susan George and Fabrizio Sabelli, *Faith and Credit: The World Bank's Secular Empire* (London, 1994), p. 106.

46 Dani Rodrik, "How Far Will International Economic Integration Go?," *Journal of Economic Perspectives* 14:1 (www.aeaweb.org/jep, 2000), pp. 177–86.

47 Quoted in Duncan Green, *Capital Punishment: Making International Finance Work for the World's Poor* (London, September 1999), p. 27.

48 Daly and Cobb, *For the Common Good*.

49 Victor Anderson, *Alternative Economic Indicators* (London, 1991).

50 United Nations Development Program, *Human Development Report 1993* (New York, 1993), p. 30.

51 Will Hutton, "New Economics Hits at Market Orthodoxy," *The Guardian*, April 19, 1993.

## CHAPTER 2

1 James Ferguson, *Dominican Republic: Beyond the Lighthouse* (London, 1992), p. 93.

2 Duncan Green, "Dogmatists in Dark Suits," *New Internationalist* (January 2000).

3 Peter Korner, Gero Maass, Thomas Siebold, Rainer Tetzlaff, *The IMF and the Debt Crisis* (London, 1986), p. 44.

4 Karel Jansen, *The World Bank and the*

*IMF: Some Issues* (London, 1994), p. 4.

5   See www.imf.org, 2002.

6   Korner et al., *The IMF and the Debt Crisis*, p. 45.

7   Ibid., p. 43.

8   www.imf.org,, 2002.

9   Overseas Development Institute, "The Inter-American Development Bank and Changing Policies for Latin America" (April 1991), p. 3.

10   Susan George, *A Fate Worse Than Debt* (London, 1988), p. 40.

11   Korner et al., *The IMF and the Debt Crisis*, p. 42.

12   Susan George and Fabrizio Sabelli, *Faith and Credit: The World Bank's Secular Empire* (London, 1994), p. 215.

13   Duncan Green, "Report on Visit to Argentina," www.cafod.org.uk/policy (January 2003).

14   *Financial Times*, August 1, 1992.

15   Arthur Schlesinger, *A Thousand Days* (New York, 1965), p. 158.

16   Korner et al., *IMF and the Debt Crisis*, appendix 2.

17   CEPAL, *Preliminary Overview of the Economy of Latin America and the Caribbean 2000* (Santiago, 2000), p. 88.

18   Joseph Stiglitz, "More Instruments and Broader Goals: Moving Toward the Post-Washington Consensus," WIDER annual lecture, January 1998, p. 5.

19   Eliana Cardoso and Ann Helwege, *Latin America's Economy: Diversity, Trends and Conflicts* (Cambridge, MA, 1992), p. 172.

20   Oxford Analytica, *Latin America in Perspective* (Boston, 1991), p. 208.

21   Catherine Caufield, *Masters of Illusion: The World Bank and the Poverty of Nations* (London, 1997).

22   Memo from Bank staff in Middle East and North Africa Department, January 2001, Bretton Woods Project, www.brettonwoodsproject.org.

23   Calculated from Alex Wilks, *Overstretched and Underloved: World Bank Faces Strategy Decisions*, Bretton Woods Project (London, February 2001).

24   www.worldbank.org/lac.

25   World Bank Articles of Agreement, Article III, Section 4, para (vii), www.worldbank.org.

26   Oxford Analytica, *Latin America in Perspective*, p. 313.

27   Paul Mosley, Jane Harrigan, and John Toye, *Aid and Power: The World Bank and Policy-Based Lending*, vol. 1 (London, 1991), p. 37.

28   Jackie Roddick, *The Dance of the Millions: Latin America and the Debt Crisis* (London, 1988), p. 56.

29   Overseas Development Institute, *The Inter-American Development Bank and Changing Policies for Latin America* (London, April 1991), p. 3.

30   www.iadb.org.

31   www.worldbank.org/lac.

32   www.iadb.org.

33   John Kenneth Galbraith, *A History of Economics* (London, 1987), p. 4.

34   www.brettonwoodsproject.org/topic/adjustment/spot.html.

35   Patricio Meller, ed., *The Latin American Development Debate: Neostructuralism, Neomonetarism and Adjustment Processes* (Boulder, CO, 1991), p. 180.

36   Talk by Hans Singer at Richmond College, London, 28 September 1994.

37   Author interview, September 1999.

38   Davison L Budhoo, *Enough Is Enough Mr. Camdessus: Open Letter of Resignation to the Managing Director of the International Monetary Fund* (New York, 1990), p. 104.

39   www.saprin.org.

40   www.saprin.org.

41   Richard Jolly, "Adjustment with a Human Face: A UNICEF Record and Perspective on the 1980s," *World Development* 19:12 (1991): 1811.

42 G. A. Cornia, R. Jolly, F. Stewart, *Adjustment with a Human Face* (Oxford, Eng., 1987).

43 Frances Stewart, "Protecting the Poor During Adjustment in Latin America and the Caribbean in the Late 1980s: How Adequate Was the World Bank Response?" (unpublished paper, Oxford, Eng., 1991).

44 World Bank chief economist for Africa, quoted in Morris Miller, *Debt and the Environment: Converging Crises* (New York, 1991), p. 70.

45 Oxfam, "Embracing the Future . . . Avoiding the Challenge of World Poverty" (unpublished paper, Oxford, Eng., September 1994), p. 2.

46 Oxfam, "Structural Adjustment and Inequality in Latin America: How IMF and World Bank Policies Have Failed the Poor" (unpublished paper, Oxford, Eng., 1994).

47 Joseph Stiglitz, *Globalization and Its Discontents* (London, 2002), p. 198.

48 Joseph Stiglitz, *Straits Times*, January 10, 2002.

49 Silvia Escóbar de Pabón, *Condicionalidad externa y desarrollo: Evaluando la estrategia Boliviana de reducción de pobreza*, CEDLA (May 2002), p. 6.

50 See, for example, *Report of the International Financial Institution Advisory Commission* (Meltzer Commission), www.house.gov/jec/imf/ifiac.

51 *The Economist*, 28 September 2002.

52 Speech given by David Dollar of the World Bank at the U.K. Department for International Development, June 2000.

53 Oxfam, "Comments on World Development Report 2000–2001" (unpublished paper, Oxford, Eng., July 2000).

54 Christian Aid, "Ignoring the Experts" (October 2001).

55 Kathleen Selvaggio, *From Debt to Poverty Eradication: What Role for Poverty Reduction Strategies?* CIDSE (Brussels, June 2001).

56 Stiglitz, *More Instruments and Broader Goals*.

57 Dani Rodrik, *Development Strategies for the Next Century* (Cambridge, MA, 2000), p. 50.

58 Rodrik, *Development Strategies*, p. 11. For other papers on the issue, see those by Brendan Martin, www.brettonwoodsproject.org/topic/knowledgebank/newleaf/newleaf0.html; Ravi Kanbur, www.people.cornell.edu/pages/sk145/papers/Disagreements.pdf; Charles Gore, "The Rise and Fall of the Washington Consensus as a Paradigm for Developing Countries," in *World Development* 28:5 (2000).

59 www.worldbank.org/publicsector/anticorrupt/cas2.htm.

60 Rodrik, *Development Strategies*, p. 36.

61 Moises Naim, "Fads and Fashion in Economic Reforms: Washington Consensus or Washington Confusion?," *Third World Quarterly* 21:3 (2000), p. 506.

62 Alex Wilks, *Overstretched and Underloved: World Bank Faces Strategy Decisions*, Bretton Woods Project (London, 2001).

63 Ibid.

64 *Multinational Monitor*, June 1990.

65 World Bank, "IDA and the World Bank: Points for Discussion" (unpublished paper, Washington, March 1996).

66 "Full Text of the Kirkpatrick Plan," *Congressional Record* (Washington, D.C., May 11, 1984).

67 Susan George and Fabrizio Sabelli, *Faith and Credit: The World Bank's Secular Empire* (London, 1994), p. 11.

68 J. M. Watt, "Voting Policy at the IADB and IBRD: El Salvador, Guatemala, Nicaragua, Mexico and Central America Desk," *Foreign Office* (October 12, 1984).

69 *The Economist*, 22 February 2003.

70  Aurélio Vianna Jr., "Fund Threatens
    Brazilian Democracy," www.bretton-
    woodsproject.org/topic/reform/
    r3103brazil.html.

71  Duncan Green, Report on Visit to
    Argentina, www.cafod.org.uk/policy
    (January 2003).

72  Joseph Stiglitz, Globalization and the
    Logic of International Collective Action:
    Reexamining the Bretton Woods Institutions,
    www.wider.unu.edu/research/1998–199
    9-5.1.publications.htm (1999).

## CHAPTER 3

1   The Guardian, 25 June 1991.

2   Economist Intelligence Unit,
    Bolivia Country Profile 1989/90 (London,
    1990), p. 6.

3   Sophia Tickell and Richard Burge,
    Bolivia Case Study (mimeo), Christian
    Aid (London, 21 May 1993), p. 2.

4   Ibid.

5   Cedoin, Informe "R" (La Paz, August
    1985), p. 2.

6   Economist Intelligence Unit, Bolivia
    Country Profile 1989/90, p. 25.

7   NACLA Report on the Americas (New York,
    July 1991), p. 28.

8   CEPAL, Balance preliminar de la economía
    de América Latina (Santiago, 1994), p. 43.

9   Latin America Press (Lima, 18 November
    1993), p. 3.

10  CEDLA, La Paz, 1993, based on INE,
    Encuesta de Hogares.

11  Ministerio de Previsión Social y Salud
    Pública, Subsistema nacional de informa-
    ción de salud 1991–92, La Paz.

12  UNICEF, The State of the World's Children
    (Oxford, Eng., 1994).

13  Interview with author, La Paz,
    October 1993.

14  NACLA Report on the Americas (New York,
    July 1991), p. 25.

15  Ibid., p. 22.

16  Interview with author, La Paz,
    October 1993.

17  Ibid.

18  Alan Riding, Mexico: Inside the Volcano
    (London, 1985), p. 156.

19  Walter Wriston, cited in Joseph Kraft,
    The Mexican Rescue (New York, 1984), p. 40.

20  CEPAL, Balance preliminar de la economía
    de América Latina y el Caribe (Santiago),
    various years.

21  InterAmerican Development Bank, Eco-
    nomic and Social Progress in Latin America
    (Washington), various years.

22  InterAmerican Development Bank,
    Economic and Social Progress in Latin Amer-
    ica 1983 (Washington, 1983), p. 115.

23  CEPAL, Balance preliminar de la economía
    de América Latina y el Caribe 1989
    (Santiago, 1989), p. 19.

24  Latinamerica Press (Lima, July 2, 1987), p. 3.

25  Victor Bulmer-Thomas, The Economic
    History of Latin America Since Indepen-
    dence (Cambridge, Eng., 1994), p. 373.
    [OK as England?]

26  CEPAL, Balance preliminar de la economía
    de América Latina y el Caribe 1993
    (Santiago, 1993), p. 47.

27  CEPAL, Balance preliminar de la economía
    de América Latina y el Caribe 1993
    (Santiago, 1996), p. 52.

28  Bulmer-Thomas, Economic History of
    Latin America, p. 373.

29  Quoted in Morris Miller, Debt and the
    Environment: Converging Crises (New
    York, 1991)

30  Bulmer-Thomas, Economic History of
    Latin America, p. 382.

31  Jackie Roddick, The Dance of the Millions:
    Latin America and the Debt Crisis (London,
    1988), p. 45.

32  InterAmerican Development Bank, *Economic and Social Progress in Latin America 1984* (Washington, 1984), p. 188.

33  CEPAL, *Balance preliminar de la economía de América Latina y el Caribe 1988* (Santiago, 1988), p. 17.

34  CEPAL, *Balance preliminar de la economía de Améria Latina y el Caribe 1987 and 1993* (Santiago, 1993).

35  InterAmerican Development Bank, *Economic and Social Progress in Latin America 1990* (Washington, D.C., 1990), p. 297.

36  Ibid., p. 267.

37  Patricio Meller, ed., *The Latin American Development Debate: Neostructuralism, Neomonetarism and Adjustment Processes* (Boulder, CO, 1991), p. 80.

38  Bulmer-Thomas, *Economic History of Latin America*, p. 394.

39  Ibid.

40  CEPAL, *Balance preliminar de la economía de América Latina y el Caribe 1989* (Santiago, 1989), p. 20.

41  InterAmerican Development Bank, *Economic and Social Progress in Latin America 1985* (Washington, D.C., 1985), p. 211.

42  CEPAL, *Balance preliminar de la economía de América Latina y el Caribe 1988* (Santiago, 1988), p. 17.

43  InterAmerican Development Bank, *Economic and Social Progress in Latin America 1987* (Washington, D.C., 1987), p. 247.

44  CEPAL, *Balance preliminar de la economía de América Latina y el Caribe 1991* (Santiago, 1991), p. 38.

45  Ibid.

46  InterAmerican Development Bank, *Economic and Social Progress in Latin America 1988* (Washington, D.C., 1988), p. 29.

47  InterAmerican Development Bank, *Economic and Social Progress in Latin America 1991* (Washington, D.C., 1991), p. 275.

48  CEPAL, *Balance preliminar de la economía de América Latina y el Caribe 1991* (Santiago, 1991), p. 38.

49  Luigi Manzetti, *Privatization South American Style* (Oxford, Eng., 1999), p. 232.

50  David Woodward, *Latin American Debt: An Assessment of Recent Developments and Prospects* (mimeo), study for Oxfam (Oxford, Eng., 18 July 1994).

51  CEPAL, *Balance preliminar de la economía de América Latina y el Caribe 1994* (Santiago, 1994), p. 54.

52. CEPAL, *Social Panorama of Latin America 2000–2001* (Santiago, 2001), p. 2.

53  Latin American Newsletters Special Report, *Poverty: An Issue Making a Comeback* (London, October 1992), p. 3.

54  Centers for Disease Control and Prevention, *The Spread of Epidemic Cholera in Latin America 1991–1993* (Atlanta, GA,1994).

55  International Labor Organization, *World Labor Report* (Geneva, 1993).

56  *Comercio Exterior* (Mexico, December 1992).

57  Caroline Moser, "Adjustment from Below: Low-Income Women, Time and the Triple Role in Guayaquil, Ecuador," in *Viva: Women and Popular Protest in Latin America*, ed. Sarah Radcliffe and Sallie Westwood (London, 1993).

## CHAPTER 4

1  CEPAL, *Balance preliminar de la economía de América Latina y el Caribe* (Santiago, various years).

2  Dani Rodrik, *Why Is There So Much Economic Insecurity in Latin America?* (Cambridge, MA, October 1999), p. 18.

3  Singer and Friedlander Investment Funds, Aztec Fund brochure and video (London, 1994)

4  CEPAL, *Preliminary Overview of the Economy of Latin America and the Caribbean 2001* (Santiago, 2001), p. 96.

5   Ibid.

6   CEPAL, *Preliminary Overview of the Economy of Latin America and the Caribbean 2001* (Santiago, 2001), p. 98.

7   World Bank, *Global Development Finance 2001* (Washington, D. C., 2002), p. 252.

8   Ibid.

9   Graciela Moguillansky and Ricardo Bielschowsky, with Claudio Pini, *Investment and Economic Reform in Latin America* (Santiago, 2001), table A-1.

10  CEPAL, *Balance preliminar de la economía de América Latina 2002* (Santiago, 2002), p. 39.

11  CEPAL, *Growth, Employment, and Equity: The Impact of the Economic Reforms in Latin America and the Caribbean, Economic Survey of Latin America and the Caribbean 1999–2000* (Santiago, 2000) p. 129.

12  *Financial Times*, February 16, 1995.

13  Quoted in Jackie Rodrick, *The Dance of the Millions: Latin America and the Debt Crisis* (London, 1988), p. 109.

14  CEPAL, *Balance preliminar de la economía de América Latina y el Caribe 1993* (Santiago, 1993), p. 35.

15  CEPAL, *Panorama económico de América Latina 1994* (Santiago, 1994), p. 18.

16  CEPAL, *Preliminary Overview of the Economy of Latin America and the Caribbean 2001* (Santiago, 2001), pp. 81, 83.

17  *The Economist*, January 7, 1995.

18  *Financial Times*, January 27, 1995.

19  Duncan Green, *Report on Visit to Argentina, January 2003* (www.cafod.org.uk/policy).

20  Author interview, July 1999.

21  Pedro Sainz and Alfredo Calcagno, *La economía brasileña ante el Plan Real y su crisis* (CEPAL, Santiago, July 1999).

22  CEPAL, *Preliminary Overview of the Economy of Latin America and the Caribbean 2001* (Santiago, 2001), p. 85.

23  Ibid., p. 86.

24  George Ann Potter, *Deeper than Debt: Economic Globalization and the Poor* (London, 2000), p. 71.

25  Alejandro Nadal, *Mexico's Debt Burden Revisited* (Center for Economic Studies, Colegio de Mexico, Mexico, 1999).

26  *Financial Times*, September 30, 1994.

27  Author interview with Marcus Faro de Castro, Department of International Relations, University of Brasilia, July 1999.

28  World Bank, press briefing, *Responding to the Crisis* (Washington, D.C., April 25, 1999).

29  For a fuller discussion of dollarization from two very different perspectives, see Jürgen Schuldt, "Latin American Official Dollarization: Political Economy Aspects," in *Dollarization in the Americas?*, ed. James Dean, Steve Globerman, and Tom Willet (Princeton, NJ, 2001), and Joint Economic Committee Staff Report, *Basics of Dollarization* (Washington, D.C., January 2000) (www.users.erols.com/kurrency/basicsup.htm).

30  Author interview with Victor Bulmer-Thomas, May 2002.

31  CEPAL, *Balance preliminar de la economía de América Latina 2002* (Santiago, 2002), p. 17.

32  Alberto Arroyo Picard et al., *Resultados del tratado de libre comercio de America del Norte en Mexico* (RMALC, Mexico, 2001).

33  CEPAL, *Preliminary Overview of the Economy of Latin America and the Caribbean 2001* (Santiago, 2001), p. 95.

34  Barbara Stallings and Wilson Peres, *Growth, Employment and Equity: The Impact of the Economic Reforms in Latin America and the Caribbean* (CEPAL, Santiago, 2000).

35  Economist Intelligence Unit, *Costa Rica Country Profile 2001* (London, 2001); Europa Publications, *South America, Central America and the Caribbean 2001 Regional Survey* (London, 2001), p. 263.

36  CEPAL, *Anuario estadístico de América Latina y el Caribe 2001* (Santiago), p. 493.

37  Quoted in John Cavanagh and John Gershman, "Free Trade Fiasco," *The Progressive*, February 1992.

38  *The Economist*, December 6, 1997.

39  CEPAL, *Latin America and the Caribbean in the World Economy 1999–2000* (Santiago, 2001), p. 98.

40  David de Pury, co-chairman of Asia Brown Boveri Group in InterAmerican Development Bank, *Latin America: The New Economic Climate* (Washington, D.C., 1992), p. 68.

41  Luigi Manzetti, *Privatization South American Style* (Oxford, Eng., 1999), p. 2.

42  Ibid., p. 106.

43  Robert Devlin, "Privatizations and Social Welfare," in *CEPAL Review 49*, p. 159.

44  CEPAL, *Balance preliminar de la economía de América Latina 2002* (Santiago, 2002), p. 40.

45  *The Economist*, December 6, 1997.

46  *Latin American Newsletters*, October 1993.

47  ICTSD, *Bridges* (Geneva, February 2002), p. 9.

48  Manzetti, *Privatization South American Style*, p. 133.

49  Ibid.

50  *Miami Herald*, March 3, 1991, quoted in David Martin, *In the Public Interest? Privatisation and Public Sector Reform* (London, 1993), p. 121.

51  Manzetti, *Privatization South American Style*, p. 114.

52  *Financial Times*, December 7, 1993.

53  *Independent on Sunday*, February 23, 1992.

54  Manzetti, *Privatization South American Style*, p. 328.

55  Latin America Monitor, *Southern Cone* (London, March 1994), p. 4.

56  *The Economist*, June 9, 2001.

57  *Latin Finance* June 2001, p. 39.

58  Author interview, January 2002.

59  www.businessweek.com/1999/99_41/b3650227.htm.

60  *Dawn*, March 25, 2002.

61  *Financial Times*, April 6, 1992.

62  *The Economist*, October 28, 2000.

63  Manzetti, *Privatization South American Style*, p. 134.

64  *Bretton Woods Update 27* (March–April 2002).

65  *The Guardian*, July 3, 1992.

66  *The Economist*, June 27, 1992.

67  *Latin Finance*, March 2001, and *The Economist*, June 16, 2001.

68  *Financial Times*, January 19, 1993.

69  *The Economist*, November 5, 1994.

70  Carla Macario, "Restructuring in Manufacturing: Case Studies of Chile, Mexico and Venezuela," *CEPAL Review 67* (April 1999).

71  Monika Queisser, "Pension Reform: Lessons from Latin America," *Policy Brief No. 15* (OECD Development Center, Paris, 1999).

72  Silvia Escóbar de Pabón, *Condicionalidad y Desarrollo: Evaluando la Estrategia Boliviana de Reducción de Pobreza* (La Paz, 2002).

73  CEPAL, *Balance preliminar de la economía de América Latina y el Caribe 1993* (Santiago, 1993), p. 33.

74  CEPAL, *Preliminary Overview of the Economy of Latin America and the Caribbean 2001* (Santiago, 2001), p. 84.

75  www.eclac.cl.

76  CEPAL, *Equity, Development and Citizenship* (Santiago, 2001), p. 55.

77  InterAmerican Development Bank, *Latin American Economic Policies* (Washington, D.C., 2002), p. 2.

78  CEPAL, *Anuario estadístico de América Latina y el Caribe 2001* (Santiago, 2001), p. 200.

79  CEPAL, *Notas de la CEPAL* (September 2002), p. 2.

80  CEPAL, *Anuario estadístico de América Latina y el Caribe 2000* (Santiago, 2001), p. 216.

81  CEPAL, *Equity, Development and Citizenship* (Santiago, 2001), p. 22.

## CHAPTER 5

1   *The Guardian*, 13 August 1993.

2   Economist Intelligence Unit, *Chile Country Profile 2001* (London, 2002), p. 37.

3   CEPAL, *Globalization and Development* (Santiago, April 2002), p. 17.

4   Ibid., p. 23.

5   See Joan Robinson, "The New Mercantilism," in *Contributions to Modern Economics* (Oxford, Eng., 1978), pp. 201–2.

6   Quoted in Tim Lang and Colin Hines, *The New Protectionism: Protecting the Future Against Free Trade* (London, 1993), p. 1.

7   *The Guardian*, September 11, 2000.

8   Fernando Fajnzylber, *Unavoidable Industrial Restructuring in Latin America* (Durham, NC, 1990), p. 47.

9   InterAmerican Development Bank, *Economic and Social Progress in Latin America 1992* (Washington, D.C., 1992)

10  Oxfam, *Rigged Rules and Double Standards* (Oxford, Eng., 2002), p. 43.

11  David Ricardo, *The Principles of Political Economy and Taxation* (London, 1992).

12  Oxfam, *Rigged Rules and Double Standards*, p. 103.

13  Quoted in Andre Gunder Frank, *Capitalism and Underdevelopment in Latin America* (New York, 1967), p. 164.

14  *The Economist*, February 17, 2001.

15  Sarah Stewart, "Colombian Flowers: The Gift of Love and Poison" (unpublished paper, 1994), p. 3.

16  *NACLA Report on the Americas* (November-December 1994), p. 27.

17  Ibid., p. 24.

18  *Multinational Monitor* (July-August 1993), p. 21.

19  *Financial Times*, June 15, 1994.

20  Author interview, San José, Costa Rica, October 1988.

21  Bradford Barham, Mary Clark, Elizabeth Katz, and Rachel Schurman, "Nontraditional Agricultural Exports in Latin America," *Latin American Research Review* 27:2 (1992), p. 47.

22  Economist Intelligence Unit, *Chile Country Profile 2001* (London, 2002).

23  CEPAL, *Latin America and the Caribbean in the World Economy 1999-2000* (Santiago, 2001), p. 185.

24  Kevin Watkins, *Fixing the Rules: North-South Issues in International Trade and the GATT Uruguay Round* (London, 1992), p. 13.

25  CEPAL, *Latin America and the Caribbean in the World Economy 1999-2000*, p. 50.

26  Fajnzylber, *Unavoidable Industrial Restructuring in Latin America*, p. 143.

27  *Latin American Weekly Report*, February 19, 2002

28  *Miami Herald*, October 18, 1993

29  Alberto Arroyo Picard et al., *Resultados del tratado de libre comercio de America del Norte en Mexico* (Mexico, 2001)

30  InterAmerican Development Bank, *Economic and Social Progress in Latin America 1992* (Washington, D.C.,1992).

31  *Financial Times*, February 11, 2002.

32  Augusta Dwyer, *On The Line: Life on the U.S.–Mexican Border* (London, 1994), p. 66.

33  *Resource Center Bulletin*, Spring 1993.

34  Harry Browne, *For Richer, for Poorer: Shaping U.S.–Mexican Integration* (London, 1994), p. 78.

35  www-ni.laprensa.com.ni/cronologi-co/2002/febrero/19/economia/economia-20020219-02.html.

36  CEPAL, *Globalization and Development*, p.25.

37  Duncan Green, *Fashion Victims* (CAFOD, London, 1998), p. 9.

38  Hubert Schmitz, *Small Shoemakers and Fordist Giants: Tale of a Supercluster* (Brighton, 1993), p. 14.

39  ABAEX, *DECEX* (Novo Hamburgo, Brazil, 1991).

40  Duncan Green, *Just How Clean Are Your Shoes?* (London, 1997).

41  CEPAL, *Economic Survey of Latin America and the Caribbean 1999–2000* (Santiago, 2000), p. 129.

42  CEPAL, *Preliminary Overview of the Economy of Latin America and the Caribbean 2001* (Santiago, 2001), p. 89; CEPAL, *Latin America and the Caribbean in the World Economy 1999–2000*, p. 73.

43  CEPAL, *Latin America and the Caribbean in the World Economy 1999–2000*, p. 88.

44  Ibid., p. 48.

45  CEPAL, *Balance preliminar de la economía de América Latina 2002* (Santiago, 2002), p. 85.

46  Ibid., p. 88.

47  Ibid., p. 53.

48  Jackie Roddick, *The Dance of the Millions: Latin America and the Debt Crisis* (London, 1988), p. 47.

49  Ricardo French-Davis, *El Comercio intra-latinoamericano y su base analítica para el nuevo decenio* (Santiago, 2001), p. 2.

50  Ricardo Ffrench-Davis and Manuel Agosín, "Liberalización comercial y desarrollo en América Latina." *Nueva Sociedad*, September-October 1994.

51  UNCTAD, *Trade and Development Report 2002* (Geneva, 2002), p. 10.

52  Ibid., p. 23.

53

54  Victor Bulmer-Thomas, "Regional Integration in Latin America and the Caribbean," *Bulletin of Latin American Research* 20:3 (2001), p. 362.

55  David Woodward, "Regional Trade Arrangements in Latin America and the Caribbean," p. 5.

56  CEPAL, *Open Regionalism in Latin America and the Caribbean: Economic Integration as a Contribution to Changing Production Patterns with Social Equity* (Santiago, 1994).

57  CEPAL, *Latin America and the Caribbean in the World Economy 1999–2000* (Santiago, 2000), p. 185.

58  CEPAL, *Anuario estadístico de América Latina y el Caribe 1992* (Santiago, 1993).

59  CEPAL, *Latin America and the Caribbean in the World Economy 1999–2000* (Santiago), p. 186.

60  *The Guardian*, January 3, 1994.

61  Browne, *For Richer for Poorer*, p. 3.

62  OECD, *Main Economic Indicators* (Paris, 2002).

63  William A. Orme Jr., *Continental Shift: Free Trade and the New North America* (Washington, D.C., 1993), p. 89.

64  Oxfam, *Rigged Rules and Double Standards*, p. 42.

65  Alberto Arroyo Picard et al., *Resultados del tratado de libre comercio*, pp. 33, 59.

66  *Latin Finance*, June 2001, p. 39.

67  This section is based on the author's field research in Mexico in July 2000; Alejandro Nadal, *The Environmental and Social Impacts of Economic Liberalization on Corn Production in Mexico* (Geneva and Oxford, 2000), and ANEC, *Los cambios estructurales en el mercado del maíz en México 1982–1999* (Mexico City, 1999).

68  *Financial Times*, 20 April 2001.

69  www.alca-ftaa.org.

70  www.asc-has.org.

71  Picard et al., *Resultados del tratado de libre comercio*, p. 9.

72  *The Economist*, April 21, 2001.

73  Nicola Phillips, "Reconfiguring Subregionalism: The Political Economy of Hemispheric Regionalism in the Americas" (unpublished paper, 2002).

74  *International Herald Tribune*, March 26, 2001.

## CHAPTER 6

1   George Psacharopoulos et al., *Poverty and Income Distribution in Latin America: The Story of the 1980s*, (Washington, D.C., 1992).

2   CEPAL, *Social Panorama of Latin America 1999–2000*, (Santiago, 2001), p. 32.

3   *ECLAC Notes*, p. 3.

4   Calculated from CEPAL, *Anuario estadístico de América Latina y el Caribe 2001* (Santiago, 2002), p. 196.

5   Calculated from CEPAL, *Anuario estadístico 2000*, p. 173.

6   Psacharopoulos et al., *Poverty and Income Distribution in Latin America*, p. ix.

7   *The Economist*, November 13, 1993.

8   CEPAL, *Social Panorama of Latin America 1999–2000* (Santiago, 2001), p. 30.

9   CEPAL, *The Equity Gap: A Second Assessment* (Santiago, May 2000), p. 51.

10  CEPAL, *Social Panorama of Latin America 1999–2000* (Santiago, 2001), p. 17.

11  *Economist*, April 17, 1990

12  CEPAL, *Equity, Development and Citizenship* (Santiago, 2001), p. 21.

13  *Financial Times*, March 26, 1993

14  United Nations Development Program, *Human Development Report 2001* (New York, 2001), p. 183.

15  CEPAL, *Equity, Development and Citizenship*, p. 67.

16  CEPAL, *Panorama social de América Latina 1993* (Santiago, 1993), p. 9.

17  CEPAL, *Social Equity and Changing Production Patterns: An Integrated Approach* (Santiago, 1992), p. 37.

18  CEPAL, *Panorama social de América Latina 1993*, p. 16.

19  CEPAL, *Social Equity and Changing Production Patterns*, p. 38.

20  CEPAL, *Preliminary Overview of the Economy of Latin America and the Caribbean 2001* (Santiago, 2001), p. 86.

21  Ibid., p. 85.

22  *The Economist*, March 21, 1998.

23  Structural Adjustment Participatory Review International Network (SAPRIN), *The Policy Roots of Economic Crisis and Poverty: A Multi-Country Participatory Assessment of Structural Adjustment* (Washington, D.C., 2001), p. 10.

24  Dani Rodrik, "Why Is There So Much Economic Insecurity in Latin America?" (unpublished paper, 1999), p. 9.

25  *El Mercurio* (Santiago), September 30, 1993.

26  Author interview, Concepción, September 1993.

27  CEPAL, *Panorama social de América Latina 1993* (Santiago, 1993), p. 8.

28  CEPAL, *Equity, Development and Citizenship*, p. 50.

29  *Buenos Aires Herald*, October 2, 1994.

30  *The Guardian*, October 28, 1993.

31  *Latin America Monitor*, December 1994.

32  Green, *Faces of Latin America*, p. 69.

33  Rolph van der Hoeven and Frances Stewart, *Social Development During Periods of Structural Adjustment in Latin America* (Geneva, 1994), p. 14.

34  CEPAL, *Social Panorama of Latin America 2000–2001* (Santiago, 2001), p. 10.

35  Eliana Cardoso and Ann Helwege, *Latin America's Economy: Diversity, Trends and Conflicts* (Cambridge, MA, 1992), p. 178.

36  Ibid., p. 173.

37  Ibid., p. 175.

38  Van der Hoeven and Stewart, *Social Development During Periods of Structural Adjustment in Latin America*, p. 24.

39  *ECLAC Notes*, September 2001.

40  Van der Hoeven and Stewart, *Social Development During Periods of Structural Adjustment in Latin America*, p. 18.

41  Kevin Watkins, *The Oxfam Poverty Report* (London, 1995), p. 79.

42  *Latinamerica Press*, June 18, 1992.

43 Deborah Poole and Gerardo Rénique, *Peru: Time of Fear* (London, 1992), p. 152.

44 CEPAL, *Social Panorama of Latin America 2000–2001* (Santiago, 2001), p. 13.

45 Peter Lloyd-Sherlock, "Failing the Needy: Public Social Spending In Latin America" (unpublished paper).

46 *The Economist*, 22 February 2003.

47 Van der Hoeven and Stewart, *Social Development During Periods of Structural Adjustment in Latin America*, p. 20.

48 International Save the Children Alliance, *El impacto de la crisis económica, el ajuste y la deuda externa sobre la niñez en América Latina* (Lima, 1992), p. 45.

49 Green, *Hidden Lives*, p. 140.

50 World Bank, *World Development Report 1993* (New York, 1993), p. 162.

51 Oxfam, "Structural Adjustment and Inequality in Latin America: How IMF and World Bank Policies Have Failed the Poor" (unpublished paper, 1994), p. 16.

52 Author interview, Mexico City, September 1992.

53 Green, *Hidden Lives*, p. 133.

54 Author interview, Santiago, Sept. 1993.

55 CEPAL, *Social Panorama of Latin America 1993* (Santiago, 1993), p. 11.

56 CEPAL, *Equity, Development, and Citizenship*, p. 67.

57 Lloyd-Sherlock, "Failing the Needy," pp. 23–26.

58 Van der Hoeven and Stewart, *Social Development During Periods of Structural Adjustment in Latin America*, p. 20.

59 CEPAL, *Social Panorama of Latin America 1999–2000* (Santiago, 2000), p. 17.

60 David Reed, *Structural Adjustment and the Environment* (London, 1992), p. 161.

61 Susan George and Fabrizio Sabelli, *Faith and Credit: The World Bank's Secular Empire* (London, 1994), p. 175.

62 Larry Summers, "Background Briefing," on ABC News, November 10, 1991.

63 *The Economist*, June 23, 2001.

64 Author interview, Tijuana, Mexico, September 1992.

65 Green, *Faces of Latin America*, p. 39.

66 Quoted in Susan George, *The Debt Boomerang* (London, 1992), p. 1.

67 Graham Hancock, *Lords of Poverty* (London, 1989), p. 132.

68 Green, *Faces of Latin America*, p. 42.

69 *Latinamerica Press*, October 28, 1993.

70 Jenny Pearce, "Central America after Hurricane Mitch," in *South America, Central America and the Caribbean Regional Survey 2001*, Europa Publications (London, 2001), p. 39.

71 Friends of the Earth U.S., *The IMF: Selling the Environment Short* (Washington, D.C., March 2000).

72 Ibid.

## CHAPTER 7

1 *Ercilla*, March 23, 1977, cited in Vergara, *Auge y caída del neoliberalismo en Chile* (Santiago, 1983) p. 96.

2 Author interview, September 1993.

3 *The Guardian*, June 15, 1994.

4 *El País*, April 8, 1991 (author's translation).

5 Luigi Manzetti, *Privatization South American Style* (Oxford, Eng., 1999), p. 92.

6 *NACLA Report on the Americas* (July 1991), p. 12.

7 *Latinamerica Press*, March 25, 1993.

8 *Financial Times*, June 7, 1993.

9 *The Economist*, October 1, 1994.

10 Ibid.

11 Joseph Collins and John Lear, *Chile's Free Market Miracle: A Second Look* (Oakland, CA, 1994), chap. 3.

12 Moíses Naim, "Latin America: Post Adjustment Blues," *Foreign Policy* no. 92 (1993), p. 138.

13 Author interview with Adrián Lajous, September 1992.

14 *Wall Street Journal*, February 5, 1991.

15 *Latinamerica Press*, December 10, 1992.

16 Author interview, May 2002.

17 Author interview, September 1992.

18 *Financial Times*, April 26, 2000.

19 *Newsweek*, July 22, 1991.

20 CEPAL, *Balance preliminar de la economía de América Latina 2002* (Santiago, 2002), p. 107.

21 InterAmerican Development Bank, *Latin American Economic Policies* (Washington, D.C., 2002), p. 1.

22 Latinobarometro poll, reported in *The Economist*, July 28, 2001.

23 Author interview, April 1990.

24 Author interview, September 1993.

25 *Bulletin of Centro Regional de Informaciones Ecuménicas*, May 3, 1993.

26 James Ferguson, *Venezuela in Focus* (London, 1994), p. 5.

27 Economist Intelligence Unit, *Ecuador Country Profile 2001* (London, 2002).

28 *Financial Times*, April 26, 2000.

29 Jorge Castañeda, *Utopia Unarmed: The Latin American Left After the Cold War* (New York, 1993), p. 367.

30 See www.worldsocialforum.org.

31 *The Guardian*, October 3, 1994.

32 *The Economist*, February 22, 2003.

## CHAPTER 8

1 Other centers of intellectual dissidence include the FLACSO network of social science research institutes (www.flacso.org) and a large number of individual authors, including Alberto Acosta, Fernando Carmona, Heinz Dietrich, and Oscar Ugarteche.

2 *The Guardian*, November 30, 1991.

3 Oxfam, *Rigged Rules and Double Standards* (Oxford, Eng., 2002), p. 112.

4 Frida Johansen, *Poverty Reduction in East Asia: The Silent Revolution*, World Bank Discussion Paper no. 203 (Washington, D.C., 1993), p. 24.

5 This section is based on Gary Gereffi and Donald L. Wyman, eds., *Manufacturing Miracles: Paths of Industrialization in Latin America and East Asia* (Princeton, NJ, 1990) and "Rethinking East Asian Industrial Policy—Past Records and Future Prospects in *Industrial Policy, Innovation, and Economic Growth: The Experience of Japan and the Asian NICs*, ed. P. K. Wong and C. Y. Ng (Singapore, 2001).

6 Gereffi and Wyman, *Manufacturing Miracles*, chap. 1.

7 Fernando Fajnzylber, *Unavoidable Industrial Restructuring in Latin America* (Durham, NC, 1990), p. 170.

8 *The Economist*, April 17, 1990.

9 Duncan Green, *Capital Punishment: Making International Finance Work for the World's Poor* (London, 1999).

10 Economist Intelligence Unit, *Taiwan Country Profile 2001* (London, 2002), p. 59; IMF, *International Financial Statistics*.

11 United Nations Development Program, *Human Development Report 1993* (New York, 1993).

12 Frances Stewart, *Income Distribution and Development*, paper delivered at UNCTAD meeting, (Bangkok, 2000), p. 8.

13 Author's correspondence with Ha-Joon Chang.

14 Carlos Fortín, "Rise and Decline of Industrialization in Latin America," *Eight Essays on the Crisis of Development in Latin America* (Amsterdam, 1991), p. 73.

15 Hubert Schmitz and Tom Hewitt, "Learning to Raise Infants," in *States or Markets?: Neoliberalism and the Development Policy Debate* (Oxford, Eng., 1991), p. 176.

16 Ajit Singh, "Asian Capitalism and the Financial Crisis," in *Global Instability: The Political Economy of World Economic Governance*, ed. Jonathan Michie and John Grieve Smith (London, 1999), p. 16.

17 Author's correspondence with Ha-Joon Chang.

18 Green, *Faces of Latin America*, chap. 1.

19 CEPAL, *Anuario estadístico de América Latina y el Caribe 2001* (Santiago, 2002), p. 531.

20 Economist Intelligence Unit, *South Korea Country Profile 2001* (London, 2002), p. 52.

21 Oxford Analytica, *Latin America in Perspective* (Boston, 1991), p. 182.

22 Ha-Joon Chang, *Kicking Away the Ladder: Development Strategy in Historical Perspective* (London, 2002).

23 Peter Evans, *Economic Governance Institutions in a Global Political Economy: Implications For Developing Countries*, paper delivered at UNCTAD X (2000), p. 9.

24 Alice Amsden, *Industrialization Under New WTO Law*, paper delivered at UNCTAD X (2000), p. 6.

25 Duncan Green, *Just How Clean Are Your Shoes?* (London, 1997), p. 20.

26 www.eclac.cl.

27 Cristóbal Kay and Robert Gwynne, "Relevance of Structuralist and Dependency Theories in the Neoliberal Period: A Latin American Perspective," *Journal of Development Studies* 16:1 (2000), p. 62.

28 See Fajnzylber, *Unavoidable Industrial Restructuring in Latin America*.

29 CEPAL, *Equity, Development and Citizenship* (2001), p. 23.

30 Ibid., p. 29.

31 Ibid., p. 24.

32 Oxford Analytica, *Latin America in Perspective*, (Boston, 1991), p. 197.

33 Author's correspondence, September 1, 1994.

34 Kay and Gwynne, *Journal of Development Studies*, p. 61.

35 Ibid., p. 62.

36 Sue Branford and Bernardo Kucinski, *Brazil: Carnival of the Oppressed* (London, 1995), p. 48.

37 This section is drawn from Sue Branford and Jan Rocha, *Cutting the Wire: The Story of the Landless Movement in Brazil* (London, 2002).

38 Author interview, August 2000.

39 www.fairtrade.net.

40 www.comerciojusto.com.mx.

41 www.forumsocialmundial.org.br.

42 Karen Hansen-Kuhn and Carlos Heredia, eds., *El marco de una alternativa al ajuste estructural* (Washington, D.C., 1994), p. 2.

43 Dani Rodrik, *Development Strategies for the Next Century* (Cambridge, MA, , 2000), p. 22.

44 See www.asc-hsa.org for details.

45 Hemispheric Social Alliance, *Alternatives for the Americas* (www.asc-hsa.org, April 2001), p. 37.

46 Ibid., p. 43.

47 Alberto Arroyo Picard et al., *Resultados del tratado de libre comercio de America del Norte en Mexico* (RMALC, Mexico City, 2001), p. 12.

48 Seminario Internacional César Jerez, *Síntesis de reflexiones y líneas alternativas* (unpublished paper, 1992), p. 8.

## CHAPTER 9

1   Susan George and Fabrizio Sabelli
    *Faith and Credit: The World Banks
    Secular Empire* (London, 1994), p. 147

2   Susan George and Fabrizio Sabelli,
    *Faith and Credit: The World Bank's Secular
    Empire* (London, 1994), p. 147.

3   CEPAL, *Preliminary Overview of the Econo-
    my of Latin America and the Caribbean
    2001* (Santiago, 2001), p. 84.

4   Calculated from CEPAL, *Anuario estadís-
    tico de América Latina y el Caribe 2001*
    (Santiago, 2002), p. 196.

5   Calculated from CEPAL, *Anuario estadís-
    tico de América Latina y el Caribe 2000*

(Santiago, 2001), p. 173.

6   CEPAL, *Social Panorama of Latin America
    2000–2001* (Santiago, 2001), p. 2.

7   Graciela Moguillansky and Ricardo
    Bielschowsky, with Claudio Pini, *Invest-
    ment and Economic Reform in Latin Ameri-
    ca* (CEPAL, Santiago, 2001), table A-1.

8   www.tradejusticemovement.org.uk.

9   Dani Rodrik, *Development Strategies for
    the Next Century* (Cambridge, MA, 2000).

10  Lucia  Hanmer, N. de Jong, R. Kurian, J.
    Mooij, "Are the DAC Targets Achievable?
    Poverty and Human Development in
    the Year 2015," *Journal of International*

# INDEX

## A

## B

## C

## D

## E

F

G

H

# I

# J

# K

# L

## M

## N

## S

## T

## U

## V

## W

## Z